DAVID
LIVINGSTONE
Africa's Greatest Explorer

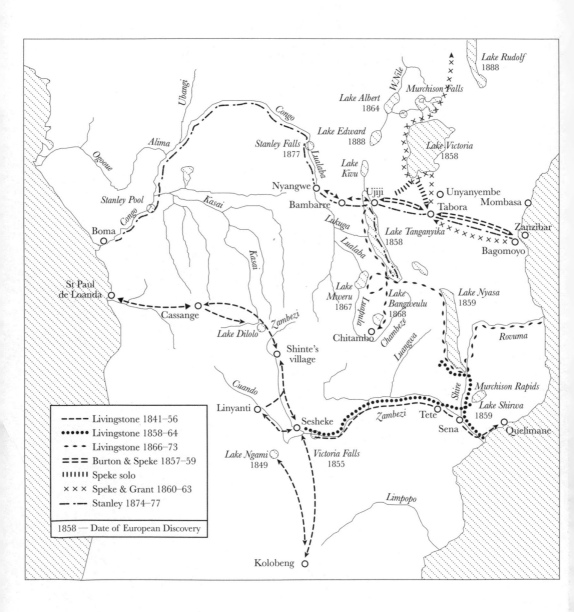

Lake Rudolf
1888

Murchison Falls

Lake Albert
1864

Lake Edward
1888

W. Nile

Stanley Falls
1877

Lake
Kivu

Lake Victoria
1858

Ubangi

Congo

Lualaba

Alima

Nyangwe

Bambarre

Ujiji

Unyanyembe

Tabora

Mombasa

Ogooue

Stanley Pool

Congo

Kasai

Lukuga

Lualaba

Lake Tanganyika
1858

Zanzibar

Bagomoyo

Boma

Kasai

Kasai

Lake
Mweru
1867

Lake
Bangweulu
1868

Lake Nyasa
1859

St Paul
de Loanda

Cassange

Zambezi

Lake Dilolo

Shinte's
village

Chitambo

Luapula

Chambeze

Luangwa

Rovuma

Cuando

Linyanti

Sesheke

Zambezi

Tete

Sena

Shire

Murchison Rapids

Lake Shirwa
1859

Quelimane

Lake Ngami
1849

Victoria Falls
1855

Limpopo

Kolobeng

- - - - Livingstone 1841–56
•••••• Livingstone 1858–64
- - - Livingstone 1866–73
=== Burton & Speke 1857–59
||||||| Speke solo
××× Speke & Grant 1860–63
-·-·- Stanley 1874–77

1858 — Date of European Discovery

DAVID LIVINGSTONE

Africa's Greatest Explorer

THE MAN, THE MISSIONARY AND THE MYTH
1813–1873

PAUL BAYLY

FONTHILL

This book is dedicated to my son, Nicholas.

Fonthill Media Limited
Fonthill Media LLC
www.fonthillmedia.com
office@fonthillmedia.com

First published in the United Kingdom 2013

British Library Cataloguing in Publication Data:
A catalogue record for this book is available from the British Library

ISBN 978-1-78155-432-6

Typeset in 9.5/13 Sabon Std
Printed and bound in England

Contents

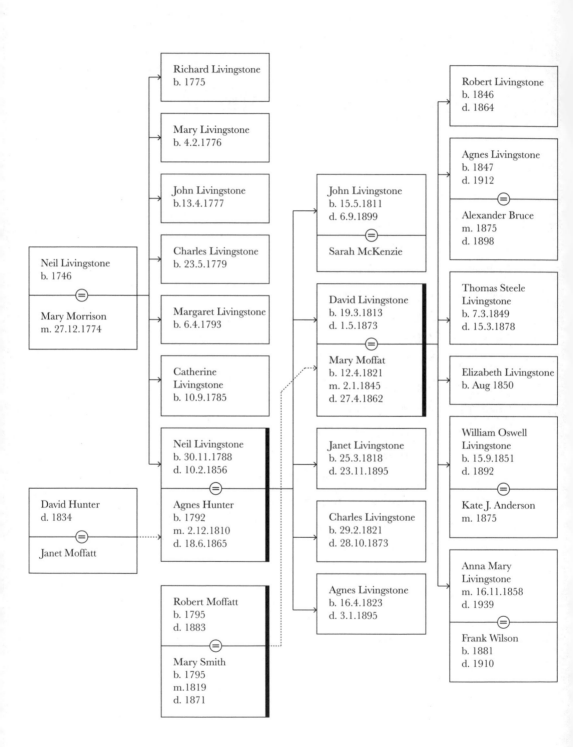

Preface and Acknowledgements

'I resolved to devote my life to the alleviation of human misery. Everyone who lives long among the African people forgets they are black and remembers that they are fellow men.'

In 1841 the 28-year-old Scottish Missionary, David Livingstone began the first of his exploratory treks into the African veld. During the course of his lifetime it has been estimated that he covered over 29,000 miles across Southern Africa uncovering what lay beyond rivers and mountain ranges where no other European had ventured. The area that he opened up covered about one million square miles of uncharted territory. It is still considered one of the toughest series of expeditions ever undertaken.

'My own inclination would be to say as little as possible about myself...' was how Livingstone began his first book, *Missionary Travels and Researches in South Africa* that chronicled his monumental journey across the interior of Africa.

Indeed, the information contained in the book, while full of observations about Africa, is scant on detail about his childhood, his private thoughts and just what motivated him.

What interested Livingstone was African people and he was one of the first to argue that the African culture should be appreciated for its richness and diversity. On today's western standards, the tribal system, so different from western or eastern models of leadership, has not measured up well on a range of selected criteria, but it has served the African nations well since time immemorial. His point was that there should not be a deliberate attempt to influence the cultures so that they more closely imitate western ones, but instead, indigenous mores and traditions should be encouraged to flourish with all their differences and interesting peculiarities.

He was an immensely curious person. In a letter to his brother-in-law, John Moffat, he shows just how wide ranging his interests were:

As you wend your way your way to the north you may feel inclined to investigate any point that comes before you. What think you of ascertaining the size of the Cape elephant? Lichtenstein heard that some were 18 feet high! See if you meet a man who measured them? Are ostriches monogamists or polygamists? You will see them; try and count their paces with your watch when at full speed and measure the length of his stride. Any information as to the cause of the migration of springbucks, wildebeests, the times, numbers. Try to discover the root and plant by which the Hottentots make their mead to ferment. Is there anything really irreligious in the boguera?[1] Or is it anything more than a political rite? Is there anything besides wool-growing that would be a profitable investment for the Bechuanas that would turn their lands to the best account and establish them in them? Take notes as to the diseases known in the country and observe the absence of pulmonary complaints (except pneumonia) so as to be able to recommend the climate to the consumptive.[2]

He made a habit of making meticulous observations of the flora and fauna of the African countryside that he was passing through. It was his habit to record his notes, sketches and maps in hard covered little books. A set of these pocket-sized books is on display at the David Livingstone Centre, Blantyre, Scotland.[3] Livingstone would later transcribe them into larger, bound family bible sized journals during periods of rest or enforced delay.

These journals contained a wealth of information and formed the basis of the two books that he published. The first, *Missionary Travels and Researches in South Africa*, was released by John Murray, London in 1857 and was an overnight bestseller. Eventually over 70,000 copies were sold worldwide with 30,000 sold in Britain alone. His next book, *The Zambezi and its Tributaries*, was published in 1865 and although not as popular as his first book, still sold well. A third book was posthumously edited by the Reverend Horace Waller and published by John Murray in 1874, *The Last Journals of David Livingstone*.

We are also fortunate that Livingstone was such a prolific writer. Over 2,000 of his letters have survived and these carefully written letters contain a wealth of information.

On first discovering the Zambezi River with William Cotton Oswell, African hunter, soldier and fellow explorer, in 1851 Livingstone's determination to open up the interior of the African continent using the rivers as highways—and his resolution for action—would eventually have a significant impact on how nations viewed other nations, the importance of maintaining cultural diversity and different forms of political organisation.

Unfortunately, in the process of opening up Africa, the virtue and good intentions of Livingstone were perverted in a way that he would not have understood: the European powers began to view the emancipation of the African peoples from poverty and strife as a mandate to impose their own kind of civilisation, by whatever means necessary. Eventually it was to lead to conflict on a scale not previously seen on the continent. But all this was in the future.

Livingstone and Oswell's discovery of the Zambezi also brought about a fundamental change in Livingstone's attitude towards missionary work. No longer did he see himself leading a relatively sedentary live nurturing his missionary flock but instead, he decided that he would explore central Africa and in the process of discovering what lay there, he could also sow the seeds of Christianity—without necessarily tending and reaping the benefits.

Livingstone did not view people as black or white, yellow or brown, but more simply as those that needed help and those that could provide it. He remained deeply concerned about the plight of 'his' people wherever he encountered them. He was one of the first to observe at first hand, the devastating effects of the so-called civilised countries' voracious demand for slaves. This led him to become an outspoken proponent against what he thought was an evil practice. In doing so, Livingstone helped to focus the determination of British public opinion to end, once and for all, this hideous trade. His message is still pertinent today with so many African nations again enslaved by poverty and despair.

The result of his explorations also led to the 'race for Africa' and by the end of the nineteenth century Britain and other European powers had successfully carved up Africa. The resulting imposition of colonial control was one factor in the gradual elimination of the cultural diversity of the continent as the servant learnt to copy his master.

Livingstone was undoubtedly one of the greatest of all explorers. Indeed, when he returned to Britain having crossed the continent of Africa in 1856, there was no man more famous in that country and perhaps in the world. But like all great men, he had great faults. He was unforgiving of those that he perceived had wronged him; he was intolerant of those who could not match his amazing physical powers; and finally and possibly worst of all, he had no compunction about distorting the truth, particularly about other people, in order to magnify his already significant achievements.

In writing this book I was keen to examine his relationship with his wife and children, who were the main casualties of his endless explorations in Africa. This is an element that has largely been overlooked in many of the biographies written about Livingstone.

His journey was a long one but it was to end in tragedy; he died alone in an unknown African village, ill and pitifully weak. But the loyalty of his servants, even after his death, resulted in his body being disguised to avoid detection and carried nearly two thousand dangerous miles overland to the British Consul of Zanzibar. They did this out of respect so that Livingstone could have a fitting burial and it serves as an inspiration about how tact and kindness can generate faithfulness among people. There could be no finer testament to the mutual love and respect that he had for the African people.

In writing a book of this type, the conundrum of what spelling to use always arises. The first difficultly was in using Livingston or Livingstone. Up to about 1852 Livingstone was sending letters to his family in Scotland using the Livingston spelling but from about this time he started, unmistakably, using Livingstone. It is not clear why he did so but in a nod to conformance I have used Livingstone throughout this book.

In regard to spellings for African names, my task has been made more difficult because of the numerous ways of spelling, with some of these differences arising from different local dialects through to Livingstone in some cases using multiple spellings or simply spellings that were wrong. I have elected to use the spellings used in his letters where they are used repetitively. For example, I have used Mebaloe rather than Mebalwe. In some cases he spelt names differently. An example is that he started using Sebitoane in his earlier letters but later adopted Sebitwane or Sebituane. I have elected to use the earlier spelling of Sebitoane. An example of incorrect spelling used by Livingstone in many letters is Oswel. In this case I have used his correct name of Oswell. As regards place names, I have occasionally used more modern place names, such as Linyanti instead of Dinyanti. Finally, in keeping with the times that this book refers to, I have used 'natives' rather than, say 'Africans', as it seemed to be more consistent with various quotes I have made throughout the book. I apologise in advance if any person is offended by the use of this term.

I started writing this book in 2001 when I was living in Zambia and over the intervening years slowly added it. There have been many friends and acquaintances that have encouraged me to continue and have, in the process, become interested in Livingstone and become keen to know more about him. In addition, and quite coincidently, I discovered one of my sister-in-laws was a direct descendent of Livingstone and indeed tucked away in a cupboard was an original edition of Livingstone's *Missionary Travels* that her great-grandmother had been given.

As is the case in any endeavour, there are a number of people I would like to acknowledge and thank. Firstly, my thanks to the helpful staff at the British Library. The British Library is major institution and truly one of the great Libraries in the world. Another magnificent institution is the Royal Geographical Society that has a fascinating collection of documents, photographs and artefacts. I also spent many useful hours in the Library of the London School of Economics, the London Missionary Society Archives, School of Oriental and African Studies, University of London and the Auckland Library, Sir George Grey Special Collections. My thanks also go to the helpful staff at the David Livingstone Centre, Blantyre and National Museums Scotland, Edinburgh. Finally, when attending the David Livingstone commemorative service at Westminster Abbey on 19 March 2013 I met two great-grandchildren of Livingstone, Neil Wilson and Elspeth Murdock. I thank them for their comments and for the family letters that Neil later provided.

It was not until I came to London in June 2012 as part of the Phoenician Ship Expedition that I was able to spend five months of concentrated research to finally start to bring this book to a conclusion. During this time I lived on board the ship in St Katharine Docks. I thank the crew and in particular Captain Philip Beale for their support and patience during this time.

Key Dates

Date	Key Event
19 March 1813	Livingstone born in Blantyre, second eldest child of Neil and Mary Livingstone
12 April 1821	Mary Moffat is born in Griquatown, Bechuanaland, eldest child of Robert Moffat and Mary Smith.
1840	Livingstone receives his medical licence from the College of Physicians and Surgeons of Glasgow
February 1840	Livingstone accepted by London Missionary Society to become a missionary
20 November 1840	Livingstone ordained as a nonconformist minister at the Albion Chapel, Finsbury, England
8 December 1840	Livingstone sails from London to Africa to begin work as a London Missionary Society missionary
September 1841	Livingstone and Edwards set out for first trip to explore area northern of Kuruman
10 February 1842	Livingstone sets out for second trip into the northern interior
21 February 1843	Livingstone sets out for third trip into the northern interior
June 1843	London Missionary Society directors authorise Edwards and Livingstone to establish of a new mission at Mabotsa
August 1843	Livingstone and Edwards leave Kuruman to establish the

	Mabotsa mission, in company of three Englishmen hunters john Robert Pringle, Captain Thomas Montague Steele and Andrew Hudson Bain
7 January 1844	Livingstone attacked by a lion and is nearly killed
2 January 1845	Livingstone marries Mary Moffat
August 1845	Livingstone establishes a new mission at Chonuane
9 January 1846	Birth of first child, Robert Moffat Livingstone, in Mabotsa, Bechuanaland (now South Africa)
13 June 1847	Birth of second child, Agnes Livingstone, in Chonuane, Bechuanaland (now South Africa)
February 1848	Livingstone establishes a new mission at Kolobeng
7 March 1849	Birth of third child Thomas Steele Livingstone in Kolobeng, Bechuanaland (now Botswana)
1st June 1849	Livingstone, William Cotton Oswell and Mungo Murray and set out to find Lake Ngami
1 August 1849	Discovery of Lake Ngami by three Europeans; Livingstone, Oswell and Murray
April 1850	Livingstone and family make another trip to Lake Ngami
4 August 1850	Birth of a fourth child Elizabeth Pyne Livingstone in Kolobeng, Bechuanaland (now Botswana) who dies six weeks later of an infection (18 Sep. 1850, Kolobeng)
26 April 1851	Livingstone, his family and Oswell depart on another trip to Lake Ngami and beyond
15 September 1851	Birth of fifth child, William Oswell Livingstone (nicknamed Zouga for the river along which he was born), Bechuanaland (now River Botetle, Botswana)
30 June 1851	Livingstone and Oswell reach the banks of Zambezi

Mid-March 1852	Livingstone and family arrive in Cape Town where family departs to Britain and Livingstone prepares to travel through central Africa
11 November 1853	Livingstone and party leave Linyanti to travel to the West coast of Africa
31 May 1854	Livingstone and party arrive in Loanda, completing the trek to the West coast of Africa
20 September 185	Livingstone and party leave Loanda for a trans-African crossing
11 September 1855	Livingstone and party arrive back at Linyanti, completing a journey of just over two thousand six hundred miles
3 November 1855	Livingstone and party depart from Linyanti to travel to the East coast of Africa
November 1855	Livingstone reaches 'Mosi-oa-tunya' or 'the smoke that thunders.' He renames them Victoria Falls in honour of the British Sovereign.
20 May 1856	Livingstone and party arrive at Quellimane on the East Coast, completing the first trans-African crossing
9 December 1856	Livingstone arrives back in Southampton to a triumphant return. Remains in Britain until 1858.
10 November 1857	Livingstone's book *Missionary Travels and Researches in South Africa* is published
14 May 1858	Arrival of the Zambezi Expedition on the on board the HMS *Pearl* at the mouth of the Zambezi
16 November 1858	Birth of sixth and last child, Anna Mary Livingstone, in Kuruman, Bechuanaland (now South Africa)
27 April 1862	Death of Mary Livingstone from fever at Shupanga, Mozambique, on the Zambezi River

4 July 1863   Livingstone receives a letter at Murchison Cataracts advising the termination of the Zambezi Expedition. Livingstone continues alone to explore Lake Nyassa.

23 July 1864   Livingstone arrives back in Britain. Remains in Britain until 1865.

April 1865   *Narrative of an Expedition to the Zambesi and its Tributaries, etc.* by David & Charles Livingstone is completed. It is published by John Murray

February 1858 Livingstone appointed Her Majesty's Consul, Inner Africa

13 August 1865 Livingstone leaves England for his final journey

19 March 1866 Livingstone leaves Zanzibar on what was to be his final trip to discover the source of the Nile.

27 October 1871 Henry Morton Stanley meets Livingstone at Ujiji on the shores of Lake Tanganyika

14 March 1872 Stanley leaves Livingstone to return to Britain

1 May 1873   Livingstone dies in Chitambo's village near the great Bangweulu swamps in modern-day Zambia, 60 years old

18 April 1874 Livingstone's remains interred in the nave of Westminster Abbey, London

December 1874 Livingstone's *Last Journals*, edited by Horace Waller, is published in two volumes by John Murray

CHAPTER 1

The Early Years

'was no thocht to be a by-ordinar laddie;
just a sulky, quiet, feckless sort o' boy.'

1.1 Blantyre Boy

The early 1800s were a turbulent time for Great Britain. The country was involved in a long and expensive war with Napoleon's France that finally came to a bloody conclusion at Waterloo in 1815. Great Britain also became embroiled in an armed dispute with the United States of America in 1812 over shipping and territorial rights and this dispute spluttered on until it was finally resolved in 1814.

In Africa the Zulu warrior king, Shaka kaSenzangakhona, founded the Zulu Empire in south-east Africa in 1816 and soon after began threatening the surrounding small British and Dutch settlements while in north-western Africa, the first colony for freed slaves was established in 1822, fittingly called Liberia.

Great Britain's society was also undergoing rapid social change as the impact of the industrial revolution swept across the country. The advent of new machines and products required new factories to produce them and as communications and transport routes improved, people from the countryside flooded into towns to have the security of a regularly paying job. The transformation was rapid; Glasgow's population over the twenty-year period from 1811 grew by 100,000 people. These people were cramped into evil smelly slums where less than fifty per cent of all children born survived to ten-years of age. About one third of these people ended up working in cotton mills.

Nowhere was this more evident than in a small town called Blantyre in Lanarkshire, about eight miles southeast of Glasgow, where in 1813 a boy was born into a family who lived in a one-room apartment on the grounds of a large cotton mill on the banks of the Clyde. His name was David Livingstone.

The Livingstone family originally came from Ulva, 'The Island of the Wolf' which is one of a cluster of islands that makes up the Hebrides, off the northwest coast of Scotland. Livingstone was proud of his lineage, 'My great-grandfather fell at the Battle of Culloden, fighting for the old line of kings, and my grandfather was a small farmer in Ulva, where my father was born.'[4]

This grandfather was called Neil and he had been a tenant farmer on Ulva but he was forced to sell the plot and seek a job on the mainland so that he could support his growing family. One of the reasons for selling up may have been due to forced 'clearances' but it is just as likely the lack of opportunity played a part in the difficult decision to uproot his family and move half way across Scotland to find employment.

The family arrived in Blantyre in 1792 which then had a population of about two thousand people. Livingstone's grandfather was fortunate to secure a job with H. Monteith and Co., owners of a large cotton mill that lay on the banks of the river Clyde. His job was an important position of trust that involved conveying large sums of money from Glasgow to the mill, a distance of about seven miles. Neil spoke both Gaelic and English and the ability to converse in both languages would have been an essential qualification given the mix of workers at Blantyre.

The Blantyre cotton works was one of hundreds across central Scotland. The mill had originally been established by an enlightened individual called David Dale who believed in providing reasonable standards of housing and ablutions and providing education for the young. In 1792 Henry and James Monteith purchased the mill and continued to expand the operations, including adding a yarn dye work, that used the Turkey Red process.[5] In 1838 the Manager, Thomas Scott, testified at a Parliamentary enquiry investigating factory working conditions that about 1,100 people worked in the mill. Of these about 300 were between the ages of thirteen and sixteen and there were thirty-three under the age of thirteen.[6]

Livingstone's father, also called Neil, was the only son of several not to enter the King's service during the Napoleonic Wars. He was first put to work in the cotton mill; later he was apprenticed to a Cotton Works' tailor, David Hunter. It was a job that he was never destined to enjoy. However, while he struggled to learn the trade, a romance started between him and the tailor's daughter, Mary Hunter that eventually led to marriage in 1810. Neil continued to persevere with tailoring for some years and after spending a period of time in Glasgow, the couple eventually returned to Blantyre. It was there that Neil decided to give it up tailoring and become a travelling tea salesman. It was not a career that was to bring him much financial reward but it was enough to enable his family to scrape along. It also provided Neil with an excellent opportunity to distribute Bibles to clients and to become more involved in church activities.

Neil and Mary had seven children in all, although two of them died in infancy. The names of the surviving children, in order, were John, David, Janet, Charles and Agnes. David, the second eldest, was born on the 19 March 1813, in Blantyre.

The dominant person in Livingstone's life from an early age was his father. He was a principled, religious man who abstained from alcohol because he did not agree with it and abhorred the use of profane language. Neil was an embodiment of an observation made about Livingstone's ancestors, 'I have searched diligently through all the traditions of our family, and I never could find that there was a dishonest man amongst our forefathers.'[7] Livingstone was fond of his father and spoke of his 'winning ways'.

It would appear that it was his father's deep religious convictions that lead Livingstone to accept the Christian faith that he was to hold to firmly throughout his life. His mother, Mary, meanwhile devoted herself to caring for the welfare of her family, a job made difficult because of the constant worry about money. She was not adverse to 'showing off' her children on Sundays, however, by dressing them up in their best.

The family shared the three-storied tenement with twenty-three other families in Shuttle Row in a bustling Blantyre. The Livingstone's apartment was on the top level and every day water and supplies would be hauled up the thirty stone steps of the spiral stairwell and every morning the chamber pots were carried down to be emptied. A photograph of Shuttle Row in the 1800s shows two women and some children at the entrance of the building staring gloomily at the camera. The building is in need of painting and the outside area leading off to the communal washhouse and ablutions is unpaved and pocket marked. There is an over-riding sense of grime, drudgery and smell.

Each apartment consisted of a large room, approximately fourteen feet by ten. There were two recesses in the room for beds. The furniture was limited to a chest of drawers and table and chairs. Within easy reach were the pots, pans, chamber pots and the treasured family bible. Clothes would nearly always be hanging up to dry in the crowded room. In this crowded space the family of two adults and five children would have worked, read and played.

Young children started work in the mills as early as six and for this reason only about ten per cent of factory children could read and write their own names. Livingstone was lucky that he was not one of them, as he continued to receive tuition at the factory-run school until he was ten-years-old. At school he learnt to read and write, using chalk and slate to practice the formal handwriting that was taught at that time.

One of the jobs that he did have to do out of school was to look after cows during the day for a local farmer. As the farmer observed, young Livingstone loved books. 'I didna' thick muckle o' that David Livingstone when he worked wi' me. He was a ye lyin' on his belly readin' a book.'[8] Like any boy, Livingstone would have enjoyed playing along the banks of the slowly moving Clyde River and exploring the area, including climbing over the ruins of Bothwell castle. They also poached salmon if they could do so safely, and his younger brother Charles was on one occasion apparently tasked with carrying a fish home inside one of his trouser legs.

Livingstone's father was particularly keen to ensure his children received a good education and took upon himself to teach them to read and write and was generally interested in literature. Livingstone also took his studies seriously and asked his father if he could learn Latin and despite their humble circumstances, Neil Livingstone agreed.

His teacher was Mike Skimming, a company employee, and he remembered the young Livingstone as 'a dour, awkward, shy young lad who was always taking notes.' He noted Livingstone's 'crocked alphabet figures.' Livingstone also made full use of library that the company provided. As Livingstone later noted, 'I read everything I could lay my hands on except novels. Scientific works and books of travel were my especial delight.'[9]

When Livingstone was seven and growing up on the banks of the Clyde, in far away Africa, in a small dusty missionary settlement called Griquatown, 800 miles north of Cape Town, the eldest daughter of a highly respected missionary, Dr Robert Moffat was born. Her name was Mary Moffat. She was to become Livingstone's wife and according to him, she 'was the best spoke in the wheel'.

1.2 Cotton Mills

Livingstone's childhood took place during the industrial revolution. This sudden economic development ushered in a long period of prosperity for Britain. It also brought about considerable social changes: the burgeoning of a middle-class; the development of places of learning throughout the country; a religious revival; and the rapid expansion of the British Empire across the globe. However, the benefits were not shared equally: for the working-class, little changed with life remaining short and brutal due to harsh working conditions.

Livingstone was sent to work in the cotton factory in 1823 at the age of ten. He was employed as 'piecer' and it was tough work; he was required to start work at six in the morning and continue to eight o'clock at night. There were two breaks during the day: forty minutes for breakfast and forty-five minutes for dinner. This corresponds to a working day of twelve and a half hours—a tough task for a young boy.

The function of a piecer was to keep a constant watch on the threads on the spinning frames to ensure that they did not break. This meant tying any weakened cotton threads together so that there were no flaws in the final product. It was also dangerous since in order to be able piece loose threads together, the piecer would have to clamber all over the working looms.

The conditions were tiring because the factories were steam-heated, since it is easier to produce fine thread in hot, moist conditions. Sometimes the temperature would be as high as eighty to ninety degrees Fahrenheit and for this reason, many workers would strip off clothes to try and keep cool. Such an environment was rumoured to have encouraged promiscuous behaviour.

There were normally four people working on each spinning machine, three piecers, who were normally boys, and an adult spinner who was responsible for production. Wages were calculated on the amount produced and so it paid for the spinner to work his team as hard as possible. This would typically include beatings for any boy who flagged.

The factories were also gloomy as there were few candles present because floating cotton fibres could be highly inflammable. Instead they relied on sunlight through numerous large factory windows. The downside was swirling breezes that stirred up floating fibres that irritated throats and noses.

Livingstone continued to take his studies after he started work. Schooling consisted of two hours tuition after work from eight to ten o'clock in the evening. Due to the long working hours only a few had the willpower to struggle along to the lessons—and Livingstone was one of them.

Livingstone later wrote that he spent part of his first pay packet on purchasing *Rudiments of Latin*. It was a subject that he first studied at the company school at ten and was to continue to do so for many years. Another favourite was Livingstone's well-thumbed pocket sized Arithmetic Book with a sewn up book spine.

Livingstone was an avid reader and took every opportunity to do so; after returning from the school he would frequently sit reading till midnight or later, if his mother would allow him. During work hours, he showed his resolve to keep educating himself by perching a book on the spinning jenny where he could catch an occasional sentence while he worked. The other boys enjoyed throwing boffins to try to knock his book off its precarious perching place. Livingstone later stated that these disruptions taught him to concentrate his mind, be it reading or writing, to the exclusion of all else. This would prove to be a useful skill when later exploring through Africa; whenever he wrote up his extensive journals, it was nearly always in the company of interested and noisy natives.

He seems to have been surprisingly well read. His preference was for books on travel and scientific works although the latter formed a source of irritation between Livingstone and his father. At that stage his father viewed all scientific matters with deep suspicion and not unnaturally, he did not want his son reading about the subject, preferring instead that the boy read about theology. There is also a story that Livingstone received a copy of the New Testament at the age of nine for repeating the whole of the 119th Psalm on two consecutive evenings and making only five mistakes in the process.[10] This is a considerable achievement. Livingstone later wrote that he 'knew Virgil and Horace better at sixteen that I do now.'[11]

He was also precocious in other respects, being particularly interested in botany, geology and zoology. These interests took him exploring all over the surrounding countryside during his occasional spare time looking for among other things, plants as described in his family's edition of *Culpepper's Herbal*. There was one incident that he liked to recall: one day he went exploring a limestone cave to collect shells. Being particularly interested in the shells that he could see in the limestone, he asked the quarryman how they came to be there. The man looked at the young boy with suspicion and then answered most discouragingly, 'When God made the rocks He made shells in them.' Nature was one of Livingstone's particular interests. He had a remarkably acute eye for observing nature and his interest only grew with age.

Despite his bookish ways, the child Livingstone was just like his peers, neither a laggard nor exceptional. A comment made about him from a childhood acquaintance summed up Livingstone as 'no thocht to be a by-ordinar laddie; just a sulky, quiet, feckless sort o' boy.'[12]

At nineteen Livingstone was promoted to spinner in the cotton factory and although his new job was hard work, he was comparatively well paid. At this time the British Parliament was debating the introduction of legislation to improve factory-working conditions. The Factory Act was finally passed in 1833. One of the reasons for the reforms was the clever way the proponents compared the treatment of mill-workers, particularly children, with that of slaves.

The Factory Act of 1833 meant that no children could work in factories under the age of nine and a maximum working week of forty-eight hours was set for those aged nine to thirteen, limited to eight hours a day. For children between thirteen and eighteen it was limited to twelve hours a day. The Act also required children under thirteen to receive elementary schooling of two hours each day.

Livingstone worked for a relatively enlightened employer and so the new legislation brought little actual change in working conditions at the Blantyre cotton works, particularly as the buildings were old and poorly ventilated.

Livingstone wrote later that: 'Looking back now on that life of toil, I cannot but feel thankful that it formed such a material part of my education; and were it possible I should like to begin life again in the same lowly style, and pass through the same hardy training.'[13] This is typical Livingstone, that is, to down play difficulties whenever writing about them, but this tough early life where so few managed to surmount the difficulties and emerge from obscurity did help to condition him for the rigours and perils that lay ahead, both as a missionary and as an explorer. It is also true that the fact that he went on to achieve national fame marked him out as an extraordinary individual and his ability to triumph over impoverished circumstances bears testimony to his depth of character and his will power.

1.3 Missionary Training

The influence of religion played an enormous part in the development of Livingstone's character during his childhood and this would eventually lead him to deciding to become a missionary. But it was not always an easy road for him to follow.

The greatest early influence on his religious development was his father who brought his family up in the Auld Kirk of Scotland although he later broke from it when Livingstone was a young man, to become a deacon of an independent church in Hamilton. The family were not intimidated by a three-mile walk to church and regularly attended Sunday services.

The influence of the church in the 1800s was considerable. Few openly disagreed with its edicts and promulgations and even fewer dared to disobey, fearing the promise of eternal damnation for those that strayed from the chosen path. This meant that Sunday church could sometimes be a harrowing experience, especially for the young. There was little warmth or spontaneity about religious practices that are evident in today's church gatherings. Instead, they were a sombre affair.

The Calvinistic approach also did not offer much hope for those who were faithful as they maintained that only the Elect would pass into heaven. These chosen few would only know this after the Holy Spirit had entered their lives.

For Livingstone, the Calvinist approach made him fearful because he knew the Holy Spirit had not reached out to him. The depth of this problem was made apparent in an admission paper that he submitted to the directors of the London Missionary Society in 1838. In his response to one question that the society asked him to address, he wrote that from the age of twelve, he was troubled by the fact that he continually sinned before the Lord. He reasoned that this not only made him unworthy of God's truth and love but, because he was unlikely to ever be able to amend his ways, he felt he was always going to be prevented from asking God for forgiveness until he could change his ways. It was an awkward argument for a child to have got into. He was also troubled by the apparent incompatibility of science and religion that was a very real issue at that time; it seemed that a person had to be in one camp or the other. He liked the sciences, particularly enjoyed scouring for animal, plant and geological specimens but he found that he was constantly questioning himself: was this interest in scientific knowledge part of the Devil's work?

These thoughts troubled him during his teenage years until he was about nineteen when he read a book that changed his thinking. *The Philosophy of a Future State* was written by Dr Thomas Dick, a science teacher and church minister. This provided him with the rationale he needed to reconcile faith and science. The impact was profound and the mists of doubt began to disappear. Livingstone later read another book by the same author, *The Philosophy of Religion*. What these books did was to bring him comfort by explaining how religion and science were friendly to each other. So great was his joy that he decided to serve God in any capacity that he could:

> I saw the duty and inestimable privilege immediately to accept salvation by Christ. Humbly believing that through sovereign mercy and grace I have been enabled so to do, and having felt in some measure its effects on my still depraved and deceitful heart, it is my desire to show my attachment to the cause of Him who died for me by devoting my life to His service.[14]

Livingstone was so pleased that he felt moved to write to the ageing Dr Dick to thank him.

Livingstone was also proud to have received religious advice from a dying man who was one of the patriarchs of Blantyre society. The man's name was Mr David

Hogg and he told the young Livingstone: 'Now, lad, make religion the every-day business of your life, and not a thing of fits and starts; for if you do, temptation and other things will get the better of you.'[15] It was excellent advice. There is no doubt that Livingstone felt he was touched by the Holy Spirit and the resulting comfort that it gave him made it easier to bear the long years of self-denial and sacrifice that characterised much of Livingstone's life and especially so, during the years of solitude while exploring the heart of Africa.

Dr Thomas Dick's books came out at about the time when there was a strong groundswell pushing for change within the Auld Kirk. Many people were unhappy with the autocratic management of the Scottish Church; local churches increasingly wanted to have a say in how they could conduct their affairs within the community while the congregations wanted to be able to influence the way their local churches were run, including the right to reject appointed ministers if they did not meet the community's expectations.

Livingstone's father was caught up in the momentum for change when he went to hear a young Canadian preacher, Henry Wilkes, a well-known liberal theologian, deliver an assault on the conservative Church of Scotland in 1832. Neil came away from that meeting troubled and after much thought, applied to join an independent church in Hamilton, near Blantyre. This church was a member of the Congregational Union that was a loose and voluntary organisation of independent churches. The guiding principle was that each church should represent the congregation's demands in how it was to be administered and this was to be achieved through the elections of church elders. The rapid growth of the Congregational Union showed how vigorous the demands for change within the Kirk were; and because it was at the vanguard of the groundswell, the Union exerted a powerful influence, and was a catalyst for change.

There was also a strong belief in the early nineteenth century that the application of Christian principles and the power of faith could achieve a change in society for a better and a more just world. After all, had not the abolishment of slavery within the British Empire by an Act of Parliament in 1833 been largely the result of determined efforts by a coalition of Protestants, Catholics and others against the powerful with vested financial interests?

The thought about becoming a missionary occurred to Livingstone when he was twenty-one, after he read an article by Karl Gutzlaff,[16] a well-known Austrian Protestant medical missionary working in China. Gutzlaff had made a general appeal to the churches of America and Britain to send missionaries to that country. It had a profound impact on Livingstone who later wrote: 'that the salvation of men ought to be the chief desire and aim of every Christian,' and so he decided 'that he would give to the cause of missions all that he might earn beyond what was required for his subsistence.'[17] Gutzlaff inspired Livingstone to think about going to China as a missionary but events conspired against this wish, particularly when the First Opium War broke out in 1839, and China became closed to Christian missionaries until the war ended in 1842.

The task of becoming a missionary was not an easy one. Livingstone had earlier told his family about his interest in studying medicine but his father would not countenance the thought unless Livingstone did so for some express purpose. When Livingstone told his father that he wanted to become a medical missionary Neil was satisfied and he agreed to support his son.

What Livingstone wanted to do was relatively new since the idea of establishing medical missions was a recent innovation resulting from experiences of missionaries in China. It was found that if an occasion arose where a missionary was able to doctor someone, it helped to embed the missionary into the local community and make his job of spreading the word of Christ and increasing the number of converts among them, easier. It is easy to be cynical now about how strong the faith of these new converts would be but at that time, the most important measure of success for any missionary was the number conversions he made.

1.4 Medical Training

Livingstone's desire to become a medical missionary meant he would need to receive a good medical education. There were few barriers for entry on academic grounds as Livingstone had been studying Latin since he was ten and was well read. However, there was one enormous obstacle to surmount; obtaining a medical training was an expensive affair and especially so for a lowly spinner. The fee for each term was twelve pounds and that was before he purchased books and paid for his lodgings. However he was resolved on his course of action and by saving very hard during the six months of summer work in the cotton mill, he was able to largely support himself. It is another example of Livingstone never wanting to give up in the face of difficulty.

On a cold winter morning in 1836, Livingstone and his father walked the seven miles through snow from Blantyre to Glasgow to find lodgings for Livingstone while he attended classes at the Andersonian University.[18] They had been provided with a list of places that might be suitable for a poor student to rent while studying in Glasgow. It is not hard to imagine the two setting off: his father would be staunchly proud to the point of gruffness while the young man would be full of hope about the future; both would be aware of the significance of the step that Livingstone was about to undertake. However, it turned out to be a depressing task; all day they looked but the lodgings were all much more than he could afford until at the end of the day, perseverance was rewarded when they at last found an affordable room. It was located in Rotten Row and cost two shillings a week.

The next day Livingstone enrolled into his various classes. The classes began on 1 November 1836 and included Greek; theology sessions given by the Reverend Dr Wardlaw; and medicine. That evening he wrote to some friends telling them how lonely he felt after his father left but that he would put 'a stout heart to a stey brae, and either mak a spune or spoil a horn.'[19] Livingstone quickly met a number of people that became life-long friends, including James Young, a young teacher at the college.

The first term finished in April 1837 and Livingstone returned to Blantyre to continue working in the cotton mill in order to save money for the next term. It must have been difficult for Livingstone to fit back in with his friends; he was in a transitional phase while his presence reminded those who had remained behind about their own lack of opportunities.

Livingstone returned to Glasgow later that year to continue his studies and ponder his future. While thinking about options, some friends advised him to join the London Missionary Society because it:

> sends neither episcopacy nor Presbyterianism or independency, but the Gospel of Christ, to the heathen—exactly agreed with my ideas. But I had never received a farthing from any one, and it was not without a pang that I offered myself, for it was not agreeable for one accustomed to work his own way to become in a measure dependent on others.[20]

Soon after Livingstone wrote to the London Missionary Society to offer his services but it was not until he was in his final year that Livingstone heard that his application had been provisionally accepted by the society. The next step was for him to travel to London to be examined by the Mission Board. He did so in September 1838, together with Joseph Moore,[21] another aspirant missionary. The prospect of being examined drew the two men together as neither had been in London before and both were, understandably, nervous about the examinations they faced. Their relationship quickly cemented and Moore became a life-long friend. Nine years later Livingstone wrote to Moore telling him that 'of all those I have met since we parted, I have seen no one I can compare to you for sincere, hearty friendship.'[22] Moore later recorded that:

> I grew daily more attached to him. If I were asked why, I should be at a lost to reply. There was truly an indescribable charm about him, which, with all his rather ungainly ways, and by no means winning face, attracted almost everyone.[23]

Together they toured the City of London in their spare time, with the ex-spinner from Blantyre looking in awe at the splendour of St Paul's Cathedral; the beauty of Westminster; the impressiveness of the Tower of London; and all the other places of renown in that great city. They both arrived in their lodgings inspired by what they had seen.

The two candidates passed the board's examination and soon after they graduated from the Andersonian University. Livingstone received passes in Practical Anatomy and Anatomy, Lectures in Surgery, Chemistry, Practical Chemistry and Material

Medica. Their success meant that the London Missionary Society accepted them both on three months' probation.

The next step was to be sent to the elderly Reverend Richard Cecil for training at the London Missionary Society College in Chipping Ongar in Essex. It is a pretty place and it made a pleasant change from Blantyre. There were a small number of students there, including Livingstone, Moore, David Watt,[24] Joseph Taylor and J. S. Cook. They all shared lodgings and were required to look after themselves.

The strong impression that his fellow students formed of Livingstone at this time was his simplicity of view, a roughness of manner, a dogged persistence in holding to his own view, and kindness.[25]

The training was held at Cecil's house and consisted of lectures on theology, studying Latin, Greek and Hebrew and reading the Classics. The curriculum, while interesting, did not provide practical training for a missionary who could reasonably expect to end up anywhere around the world in the company of foreign and sometimes primitive people. They were also required to write sermons and after correction by the Reverend, would be committed to memory. However, this is not so easily done as Livingstone found out when he was unexpectedly called upon to deliver his first sermon for a minister who had suddenly fallen ill. It turned out to be a most unhappy experience; after entering the pulpit and reading the chosen biblical text, he found he had completely forgotten the sermon he had memorised. There were a few moments of panic and embarrassment before he suddenly blurted out to the congregation, 'Friends, I have forgotten all that I had to say,' and then fled from the church.

The Reverend carefully evaluated Livingstone's potential as a missionary and by January 1839, he had only formed a lukewarm opinion about his young Scottish charge:

> His heaviness of manner, united as it is with a rusticity, not likely to be removed, still strikes me as having importance, but he has sense and quiet vigour; his temper is good and his character substantial, so that I do not like the thought of his being rejected.[26]

The London Missionary Society considered Cecil's report and at one point in the meeting, a decision was made against him. Fortunately there was one to plead that they should give him an extension to see if he might improve.

Livingstone stayed on in Chipping Ongar and battled on. Cecil noted in another letter, written in February 1839, that Livingstone was 'worthy but remote from brilliant.' The picture that emerges about him from this time from friends and acquaintances suggests that he was a rather dour and serious young man. Walter Inglis later described Livingstone in this way: 'I have to admit he was no bonny. His face wore at all times the strongly marked lines of potent will. I never recollect of him relaxing into abandon of youthful frolic or play.'[27] These comments should be seen in their proper context. Livingstone was at a disadvantage to the other students since his was very much a Scottish working-class background while many of the others came from English middle-class families.

He was finally accepted in June 1839 and he was ordained along with William Ross on 20 November 1840 at the Albion Chapel, Moorgate Street in London. It had been hard work.

The question then arose—where to be posted? The first suggestion made by London Missionary Society directors was the West Indies. Livingstone recoiled from the idea. After all, as he argued in a letter to the London Missionary Society, the two years he had spent studying medicine would not be fully utilised since there were already a number of qualified doctors working there, and besides, it would be too 'like the ministry at home'.[28] Livingstone wanted a tougher challenge and suggested that he be sent to South Africa, 'being desirous to enter upon that sphere of labour and, I trust, that only, in which I may be able most efficiently to advance the great cause of our Blessed Redeemer'. The directors agreed with his suggestion and wrote to him later that month to say that he would continue his medical studies in London until early 1841, in order to prepare himself for a posting in either South Africa or the South Seas.

Livingstone arrived in London on the 2 January 1841 and took up lodgings at a London Missionary Society boarding house for young missionaries in Aldersgate. His goal was to further his medical and scientific knowledge and skills. He also joined the church in Falcon Square, London. The minister was a Dr Bennett and his son was also studying medicine.[29]

It was during this time that Livingstone first met Dr Robert Moffat, his future father-in-law. Moffat was at that time forty-four-years-old and working for the London Missionary Society. He was a physically impressive man and was widely considered a giant in missionary circles for his missionary and literary achievements in South Africa.

Moffat's background closely mirrored Livingstone's own humble Scottish beginnings and so it was probably a feeling of a kindred spirit that initially drew the two men together. He had been born at Ormiston in East Lothian and had started out as a nursery gardener, teaching himself Latin in his spare time. He later moved to Manchester before deciding he wanted to become a missionary. He applied and was accepted by the London Missionary Society in 1813. It was while waiting to start his missionary training that he struck up a romance with the daughter of his employer, Mary Smith. Their marriage was to be solid partnership that lasted over fifty years, surviving the many hardships they faced together in Africa.

Livingstone and Moffat struck up a lasting friendship and Moffat later recorded how it started:

I had occasion to call for someone at Mrs Sewell's, a boarding-house for young missionaries in Aldersgate Street, where Livingstone lived. I observed soon that this young man was interested in my story, that he would sometimes come quietly and ask me a question or two, and that he was always desirous to know where I was going to speak in public, and attended on these occasions. By and by he asked me whether I thought he would do for Africa. I said I believed he would, if he would not go to an old station, but would advance to unoccupied ground, specifying the vast plain to the north, where I had sometimes seen, in the morning sun, the smoke of a thousand villages, where no missionary had ever been. At last Livingstone said: 'What is the use of my waiting for the end of this abominable opium war? I will go at once to Africa.' The Directors concurred and Africa became his sphere.[30]

The influence that Moffat was to exercise over Livingstone was considerable. It was further strengthened when Livingstone later married Moffat's daughter, Mary, in 1845.

While in London Livingstone went to a public meeting organised by the *Society for the Extinction of the Slave Trade and for the Civilisation of Africa*. This society was actively campaigning for the full abolishment of all forms of slavery as the Moresby Treaty signed in 1822 by the Omani Arabs, who controlled the slave market in Zanzibar, had only made it illegal for them to sell slaves to Christian countries but not to other Arabs.

Britain had established a number of diplomatic relations with countries where there were active slave markets and sent consuls to monitor the local situation. The Arabs and Portuguese largely ignored these slaving restrictions and continued to capture and trade huge numbers of slaves across the African continent. On the east coast of Africa, large slaving caravans started out from places like Bagamoyo on the coast, travelling on foot as far as Lake Tanganyika, a distance of over 1,000 miles, buying slaves from local rulers, or when convenient, capturing them. The slaves were then chained together and used to carry ivory back to the coast where they would be packed into dhows and taken to Zanzibar.

A huge crowd of over 4,000 people had assembled in the Exeter Hall on The Strand, London, to hear a number of speakers, led by the Prince Consort. The meeting had an enormous impact on Livingstone, particularly when the well-known abolitionist, Thomas Buxton, a keynote speaker argued passionately for change:

notwithstanding all the measures hitherto adopted for the suppression of the foreign trade in slaves, the traffic has increased, under circumstances of aggravated horror, and prevails to an extent imperiously calling for the strenuous and combined exertion of the whole Christian community to effect its extinction.[31]

He also spoke about the need for commerce to help open Africa up, the so-called 'positive policy for Africa'. It was a practical message and was consequently endorsed at the meeting and led to the establishment of the Niger Expedition.[32] As it happened, the expedition was a disaster with large loss of life and with little to show for it. However, Buxton's point was that there was an urgent need for Christianity and commerce to work together to open up the African continent. One reason for offering genuine trade opportunities to the tribes was that it was thought it would in time lead to a reduction in the slave trade that raged throughout Africa. Livingstone agreed with his argument and later vigorously expounded this same view. Within the missionary circles, however, Buxton's idea about missionaries working alongside traders was thought repugnant; trading was considered a very undesirable occupation and certainly not one that any missionary would want to be associated with.

Livingstone was exceedingly busy with his work and the strain of attending lectures at the British and Foreign Medical School, Charing Cross Hospital and Moorfields Hospital for the Blind took their toll. He fell sick. It was probably hepatitis as he complained that his infected lungs and liver were the result of 'too much effluvia of sick chambers, dissecting rooms etc.'[33] It was serious enough for Livingstone to be sent home to Scotland for convalescence. The change did him good and he was soon back in London to continue his studies.

Livingstone did not have much time for socialising and certainly his experience with women was very limited. In the paper he had submitted to the London Missionary Society, his answer to a question about marriage was to the point: 'Unmarried, under no engagement relating to marriage, never made proposals of marriage, nor conducted myself so to any women as to cause her to suspect that I intended anything relating to marriage...'[34] The only amorous pursuit we know about occurred when he was a student at Ongar. She was called Catherine Ridley. The fact that she was a middle-class lady made Livingstone with his working-class background feel uncomfortable in her presence. He admitted as much in a letter telling her he was 'not very well acquainted with the feelings of those who have been ladies all their lives.'[35] In any event the relationship failed to flower: it seemed Miss Ridley preferred the company of another young student, Thomas Prentice. Livingstone would probably have continued with his busy schedule that did not leave time to pursue any likely marriage prospects but after it was decided that he would go to South Africa, the Moffat's became insistent that he should get married before going. It was good advice because it could be very lonely for a young man in some remote area where the chances of meeting someone suitable were very slim. Besides, a hard-working wife would be very useful to a young missionary trying to establish a mission. The Moffat's went so far as to even suggest what they thought might be a suitable companion for him; a Miss Collier. She was ten years older than Livingstone and the thought of marrying her somewhat distressed him.

Livingstone travelled back to Scotland in November 1840 to sit the medical exams required for admission as a Licentiate of the Faculty of Physicians and Surgeons of Glasgow. He could have sat similar exams in London at the Royal College of Surgeons but the directors of the London Missionary Society were unwilling to pay the higher fees demanded by the College.

The examination included the presentation of a thesis and Livingstone decided on the use of a stethoscope. He nearly failed the examination. Livingstone later wrote how he had 'unwittingly procured for myself an examination more severe than usual, in consequence of a difference of opinion between me and the examiners on the use of the stethoscope.'[36] It is indicative of his pugnacious and generally difficult nature that became increasingly apparent in later years.

This trip was also the last opportunity for Livingstone to see his parents. A single night was all there was available to them to say their farewells and Livingstone wanted to sit up all night talking to his family. However, his mother would not allow it. His sister Janet recalled the occasion:

> I remember my father and him talking over the prospects of Christian Missions. They agreed that the time would come when rich men and great men would think it an honour to support whole stations of missionaries, instead of spending their money on hounds and horses. On the morning of 17th November we got up at five o'clock. My mother made coffee. David read the 121st and 135th Psalm, and prayed. My father and he walked to Glasgow on a bleak morning to catch the Liverpool steamer.[37]

It was the last time the peripatetic Livingstone saw his father.

Livingstone returned to London and on the 20 November 1840 he was ordained as a nonconformist minister at the Albion Chapel in Finsbury. This type of ordination meant that he would only be recognised by other non-conformist denominations: he would not be able to preach in Anglican and Catholic churches. There was little time for him to relax after the ceremony because he was due to depart to South Africa on the 8th of December, on a barque. However, in between packing, he sat down to write a farewell letter to his mother. The tone of it is unusual and one can only wonder what Livingstone was thinking about when he was writing it:

> Now, however, as I am sorry to learn your health and strength is declining, and as we are separated for some time, who knows but it is forever … I now take this opportunity to draw your mind and direct my own to that subject which of all others, concerns us most, viz that of eternity … You have had many trails in passing through life, I believe it has been to you one continual long struggle with poverty for many years, perhaps this may still be your lot, this may have been temptation, you may have felt it was impossible you could bestow much attention on the concerns of the soul, but this just exactly is what you should certainly have felt…[38]

It was now time for the great African adventure to begin that would take him over much of southern Africa. Livingstone at twenty-seven years of age was resolute, if not a little lonely after the recent parting from his beloved family. He was also just another unknown missionary quietly setting out upon God's work; when he returned sixteen years later, he would be acclaimed by cheering crowds throughout Britain as a famous explorer.

CHAPTER 2

Missionary Expectations

'The smoke of a thousand villages'

2.1 Set Sail to Africa

The African continent was probably first circumnavigated by the Phoenicians in about 600 BC. In 440 BC Herodotus described the voyage:

> Libya (the ancient name for Africa) is demonstrably surrounded by water, except for the bit of it that forms the boundary with Asia. King Necho of Egypt was the first to discover this, as far as we know; after he abandoned the digging of the canal from the Nile to the Arabian Gulf, his next project was to despatch ships with Phoenician crews with instructions to return via the Pillars of Heracles into the northern sea and so back to Egypt. So the Phoenicians set out from the Red Sea and sailed into the sea to the south. Every autumn, they would come ashore, cultivate whatever bit of Libya they had reached in their voyage, and wait for harvest-time; then, when they had gathered in their crops, they would put to sea again. Consequently it was over two years before they rounded the Pillars of Heracles and arrived back in Egypt. They made a claim which I personally do not myself believe, although someone else might—that as they were sailing around Libya they had the sun on their right. This is how information about Libya was first gained.[1]

It was not until the fifteenth century that the shipping route around Africa became widely used, first by the Portuguese, and later by British and other sailors. But while the coastline was accurately mapped, the hinterland of Africa was still largely unexplored when Livingstone arrived in South Africa in 1841. Great European explorers had preceded him, including: James 'Ethiopian' Bruce who discovered the source of the Blue Nile; Mungo Park who chartered the Niger River; René Caillié who was the first European to enter Timbuktu; Richard Burton and John Speke who together discovered Lake Tanganyika. Speke also traced the source of the White Nile although there were many, including Livingstone, who disagreed that its source was Lake Victoria. But significant as these achievements were, details about the interior of the 'Dark Continent' were largely drawn from rumour and imagination. This only added to the fascination about Africa that was then, along with Antarctica the only remaining continents to be explored fully.

The topography of Africa made travel difficult. The easiest route to the interior appeared to be by water, but there was a lack of natural harbours on the coast. Secondly, the great rivers such as the Congo, Niger, Orange and the Zambezi do not allow for it because it entails crossing braided deltas, cataracts and tremendous variations in depth and flow that all act as impediments to river transportation at different times of the year. Travel overland was also extremely difficult because of the presence of the tsetse fly that brought death to livestock, particularly oxen that were the main form of transport; and mosquitos that spread malaria. At that time the cause of malaria, the 'African disease', was not understood. The other big killer of both natives and Europeans was dysentery, a parasite borne disease. These factors meant that Africa surrendered its secrets slowly and only at great loss of human life, giving rise to the familiar expression 'The White Man's Grave'.

Livingstone sailed to South Africa aboard the barque *George*. He was a man who liked to keep busy and made full use of his time during the fourteen-week voyage to South Africa. The ship's captain, Captain Donaldson, taught him how to navigate using a quadrant and he also learnt the basics of Setswana, using Moffat's newly published Sitchuana[2] Testament. His ability to learn languages is evident from the description of Sechuana words he detailed in his letter to his fellow student Prentice. It was a skill that proved to be essential to his future success.[3] He later noted: 'In eight years I had upwards of seven thousand [Sechuana] words and rejected many others either as uncouth or to me quite useless.'[4]

It was an eventful trip; during a severe storm their foremast was split and the Captain put into port at Rio de Janeiro to have it repaired and to get fresh water.[5] Livingstone did not like the place as he was shocked by the amount of drinking and womanising that went on in the waterfront bars. Livingstone, recently ordained and full of the confidence, decided to do something about it; one evening he visited a bar of particular disrepute and to the amazement of the drunken sailors, he started handing out temperance tracts. It was both a brave and foolhardy thing to do as it could have ended up very nastily, particularly as at one point he had 'about twenty ruffians around, some of them drunk and swearing'.[6] But he was lucky and the pluck that he displayed impressed his audience.

The voyage was also marred by an ugly incident between Livingstone and William Ross, a fellow missionary. At 38, Ross was setting out on his missionary work having started his career as a farm servant. It appears that Mrs Ross suffered very badly from seasickness and Livingstone felt compelled to try and help her.

His constant attention provoked the jealous rage of her husband.[7] Ross alleged that Livingstone was flirting with his wife, or in the vernacular of the time, 'had imposed on his wife'.[8] Angry words were exchanged with Livingstone describing Ross as a man with 'an exceedingly contracted mind' and 'is mule-headed beyond calculation'[9] while Ross countered with the comment that Livingstone had little hope of getting married because he was such an ugly and boring young man. Livingstone later wrote somewhat naïvely to Moffat that there might have been some justification in Mr Ross's accusations since it was true that he had paid much more attention to Mrs Ross than her husband.[10]

2.2 Cape Town

On the 15 March 1841, the *George* weighed anchor in Simon's Bay[11] and Livingstone immediately set out for Cape Town and arrived there two days later.[12] He stayed in Cape Town for about a month, lodging with a fellow Scot, Dr John Philip, who was the London Missionary Society's Secretary in South Africa. Philip had been Superintendent in South Africa since 1820 and was a well-known strong supporter of the native Khoi peoples, who were also known as the Hottentots or Bushman.[13] Moffat held a grave dislike for Philip and had already convinced Livingstone that Philip was a meddler and could not be trusted. It was therefore with some surprise that Dr Philip did not appear to be anything like what Livingstone had expected; he seemed genuine in his concern for the oppressed tribes in Southern Africa and took every opportunity to urge for the creation of areas reserved specifically for the natives. He also saw the London Missionary Society's role as essentially one of promoting civilisation in that part of the world.[14] Livingstone agreed with this view as he did not subscribe to 'Colonial feelings' but 'I am and always have been on the side of civil and religious liberty.'[15]

Cape Town presented the first opportunity for Livingstone to observe missionaries in the field. He was not very impressed for he saw that it was a much-divided group; there were those that supported the colonists while the others sympathised with the natives. It made for a divisive and unfriendly atmosphere and when Philip invited Livingstone to preach at a Sunday service, he made the most of the opportunity to castigate the congregation. The result was a controversial sermon: some of the parishioners responded by making accusations of heterodoxy against him while the rest, according to Livingstone:

> requested the notes of my sermon, expressing a determination to act more than they had done on the principle I had inculcated. My theme was the necessity of adopting the benevolence of the Son of God as the governing principle of our conduct.[16]

It is difficult to imagine the notes of a naïve young preacher would be eagerly sought after. It also seems Livingstone's oratorical skills had not improved much since his days at Ongar. In a letter to his friend Moore, written soon after he arrived in South Africa, he lamented, 'I am a very poor preacher, having a bad delivery, and some of them said if they knew I was going to preach again they would not enter the chapel.'[17] His delivery was not helped by the fact that he spoke with a thick Scottish accent.

Around this time Livingstone began an important friendship with a Dr Thomas Maclear.[18] Maclear was practising as a doctor in the Cape but had taken up astronomy as a hobby and had become increasingly interested in the subject. This interest was rewarded when he was later appointed Astronomer Royal of the Cape in recognition of his work. Livingstone asked him to teach him how to use a sextant and other instruments required for navigation to complement his knowledge of the use of a quadrant that he had learnt while sailing to South Africa. The friendship grew over the succeeding years and Livingstone made a point of regularly sending Maclear details of his observations and maps that he made during his subsequent travels.

Livingstone's first impressions of the African continent were favourable as he observed in a letter to his parents:

> The scenery is very fine. The white sand in some places near the beach drifted up in large wreaths exactly like snow. One might imagine himself in Scotland were there not the hot sun overhead. The woods present an aspect of strangeness, for everywhere the eye meets the foreign-looking tree from which the bitter aloes is extracted, popping up its head among the mimosa bushes and stunted acacias. Beautiful humming birds fly about in great numbers, sucking the nectar from the flowers, which are in great abundance and very beautiful.[19]

Livingstone showed his deep concern about his family from the moment he arrived in South Africa and continued to do so throughout his life. He wrote to his sisters Janet and Agnes and suggested they should consider moving to America where there were better opportunities. In the meantime he made good on his promise to send them money by drawing down an advance on his London Missionary Society salary.[20]

2.3 Trip to Kuruman

On the 20 May 1841, he again boarded the *George* to sail to Algoa Bay, in Port Elizabeth, to start a five hundred and thirty mile journey northwards to Kuruman in Bechuanaland.[21] Mr and Mrs Ross accompanied Livingstone but in spite of them he was able to enjoy himself. It was a long, slow journey on an ox-wagon. Each wagon carried up to a ton of supplies and was drawn by fourteen oxen. These animals lumbered along, averaging between ten to twenty miles a day. A driver would normally walk alongside the beasts, cracking a long whip made of rhinoceros hide, over the backs of the oxen to urge them on. The slow pace suited Livingstone as it allowed him to indulge in one of his favourite childhood pastimes; that of observing nature. He also enjoyed his first real sense of freedom on the African veld: they could travel as fast as they wanted to, stopping to hunt when required and camping in places of their choice. The only thing he had to grumble about was that he found it difficult to read and study local languages during the journey.

Their route traced a line of established London Missionary Society stations, the first being Bethelsdorp Station, about nine miles north-west of Port Elizabeth. In time they arrived at Griquatown (about 110 miles south of Kuruman) where there were missionaries. The Griquas were a tribe of half-caste Dutch and Hottentots who spoke Dutch. However, they were shunned by the whites and rejected by their mother tribe. This forced them to form communities of their own and in time they gained considerable power over the Bantu nation through their ability to acquire arms from the settlers. It was here that Livingstone first observed the employment of native 'missionaries' to spread the Gospel to the local tribes.

The ox-wagons pulled into Kuruman on 31 July 1841[22] and Robert Hamilton and Rogers Edwards[23] greeted the travellers. Kuruman was the most northerly established mission that the London Missionary Society operated in South Africa. Dr Moffat ran the Kuruman Mission but he and his family were still in Britain. It felt good to have arrived at last and Livingstone was full of hope. The Edwards family kindly invited him to stay with them and he was initially quite attached to them, noting Edwards was an 'excellent friend'.[24] Sadly, their friendship was not to last.

Livingstone had talked to Moffat when in London at some length about Africa and missionary work and he had built up a picture of what Kuruman was like. The reality was very different from what he had expected. For a start, it looked like a replica of a small English country village with its main street lined in trees. There were stone buildings, including a school, workshops and most importantly for any mission, a large church. There was also a well-established orchard that was watered by a large spring near the town's station, known as the 'Eye of Kuruman'. Kuruman, known to the natives as Sunday,[25] was a pretty place but it was uncomfortably hot during the summer months.

Livingstone was surprised and disappointed to find out that the missionaries stationed at Kuruman did not seem to have been very successful in their work. One problem was that the area surrounding Kuruman was not heavily populated. Livingstone thought there were just 700 Bechuana living in the immediate area and 1,300 to 1,400 people within fourteen miles of the mission.[26] It was nothing like the image that Moffat had so successfully conjured up of a populous nation, where there could be seen 'in the morning sun, the smoke of a thousand villages.' He concluded that the lack of a native population did not warrant such an elaborate mission, or indeed the numbers of missionaries that lived there. The community at Kuruman also seemed lethargic and indecisive although this can probably be ascribed to the fact that Moffat was away and he was the main driving force behind the Kuruman Mission.

Kuruman had a number of Scottish missionaries and it was an unsettled community. The Scots have been described as 'dogged and penurious and cautious'[27] and Livingstone was no exception. When Livingstone foolishly told the missionaries what he thought about their apparent failings they were of course not impressed. He was particularly scathing about the fact that there seemed to be only about six natives who could truly be called Christians although in time there was thought to be about forty natives who became committed Christians. These comments are another example of his tactlessness. Their reaction and irritation was understandable; a new and inexperienced missionary arrives and quickly starts criticising those who had been struggling over a period of years to develop the mission. What experience and success did he have? The answer of course was none.

The church services were an interesting spectacle; over three hundred natives normally attended church services. But it was not always a happy occasion; in response to warnings about the promise of eternal damnation for those that chose not to follow God's path, the congregation would shrink away in terror; some of the Bechuanas would hide their faces under their karosses while others would fall to the floor and creep around under the pews. More distracting would be those that actually ran out of the church and disappeared into the distance, 'fleeing with all their might.'[28]

Livingstone had not been given any instructions on what to do when he arrived and so he was free to do what he wanted. One of the first tasks that he set himself was to improve his knowledge of the local language, which he quickly mastered. Later on he carried a phrase book that contained notes about nine different African languages.

2.4 First Explorations North

It was not long before Livingstone started hungrily eying the vast expanse to the north. Moffat had advised him that he should consider establishing his own mission and this fitted exactly into Livingstone's plans—he was not the type that wanted to live under another man's shadow. He saw his chance when Edwards got permission from the London Missionary Society to travel north with the purpose of finding a suitable site to establish another mission. Edwards asked

Livingstone to accompany him, much to Livingstone's delight. The pair did not waste any time in preparation, leaving Kuruman in September 1841. They were away for three months.

Edwards and Livingstone passed through numerous villages as they slowly travelled north. The mud and thatched huts, with dung-smeared floors, were surrounded by high thorn fences to keep hungry predators away from their cattle and sheep. Men and women, dressed in their karosses, went about their business while young children, naked, played in the clay. They also encountered a number of tribes; Bakhatla-baMmanaana near Mabotsa, Bakwena at Shokwane and Dihubaruba, Bangwaketse at Setlagole and Barolong at Lotlhakane.[29] They discovered that all these tribes lived in permanent fear of a tribe called the Matabele, under the leadership of Moselikatse.[30] The Matabele had only moved into the area further north about twenty years earlier. How they came to be there is an important part of southern African history.

It all started when Dingiswayo, chief of the Mtetwa, set out to become the paramount chief in north-eastern Natal. His success depended on the skill of his army and so he implemented a number of military reforms to improve its effectiveness, including the reorganisation of his regiments based on age groupings. Then in 1810 he called on a twenty-three year old warrior to become his new military commander. His name was Shaka and he was a military genius. At that time warfare resembled more of a social outing than a battle where at a prearranged time and place, the armies and attendants would converge. Warriors would be chosen from each army to fight in single combat and they would be cheered on by the other warriors and women folk. Victory would be awarded to the army whose champion prevailed.

This arrangement seemed foolish for Shaka who believed war was about armies locked in combat. And so he continued the military reforms that Dingiswayo had made. First, he improved on the manoeuvrability of the 'horns and chest' formations that were commonly used, by demanding speed and discipline never before seen to encircle and close with the enemy. The purpose was to butcher them in hand-to-hand combat. This type of tactics meant that there was no need for a throwing spear and so he replaced it with a short assegai that was designed for close combat. He also drilled his soldiers remorselessly until they were superbly trained and disciplined. Nothing seemed to miss his fanatical attention to detail and in time he built the most efficient and feared fighting machine seen in southern Africa.

Shaka set out on the death of Dingiswayo to expand the empire using his tribe, the Zulus, as its core. There were many that opposed him but they were soon destroyed in battle. His success grew and there seemed to be nobody, or nothing, that escaped the power and fury of Shaka. The remnants of those defeated in battle and all others that were unwilling to submit to him were therefore forced to flee. It was a grim and bloody time and it later became known in seZulu as the

'Mfecane', or the 'wars of wandering'. These defeated tribes were driven towards all the points on the compass and being often powerful and well-armed, they fell upon tribes living in other areas, causing further displacement. One of the occupying forces was a branch of the Zulus, called the Matabele. Edwards and Livingstone were amazed at the fear with which this tribe were held but they were both powerless to do anything about it.

Their trek was successful in a number of ways. Firstly, they agreed on a possible site for a mission at a place called Mabotsa. It lay about two hundred miles northeast of Kuruman in the country of the Bakhatla[31] whose chief was Moseealele. The tribe was thought to number about two thousand people.[32] But they were under no illusions about how difficult it was going to be living there as they had passed through hot, desert-like country where water was difficult to find.

Edwards and Livingstone successfully completed their arduous trip of over 700 miles through difficult terrain. This included travelling 250 miles due north, which was thought to be further than any missionary had gone, and this gave them both the confidence to return north.[34]

2.5 Second Exploration North

Livingstone only stayed about a month in Kuruman before he set off north again on 10 February 1842. The ostensible purpose of this second trip was first, to improve his command of Bechuana and secondly, to test his idea of using native teachers to help him in his work of spreading the Gospel in an area where the community was well spread out. He had observed how the Griqua missionaries had used them and had found them useful. Livingstone knew he needed to get approval to use them but it would not be easy because the Griqua and Kuruman missionary communities were deeply divided over this issue.[33]

The missionaries at Kuruman generally disagreed with the policy of using native missionaries, apparently led by Moffat and Edwards, arguing that natives could not be relied upon to give a complete and accurate account of the Bible because they lacked proper training. The Griqua missionaries countered with an equally strong argument: native teachers used their mother tongue to spread the Word and this lead to an increased number of conversions to Christianity. Another reason that was advocated was that native teachers were more trusted than white men who were generally regarded with suspicion. This issue continued to fester throughout the time Livingstone remained a missionary.

The first person he selected for training by a fellow native was one of the chiefs of the Bakwains, called Bubi. These Bakwains lived in a place that lay about two hundred and sixty miles north-northwest of Kuruman. It ended in disappointment as far as the experiment was concerned because Livingstone's native teacher fell sick with fever soon after he started work, forcing Livingstone to withdraw him so that he could be treated properly. But this disappointment was offset by Livingstone's growing influence among the natives. He described the reasons why:

> The missionaries solicited their permission to do what they did, and this was the very way to make them show off their airs, for they are so disobliging; if they perceive any one is the least dependent upon them, they immediately begin to tyrannise. A more mean and selfish vice certainly does not exist in the world. I am trying a different plan with them. I make my presence with any one of them a favour, and when they show any impudence, I threaten to leave them, and if they don't amend, I put my threat into execution. By a bold, free course among them I have had not the least difficulty in managing the most fierce. They are in one sense fierce, and in another the greatest cowards in the world. A kick would, I am persuaded, quell the courage of the bravest of them. Add to this the report which many of them verily believe, that I am a great wizard, and you will understand how I can with ease visit any of them. Those who do not love, fear me, and so truly in their eyes am I possessed of supernatural power, some have not hesitated to affirm I am capable of even raising the dead![35]

His robust approach meant that Livingstone was able to travel surprisingly easily throughout the area with only natives for company. His knowledge of medicine was also greatly sought after. As the word got around, people would walk great distances to see if he could heal them. The prevalent diseases were ophthalmia, rheumatism and indigestion.

On this second trip, Livingstone proceeded further north than he had previously with Edwards, to see the Bamangwato who lived about four hundred and ten miles north of Kuruman. He explored some of the countryside while there and he got to within ten days journey of Lake Ngami although he did not know it. At that time, the lake was still undiscovered although many knew of its existence. He may have been tempted to continue but his party had to travel part of the journey on foot when his oxen fell sick. It was his companions' first experience of Livingstone's powerful pedestrian powers.

He was away for only five months on this second journey but he had already established a strong presence among the Bechuana tribes. When he arrived back in Kuruman in June 1842 he was disappointed to find that he had still not received any instructions from London on what he was to do. Livingstone had grown in confidence and he therefore resolved to immediately travel north again. However, a tribal war suddenly broke out which forced him to stay at Kuruman for seven long months. It was not a happy time because he did not fit easily into missionary society with his abrupt and outspoken manner. But the fault was not all his because in many ways, the missionary community set a poor example to their Christian flock: they indulged in acrimonious gossip about each other and jealousies and petty squabbles were common. Livingstone was therefore pleased to finally leave Kuruman.

2.6 Third Northern Exploratory Trip

Livingstone set out for his third trip into the northern interior on 21 February 1843. On this journey he passed up through Bakhatla country as he wanted to meet Sechele, a chief of another part of the Bakwain tribe. He was a powerful figure and it was important that they got on well together. Sechele was already annoyed that Livingstone had not come to see him on his previous journeys but luck was on Livingstone's side for when he arrived in Sechele's village, he found the chief greatly agitated because his only child was sick. Livingstone immediately set to work to treat his child together with another child of one of Sechele's ministers. The children were successfully cured and Sechele was relieved and grateful. It was the beginning of a strong friendship between the two men.

Sechele was interested in Livingstone's message about Christ and was soon asking him some very awkward questions with typical African simplicity. One of them was why a message that seemed so important to the white man had not being brought to Africa earlier, especially as there was no hope of salvation for Sechele's ancestors. Livingstone replied unconvincingly that the distance and difficulty of travel in Africa had prevented it.[36]

Livingstone enjoyed these exploratory trips. A prolific writer, he wrote about what he saw. Describing the tribal system, he noted with a touch of humour that:

> the people are all under the feudal system of government, the chieftainship is hereditary, and although the chief is usually the greatest ass, and the most insignificant of the tribe in appearance, the people pay a deference to him which is truly astonishing.[37]

On another occasion he wrote to his sister to allay her fears about what he might be eating:

> Janet, I suppose, will feel anxious to know what the dinner was; Well, we boiled a piece of the flesh of a rhinosuoss, which is toughness itself. The night previous, the meat was our supper, & porridge made of Indian corn & gravy of the meat made a very good dinner the next day.[38]

Livingstone enjoyed the company of the natives. This was evident from the apparent ease with which he travelled through the country, preaching and treating aliments. However, there were no early missionary successes: he was not even able to convince his closest native attendants about the importance of Christianity.

When one of his native companions called Sehamy died, Livingstone was distraught and poured his feelings out into a letter to his sister Janet:

> Poor Sehamy, where art thou now? Where lodges thy soul tonight? Didst thou think of what I told thee as thou turnedst from side to side in distress? I could now do anything for thee. I could weep for thy soul. But now nothing can be done. Thy fate is fixed. O, am I guilty of the blood of thy soul, my poor dear Sehamy? If so, how shall I look upon thee in the Judgement? But I told thee of a Saviour. O, didst thou think of Him, and did He lead thee through the dark valley, did He comfort as He only can? Help me, O Lord Jesus, to be faithful to everyone. O remember me, & let me not be guilty of the blood of souls.[39]

Livingstone arrived back in Kuruman in June 1843 and soon after a letter arrived from the directors authorising Edwards and Livingstone to establish a new mission at Mabotsa. However, they also suggested that the pair should wait for Moffat to arrive back in Kuruman so that a district committee could be formed to discuss the site of the proposed mission and how it could best be managed. These suggestions filled the independent Livingstone with dread; from his experiences with the missionaries at Kuruman, Livingstone knew it would be a long and frustrating process. Edwards had the same concern and so the two men decided to go ahead and establish a new mission without waiting for Moffat. It was in fact a brave decision for Edwards because he had never before acted without the approval of the society; for Livingstone, the independent course of action that he suggested was typical of him. Livingstone was, however, somewhat troubled by his own motivation in wanting to quickly establish his own mission: 'some of the brethren do not hesitate to tell the natives that my object is to obtain the applause of men. This bothers me, for I sometimes suspect my own motives.'[40] He was acknowledging somewhat guiltily that he sought both missionary success and its acknowledgement.

2.7 Mabotsa: A Missionary Beginning

Livingstone and Edwards initially planned to leave Kuruman in August 1843 but they delayed their departure for the arrival of three Englishmen. These three men were hunters; John Robert Pringle, Captain Thomas Montague Steele[41] and Andrew Hudson Bain.

It turned out that they were all stationed in India and had come to Africa on leave to do some big-game hunting, a common practice for wealthy young men. When they heard about the missionaries proposed journey, they asked that they be allowed to accompany them on their two-hundred-and-fifty-mile journey north. Livingstone did not enjoy their company, noting how ill-suited they all were in travelling in this part of Africa and their apparent spendthrift. He also disapproved of their sport, 'Their object in coming up to this part of the country is simply to kill animals. They frequently do so, & then leave their carcases to be destroyed by the vultures.'[42] Despite this rocky start one of the hunters, Steele, later became a close friend of Livingstone and a pall-bearer at his funeral.

Livingstone and Edwards arrived in the Mabotsa in late August 1843 and immediately got down to the business of establishing a mission. They had brought Mebaloe[43], a native teacher from Kuruman who was in training to become a missionary to assist them. The first thing to do was to gain formal approval from the natives to establish a mission in their area. The chief of the Bakhalta, Moseealele, called a meeting of his tribe to discuss whether they should allow the missionaries to live and work among them. The general reaction was favourable and in consequence Moseealele agreed to the missionaries' request.

The spot where the missionaries wanted to build was in an area where the Bakhalta also thought it would be suitable to relocate to. It was in a valley surrounded by tall peaks. The name of the mountain range immediately behind the peak was called Mabotsa, which meant 'marriage feast', and this became the name of the mission.[44] On the issue of acquiring land, the missionaries insisted that it should be paid for since they did not want to feel beholden to Moseealele. Accordingly, a legal document was drawn up and signed. The consideration was a gun, powder, lead and beads, worth a princely sum of four pounds.

The first building Edwards and Livingstone put up was a substantial building, fully fifty-two feet by twenty that became the church. Other buildings soon followed.

Edwards and Livingstone were hopeful about the future of their new mission although they were honest about why the Bakhatla had given them permission to establish a mission among them as Livingstone explained in a letter to Dr Arthur Tidman, Foreign Secretary of the London Missionary Society:

> They wish the residence of white men, not from any desire to know the Gospel, but merely, as some of them afterwards expressed it, 'That by our presence and prayers they may get plenty of rain, beads, guns &c. &c.'[45]

The London Missionary Society acknowledged the establishment of a new mission by publishing a ridiculous picture in their missionary magazine showing the two men wearing formal dress, complete with top hat, negotiating with the chief and his ministers and surrounded by a large crowd of natives. There seemed to be only one dissenting voice, Livingstone's acquaintance in Cape Town, the Reverend Dr Philip, who was concerned about the safety of the two missionaries 'because Mosilikatze was behind the Cashan mountains thirsting for the blood of the first white man who should fall into his hands, and no man would in his sober senses build his house on the crater of a volcano.'[46]

Edwards and Livingstone quickly settled down at Mabotsa but among other things, their age difference portended trouble between them. Edwards was eighteen years older than Livingstone and the establishment of Mabotsa was his big chance to show the directors of the London Missionary Society that he was capable of establishing a mission. He hoped that if he was successful, it would lead him to be promoted from 'artisan missionary' to full missionary status. By contrast, Livingstone increasingly viewed Mabotsa as his mission and as his opportunity to show that he was no ordinary missionary but a pioneer who was willing to go and work where no other had set foot. By this time Livingstone had spent over thirteen months travelling out of the twenty-eight months he was stationed in Kuruman. The directors had been very lenient with him in allowing him to travel as freely as they did and they were pleased to at last see Livingstone settle into a missionary post at Mabotsa.

Edwards and Livingstone were only about a month there when word came that Moffat and his family were on their way back to Kuruman. Both men decided it would be appropriate to meet him at Kuruman and so they departed south soon after. But it turned out that no one knew when to expect them; Livingstone ever busy, took the opportunity to write about the establishment of their new mission at Mabotsa. He sent a detailed report to the directors, purposefully omitting any mention about the significant part that Edwards had played in the affair. This was embarrassing for Livingstone when the London Missionary Society later published a complete version of his report. It also upset Edwards who was looking for recognition of his missionary work and spirit.

At the end of November 1843, word reached the mission that Moffat and his family were on their way to Kuruman. This was met with communal joy and relief. Livingstone, never very patient, decided he would go and meet them *en route*. He ended up riding nearly one-hundred-and-fifty miles to do so, racing his horse up to the caravan as if 'at Ascot or the Derby' to the enjoyment of the travellers. But this apparent keenness probably masked a sense of guilt arising from Edwards and Livingstone's decision to go ahead and establish Mabotsa without the permission of the district committee. Moffat, however, was impressed by the apparent enthusiasm that Livingstone showed. The slow trip back to Kuruman was a perfect opportunity for the two men to discuss the situation at Kuruman and future of the missionaries in southern Africa. Moffat later wrote warmly of Livingstone's enthusiasm,

> Such a visitant as Mr. Livingstone in the wide wilderness was to us a most refreshing circumstance. Few can conceive of the hallowed feeling his presence produced, direct from the station and people to whom all our fondest affections were bending.[47]

One thing that was clarified during the long ride back to Kuruman was the issue of native teachers. Contrary to popular view Moffat was not opposed to their use at outstations. This enlightened view meant missionaries would be able to rely on native helpers to establish new missions and help ease the daily grind of surviving in a harsh environment.[48]

It was also the first time Livingstone met Moffat's children. His eye soon fell upon Mary who at twenty-three years of age, was at a very eligible age for marriage. Mary also had time to closely observe the fit, young missionary and draw her own conclusions about his nature and prospects. Moffat later claimed that Livingstone was immediately 'smitten with Mary's charms' and although this is possible, Livingstone's subsequent comments about Mary suggested that he was more interested in the practicality of having a wife.[49]

The Moffat party included Walter Inglis[50] and William Ashton[51] and their wives. Inglis was a former Ongar student friend of Livingstone and they rejoiced in having the opportunity to meet up again in such difference circumstances. The happy party eventually reached Kuruman on 13 December 1843, particularly for Moffat as he had been in England since June 1839 and was keen to get back into proper missionary work.[52]

One of the first things Moffat organised on his return to Kuruman was a meeting of a newly formed 'district committee of the Griqua and Bechuana Missions'.[53] The London Missionary Society appointed missionaries from a range of denominations, such as Presbyterians, Episcopalians, and Independents who operated across the region. Each mission felt that its own work was equally important and deserving of funding but for the directors of the London Missionary Society, trying to judge how monies and resources should be allocated was an impossible task given the distance and communication difficulties. District committees were established to make decisions about funding priorities but this was not an easy task. At the inaugural meeting presided over by Moffat, Inglis, newly arrived, demanded to be a spectator 'because he is an Independent'[54], and did not want to become a member of the district committee. Livingstone moved a motion to have Inglis removed from the meeting on the basis that only members could be present. While the minutes of the meeting are unclear about the outcome it was certainly the beginning of a complete breakdown in Livingstone's relationship with this particular missionary. There were to be others.

2.8 Lion Attack

With the approval of Moffat, Livingstone and the Edwards family immediately left after the district committee meeting to travel back to Mabotsa. Their first task was to build houses and a watercourse to ensure their mission had a reliable water supply for irrigating the vegetable gardens. However, care had to be taken in moving around the area to find materials because there was a large pride of lions prowling the territory. Livingstone had already seen a woman eaten by a lion two years earlier in a particularly gruesome and bloody affair. Suddenly on about 7 January 1844,[55] some natives came running up to Livingstone yelling for his help. Lions had attacked their flock of sheep and killed nine sheep and goats in broad daylight. Livingstone provided a graphic account of the incident in his book, *Missionary Travels*. He and others dropped their tools and Livingstone, pausing to pick up his rifle, set off after the lions. When he came across a large lion he immediately fired both barrels at the beast but only succeeded in wounding it. The enraged beast sprang upon Livingstone and fastening his great jaws on Livingstone's arm, shook him 'as a cat does a mouse.'[56] The upper humus was crushed and the flesh torn and punctured by the lion's teeth; while it was doing so a faithful servant, Mebaloe, came panting up with another gun. He aimed and fired and although he missed, the lion's attention was sufficiently diverted by this new threat that it charged the hapless servant. Total confusion broke out: Mebaloe was attacked and his thigh was mauled; when another servant intervened by throwing a spear at the lion, he too was pounced upon and his shoulder bitten. Then suddenly the lion fell dead, apparently dying of the wounds that Livingstone had inflicted.

This version conflicts with the description that Livingstone provided in his letters to both Moffat (15 February 1844) and his parents (27 April 1844). In these letters he makes it clear that the natives had wounded the lion, not Livingstone;

> They [natives] surrounded him several times, but he managed to break through the circle. I then got tired, & coming home had to come near to the end of the hill. They were then close upon the lion & had wounded him. He rushed out from the bushes which concealed him from view, & bit me in the arm so as to break the bone.

Clearly Livingstone had re-written the facts to make a more interesting account of his brush with death when he sat down to write *Missionary Travels* thirteen years later, describing how 'beyond crunching the bone into splinters, eleven of his teeth had penetrated the upper part of my arm.'

Regardless of the facts Livingstone made light of the incident in his letter to Moffat[57] but his wounds were severe and the situation bad. He was two-hundred-and-fifty miles from Kuruman—normally about a two week trip—which was the nearest place where he might expect to get reasonable medical care. But it was not a journey he could contemplate in his condition and that meant that he would have to stay where he was. Edwards and his family were of course there but they did not have any medical knowledge or skill. This forced Livingstone to be both doctor and patient as he supervised the setting of his arm. It was an agonizing operation performed without anaesthetic as rough hands worked the crushed limb back into place. He then had to wait patiently for the injury to heal, a process that was protracted due to the wound copiously discharging which prevented the fusing of the fragments of bone. Edwards noted in a letter to the directors of the London Missionary Society how he and the native servants had attended Livingstone for three months but 'His sufferings were dreadful and called for all our sympathies and all we could do for him.'[58]

Livingstone was lucky that the injury mended surprisingly well, due in part to maggots in the wound that helped to keep it clean.[59] The only long-term damage was that he was unable to raise his arm above his shoulder and this made it impossible for him to shoot from his right shoulder.[60]

CHAPTER 3

Marriage

'She exchanged one great name for another, and honoured both'

3.1 The Moffat Family

The London Missionary Society's decision to extend their missionary work north of the Orange River led to Cornelius Kramer and William Anderson establishing the first of many missionary stations, in Griquatown in 1804.[1]

In 1821 the Scottish missionary Dr Robert Moffat (1795-1883) and his wife Mary (1795-1870), travelled to Griquatown from Cape Town. It was while they stayed at the Lattakoo Mission Station that Mary Moffat gave birth to her first-born, a daughter, also called Mary. She was the first of ten children.

At the time of Mary's birth, the Moffats were *en route* for their London Missionary Station in Kuruman. Moffat, together with Robert Hamilton had established one of the best-known missionary stations in southern Africa. Kuruman was sometimes majestically referred to as 'the fountain of Christianity'.

Moffat decided early on in his missionary career to treat all natives as equals, without fear or favour. In time his strong will and towering presence enabled him to become friends with a wide range of people, including Moselikatse, the much feared chief of the Matabele.

Moffat's wife also developed into an important part of the Moffat missionary team, although at first she did not care for the natives, describing them as having 'extreme selfishness, idleness, obstinate stupidity and want of sensibility.' With time, she grew more relaxed in the company of natives but always maintained a Victorian reserve.

Their daughter Mary grew up very much a white girl living in an African environment. Although there are few references to Mary as a young child, it is clear that she was fond of her sister Ann. At the time of Ann's birth the Moffats took in two Khoisan babies that were about to be buried with their dead mother. These babies grew up with Mary and her siblings and one of the babies, a girl, became a close life-long friend of Mary. The Moffats later rescued another abandoned Bechuana baby, whom they christened Sarah Roby. She remained with the Moffat family, even accompanying them on their trip to Britain in 1839.

The most important person in the Moffat children's early lives was their mother, who was efficient, exacting and matriarchal. She set high standards for herself and her family; was courageous, frequently undertaking long journeys without her husband who was often away conducting his missionary work; but was stiff and humourless. The only time she appears to have really enjoyed herself is when she was travelling by ox-wagon where the open spaces and simplicity of travel seemed to have a relaxing effect on her.

In June 1830 the Moffats took their two eldest children, Mary, then nine-years-old, and Ann, to the Cape to enrol them into school. They were enrolled in the beginning of September 1830 into Salem, a Wesleyan school near Grahamstown in the eastern part of the Cape Colony.[2] Mary's mother noted with some satisfaction that 'the strict attention paid to the religious instruction of the children compensates for the want of some advantages; the cheapness of the school and its comparative contiguity to our own part of the country are also inducements to have them there, as keeping them at home is beyond all doubt highly improper.'[3] In the same letter her mother noted it would be two or three years before she saw them again and their father, many years. It was in fact not until early 1833 that Mary Moffat was able to make a return trip to see how her daughters were progressing at Salem and also to enrol their third eldest child, Robert, into school.[4]

Mary's education was traditional: she spent five years at Salem. The Moffats were keen for her, in due time, to become an infant school teacher in Kuruman as this was already being discussed in 1833 when Mary was just twelve-years-old.

In 1835 Mary Moffat made another return to the Cape. One of the main reasons for making the journey this time was her very poor health and it was felt that she would recover better if she lived for a while on the coast. In early January 1836, she called into Salem to pick up her three children. Mary Moffat had decided to send her three children to Cape Town for further education.[5] In Mary's case she received informal teacher training.

In 1838 Moffat joined his family in Cape Town and they all boarded a ship to London. There were two reasons for making the voyage; the first was Mary Moffat's continuing poor health as it was apparent she had never fully recovered from her illness in 1835. The second reason was Moffat had completed his translation of the New Testament into Setswana and he decided to have the book published in England. It was twenty years since Robert and Mary Moffat had been in England and much had changed in the intervening years.[6] The Moffat family remained in England for five years and during most of that time Robert Moffat was deeply engaged in giving public lectures and sermons while his wife looked after her family and enjoyed life with family and friends.

The Moffats were stalwarts of the London Missionary Society and it was inevitable that any new missionary wanting to work in Africa should meet them. In time they were introduced to two aspiring Scottish missionaries, William Ross, whom Mary Moffat liked, and David Livingstone. Writing to her brother, Mary Moffat noted, 'I have done what I could to persuade Livingstone to marry, but he seems to decline it.'[7] Little did she know that she had just met her future son-in-law.

When Ross and Livingstone sailed for Africa in 1840 they took with them five hundred copies of Moffat's New Testament in the Setswana language. Moffat had also been working on the translation of the Psalms and a selection of Scripture lessons that he thought would be suitable for use in the churches in Bechuanaland. These works were later sent out to South Africa.[8]

Moffat was tireless and in the spring of 1842, published *Missionary Labours and Scenes in South Africa*.[9] It was an immediate commercial success. After his book was published he decided to return to South Africa with his family as he was keen to continue his missionary work, and in late 1842 he began a large number of valedictory meetings in Scotland and England. The public popularity of Moffat throughout Britain was not to be outdone until his son-in-law, Livingstone, first returned to Britain thirteen years later in 1856.

After attending a succession of tiring public events, the Moffat family boarded a ship, *Fortitude* and returned to South Africa in early 1843. Accompanying them were two other missionaries, Inglis and Ashton, together with their wives. The Moffat party arrived back in Kuruman on 10 December 1843 to a very warm welcome after a five-year absence.[10] Within a few weeks of their arrival their daughter Mary assumed responsibility for the infant school in Kuruman while Ashton took charge of the day school.[11]

3.2 The Indomitable Mrs Livingstone

Mary was determined and doughty. In her photograph, she looks capable and resolute. She was a local who knew how to maintain a household in a harsh climate, competently and uncomplainingly. Livingstone, a relative newcomer, was impressed by the fact that 'Mary speaks the language like a Native without knowing as so much of it as your servant [Livingstone]. I have a foreign accent, a heelandman. The Native children are fond of her and maybe, so am I.'[12]

In early July 1844, Livingstone decided to go to Kuruman in order to fully recuperate from the lion attack and to have a change of scene. He had been writing to Mary continuously since meeting her six months earlier and within three weeks of his return to Kuruman, Livingstone proposed to her under an Almond tree that grew in Kuruman.[13] She immediately accepted.

The newly engaged Livingstone returned to Mabotsa in August 1844, fired up to complete the construction of his house and a school. Livingstone seems to have enjoyed being architect and builder, writing enthusiastically to Mary about his progress. 'The walls are nearly finished, although the dimensions are 52 feet by 20 feet outside, or about the same size as that in which you now reside.' The buildings were constructed of stone to waist height and then completed with mud walls and finished with a wooden roof. Unfortunately the construction was not without its mishaps. At one stage he fell off the roof and had to grab a rafter with his stiff arm to break his fall. He was fortunate not to break it. A local trader, Buba[14] bound it up for Livingstone to stop the swelling, using 'splints, gum, white of egg, & sugar of lead, and a few days' rest put all to rights.'[15]

On 9 January 1845 they got married in Kuruman in the little stone church that had been built by Moffat, Robert Hamilton and their Bechuana helpers. Livingstone was thirty-one and Mary was twenty-three. Mary's wedding present to her new husband was a polyglot Bible, containing the Old and New Testaments. Her wedding gift inscription reads, 'To David Livingstone from his affectionate Mary. Jan 9th 1845.' It was a no-nonsense start to the marriage.

Livingstone was required to obtain permission from the directors of the London Missionary Society to marry Mary but it was not until December 1845 that Livingstone dutifully wrote to them:

> Various considerations connected with this new sphere of labour, and which to you need not be specified in detail, having lead me to the conclusion that it was my duty to enter into the marriage relation, I have made the necessary arrangements for union with Mary, the eldest daughter of Mr Moffat, in the beginning of January 1845. It was not without much serious consideration & earnest prayer I came to the above decision, and if I have not deceived myself I was in some measure guided by a desire that the Divine glory might be promoted in my increased usefulness. I hope this will be considered a sufficient notification of the changes contemplated, and that it will meet with the approbation of the Directors.[16]

It would at first appear to have been a marriage of convenience but it was a good pairing. She was the plain eldest daughter of an eminent missionary and could be expected to withstand the rigours and hardship of that type of life having being brought up in Africa. Physically she was of stout build and strong although she already showed the first signs of a tendency towards corpulence. She was also educated and this would be useful both for keeping house and in Livingstone's work. One of the problems Livingstone had already encountered was that it was difficult to talk with the natives about bigamy and fornication as a single man without raising suspicions about his purpose.

Livingstone was not an easy person to get on with but Mary was tough in her own way. Livingstone summed up his feelings about her when he wrote to a friend describing the ideal missionary wife: 'a plain common sense woman, not romantic.

Mine is a matter of fact lady, a little thick black haired girl, sturdy and all that I want.'[17] This description fits photographs of Mary.

For Mary, Livingstone presented a respectable way to get out of the Moffat household, away from her domineering mother and start her own married life. After all there were unlikely to be many marriage offers in such a far-flung place as Kuruman—for either person.

Much has been written about their marriage but they seem to have been genuinely fond of each other. Livingstone, in the typical Victorian manner, is formal in his letters to her although small glimpses of their playfulness occasionally appear, 'don't forget to write a long letter, the longer the better, although it may contain nonsense.'[18]

In typical missionary style, wives of missionaries expected to be left for long periods while their husbands pursued their work among the natives. In Mary's case, she was often left for extended periods during their successive missionary moves. Her sister, Ann, would visit Mary if possible and on one occasion while Livingstone was away building them a house in Chonuane, Ann stayed with her sister for a few months.[19] Unfortunately, this was the exception and Mary had to endure long periods of loneliness.

The marriage started out well. Livingstone was pleased to be married as it gave him companionship, a well-kept home, status within the missionary community, and in time, a family to enjoy. In October 1845 Livingstone wrote to his parents saying, 'Mary sends you her kindest love. We are happy & contented in each other.'[20]

It is of course difficult to know what each of them wanted from their marriage. Mary would have known her job was to put food on the table, keep a clean house, support Livingstone in his missionary career and in time provide children. In Livingstone's case, it is much more difficult to understand what his views on marriage were. He does provide a clue in a letter he wrote three years after his marriage to the Reverend D. G. Watt, who had lost his wife soon after their marriage. He advised Watt unenthusiastically, that 'Having been married the conjugal state may again be desirable but I would not go much out of my way for that object.'[21]

The way the couple interacted, particularly as their family grew, can be clearly ascertained from a letter that Livingstone wrote to his sister in April 1849, shortly after the birth of Thomas Steele Livingstone. It shows they had an effective working partnership. It is also one of the few passages where Livingstone describes at some length their family situation.

Mary with the young brood set off for Kuruman. I went four days with them and then returned on pack ox, and here I sit in the house alone, no matrimonial music ringing in my ears, no washing, no skirling & putting to bed, no nothing but a large sheet of paper which I must fill with either sense or nonsense before I lay me down to sleep. And first of all I must pay off a score I have contracted with my rib [Mary]. She got quite into a fever and blushed up to the ears lately when she found out I could not remember whether I had thanked you for all the fine things you had sent us in Mr Drummond's box. I think I did, but not being quite certain she wished me to write immediately on the point. I got out of the difficulty by promising to write as soon as she went away. The gown Mother sent she had on last Sunday she was with us, and wonderfully pleased she was with it. Intends to order her next by you. Your taste & knowledge of what is good pleases mightily…On 7th of last month [March 1849] we had another son added to the stock. We have called him Thomas Steel after a gentleman who wished us to do so… Mary is so much and so continually occupied with the children you need not expect much from her in the way of writing. She tried to put in a bit in one letter lately, & it seems I sealed it before she finished what she meant to say. She has all the household affairs to manage besides.[22]

On another occasion Livingstone noted in a letter to his sister Agnes:

Mary sends profound love to you all. It must be very deep, for she has this minute been finding fault with me for omitting it in some letters sent off last year. [23]

The common perception is that Livingstone was an uncaring husband but an examination of his letters does not support this. For example, his letters written after his family sailed from Cape Town for England in April 1852 show his deep longing—and perhaps some guilt—about their separation. He sent his wife two touching letters and in one of them he describes how he was feeling and articulates his thoughts about Mary, marriage and children:

How I miss you now, and the dear children! My heart yearns incessantly over you. How many thoughts of the past crowd into my mind! I feel as if I would treat you all much more tenderly and loving than ever. You have been a great blessing to me. You attended to my comfort in many many ways. May God bless you for all your kindnesses! I see nothing now to be compared with that sunburnt one which has so often greeted me with its kind look. Let us do our duty to our Saviour, and we shall meet again. I wish that time were now. You may read the letters over again which I wrote at Mabotsa,[24] the sweet time you know. As I told you before, I tell you again, they are true, true; there is not a bit of hypocrisy in them I never show all my feelings; but I can say truly, my dearest, that I loved you when I married you, and the longer I lived with you, I loved you the better.[25]

Livingstone described Mary in a letter to his mother as 'amiable & good-tempered.' He was also pleased with his in-laws, 'and my new connections pious, which you consider to be the best certificate of character. I cannot perceive that the attentions paid to my father-in-law at home have spoiled him.'[26]

Livingstone evidently enjoyed a close relationship with his father-in-law, as his many letters are warm, full of detail, whether it is discussing the pronunciation of native words, use of different native plants or observations about people. In one of his letters in July 1850 Livingstone playfully chides Moffat about their correspondence:

> I wonder you are not ashamed when you get one of my magnificent letters into your hands. They are perfect newspapers in size, while yours are mere ladies' notes. However, I am thankful for them when they come, and this I may as well tell you shews that I am a good-natured fellow upon the whole. My wife does not praise me, so I must sound my own trumpet, or it will lie unsounded, which would be a great pity.[27]

Livingstone's close relationship with his father-in-law was not reciprocated with his mother-in-law. There is no evidence to suggest that Mary Moffat was against the marriage of Livingstone and Mary, indeed she may have wondered if Mary would get married at all. But they certainly did not have a close relationship. Mary Moffat did not approve of the risks that Livingstone later placed upon his family and was vocal about this fact. She was clearly angry when Livingstone took his family on perilous exploratory trips but he seemed blind to the obvious risks associated with trekking into the wilderness. It seems extreme in this day and age to imagine taking a heavily pregnant wife and young children on these types of journeys, but even in the 1850s, Mary Moffat was not alone in her concerns; Livingstone's actions were subject to opprobrium from his peers.

Livingstone acknowledged this and naughtily noted in a letter to Moffat, 'From the way Mrs. M. has written to us for some time past, I expect to be obliged to pull down my breeches as soon as we reach Kuruman and get my bottom warmed with the "Taws". I can't please everyone, and least of all those who know not the objects I have in view.'[28]

Mary Moffat felt compelled on a number of occasions to visit her daughter because of fears over Mary's health. However, offsetting her concern with the welfare of the Livingstone family is her resonating joy at the good missionary work that Livingstone was undertaking.[29]

This constant warring continued through his marriage. For example, in 1852 after the Livingstone family arrived in the Cape, he wrote to Moffat but could not resist including an unkind jibe at his mother-in-law, 'Mamary has not given me a "touching up" since I came here. Hope she ain't dead. All present kind salutations to her & little Mrs [Robert] Moffat.'[30] Moffat's response to Livingstone's comments has not survived.

Livingstone was clearly an active member of the Moffat family, often providing advice in letters to Moffat about Mary's siblings, their education and work and marriage prospects. In a letter Mary Moffat sent to a friend she described the decision making process that led to her placing her two youngest girls into school in the Cape. 'Before I left home, my husband and Livingstone has been pressing on my attention very closely the propriety of sending the two little girls.'[31]

In regard to managing money—a common complaint in many marriages—Livingstone's later explorations placed a large strain on his modest salary of £100 per annum. The on-going costs were significant, even though a wealthy fellow explorer Oswell did on two occasions, significantly underwrite the cost of the expeditions. Livingstone estimated his loss of oxen to the tsetse fly on his third expedition to Lake Ngami in 1843 amounted to £47 'and about as much more in extra wages & expenses.'[32] This was on top of a wagon, supplies and oxen worth some £162 that Oswell gave to Livingstone to help defray some of the expedition costs.[33] These explorations meant there was barely sufficient money to support his family and certainly nothing left for luxuries.

It is difficult to know what Mary thought about this expenditure—perhaps she was just resigned to going along with it as a way to try and keep her husband happy. Even a trip to the Cape was expensive—Livingstone estimated it cost them between £60 and £70. By way of comparison, this was more than the amount, £50, that had been advanced to another missionary, Joseph Gill, to pay for the travelling costs of sailing back to England.[34] These expenses explain why he was sensitive to how the London Missionary Society would financially support him when he later sent Mary and the children back to England in 1852. Soon after he wrote ominously to his father-in-law; 'If they crimp my wife and family in England they will hear thunder.'[35] As it happened the London Missionary Society generously agreed to pay an allowance to Mary of £120 per annum.

Mary was frequently unwell during the early years of her marriage, living in harsh and at times, brutal conditions. We know that while suffering from the effects of the drought at Kolobeng there were long periods where they had no vegetables to eat and this necessitated Mary taking herself and the children off to Kuruman where there was food and parental support. Livingstone recorded in a note to his father-in-law, in early 1850, 'Mary often poorly, but not knocked up.'[36] This type of living was a contributing reason for Mary being afflicted more than once with partial paralysis of her face. It may have also started her gradual decline in health.

This later became evident when back in England she had a relapse in December 1853 while staying at the home of Isaac Braithwaite, an old family friend in Kendal, Westmorland. She became seriously ill. Livingstone heard about it much later and hoped it was not chronic.[37] A month later Mary wrote to Tidman, 'I am happy to say that I am so far recovered as to be able to move about again ... my illness has been long and severe.'[38]

3.3 Married and in Mabotsa

The couple returned to Mabotsa at the end of March. They quickly settled down into the familiar routine of married missionary life: Mary ran the missionary school for the natives while Livingstone carried out his pastoral, educational and when required, medical services.

For Livingstone the change must have been both extraordinary and satisfying. The most important thing was that there was now another pair of hands to help out—and Mary was very capable. Nonetheless, it continued to be a daily battle for survival and at times keeping house and garden and ensuring there was sufficient food and water took priority over missionary affairs.

Mary soon had a local school up and running in Mabotsa. The native children were initially in awe of this white woman teacher but Mary quickly had them learning to write and read. The children attended when they could but their attendance usually came second to completing jobs such as looking after the animals, crops and younger siblings and fetching water and firewood. As a consequence the school roll fluctuated daily. Mary also worked with the native women, teaching those who were interested to read and sew. When she was not teaching, she was tending to their garden, cooking and washing, repairing clothes, making soap and undertaking all the other innumerable activities that make a household function efficiently. They also had time for each other for Mary was soon pregnant with their first child.

The difficulty in maintaining a busy mission is apparent in a letter that Livingstone wrote to Moffat three months after he and Mary were married:

> The plough is in process of resuscitation, and though Mr E. [Edwards] consigned it to 'old iron' I feel sanguine it will soon be of more use than that material. Not having the instruments for boring or drilling holes for rivets I have taken the essential portions & let them into a log of murutu of this shape [drawing inserted]. The different portions are firmly screwed to it, & tomorrow we shall put in a new beam of white ash, much thicker than the old, but with the old wheel & coulter irons. Mr Milligan gave me an idea of the shape, or I should have gone wrong altogether. I had the handles in when he came, & as I was doing it simply from my recollection of the shape of a plough, I have the centre of the handles right in the centre of the plough, & not chiefly on the furrow side as it ought to be. Will you send the iron which runs from the handles to the beam, which you shewed me in the printing office? The one you made is entirely gone.[39]

Livingstone had not given up the idea of persuading others about using native teachers. He had written to the London Missionary Society directors as early as June 1843 urging that the natives be employed in such a capacity.[40] The independence that he had at Mabotsa gave him the opportunity to explore the idea further and he thought about establishing a training seminary for this purpose. When he broached the idea to the district council in Kuruman, he received a very lukewarm response; when he tried again, there were suggestions that Livingstone's sole motivation was that he wanted to become a 'professor'. The slur infuriated Livingstone and he immediately dropped the idea for the time being. It was the start of an increasing enmity between him and his missionary brethren in Kuruman. But he was determined to try out his ideas and so he started one anyway. It was a practical approach to his problem but it was a short-lived project because of his deteriorating relationship with Edwards at Mabotsa.

3.4 Edwards and Livingstone—Partners no More

Mr and Mrs Edwards had shown Livingstone much kindness when he first reached Kuruman by inviting him to stay with them. This relationship had matured and when Edwards invited Livingstone to journey north in order to establish a new mission, Livingstone gladly accepted.

Unfortunately it was not long before their relationship started to sour. It is not difficult to understand how this might happen in an unrelenting environment. Any unguarded comments, petty jealousies and perceived slights, if not quickly addressed, would have festered and resulted in a quickly deteriorating relationship.

It was always expected that Edwards would be in charge of the new mission— he was much older than Livingstone—Edwards was 49 and seventeen-years older than Livingstone. Unfortunately for them both, Livingstone did not see it that way. In a letter to his mother, Livingstone made it quite clear what he thought of Edwards' *vis-à-vis* his own position, 'he is mightily offended with me because the directors don't in the Magazine make him the great man of this mission.'[41]

They seemed to have argued about everything. Little incidents caused ructions, letters were written and accusations traded with Edwards claiming that Livingstone's 'conduct has been dishonest, dishonourable, & mischievous; there never has occurred an instance of conduct so base between one missionary & another, I don't believe there is another instance on record'[42] and that Livingstone wanted everything to be run in his own way. Livingstone countered that Edwards had attempted to 'impugn my veracity'.[43] One thing that Edwards felt particularly bitter about was that Livingstone had occasionally chosen to support the natives over certain issues rather than him. One example was a dispute between Mrs Edwards and her servant, Mebaloe's wife. Edwards believed Livingstone had quietly gone to the natives to seek information about the dispute without telling him what he was doing.[44] As a consequence, Edwards thought that this had undermined his authority within the community, as well as undermining Edwards' own confidence.

Livingstone wrote to Moffat from Mabotsa on the 1 April 1845, just seven months after Edwards and Livingstone had established the Mabotsa mission, to present his side of the situation. In that letter Livingstone raised the possibility with Moffat that Edwards had been trading, a serious charge against a missionary, quoting in a letter 'O, Mr Edwards has turned trader now; his man brought a fine large tusk (*this is No. 2)* from the Bakwains for him. If it were not for our difference I should ask an explanation from Mr E., and caution him against appearing to degrade the missionary character.'[45] In early May 1845 Livingstone wrote again to Moffat and raised the possibility of him and Mary leaving Mabotsa to establish a new mission.[46]

Edwards later decamped from Mabotsa in order to present his complaints to 'a Committee of the brethren',[47] presumably at Kuruman, although according to Schapera, he had gone to live with French missionaries at Motito.

It was a sorry parting of the ways of two men who both came to look foolish in the process. Unfortunately, Livingstone seems to have come out of the affair worst by displaying a spiteful and uncharitable attitude towards Edwards, This was particularly evident in long letters he wrote to the London Missionary Society directors complaining about Edwards, and in his letters to Moffat.[48] The London Missionary Society, not for the last time, was very perturbed about the turn of events and wrote to Livingstone about it:

We perused with deep and painful concern the principal portion of your letter dated in October last [1846], explanatory of the circumstances which led to your separating from Mr. Edwards and your removal to another station.

Unfortunately for Edwards the London Missionary Society then went on to take the side of Livingstone.

From our previous knowledge of your character and disposition, we are inclined to take the most favourable views of your conduct in this transaction, though we should feel it unjust to pass any positive opinion on the proceedings of Mr. Edwards from whom no communication on the subject has been received.[49]

Clearly the directors did not know their man, as this was the beginning of a pattern of Livingstone falling out with his fellow brethren.

It seems Livingstone had already decided in principle to move from Mabotsa while staying at Kuruman for his wedding but he withheld this information from Edwards. The reasons for doing so were clearly spelt out in a letter Livingstone wrote to his friend Pyne from Ongar:

At Mabotsa matters go on pretty well. But I don't expect to remain there long. The sphere is too small for two missionaries. As I am the younger I purpose to go on to the Bakwains of either Bubi or Sechele. If I remain at Mabotsa the utmost I could hope for would be the part of introduction of the gospel to a tribe, while by going to another it would be an introduction of the gospel wholly by my instrumentality.[50]

These comments are very illustrative of Livingstone's personality: a lack of transparency in dealing with others and an unwillingness to share success. When Edwards eventually found out that Livingstone intended leaving, he regretted what had occurred.[51] Livingstone gleefully pointed out that Edwards' remorsefulness only indicated his guilt in the whole affair.

The Bakhatla soon got to hear of Livingstone's plans and were upset with the thought of Livingstone leaving them, as he was well regarded and respected.[52] They offered to build him another house close by as an inducement to get him to stay. Despite their entreaties, Livingstone realised his chances of missionary success with the Bakhalta was very small. Indeed, in the time he had spent with them he had not made a single Christian convert. One reason was that the Bakhaltas viewed Christianity as something to be feared because it appeared to threaten their culture, including the practice of polygamy. Therefore, he knew the tribe's concern was not that Livingstone the missionary was leaving but Livingstone the man who had many useful skills, was shifting away.

Livingstone left Mary in Mabotsa and headed north in late August 1845 with the intention of finding an appropriate site to establish another mission. It was a decision taken without either the agreement of his colleagues in Kuruman or the approval of the London Missionary Society directors but that was of little concern to Livingstone.

3.5 Chonuane: A Second Start

Livingstone was undaunted by the challenge of establishing a new mission and having to build another house, his second in as many years. He was well aware of his general unpopularity with his fellow missionaries and the further he could be away from missionary politics the better. However, there was a significant financial cost to moving and it was more than he could afford on his meagre salary of one hundred pounds per annum. Furthermore, Mary was expecting their first child and he was therefore forced to write to the directors asking to borrow thirty pounds. It was a difficult thing for a proud man like Livingstone to do.

Livingstone chose to establish his new mission at a site that lay about forty miles north of Mabotsa, at a place called Chonuane.[53] The Bakwains, who numbered about three thousand five hundred people, inhabited the area.[54] Livingstone had been impressed by their intelligence and friendliness when he had visited them on previous trips.

Livingstone's first task was to decide which of the two competing chiefs of the Bakwains he would settle with. This was an issue of patronage and he finally decided to settle down with Sechele's section of the tribe, as the chief seemed genuinely keen to have a missionary settle down among his people. It was a lucky decision as soon after Bubi, the competing chief, died by blowing himself up when, following a poor elephant hunting trip, he had all the gunpowder in the town—about ten to twelve pounds—piled up so a medicine men could incant over it using burning sticks.[55] In the spectacular explosion that followed, Bubi and many of his close advisors were blown to bits. Sechele rapidly seized the opportunity to successfully unite the tribe under his chieftainship.

Sechele quickly made Livingstone welcome but was surprised when Livingstone insisted on purchasing land for his mission. Livingstone drew up a contract and both of them signed this document. The chief received a gun, some ammunition and beads in exchange.[56]

Sechele was a highly intelligent man who later became a powerful influence in the creation of Botswana as an independent republic. He was also intrigued by this strange religious message that Livingstone talked about. When he saw the doctor reading from a book one day, he asked that he be taught to read. He astounded his teacher when he learnt the English alphabet within two days.[57] This remarkable progress continued and in the space of a few weeks he was reading simple books.

Livingstone's experience at Mabotsa had taught him two things: firstly, the support of the chief was essential to making Christian converts. Secondly, native agents could be useful in helping to spread the word of the Gospel. In the Bakwain chief, Sechele, he had a strong chief who was outwardly interested in Christianity. As regards using native teachers, he had Mebaloe, his missionary assistant from Mabotsa and a new native teacher Paul, who had joined them from Kuruman. At last it seemed Livingstone had two men who seemed reliable. It portended well for the future but sadly it was a misplaced hope.

Livingstone's immediate priority was to start building a house in Chounane, with a view to having it completed by December or January 1846, while Mary remained in Mabotsa. There was a good reason for his urgency—Mary was expecting to give birth about this time. The house ended up being reasonably substantial—sixty-four feet by twenty.[58] Livingstone took some door and window frames from his house in Mabotsa and with Mebaloe's assistance, they quickly got to work building a house and establishing a garden.[59] The importance of the latter cannot be over-estimated; it was an essential food source. Livingstone was proud about the way his garden developed and frequently described the progress in his many letters to Moffat.

We have sown a great many garden seeds presented to us by Mr Methuen.[60] The endive, spin[a]ch, turnip, mangold wurzel & Knight's cabbage have come through the ground, also some lettuces & carrots, so we shall have vegetables. I have got three large Swedish turnips, intend them for seed. None of our onions have come up, the seed seems bad. I am very sorry the olive is dead, but there is hope in the roots. There are wild olives at the bottom of our garden at Chonuane. The soil is black deposit, with at some parts small portions of limestone intermixed. The banks of the stream are clayey. The water is small, but it will serve.[61]

Mary was also a keen gardener and Livingstone was quick to acknowledge that she knew more about gardening than he did.[62]

Mary gave birth to a son on 9 January 1846 in Mabotsa, which coincidentally happened to be the date of their first wedding anniversary. Livingstone was on hand and helped deliver his first-born child. He was the eldest of six children (three boys and three girls) that Livingstone and Mary eventually had. Livingstone toyed with the idea of calling him Neil[63] but in the end the baby was named Robert Moffat Livingstone.[64]

The first real description of Robert comes from Livingstone in a letter to his father-in-law in October 1847, when Robert was just twenty-two months old:

Robert is rather a consequential sort of gentleman. He won't even bestow a look on the chief, and if any of the people presume to salute him by touching him, he either walks past scornfully or lifts up a stick to keep them at a distance. You might see him lifting up a stick to those he could not strike above the knee, yet he roars out Murder if a kid looks at him. Seems to like English better than Sichuana, and is very fond of this little sister.[65]

Three years later in May 1849, Livingstone made a further observation about Robert.

He speaks the Native language well, but feels much at a loss in English. Never addresses us in it, and as we wish him to know the English we prefer to hear it though we lose much of his prattle or want of words. He is excessively obstinate at times. Never saw one so very determined at his age. It often causes us sorrow.[66]

When the London Missionary Society directors finally got to hear about Livingstone's movements, the Secretary again wrote and told him belatedly that 'they have sanctioned your removal to Chonuane, in the strong hope that you will there be able to bestow your undivided attention on the work, enjoy the peace of God in your heart, and largely experience His blessing on your labours.'[67]

Livingstone also seemed happy enough, informing Moffat in September 1845 that 'nothing is like the preaching of the Word. Dogged perseverance at this is infinitely preferable to doctoring, tinkering, or anything else.'[68] However, a pattern of being on the move had been established and it was not long before Livingstone grew restless to explore the surrounding region. He restrained himself long enough to make his house habitable for Mary and Robert and in July 1846 he set off east to go into the Boer Republic in Transvaal.

3.6 Contact with the Boers

The Boers were well established in what is now known as Transvaal and the Orange Free State at the time of Livingstone's visit. They had moved into this area as a result of the British Government's decision to abolish slavery in the Cape Colony in 1834. The Boers were outraged at the Government's proclamation since they viewed the natives like the original 'sons of Ham' who were born to be slave labour. But on the law being passed they were forced to either comply or leave. And leave they did, heading north out of the Cape in the thousands. The largest of these 'migrations' became known as the 'Great Trek' under the leadership of Louis Trichardt in 1835. It was a long and dangerous journey but beyond the Orange and the Great Fish rivers, they were free to rule as they liked. They divided the region up into districts and appointed district commandants to rule over them and soon after they began exerting their control over the tribes that inhabited the area. This was achieved by the familiar divide and rule strategy of setting one tribe against another as well as raiding tribes to plunder livestock, and more distressingly, children. These native children would then be 'officially' registered as orphans and this meant that they would become free labour for the person holding the registration papers. Ownership was transferable on payment of a transfer fee. The Boers also demanded that the chiefs provide free labour whenever it was required. Livingstone was to write:

> Nor have the Boers any wish to conceal the meanness of thus employing unpaid labour; on the contrary, every one of them … lauded his own humanity and justice in making such an equitable regulation. We make the people work for us, in consideration of allowing them to live in our country.

These quasi-forms of slavery carried out under official pretences shocked Livingstone, making him bitterly opposed to the Boers. When Livingstone tackled one commandant about this type of abuse, he was told that he did not know anything about it but 'promised to investigate the matter and apply the law in case.'[69]

The Boers correctly reasoned that given the growing international condemnation against slavery, it was best that this type of 'official' practice be kept as quiet as possible. It was therefore in their interest to keep any missionaries—and particularly British ones—out of their area of jurisdiction. A convenient excuse for doing so was to accuse the missionaries of arming the natives and so inevitably they alleged that Livingstone was involved. There may have been some justification in their accusation for if Livingstone was not actively involved in the arming of them, he certainly turned a blind eye to the acquisition of guns by Sechele. It is possible that they may also have heard Livingstone had sold Sechele a gun for his land holding at Chonuane and extrapolated this into an accusation that Livingstone was helping Sechele to obtain guns.

In July 1846 Livingstone crossed the Marico river and headed up to a large tribe ruled by a chief called Mokgatle. He then crossed the Limpopo river and met a Boer commandant, Gert Kruger. It was a tense meeting because Kruger had written to Livingstone five months earlier, in February 1846 asking him what his intentions were. During the meeting Kruger made an implied threat that the Boers would come and seize all the guns from Sechele's tribe[70] as the Boers had received a report that Sechele had procured a cannon.[71] Kruger made it clear that arming the tribes posed an unacceptable threat to the Boers and they had resolved to attack the Bakwain tribe before they grew too powerful. Livingstone was shocked to hear of their plans and it took all his persuasive powers to stop the attack. It was an uneasy truce and Livingstone returned to Chonuane troubled by what he had seen.

On his return Livingstone put his concerns to one side and busied himself in developing his mission and missionary work. This included building another large school (forty-eight feet by twenty)[72] and continuing his biblical lessons with Sechele. The obvious interest that the chief and his five wives took in Christianity guaranteed a large turnout for Livingstone's Sunday church services.

In September 1846 Mrs Moffat arrived in Chonuane, ostensibly to check on the health of her daughter. Mary's three other siblings, John, Elizabeth, and Jean also accompanied their mother. According to John who later wrote *The lives of Robert and Mary Moffat* his mother undertook this trip because 'her mother-heart was anxious about the daughter now enduring sickness and hardship in a new mission.'[73]

Mary Moffat brought much need resupplies as the area around Chonuane was wilting in the heat. Mary was also fading, trying to maintain her wifely and teaching duties while also looking after Robert. It must have been an uncomfortable visit for Livingstone as he would only be too well aware of the anxiety his mother-in-law must have felt in order to have made such a long journey north to Chonuane. Her fears about the dangers of Mary and Livingstone living in such a remote place—the furthest north of all missionaries in South Africa— was underscored when Robert fell seriously ill with pneumonia soon after Mary Moffat had returned to Kuruman.

In early October 1846 Livingstone wrote to his father-in-law requesting him to purchase a wagon.[74] On its arrival he immediately set to work preparing for another exploratory trip and in early November 1846 they ventured again eastward. Mary and their ten-month old baby Robert accompanied Livingstone on this trip. One reason for them all to go was to escape the drought that now gripped the land around Chonuane. It was proving to be a harsh place to live and certainly harder than Mabotsa as Livingstone acknowledged in a letter to his brother Charles.[75] In his last letter to Moffat before departing, Livingstone noted their entire corn crop was lost due to lack of rains.[76] The recent visit by his mother-in-law may also have contributed to his decision to see if they could find somewhere better to live.

They went by ox-wagon and they travelled further east into Transvaal than Livingstone had done on his previous trip.[77] They were away for about six weeks meeting many tribes who had never met a missionary before. On the way back Livingstone stopped to have a second meeting with Kruger. It was barely civil with the two men treating each other with mutual suspicion and hostility. Livingstone had hoped to settle one of his native teachers with one of the larger tribes in the area but this could only happen with the approval of the Boer commandant and Kruger had no intention of giving it. Frustrated, Livingstone returned to Chonuane and battled on with his missionary work amid growing starvation. The drought soon became so critical for the Bakwains that Sechele was forced to move his tribe to a place called Kolobeng where water was more plentiful.[78] This provided a valid reason for Livingstone to make a change. However, before doing so, in March 1847 Livingstone returned to Kuruman to attend another meeting of the district committee. At the meeting Livingstone got annoyed when Ross, his former colleague, proposed a motion calling on Livingstone to explain why he had moved to Chonuane without getting permission from the district committee. Although the motion did not get debated, Livingstone became fully aware of his unpopularity among his brethren and knew he must remain with the Bakwains for the time being.

Two months later both Mary and Livingstone were back in Kuruman for the birth of their second child. Their first daughter was born on 13 June 1847[79] and was called Agnes, although the natives invariably called her Nannee.[80] Mary Moffat was shocked at their appearance and later wrote, 'The Livingstones came out last year, half withered away with fatigue and privation. I laboured hard to fetch up their strength, and sent Mary back with their children like roses.'[81]

Soon after they returned to Chonuane and began the depressing task of again packing up their belongings in order to follow the Bakwains north to Kolobeng. The family faced a considerable challenge—and hardship—as they would again be starting from scratch.

CHAPTER 4

A Fresh Start

'The Love of Christ constraineth us.' St. Paul
'The Love of Christ compelled me.'

Livingstone 1873

4.1 Kolobeng: A Third Fresh Start

Livingstone had a triumvirate of brethren who were opposed to him: Edwards, Inglis and Ross. His letters from this time, particularly to Moffat, are full of accusations and he makes contrary statements about perceived injustices. For his father-in-law, it must have been both saddening and wearying to have to read these letters.

In August 1847 Livingstone prepared to relocate his family to Kolobeng and establish a new mission there among Sechele's Bakwain people who had already left Chonuane. Kolobeng means 'the haunt of the wild boar'. It lay about two hundred and seventy miles north east of Kuruman and about forty miles north-west of Chonuane in what is today Botswana.[1] The mission was situated on the edge of the Kalahari Desert, but in spite of this the land was fertile and there was water—or seemed to be. For Livingstone, Kolobeng provided a convenient base to expand his missionary work into the well-populated area further to the east.[2]

Mary again remained in Chonuane with their native teacher Paul, while Livingstone and Mebaloe went ahead to start building huts. Later Livingstone, Mary and their native helpers, Mebaloe, Paul, Isaac and Friday[3] formed the nucleus of the mission at Kolobeng.

Sechele announced that his people would build a church in their new station to demonstrate his personal commitment to Christ. A school followed soon after so that the mission was rapidly advanced.[4] If this aspect was fast, Livingstone's request to the London Missionary Society to approve the change of mission was not, as it was not until February 1848 that Livingstone finally wrote to his friend Watt of the London Missionary Society. 'My date [13 February 1848] will show you if you have not received my last letter that we are now in a different locality from that to which I suppose you have been accustomed.'[5] In doing so Livingstone again presented the London Missionary Society directors with a *fait accompli* and they were forced to respond to Livingstone in November 1848 and agree to his re-settlement, 'we hope we may now regard you as permanently settled, knowing well the disadvantages attending frequent changes of this nature.'[6] Kolobeng thus became the London Missionary Society's most distantly established mission in southern Africa, a fact that Livingstone liked to tell people about.

The most important task facing the Livingstone family was to build proper shelter as they had only built temporary huts. Livingstone set about it promptly but nonetheless it took about a year to complete the house,[7] as Livingstone's attention was continually diverted to overseeing Sechele's church and school building programme. Livingstone chose a rocky knoll overlooking the river on which to build his new dwelling. Their new house was another large building, approximately fifty-feet long and twenty-feet wide, with an attached workshop. The size amazed the Bakwains and they kept asking him why it was necessary to have such a 'large cave' when so few people lived in it. In the meantime, the uncomplaining Mary lived in a wood and mud hut bringing up their two children. The physical conditions were tough as the hut offered little protection against either the heat or the cold. Even Livingstone, famously inured to hardship, noted in a letter to his parents how they froze at night during the wet season while during the day the hut would be full of swarming flies that settled onto the faces and particularly the eyes, of their young children.[8] He also confided to Moffat that, 'Mary is troubled with shooting pains in the chest. Had sore eyes but not severely, & is now recovered. She got them from the little one.'[9]

Mary not only had to look after her family, but she was also kept busy running her infant and sewing school[10] for about sixty to eighty pupils.[11] She was exhausted by the strain and this was evident when Livingstone and his family later travelled to Kuruman for supplies. One old woman who knew Mary exclaimed loudly to Livingstone's embarrassment, 'Bless me! How lean she is! Has he starved her? Is there no food in the country to which she has been?'

Despite their difficulties Livingstone continued his missionary work during the day while at night he would typically sit down to write a letter before falling asleep. There was little time to play with his children, something that he later regretted. This meant Mary largely brought up his children.

Livingstone did not often refer to his children in his letters but an example is from 1849 when they were living in Kolobeng where he described a familiar family scene. 'Robert is now singing at the top of his voice at my elbow, and Nanee [Agnes] has just gone to the land of Nod from running around first to one leg then another for the amusement of biting it'.

Livingstone's work schedule followed a familiar pattern: missionary activities took place during the morning, including teaching most of the influential members of the tribe how to read. Sechele and his wives outshone the others. In the afternoons, daily chores would be carried out and these included gardening and repairing buildings and watercourses until it was time for evening services. Livingstone's favourite preaching topics included 'the love of Christ, the Fatherhood of God, the resurrection, and the last judgement.'[12] Livingstone used a 'magic lantern' to illustrate and explain parts of the bible.[13] A magic lantern was an early type of image projector through which images, backlit by a candle, could be displayed. The one Livingstone used stood about one-and-a-half feet high. He used it to good effect to build interest in Christianity and by June 1848 between 100 and 150 members of the tribe regularly attended church services on Sundays.[14]

A year after being in Kolobeng, Livingstone was able to report to the London Missionary Society directors with some degree of satisfaction that he had persuaded Sechele to give up polygamy. This was the first step towards getting Sechele to become a Christian. The chief's practical solution was to send his superfluous wives back to their respective families. It was a testing time for Sechele for when the tribe heard about his decision, they were most unhappy about it. One reason was because it was deeply humiliating for a married woman to be divorced. The tribal elders simply could not understand why a religion that preached love and forgiveness should also require a husband to only have one wife, when clearly he loved more. Sechele's decision to enter into a monogamous relationship was one of the factors that slowly isolated Livingstone from the rest of the tribe because they saw it as an unwarranted attack on their customs and traditions. In time this lack of tribal support eventually contributed to the failure of Livingstone's missionary work with the Bakwains.

Sechele was baptized on the 1 October 1848.[15] It had taken Livingstone over two-and-a-half years of patient missionary work to get Sechele to fully accept Christianity and it was over seven years since he first set foot in Africa. For the occasion, Sechele, fittingly, was dressed in a cloak and sat in one of two baptismal chairs that had recently arrived from Birmingham.

Livingstone was understandably proud of his achievement because it was his first, and as it turned out, only convert. But while Livingstone was enjoying his success, his first convert suffered grievously for his decision. His tribe openly taunted their chief about his decision to take up this new religion. The problem was that the Bakwains now thought Sechele had become a 'white man' who they still thought ate human brains. The open hostility was a serious challenge to the chief as previously a disrespectful member of the tribe would have been expelled from the tribe or killed out of hand. Livingstone also had to endure the same level of disrespect although this did not worry him.

Livingstone made another trip eastward, leaving Kolobeng on 5 December 1848.[16] In the course of that trip he had a particularly unpleasant meeting with Andries Potgieter,[17] the chief commandant of the Boers on about 13 December 1848.

The main concern of the Boers at that time was the possibility that the British Government would take possession of land presently occupied by them. This concern was genuine and arose following a recent confrontation with the British.

The British governor, Sir Harry Smith[18] had resolutely dealt to the Boers when he took command of a military expedition and crossed the Orange River without warning and engaged the Boers. Andries Pretorius[19] led the Boer force and a pitched battle was fought on 29 August 1848 in what became known as the Battle of Boomplaats. The result was the annexation of what became known as the Orange Free State. Many Boers opted to stay and live under British rule but the more intransigent ones crossed the Vaal river to carve out a new homeland in the territory of the Bechwana and Bapedi tribes. This immediately brought the Boers into conflict with the missionaries in the Bechwana area, particularly when the missionaries saw first-hand how harshly the Boers treated the natives.[20]

In a letter to Moffat he described his encounter with Andries Potgieter.

> Paul & I went lately in order to erect a temporary building at Mokhatla's in which he might place his family. We found Potgieter close by, and somewhat opposed to our work from an idea that we had come to take possession of the land for the English Govt. We could scarcely get an opportunity to reason with him on the absurdity of this supposition, for an individual from Holland, whom I take to be a Jesuit, would scarcely allow us to speak three words without screaming out at the top of his voice that missionaries were like a cancer & ought to be shot, & a thousand other things which perhaps happily for me I did not understand.[21]

This meant Livingstone had to again abandon his plan of settling a native teacher with the Mokhatla people. He also learnt that some French missionaries had previously tried to settle five native teachers in the same area but Kruger had torn up their letters of introduction and chased the teachers away.

Livingstone returned to Kolobeng where Mary had remained behind as she was pregnant again. By January 1849 she was suffering pre-natal sickness and in a letter Livingstone sent to Moffat he confided:

> Mary is much as usual—frequently tired & troubled with pains of different sorts. These can be troublesome when she sits up long in one position. Cannot write her Mamma at present, & is quite excusable. Wish much I have some chloroform. From the accounts I see of its operation I expect the old ladies will be wishing they could begin again. It is uniformly safe for both mother and child, and the recovery is much accelerated.[22]

On 7 March 1849, while still in Kolobeng, Mary delivered another boy after only three hours of labour. They named him Thomas Steele Livingstone after Livingstone's good friend. Livingstone laconically recorded, 'Seems to be a strong chap. Cries very little. His share is not missed, for the other two when both at it afford music enough for one house.'[23]

In May of 1849, Livingstone wrote to the London Missionary Society directors saying that it was very difficult for everybody living around Kolobeng as the area was in the grip of a new drought that was to continue for three long years. The failure of the crops forced the natives to hunt game almost continuously. Livingstone lamented the fact that they even searched for food on the Sabbath although he could not bring himself to blame them.

Livingstone's precarious situation was further compounded when Potgieter wrote to Ross, as Secretary of the district committee in January 1849, demanding the permanent recall of Livingstone from Kolobeng.[24] The Boers also ominously threatened to take their own measures if the district committee failed to take the necessary steps.[25]

The Boers further increased the pressure two months later when they sent a delegation to Kuruman demanding the recall of Livingstone,[26] by making the serious allegation that he had sold Sechele five hundred guns and a cannon. While the allegations were unproven, they were damaging to Livingstone as some of his brethren thought that the wayward missionary might have been involved in gun running in some way. The district committee prevaricated but it seemed inevitable to all that Livingstone and his family would soon have to leave Kolobeng.

If Livingstone was unworried about these events, there was something he noticed that did worry him—one of Sechele's former wives was pregnant. He asked the chief whether he was the father and shyly Sechele confirmed that he was, admitting that he had slept with her twice[27] in January 1849.[28] This was about three months after his baptism and it came as a real body blow to Livingstone. Sechele was deeply repentant, and Livingstone's punishment was to suspend Sechele from Christian fellowship for a time. Worse was to follow when Livingstone learnt that Isaac, son of one his native teachers, Paul, had seduced a Hottentot woman who was an early member of the Kuruman congregation. When Isaac was confronted he was not in the least bit repentant about his conquest—and soon disappeared from Kolobeng.[29]

To make matters worse Livingstone learnt that the sexual predations of Sechele and Isaac were common knowledge among the Bakwains. The realisation that he had been made a fool fell like a hammer blow. Livingstone immediately contemplated leaving the tribe as soon as possible and this time Mary was in agreement.

> The conclusion to which I came immediately was, he [Sechele] has apostatized, and if he has become our enemy I may as well leave and try some other tribe. Mary said, 'Let us both go now'.[30]

4.2 Discovery of Lake Ngami

Livingstone had been thinking for some time about exploring the region north of Kolobeng as his plans to work eastward were being actively thwarted by the Boers.

The existence of a large lake on the other side of the Kalahari Desert was becoming increasingly well-known although no European had yet succeeded in reaching it. Livingstone decided that he would be the first. He also wanted to go and meet a very powerful chief called Sebitoane who lived north of the lake. It was rumoured that he had created a small empire in the interior of Africa. His desire was heightened when he had seven visitors from the Ngami lake region call upon him in early May 1849, and who subsequently invited Livingstone to visit them.[31]

The lake was known as Ngami and lay about eight hundred and fifty miles northeast of Kuruman. The only difficulty was the vast Kalahari Desert—about 120 miles of waterless desert—that lay between Kolobeng and the lake. Only the Kalahari bushmen and Bakalahari had the skills to pass through this area.

The type of expedition that Livingstone envisaged would need to be substantial and self-sufficient. He could not hope to pay for its cost on his meagre salary of one hundred pounds per annum and it was therefore essential that he get a sponsor. He knew that Moffat had been given four hundred pounds to mount such an expedition and Livingstone had written to him on a number of occasions suggesting that they should attempt the trip together. Moffat, however, was continually occupied with missionary matters and it became clear to Livingstone that it was unlikely that Moffat would ever make the trip. Livingstone had also written to a wealthy Englishman who had a passion for travel. His name was William Cotton Oswell. Oswell had briefly stayed with Livingstone at Mabotsa while on a hunting trip and Livingstone thought he seemed like the type of man that would be interested in making a crossing of the Kalahari. He was therefore delighted when he received a letter from Oswell informing him that he and another English hunting friend, Mungo Murray, would be arriving in Kolobeng in late May 1849 with the intention of making the crossing with him. Oswell also happily agreed to underwrite the cost of the expedition, and when he arrived he presented Livingstone with a wagon worth £50.[32] This was the first of two wagons that he eventually gave to Livingstone. All preparations were soon completed and on 1 June 1849 Livingstone and his two English companions and their native escorts set off on ox-wagons.

They decided not to attempt what had already failed—trying to cross the Kalahari Desert—but instead circumnavigate the desert as much as possible by travelling up the north-eastern border of the Kalahari. For the next month, they moved slowly across the fringes of the desert using local guides. At one stage a hyena startled seventeen oxen into flight but they were eventually rounded up and returned to the party by members of the Bamangwato. Their chief, Sekgoma, delivered a stern warning that they should turn back. They were not to be deterred, however, and continued their slow journey north. They were all amazed by the vastness of the desert. At times it was covered in shrubbery and in other places it is perfectly flat. The glare from the soft white sand made navigation difficult and Livingstone marvelled at his guide's ability to move confidently across the country. Unfortunately even their guide was not infallible as Oswell and Murray found out when they went off hunting eland. It seems that when they started moving quickly over the country in pursuit of game, the guide lost his way. All day they roamed around completely lost until nightfall fell and they could make out lights in the distance. On another evening, just as dusk was falling, they unexpectedly came across a large lake. The setting rays cast a beautiful blue hue over it and Oswell, overjoyed, threw his hat into the air and cheered loudly. Murray and Livingstone also believed that they had discovered a lake, the existence of which was not previously known. They could also see elephants in the distance and Oswell immediately began saddling up his horse to go hunting. But they had been deceived by a mirage for what they had found was the first of a number of huge saltpans that can be found in north-eastern Botswana. These saltpans are magnificent, being vast flat areas of salt encrustations that reflect light to bewitch the beholder. Their guides chuckled at the white men's folly.

The party continued pushing north and on the 4 July 1848, after covering 300 miles, they reached the Zouga River.[33] It was rumoured to flow out of Lake Ngami and so they turned west and followed the course of the river. It was a pleasant journey plodding along the gently curving banks of the Zouga River that were lined with many gigantic Baobab trees. It reminded Livingstone of the banks of the River Clyde.[34] After several days they came across a tribe called the Bakoba[35] who lived on the banks of the river. The tribe was widely known not to carry arms and that meant they had to submit to every raiding party that swept through the area. This Quaker-like behaviour delighted Livingstone and he enthused about them, writing that they seemed the most receptive to his Christian message of all of the people that he had so far encountered in Africa. The chief of the Bakoba ordered his people to assist the explorers by providing them with canoes so that they could paddle up the river. These canoes were hollowed out of logs using adzes and were a source of great pride for their owners. After a couple of days paddling, they soon came across a confluence that marked the junction of the rivers Tamanak'le and Zouga. When Livingstone enquired he became excited by the reply: 'Whence the Tamanak'le came?

> 'Oh! From a country full of rivers,—so many, no one can tell their number, and full of large trees.' This was the first confirmation of statements I had heard from the Bakwains ... that the country beyond was not the 'large and sandy plateau' of the philosophers. The prospect of a highway, capable of being traversed by boats to an entirely unexplored and very populous region, grew from that time forward stronger and stronger in my mind; so much so, that when we actually came to the lake, this idea occupied such a large portion of my mental vision, that the actual discovery seemed but of little importance.[36]

The excitement that Livingstone felt remained with him and over the succeeding years he slowly organised his thoughts into a strategy for opening up Africa using the great rivers as highways to penetrate the interior.

Their efforts were rewarded when on 1 August 1849 the three Europeans first looked on Lake Ngami. It was a moment of euphoria as they realised they had achieved a place in history. Enquiries from the natives revealed that it took several days to walk around it and Livingstone estimated the lake might be about seventy miles long.[37] Today, the lake has reduced to no more than a marshy plain due to desertification.

Livingstone had planned to go on and meet the paramount chief of the Makololo tribe, Sebitoane, who lived about two hundred miles north of the lake. However, he was prevented from doing so by an ambitious half-chief, Leculathebe, who refused both guides and passage through his land since he feared that Sebitoane would obtain guns from the traders. Livingstone was not so easily deterred and he set about building a raft. In doing so, he spent many hours standing in the Zouga River unsuccessfully trying to build a raft out of dry wood. When he was later told that there were many crocodiles in the river, he realised how lucky he was not to have been attacked. The river was only fifty or sixty yards wide and Livingstone noted:

I could easily have swam across, and fain would have done it, but landing start naked and bullying the Bakoba for the loan of a boat would scarcely be the thing for a messenger of Peace. [38]

In fact Livingstone only gave up on his plan when Oswell, startled by Livingstone's determined behaviour, offered to bring a boat up from the Cape on their next trip. They were also worried that the wet season was fast approaching which would make travel difficult and so, with satisfied hearts, they returned to Kolobeng.

The party arrived back in Kolobeng after their six hundred mile journey on 9 October 1849.[39] They had been away for just over four months, about six weeks longer than they had estimated.

The area around Kolobeng was still in the grip of a drought, and Mary, busy bringing up her three children and trying to maintain her regular school classes, was struggling to survive alongside the Bakwains. Her anxiety must have been acute for there was a very real risk that Livingstone and his companions would fail and die in the wildness. There is no record of how Mary coped during this long absence, the first of many. The only time we hear about Mary during this period is when Livingstone mentions her in his letters to family and friends. When Mary had time, she occasionally added a footnote to a letter but they were brief and often concerned with obtaining household supplies, clothing and the health of the children.

If Mary was anxious for them, Livingstone arrived back exhilarated about their achievement. He wasted no time in informing the London Missionary Society about their discovery and Captain Steele, who passed the news onto the Royal Geographical Society.[40] Livingstone was worried that Oswell might try to claim all the recognition as he had financed the expedition but he could not have been more wrong since Oswell was quite happy to stay in the background. This was due to his characteristic generosity. Later overtures were made to Oswell by a representative of the Royal Geographical Society saying that they needed some form of written statement so that his contribution could also be recognised, he still demurred saying 'give it to Livingstone for he wants much more than I do.'

Recognition was not slow in coming since they had not only discovered Lake Ngami but the party had succeeded in travelling through the Kalahari Desert where a number of other well-equipped expeditions had failed. This trip enabled Livingstone to quickly establish his reputation as an explorer. In May 1850, the Royal Geographical Society awarded him one half of the 1849 Royal Premium, being a gift of twenty-five guineas from Queen Victoria. The citation noted that the award was 'for his successful journey, in company with Messrs Oswell and Murray, across the Southern African Desert, for the Discovery of an interesting Country, a fine River, and an extensive inland Lake.'[41] Livingstone used this money to purchase a chronometer watch for determining latitudes by observing the occultation of the stars by the moon.[42]

4.3 A Second Trip to Lake Ngami

Livingstone was keen to make another attempt to see Sebitoane but during the early part of 1850, he and Mary concentrated on just trying to survive in Kolobeng because of the continuing drought. It finally broke after four long, difficult years when the rainy season finally arrived.

Livingstone was increasingly troubled by his uvula that was causing him difficulties when speaking.[43] They discussed going to the Cape to have it removed, but in the end he chose to stay in Kolobeng. He also did not want to go to Kuruman because of his deteriorating relationship with the other missionaries. It seems he was normally on the wrong side of the politics that circulated and festered within this small isolated missionary community. In a letter Livingstone wrote to Moffat dated 8 July 1850 he complained 'there is no more Christian affection between most if not all the brethren and me than between my riding-ox and his grandmother'.[44]

In frustration he finally decided to go north again but instead of waiting for Oswell as had been arranged, he packed his family into an ox-wagon and set off on the six hundred mile journey north in April 1850. It has never been properly understood while he did not to wait for Oswell to join them. As it happened Oswell arrived in Kolobeng in May 1850 to find to his surprise that the Livingstones had departed a month previously. Oswell was a generous man but even he must have reflected on the strange behaviour of his friend.

Sechele, one wife and about twenty native followers accompanied the Livingstone family. Sechele was interested in investigating trade opportunities. He may have also have wanted some time away from his tribe who were still unhappy with his Christian conversion.

On Livingstone's first trip to Lake Ngami with Oswell and Murray the Bamangwato chief Sekgoma, who lived in Shoshong, had deliberately impeded their progress. Sekgoma controlled the ivory trade coming out of the north and he realised that if any white men opened up a route north through the Kalahari Desert then it would only be a matter of time before traders followed. Consequently he ordered water holes to be filled in and this had contributed to the suffering that Livingstone, Oswell and Murray had endured. This time Livingstone decided he would visit Sekgoma. It was a brave thing to do, but as Livingstone knew, a man travelling with his family does not pose a threat. They were in luck as Sekgoma was suffering with an ulcer and Livingstone was able to use his medical skills to successfully treat him. The chief's gratitude was quick in coming for he ordered his men to unblock the wells and provided Livingstone with guides as they set out for the Zouga River.

Oswell, in a gentlemanly fashion, followed Livingstone and occupied himself with hunting along the Zouga River until he met the Livingstones returning from their expedition.[45] It must have been an uncomfortable and unexpected rendezvous for Livingstone. Livingstone's selfish motive becomes clear when he later wrote to Moffat, 'Oswel was excessively anxious that I should promise to let him accompany me next year, but I declined, yet I don't know how to get rid of him.'[46] Livingstone was in no mood to share his success.

It is also difficult to understand why Livingstone decided to take his family along as Mary, 'the great Irish Manufactory' as Livingstone unkindly put it, was pregnant again. The children, Robert, Agnes and Thomas required constant care because of their age and travelling through the Kalahari Desert, previously thought impassable, was certainly no place for them to be. One can only conclude that Livingstone seemed completely impervious to their plight. However, he did succeed in bringing his family to the shores of Lake Ngami and in doing so they became the first European family to visit the lake. Unfortunately this success was quickly forgotten when his children and some of his servants caught a malarial fever while they were camped on the shore of the lake. No doubt the poor diet and rough living that they had experienced on the trip had affected the resistance of the young ones. They soon became so ill that Livingstone knew that he would have to go back. 'Thomas had it in the remittent form, & Agnes in the intermittent.'[47] Livingstone prescribed quinine as a treatment and it seemed to work, but nonetheless disappointed, Livingstone abandoned his plans of visiting Sebitoane and set off back to Kolobeng.

The party had another difficult passage back to Kolobeng, during which Livingstone lost nine oxen.[48] The family survived what could have been a very nasty accident when one day the wagon they were travelling on cartwheeled into a disguised pit that had been dug to capture game.[49] It was something that Mary had long feared would happen but when it did happen, she exclaimed, 'Is this all?'[50] They were also constantly short of water and exhausted from the unrelenting heat. Mary was in her very last stage of her pregnancy and it was surprising that she did not have a miscarriage. When they arrived back at Kolobeng at the end of July 1850, she was expecting to give birth literally at any moment. It was a remarkable feat of endurance by a woman in having to put up with the constant, uncomfortable movement of travelling on an unsprung ox-wagon.

Mary gave birth a mere seven days arriving back from their 1,200 mile journey,[51] delivering their fourth child, a daughter called Elizabeth Pyne Livingstone.[52] Sadly the baby did not survive long: a mere six weeks as she and the other children caught an epidemic that was raging through the Bakwains.[53] Elizabeth was buried in a grove of nearby mimosa trees.

Meanwhile Mary, weakened by the pregnancy, soon became ill. Shivering and earache was followed by a paralysis of the right side of her face. Livingstone tried cupping behind her ear but she could not bear a second treatment.[54] It was obvious, even to Doctor Livingstone, that it was time that his wife and children got some proper care. Fortunately Mary Moffat had heard about their return and ever perceptive, gathered supplies and immediately set out for Kolobeng to replenish the Livingstone's meagre stores, arriving there on 15 October 1850. During the intervening time Mary gradually recovered from her paralysis. However, such was the state of the family, with the children particularly thin, that Mary Moffat was able to successfully prevail upon them to return to Kuruman with her for rest and recuperation.[55]

They all travelled south to Kuruman in November 1850 and remained there until February 1851 recovering. However, it was an unhappy time, mainly because Livingstone did not fit easily back into missionary society, as attested by his description of the state of affairs then existing in South Africa.

> Mr Moffat is busy with the translation of the whole Bible, a great work and likely to be of permanent benefit to the people ... This is the only great work at present going on in the South African field. A remarkable deadness afflicts the whole country. There are no candidates, no conversations.[56]

There was talk about them making a journey to the Cape to get essential supplies and also to enable Livingstone to get his uvula operated on but in the end Livingstone dismissed the idea, as he was keen to head back north again.[57]

While in Kuruman Livingstone discussed with his parents-in-law his plans to establish a new mission as the Bakwains were preparing to move further 'up the Kolobeng'[58] due to the continuing lack of water. The Moffats were naturally very concerned about Livingstone relocating his family once again and undertaking further explorations, as it was clearly having an impact on the health of the ever-faithful Mary and the children. Mary Moffat in particular, argued vehemently against Livingstone taking his family on further explorations.

The situation became further inflamed when soon after their return to Kolobeng, Mary's mother subsequently discovered that her son-in-law had decided to ignore her advice and take his family on another trip north. She wrote to him, demanding with righteous indignation, that he explain why he wanted to put his family at further risk:

> Before you left the Kuruman I did all I dared to do to broach the subject of your intended journey, and thus bring on a candid discussion, more especially with regard to Mary's accompanying you with those dear children ... But to my dismay I now get a letter [from Mary], in which she writes, 'I must again wend my weary way to the far interior, perhaps to be confined in the field'. O Livingstone, what do you mean? Was it not enough that you lost one lovely babe, and scarcely saved the others, while the mother came home threatened with paralysis? And will you again expose her & them in those sickly regions on an exploring expedition? All the world will condemn the cruelty of the thing to say nothing of the indecorousness of it.[59]

Livingstone's thoughtlessness was strange and as a Doctor, he should also have known better.

The quote from a letter Mary sent to her mother, now lost, gives the sharpest indication on what Mary thought about having to accompany Livingstone once more to the north: 'I must again wend my weary way to the far interior, perhaps to be confined in the field'. The bitter loss of their daughter, Elizabeth Pyne must have been raw with Mary. She also knew she was already pregnant again. Would this as yet unborn child survive or go the same way as Elizabeth?

The letter from his mother-in-law incensed Livingstone, especially as she added: 'Had you found a place to which you wished to go and commence missionary operations, the case would be altered.' This last comment cut deeply since she had dared to write what people only privately thought about Livingstone's seemingly itinerant approach to his missionary work. And so, unsurprisingly he ignored her advice. There was certainly an element of spite in his decision and justified, perhaps, because one of the purposes of the trip was to identify a healthy site on which to establish a new mission.[60] It appears Mary had by now also accepted the need to move.[61]

It seems Moffat kept himself somewhat aloof from his wife's entreaties to her son-in-law. Moffat wrote to a friend in March 1851, 'The Livingstones were some months with us, and have returned improved in health. It is probable that he will visit the lake, or rather Sebitoane, the ensuring winter, accompanied by Mr. Oswell.'[62]

4.4 A Third Trip to Lake Ngami and Meeting Sebitoane

Livingstone's failure to reach the Makololo on his second trip persuaded him to wait for Oswell who had promised to fully equip a third expedition. Oswell duly arrived with all the equipment and provisions. Oswell's generous spirit shows what an exceptionally tolerant and forgiving nature he had.

The caravan set off from Kolobeng on about 26 April 1851. It included Oswell who had gone ahead and the Livingstones, who followed in their ox-wagon. Livingstone and Oswell were determined to reach the Makololo. Mary was just following her husband, and the children were there for the adventure.

When they eventually met up with Oswell they found him recovering from another of a long list of close escapes. The latest incident occurred when a lion jumped onto his horse. In the ensuing *mêlée*, the panicked horse wheeled around a wait-a-bit thorn bush and Oswell was thrown to the ground and knocked out. When he came to he found his dogs had bailed up the lion only thirty yards away.[63] Livingstone later wrote what a remarkably brave man Oswell was.

They followed the same path that they had first used to travel up through the Kalahari Desert—the north-easterly circular route. The area was more drought-affected than previously, 'There is not a single flower to be seen now, everything is withered. Never saw it so excessively dry. The grass crumbles in the hand to powder.'[64] They had also taken the precaution of sending several men ahead to deepen the wells. All went well until they reached the Chukutsa pan where they decided to branch off northward rather than westward as they had previously done.[65] The reason was that they wanted to take a more direct route to where Sebitoane lived. Little was known about this country and it was therefore essential that they hire a reliable guide. Luck was on their side because they came across a Bushman who needed his gun repaired and a few days later another who offered his skills as an interpreter if Livingstone would also repair his gun.[66] Livingstone successfully repaired both weapons and the grateful Bushmen offered to lead them over the wastelands to where they wanted to go. However, they warned them with some foreboding that they should not expect to get any water for at least a month. It required a courageous decision but they considered the risks and decided to chance it.

Despite the warning the country they passed through was much more depressing than they expected: the never-ending vista is one of scrub and deep sand. Nothing seemed to move in the landscape. On they plodded with a guide who seemed more interested in following elephants. They constantly worried about water. Then one morning they were horrified to find that their guide had slipped away during the night. There was nothing else to do but to continue in the direction that they had been heading. The situation was quickly becoming grim when suddenly they came across a trail and in the distance they could see birds. It meant water and so they unyoked the thirsty oxen and these promptly rushed off as they could smell the water. They were followed by some of their servants while Oswell and Livingstone and his family remained with the wagon. Their only hope was the servants would return with some water. Livingstone sat down to write up his journal and he recorded just how worried he was:

> The supply of water in the wagons had been wasted by one of our servants, and by the afternoon only a small portion remained for our children. This was a bitterly anxious night; and next morning, the less there was of water, the more thirsty the little rogues became. The idea of them perishing before our eyes was terrible; it would almost have been a relief to me to have been reproached with being the entire cause of the catastrophe, but not one syllable of upbraiding was uttered by their mother, though the tearful eye told the agony within. In the afternoon of the fifth day, to our inexpressible relief, some of the men returned with a supply of that fluid of which we had never before felt the true value.[67]

Livingstone and his party, once more refreshed, set off on a north-westerly bearing for the Chobe river[68] which lay about one hundred and seventy miles away. The intervening countryside quickly changed from dry desert to marshlands and watercourses that had to be carefully crossed. They reached the Chobe in late September 1851 and to their surprise found some Makololo were waiting, ready to take them to their chief. Sebitoane had received word that white men were travelling to meet him.

It was impossible to ferry the wagons over the river and so Livingstone and Oswell decided to board some canoes to travel thirty miles down the river to met Sebitoane. Mary and her three children were left behind together with their Bakwana drivers and helpers. It was a brutal thing for Livingstone to do; his wife was seven months pregnant and he was leaving her to look after their three little children. Left in the wild, she would be unlikely to be able to do so properly if there were complications with her pregnancy. Oswell noted Mary was heartbroken and fearful 'when it was proposed to leave her behind'.

This decision would also mean Mary and the children would be stranded as the tsetse was slowly but surely decimating their oxen. Twelve had already died and a similar number were failing from the tsetse 'sleeping sickness'. The tsetse fly did not only attack oxen; anyone who has been bitten by this ferocious insect never forgets the experience—both the bite and the painful swelling.

Mary's father Moffat was meanwhile, perceptively, again writing to his friend Dr Bruce, 'Livingstone and Oswell were in Sebitoane's country by last accounts, north-east of the Ngami lake. Think only what a journey for a wife and children. We shall wonder and be very thankful if they all come back safe.'[69]

Sebitoane had been living at his southern capital in Linyanti but when word was brought to him of the imminent arrival of his two visitors he moved down the Chobe to greet them. The auspicious meeting took place on an island in the middle of the river.

Livingstone described how as they approached the island in their canoes, they were greeted by the sounds of sweet singing that reminded him of choral music. On landing, a 'thin wiry framed man about 5ft 10in height and slightly bald' stepped forward to greet them. This was Sebitoane. He had already been informed that his guests had lost a number of their oxen and on greeting Livingstone and Oswell, immediately told them 'Your cattle are all bitten by the tsetse and will certainly die; but never mind, I have oxen and will give you as many as you need.'[70] He also presented his guests with an ox and a jar of honey. Since it was late, the two weary travellers were led away to a place to sleep.

Sometime during that first night Sebitoane quietly entered the hut where Livingstone lay sleeping. Livingstone woke up and was soon avidly taking notes while Sebitoane told him his life story. One can easily imagine the scene; two men, one white and the other black, whispering away in the middle of the night while the others slept and with the only other sounds being that of the African night. And what a story it was from a man who was revered for being a great warrior and a powerful chief: his tribe had originally lived in the area around Kuruman but in 1824, a big battle was fought between the Griquas and a large army made up of a coalition of tribes. Numbers had proved no match for guns and the Griquas had routed their enemies. Sebitoane was forced to flee north with a small band of followers. They fought a number of battles, often against overwhelming odds as they moved north, including the Matabele under Moselikatse. He then took his growing tribe west to the area between the Chobe and Zambezi. But the Matabele, who were intent on avenging their defeat, followed them. Sebitoane saw an opportunity to destroy them and cunningly set a trap for them by having some of his men ferry the Matabele onto an island in the middle of the Zambezi. They were then stranded there and Sebitoane left them to the point of starvation. He then crossed over to the island with his warriors and slaughtered the men but spared the women and children who were then adopted into his tribe. With his immediate enemies destroyed, he settled down in the area because it could be defended as swamps and rivers surrounded them. The only problem was that malaria and other diseases were slowly decimating the Makololo. Livingstone noted in his journal details about the general appearance of the Makololo:

> The fever frequently attacks the bowels, producing bloody stools and great pain ... a weal extending half round the body under the ribs comes out. The people report the whole country is excessively sickly, and the appearance of the Makololo as contrasted with the aboriginal inhabitants fully confirms the assertion. The Makololo are all sickly looking & yellow with spare habits of body, while the Makalaka are stout and their frames are gigantic in proportion.[71]

Venereal diseases, including 'Manasa' or syphilis, were also rife among the Makololo. It had been introduced from the tribes in the south and was slowly being passed inexorably up through central Africa.

Sebitoane accompanied Livingstone and Oswell back to their camp where Mary was eagerly waiting for them. Sebitoane knew about the special relationship between the chief of the powerful Matabele, Moselikatse, and the great Bwana, Moffat. He also knew that Livingstone's wife was the daughter of 'Moshete of the Bechuanas', as Moffat was known. Sebitoane was very keen to meet Mary, and also to have this particular white man and his family settle down and live amongst them since the Livingstone family would be an effective shield against future attacks by Moselikatse. Sebitoane also cunningly thought it would mean that he would be able to acquire guns through him.

The friendship that Sebitoane and Livingstone enjoyed was sadly short-lived as the old warrior caught an 'inflammation of the lungs'[72] or pneumonia about three weeks after they arrived. His condition was aggravated by a chest injury that he received in one of his many battles. Livingstone knew that Sebitoane needed proper medical help if he was to have a chance of survival but Livingstone feared for his family should he attempt to treat him and fail for it was likely the tribe would blame him for their chief's death and demand retribution. It was a wise decision. Sebitoane weakened quickly. Livingstone visited him as often as he could and on one particular Sunday after the family had held a small church service, Livingstone again called on Sebitoane along with his eldest boy, Robert. Seeing the young lad, Sebitoane called out to him: 'Come near and see if I am any longer a man' and then later he added quietly, 'I am done.' They left soon after but not before Sebitoane 'raised himself up & told the people to take Robert to his chief wife and give him some milk.' It turned out that it was the last time Livingstone saw him alive. Livingstone was obviously deeply affected by his encounter with Sebitoane, writing, 'I never felt so sorry for the death of any black man before.'[73] And that 'he was unquestionably the greatest man in all that country.'[74] But it was a mutual admiration for Livingstone was also to be admired: he was a strangely intense man who possessed a quiet dignity.

4.5 Finding the Zambezi River

On his death, Sebitoane's daughter, Ma-mochisane was named chief. However, there was a brother who thought he had a better claim to the chieftainship and the two travellers could see trouble brewing so they thought it would be best to get away until the situation was resolved. They therefore sought permission from Ma-mochisane to travel around the region, saying they wished to search for a suitable site to build a mission. They immediately set out to see a large river that they had been told about which lay about one hundred and thirty miles to the north-east.

The 'large river' was in fact the mighty Zambezi[75] and they were not at all prepared for the sight that appeared before their eyes on the 30 June 1851. Here in the middle of the African continent was a deep and fast flowing river; at that point it was 300 to 500 hundred yards wide. Livingstone was amazed; Oswell said he had never seen such an impressive river: not even the Ganges could compare with this body of water. The Makololo also told Oswell and Livingstone about some enormous falls, Mosi-oe-tunya, eighty miles downstream, where the spray from the falls could be seen from ten to fifteen miles away.[76] The temptation to go and see it must have been difficult to resist but for some reason they chose not to. This decision meant Victoria Falls remained undiscovered for another few years, in a triumph that Livingstone was to savour alone.

Livingstone and Oswell were able to move around with the Mokololo, noting how the natives used the river as a major highway. They moved north by canoe and were impressed by the people living on the river, both in number and size. 'They are inhabited by a black race. They are deep chested, and their muscular system is strongly developed. The Bechuna who live among them appear a puny sickly set in comparison, and they are fast dying out.'[77]

They discussed the course of the river with the locals and this led both Oswell and Livingstone to conclude, accurately, that the Zambezi flows pass Tete, which lies over 300 hundred miles from the east coast, and out to the sea somewhere south of Quelimane in Mozambique.[78] The idea of river highways immediately crystallised in Livingstone's mind for he could see a way to open up the interior of Africa to commerce and civilisation. Here was the way to put into practice the idea that Burton had first eruditely proposed at a meeting that Livingstone had attended in 1840.

Livingstone and Oswell soon returned to Linyanti. Livingstone already knew that he would not try to establish a mission with the Makololo because of the widespread fever and malaria. The tsetse fly would also mean that travel would be all but confined to foot or by canoe. Instead Livingstone was now excited about exploring the Zambezi to see whether it would serve his purpose of opening the interior. It also meant he would not have to think about establishing another mission but instead he could become a type of roving missionary spreading the Gospel in unexplored regions.

The only problem he had with this scheme was that there was no place for his family or his friend Oswell. Livingstone's family had grown on this trip as Mary had given quickly and easily given birth to their fifth child, on 15 September 1851 on the shaded banks of the Zouga.[79] They named him Charles but later they more fittingly renamed him in honour of their erstwhile travelling companion and friend. 'As he [Oswell] seemed very fond of our little baby, we altered our intentions and calling him William Oswel instead of Charles. It was the only thing we could do to shew our gratitude, and he seemed much pleased with it.'[80] Livingstone had first suggested that they call him Zouga for the river along which he was born but Mary objected. Instead Zouga became Williams's nickname.

With regard to his family, Livingstone calculated that he would need up to two years to explore the region to identify an appropriate missionary site. Co-incidentally it was nearing the time to send the children for proper schooling; Robert was by then five years old. He and Mary agreed that they would send the children to England rather than Scotland, as Livingstone felt the Scottish climate might be too cold for the children. This of course meant Mary would have to accompany the children. However, before any final decision could be made Livingstone knew he first needed to obtain the approval of the London Missionary Society directors to his plan.

With regard to Oswell, Livingstone realised his days of joint expeditions were over. Oswell had served his purpose and he was not yet ready to confide in Oswell about what he was planning. One advantage of Livingstone's plans was that he would not have to share any accolades for other discoveries he might make.

4.6 Slavery

It was on this trip that Livingstone first saw the evidence that the slave trade stretched into the heart of Africa. He had previously observed that some of the Makololo proudly wore pieces of European clothing and on making enquiries he was dismayed to discover that his new native friends were actively involved in the slave trade. The waterfall, Mosi-oa-tunya, which lay about eighty miles to the east, had blocked the penetration of slavers, including the Portuguese and the Mambari,[81] into the area but by 1850 they had managed to get up past this obstacle and reach the Makololo. The slavers arrived 'carrying great quantities of English manufactured goods, viz. blue striped and printed cottons, blue, red and green baize, and a few very old Portuguese muskets also.'[82] What they wanted in exchange for these goods were boys of about fourteen years of age. According to Livingstone, the Mambari stayed with the Makololo for several months and finally persuaded them to go out on marauding expeditions against other smaller tribes. On one of these forays Sebitoane's Makololo sold about thirty captive children to Portuguese slave traders who were returning to the east coast while the Mambari led away about two hundred boys and girls in chains to the west. 'The price of a boy was one old Portuguese musket or nine yards of cloth.'[83] The business was good and the Mambari and Portuguese slave traders promised to return for more.

The slave trade developed out of a thriving trading pattern that had been established in Africa for many centuries before the slave merchants had started to penetrate into the interior. Initially, trade had centred on the need to obtain salt and iron products, such as hoes and axes for agricultural purposes. However, the Arab and European traders wanted ivory, something that was of little value to the natives. Later the demand for slaves grew as the colonial powers needed labour to work in the cotton plantations and sugar cane fields in the Americas.

The Makololo were the most powerful tribe in the area and so not surprisingly, in time, they routinely sold slaves in exchange for beads, guns and clothing. However, the Makololo were new to the practice; other powerful tribes had been active for many years. One such tribe was the Wa-Yao[84] in the Shire Highlands in what is today, modern Malawi. They ruthlessly exploited the neighbouring tribes. The Wa-Yao began acquiring slaves through trade but over time, they slowly became more powerful and soon they were mounting large expeditions to capture slaves in battle. Soon everyone feared the Wa-Yao and as the neighbouring tribes slowly became depleted, the Wa-Yao had to send large raiding parties further and further inland. Eventually the tribe became so powerful that not even the slave traders themselves dared enter their territory without their permission. When the Europeans came, led by the missionaries, the Wa-Yao grew increasingly hostile as the Europeans represented a threat to their profitable practice.

The demand for slaves led to an informal partnership between the Zanzibari Arabs and the Swahili traders and they frequently formed slave-trading parties. The people became renowned for their ruthlessness and callous disregard for human life. They were also very active; by the 1850s, slaving parties from the east coast had met up with similar parties travelling inland from the west coast.

The impact of these forays was severe; whole areas became denuded of people as the tribes retreated further into the most inaccessible places out of fear. The stability of the village life that made agriculture and production of specialised goods possible was shattered. No one could trust their neighbours and any stranger was looked upon as a potential enemy and if possible, attacked.

The cruelty of the trade was unimaginable. Slaves would be secured with neck irons with loops that were threaded with fourteen foot of iron chain. Many of the adults were also yoked in pairs with a heavy wooden pole that was fastened around the neck of each slave by a riveted iron rod. At night a leg iron would be placed on each slave and massive solid bolts and locks used to shackle the slaves to posts as an added precaution against escape.

Long lines of dejected captives would tramp through the countryside, all heading to the coast and an eventual slave market. Those that faltered would be beaten mercilessly with hippo hide whips; those that could not keep up would be executed. If a slave was lucky, the execution would be a quick release; for others they would be tied to a tree and left to starve to death as a warning to others not to fall behind. The brutality with which the prisoners were treated meant many perished *en route* and the losses were alarming high.

The principal clearing houses for slaves was Zanzibar and Mombasa although the former was by far the largest. The British authorities, when they started to take an interest, estimated that by the end of the 1840s, between 40,000 and 45,000 slaves were annually being sold through these two markets.

Livingstone thought deeply about how to replace this illegitimate form of commerce with legitimate trade. For a missionary he showed extraordinary foresight and practical sense in how the problem of slavery could be addressed. He noted that the Makololo preferred to trade goods such as ivory, a product that had little value for the Makololo but had great commercial value in the Cape, rather than slaves to obtain the English goods that they desired. The Makololo had told Livingstone and Oswell that 900 elephants had been killed on the banks of Zouga in the last three years but most of the ivory lay 'rotting in the sun.'[85] While camped on the banks of the Zouga with his family and Oswell, Livingstone set out in a letter to his parents a remarkably modern template on how to open up trading opportunities:

> But let a legitimate trade be once established, all these articles would be kept for the trader. They readily acquire the habit of saving articles for him which would otherwise run to waste. The slave trader is never longed for by the poorer classes, but all classes are glad to obtain the visits of English traders. If it is profitable for those engaged in the trade on the coast to pass along picking up ivory, wax, &c, would it not be much more advantageous to come up the Zambesi and receive such articles from the producers themselves? I venture to give these hints, though entirely ignorant of the trade to which I refer, and I feel assured that if Christian merchants would establish a legitimate commerce on the Zambesi they would soon drive slave dealers out of the market, and would certainly be no losers in the end.[86]

Livingstone would be continually appalled at both the extent and viciousness of the traffic in human lives.

CHAPTER 5

The Journey to Loanda

'I am a missionary heart & soul'

5.1 Missionary or Explorer?

Much has been made of the fact that Livingstone was more of an explorer than a missionary, particularly given his little apparent success in converting the natives to Christianity. This conclusion is wrong as Livingstone saw himself first and foremost a missionary, and that missionary work could be achieved in a number of ways. In a letter to his sister, Agnes, in 1850, he clearly sets out his mission in life. 'I told Charles in answer to his invitation to turn Yankee [pastor] that I am a missionary heart & soul. God had an only son, and he was a missionary & a physician. A poor, poor imitation of Him I am or rather wish to be. In this service I hope to live, in it I wish to die.'[1] He was to achieve his wish.

The size and length of the Zambezi, Africa's fourth longest river at over 2,300 miles, fascinated Livingstone. He was particularly interested when told about another river of about the same size 400 miles north of Linyanti. He closely questioned the Makololo and drew about sixty maps of the surrounding area based on his conversations with them.

The party set off back to Kolobeng but instead of using the shortcut that they had followed north with nearly disastrous consequences, they decided to use the path that Livingstone and Oswell had pioneered.

It must have been an uneasy and deeply contemplative journey back to Kolobeng. Livingstone and Mary would have spent many hours sitting on the bench seat of their wagon discussing the merits and ramifications of what he was planning, while they slowly trundled along. She would, of course, have been fearful of losing Livingstone if he set out on his exploring ways, as death was an real prospect in that region; he would have talked about the need to open up highways to enable Christians to spread into the interior but this first required someone to uncover central Africa's hidden secrets. In the end, they decided that

Mary would take the children back to England while Livingstone did what he had to do.

They would also have discussed the on-going Kaffir or Xhosa Wars.[2] These wars were between the Xhosa and the whites—both Boers and British—and dragged on through the 1800s. The Xhosa were a powerful tribe that had steadily expanded, migrating slowly westward towards the Port Elizabeth area. But their expansion was checked when they came up against the Dutch settlers who moved north-east from the Cape Colony during the 1830s and 1840s to escape British control, in what later became known as the Great Trek. There was soon fierce competition for land and water. The raids and counter-raids were largely indecisive because although the whites had guns and horses, the Xhosa had the advantage of numbers.

In December 1850 war broke out again with the Xhosa but this time the British army was involved. The army was under the command of Sir Henry Smith but it was not strong enough to subdue the Xhosa as the force was too small. The Boers were also active and persecuted the natives with great ferocity at any opportunity.

These wars caused great suffering for the natives. It also affected the work that the missionaries were able to perform as the Boers limited the places the missionaries could work. Mary Moffat gave this as one of the reasons for Livingstone wanting to return to the Lake Ngami area in June 1851. 'Livingstone is again away to the Lake [Ngami], intending to seek a field there, or rather beyond it. He seems determined to get out of the reach of the Boers.'[3]

The Livingstone family arrived back in Kolobeng on 27 November 1851 after an easy journey where, for a change, water had been plentiful. Their minds where made up and the Livingstones only paused at Kolobeng for about a week, just long enough to pack their belongings before setting out to trek down to the Cape. Livingstone wrote a hurried note to Moffat to tell them to expect them in Kuruman and requesting new axles and oxen, as 'We shall pass Southwards to the Cape as quickly as we can.'[4]

It was a sad time leaving Kolobeng because the family had been relatively happy there—despite the drought—and Mary had enjoyed making a proper home for her family. But as soon as all was ready, they headed to Kuruman where Mary and the children said a tearful goodbye to the Moffat family. It must have been heart wrenching—and difficult—because Livingstone's in-laws could not have approved of his decision to leave his family to go wandering again in the dangerous interior of Africa. After all, was he not a missionary? When the farewells were over, they again mounted their wagon and set out on the long road south to Cape Town.

Livingstone hoped his large family in Scotland might make the transition for Mary and their children easier when they arrived back in Britain. An anxious Mary was also clearly hoping so and asked Livingstone to mention it to his sister Agnes when he wrote to her shortly before they left Kuruman. 'Mary however puts in a word now as to her coming home, and asks what our poor children are to do in the vacations. Perhaps you will see her before long, and then you can talk over matters.'[5]

They also said farewell to Oswell in Kuruman who was also travelling back to England. Livingstone had made a true friend. This is Livingstone at his best when he described Oswell in the same letter to Agnes:

> Mr Oswel left us on Friday last. We felt as if we had lost a brother. He is not what you would call pious, but is very upright & honourable and has a good deal of reverence for the Church of England. His brother is a clergyman of that church.[6] Well, before he parted he requested us as a favour to draw upon him for as much money as we should need. 'Take as much of my money as you wish, either now or at any future time.' He asked for your address, and I told him you were not rich enough to entertain a gentleman but would be very glad to see him, he goes home now, and will probably call upon you. You may volunteer to shew him the sights about Hamilton. He is very civil and exceedingly kind, and one of the bravest men alive.[7]

The Livingstone family arrived back in Cape Town in the middle of March 1852[8] and there they made an unusual sight. It was over eleven years since Livingstone had last been in Cape Town. As Livingstone noted, 'the costumes of the whole party were somewhat on the style of Robinson Crusoe.' Fortunately, Oswell was also in town and seeing their predicament, generously paid for some new clothes for all of the family and also helped Livingstone to rent a house. Livingstone related how difficult he found using stairs and kept wanting to 'come down as one descends a ladder.'[9]

Livingstone's immediate priority was to arrange passage on a ship for his family for he was now eager for his family to leave so that he could prepare for his own journey. However, one of the first things he had to do was to write to the secretary of the London Missionary Society to explain why he was sending his family back to England:

> The swampy, boggy nature of a region more than two hundred miles in breadth, the tsetse, the death of Sebitoane, the deep rivers, and the fever, prevented our proceeding at once to a part of the salubrity of which we could entertain a hope. The impropriety of removing the people from the only defences against the annual forays of the Matebele, and the fact the Sebitoane's people ... have nearly all fallen victims to the fever, led me to the conclusion that separation from my family had become absolutely necessary—for though I may be justified in risking my own life in the service of our Master, I may not use the same freedom with the lives of my wife and children.[10]

He went then on to ask Tidman, 'If I am spared for two years I may be permitted to establish a mission, and also to find a way to the Sea on either the East or the West Coast.'[11] The directors must have wondered that given the conditions that Livingstone had carefully described, and little consequent possibility of success, just what was Livingstone trying to achieve by these changes and for what purpose?

While in Cape Town Livingstone became upset and annoyed when had to listen to local missionaries tell him how rich the 'interior missionaries' were. Moffat in particular was singled out as someone who was thought to be wealthy. This prevalent view was far from the truth. Indeed, as he acknowledged to Moffat, he was only able to afford the trip south because of the generosity of Oswell. Livingstone could not even afford to pay for the repairs to his wagon and ended up giving it away to his brother-in-law, John Moffat.[12] Livingstone also noticed how well dressed and provisioned the Cape missionaries and their families were, and how unwilling they seemed to want to assist their brethren who lived in the interior. If ever Livingstone needed a further reason to leave the London Missionary Society, then this last episode provided one.

Livingstone immediately began to prepare for his expedition. He was surprised to discover that he seemed to be reasonably well known in the Cape, 'Lots of people know me of whom I know nothing, and were we to accept their invitations we should not be much at home.'[13] One of the people he did call upon was Thomas Maclear who carefully checked Livingstone and Oswell's observations and 'found us only 10° wide of the longitude.'[14] This gave Livingstone confidence that he could take accurate readings on his subsequent explorations.

However, not all the attention was welcomed. He also wanted to leave Cape Town as soon as possible because many people intensively disliked the missionaries, 'The feeling is very strong against us here.'[15] In Livingstone's case he was widely known to be a supporter of the natives and rumoured to have supplied the Bakwains with guns and ammunition. Livingstone had to apply to the Government to get permission to buy seventy-five pounds of gunpowder, 100 pounds of lead and three guns to take beyond the borders of the Cape Colony but these rumours were particularly damaging and meant the British Government officials were unwilling to give him all the guns and ammunition that he wanted, particularly as another Kaffir War was being fought at the time. The authorities eventually relented and issued him with a licence but only after much talk and negotiation.[16]

Livingstone was also limited in what he could buy because he had little money, which meant his provisions were insufficient when considering the magnitude of what he was contemplating. This deficiency was dismissed when Livingstone cheerfully announced that that it was unwise to carry too much since it only encouraged the avarice of the tribes that he would encounter. The apparent lack of provisions was, however, compensated by the man himself. He was forty years of age, fit and strong. He possessed a remarkable determination to succeed and an iron will. He was also a person who could endure hardships and privations that would deter the hardest of men. In fact, he seemed to relish a situation where the going became difficult and at times, desperate, since he would often be at his best, displaying courage and fortitude. He would later write:

I have drunk water swarming with insects, thick with mud, putrid with rhinoceroses' urine and buffalo dung, and no stinted draughts of it either, and yet felt no inconvenience from it.

He was a man who understood nature and was happy to live from the land. For most of his journeys, his staple fare was native food, the base of which is crushed corn or mealie and cassava. This type of food, still the staple food across much of Africa today, is filling but has little nutritional value. It also requires a tangy sauce to make it more appealing as it is bland by itself.

He also had the advantage of having worked among the natives for many years and he could communicate with them exceedingly well because he understood how they thought and how to handle them so as to get the best out of them. A frank attitude and generous spirit, combined with a sense of humour is what endeared him most to the natives that he encountered.

In between collecting all the provisions he required, often in the face of open hostility, he found time to get his uvula 'cut off.'[17] This had been causing him problems for some time. He was also successfully prevailed upon to provide a copy of his *Notes of a Tour to the River Sesheke, in the Region North of Lake Ngami*. This work was published in the *S.A. Commercial Advertiser* on 1 April 1852.[18]

It took some time to get a passage on a ship to London as the ships were fully booked. Eventually Mary and the children sailed on the *Trafalgar*, on 23 April 1852. It was, predictably, a sad farewell, as they did not know when they would be reunited. 'It was only with the greatest difficulty I could restrain my sorrow in parting; had I given way in the least, I should have burst into a regular roar.'[19] However, he wrote that while it was a tearful parting, he did not doubt that he was doing the right thing.[20]

Livingstone was clearly starting to position himself as an explorer but his missionary zeal also underlined his purpose. The London Missionary Society seemed to agree as Tidman wrote to Livingstone in April 1852, in a postscript noting:

We have sent extracts from your correspondence to the [Royal] Geographical Society, and shall be happy to furnish that Society with such information as it comes to hand; but in order to give additional attraction to your reports, we would suggest that you keep a regular journal recording any remarkable events, notices of the manners and customs of the different tribes, the natural history of the country, and other topics which as the result of observation at the time are more likely to prove of permanent interest and value than the more vague and general impressions conveyed in a hastily written letter.[21]

With this encouragement Livingstone started keep more detailed and accurate journals that in time become comprehensive, detailing people, their customs and social mores and an extraordinary range of fauna and flora.

Then, just before he was leaving, he accused the Kolobeng postmaster, James Walker, with overcharging for postage. He did this by taking six letters to the Postmaster General in the Cape and pointing out specimens of Walker's overcharging.'[22] Walker threatened Livingstone with a court action for defamation of character and rather than wait for the case to heard, Livingstone settled out of court. It cost him £13.

5.2 Trip to Linyanti

After a busy two months in Cape Town, he finally left on the 8 June 1852. He made a slow journey north with frequent stops due to the fact that his wagon was well overloaded. He reached Griquatown on the 15 August 1852 and a fortnight later he was in Kuruman.[23] It was while he was staying there that he received news that a six hundred strong commando force of Boers together with another seven hundred friendly natives under command of Pieter Scholtz,[24] Commandant of the Marico district, had gutted his home in Kolobeng. He calculated that had he travelled at his normal rate, he would have been there when the place was attacked. He was thankful not to have become involved in the *mêlée*.

Livingstone wrote to Mary at this time and gave a detailed description of the apparent damage, saying that they smashed what they could not carry off, and took his cattle with them. However, Livingstone never visited Kolobeng and he was relying on hearsay.[25]

On the basis of this report there was little that he could do except to make a formal protest to Lieutenant Governor Darling. In his letter to the governor Livingstone claimed to have lost personal property of £335, a substantial figure.[26] The action shows Livingstone in a poor light; he wrote and complained to the governor before he had an opportunity to verify the facts. As it later turned out his house had not been destroyed.

According to Livingstone the target of the raid was Sechele who the Boers had claimed, 'had allowed Englishmen to proceed to the North.'[27] This excuse does not seem to be plausible. It is more likely to have been related to the fact that Sechele was sheltering Mosseealele and some of his Bakhalta tribe from the Boers. The force arrived at Kolobeng and after some of the Boers attended the church service on Sunday where Mebaloe was preaching, they then informed Sechele that they would attack next day. At first light they launched their attack. It was a vicious struggle but weight of arms prevailed; sixty Bakwains were killed although this figure was later increased to 120 people[28] as a number of the injured died. Scores of women and children were also carried off as booty—one estimate was that as many as two hundred women and four hundred children were captured. Even allowing for the usual inflation in figures, the Bakwains had suffered a humiliating defeat. But the affair was not entirely one-sided as Sechele claimed his people killed thirty-five Boers.[29] The Boers disagreed, saying that only four men were killed and five wounded.[30] It was also reported that the commando force stole up to three thousand head of cattle, wagons and other possessions.

Livingstone also received word that the Boers were determined to stop him travelling north and when he heard this he became furious. In his anger, he wrote menacingly: 'should I meet them it would be like meeting a bear bereaved of her whelps.' But he knew it would be foolish to attempt to pass up through that area with bands of armed men roving the countryside. He therefore wisely decided to stay in Kuruman and let the situation settle down.

Livingstone had initially decided to leave in November 1852 but because of the unsettled situation it was not until late December 1852[31] that his small party finally left Kuruman. Accompanying him were three natives who acted as drivers and a West Indian half-caste, called George Fleming.[32] Fleming had been encouraged to come along to investigate what trade could be started with the Makololo as Livingstone hoped that this would help to discourage the slave trade.

Livingstone had intended to first travel to Kolobeng to inspect the damage caused by the Boers. The Kaffir War was still raging, but to his surprise he received word that the Boers had decided to make peace with Sechele by returning one of his children, Kgari, then aged 'about three or four' who had been captured during the attack. The meeting point was held at Livingstone's house. This was the first time that Livingstone had word that his house had not been destroyed, as he acknowledged in a letter to Mary—it is hard to understand what she might have made of this conflicting news about her former home.[33] Livingstone also said he had heard that the Boers where planning another attack on another tribe nearby and he thought it would be unwise to be there when they arrived and so he gave orders that his house and all its contents be burnt while he pressed on north. Nevertheless, he found time to record the names of those missing from each tribe, 123 children from the Bakwains alone,[34] as he progressed north and sent these details to Moffat.[35]

They also hunted for food on the way:

We have killed on the journey, two Bustards & one zebra, three stein bucks, three Redbucks or Palahs, one eiland, two giraffes and two black Rhinoceros. The black Rhinocerous were five feet four inches high at the shoulder and ten feet from point of nose to the insertion of the tail. The Giraffe females were fourteen feet high from forefoot to point of horns. Six serpents.[36]

The party normally ate game meat:

> We have had zebra for some time back. It smells just as a horse does, and is not nice till one gets used to it, and even then though we get to like it we don't prefer it. Other kinds of flesh may be eaten after they are green & maggotty, but this when rancid is very nasty.[37]

Fortunately there were the occasional treats when for example Fleming produced a plum pudding,

It was not all easy travelling. Livingstone had a horse collapse underneath of him and had to walk thirty miles.[38] On another occasion the oxen managed to escape and it took them five days to recapture them. Livingstone and his companions only survived because they dug out an old well and found some water.[39]

The party made steady progress but as February turned into March 1853 the temperatures kept soaring as they wound up through the now familiar route through the Kalahari Desert:

> 148 degrees in direct sun; 138 degrees three inches beneath the soil.[40] The desert quickly became searingly hot.[41]

While passing near the Ntwetwe Pan they passed an enormous baobab tree, now known as 'Chapman's Baobab'.[42] Travellers used it as a mail tree where letters could be safely stored and later collected by their owners.

It is interesting to look at the state of Livingstone's mind at this time. He initially suffered doubts about the enormity of his decision to send his family back to England as he began to move away from civilisation:

> Am I on my way to die in Sebitoane's country? Have I seen the last of my wife & children? The breaking up of all my connections with earth, leaving this fair & beautiful world & knowing so little of it? ... O if Jesus speak one word of peace that will establish in thy breast an everlasting calm ... I have done nothing for thee yet, and I would like to do something.[43]

Soon after he is all business instructing Mary in a letter to settle his accounts, ordering a number of books on medicine and natural history, and also interestingly, Gesenius's *Hebrew Lexicon* and Mrs Stowes's *Uncle Tom's Cabin*. He asked Mary to ensure a Newman thermometer was included with the books. This type of thermometer is used to determine altitude by measuring the temperature at which water boils at different locations.[44]

The party made slow progress north, and at one point they halted for nearly two months as everyone, excluding Livingstone and a native, had fallen ill with fever. Livingstone had to care for them all and patiently did so. They then entered the Chobe basin and found the country flooded, extending out about twenty miles from the river.[45] This posed a real problem for the oxen and it was only with great difficulty that they succeeded in getting the wagons through the rivers and floodplains. Often man and beast would spend hours floundering around in water heaving and pushing. They continued to straggle north but his helpers became increasingly disillusioned forcing their way through the swamps that surrounded the Chobe. Eventually his Bushmen guides deserted him. Undeterred, he spent several days trying to push a path through to the river but the vegetation was so dense that he was thwarted at every turn. The flooding meant that the party could not head to Linyanti as intended so instead they headed north before turning east towards Sesheke. Taking just one companion, Livingstone battled on, cut, bruised and bleeding, until after several days, his perseverance was rewarded—they stumbled onto the river. A pontoon was rigged up and Livingstone and his helper mounted the river craft and floated twenty miles down the river towards Linyanti. They dodged hippopotamus and malevolent crocodiles that coldly eyed them from the water. To their enormous relief they found some Makololo waiting on the riverbank as they had heard about their difficulties and two parties had set out to find them.[46] The natives were astonished to see them arrive from the direction they had come from as they thought the Chobe was impenetrable and anxious questions were asked if the Boers or any other people knew about their route.

News quickly spread of their arrival with Livingstone later writing it was as if 'I had fallen on them as if from a cloud, yet came riding on a hippopotamus' (pontoon).'[47]

Livingstone found that Sebitoane's chosen successor, Ma-mochisane, had happily abdicated in favour of her brother Sekeletu who was then about eighteen-years of age.[48] The welcome that Livingstone received at Linyanti was tumultuous. One old man roared out to the assembled crowd, 'Don't I see the white man? Don't I see the comrade of Sebitoane? Don't I see the father of Sekeletu?' Livingstone was happy to be back among his native friends. The gifts that Livingstone had brought with him were also welcome. They included three goats, the remains of a small herd of a superior breed of oxen that had been requested by the dying Sebitoane; and larger breeds of domestic fowls and cats. The thoughtfulness of these gifts and the considerable trouble he went to in bringing them safely to the Makololo helped to cement a strong relationship with the tribe. Sekeletu reciprocated by presenting Livingstone with an oxen and an elephant tusk.

Livingstone was asked what his purpose was. He told the Makololo that he wanted to explore the upper Zambezi to see if he might find a suitable place to establish a mission. He was being less than truthful, but it was a convenient excuse for he had no intention of settling down just yet. Instead he was looking forward to exploring the region and making his way out to either coast.

It was while staying with Sekeletu that Livingstone had the first of his many malarial attacks. It seems incredible that he had not been previously affected given all the time he had been in the region. The first attack was on 30 May 1853 and was rapidly followed by eight other attacks, some of which were accompanied by large discharges of blood. He tried using native remedies but gave up in favour of his own medicines.[49]

Livingstone inspected the cattle and oxen that he had been forced to leave behind on his previous journey as some of them had been bitten by the tsetse fly. Those that had not already died were all in very poor health and in seeing this first hand, he realised what a scourge this insect presented for Europeans who wanted to settle in any areas inhabited by the tsetse fly.

5.3 Barotse Floodplain

Livingstone was keen to start exploring some of the surrounding area. He got his opportunity about a month after he arrived when Sekeletu decided to make his first grand tour around his kingdom since he became chief of the Makololo.

Their nine-week trip started with much excitement when Livingstone was unwittingly involved in an assassination attempt on Sekeletu. It occurred when they entered the village of Mpepe which lay about sixty miles north of Linyanti. Mpepe was a cousin of Sekeletu and thought he had a better claim to the chieftainship than Sekeletu by virtue of the fact that he had been Sebitoane's military commander. He had also been favoured by Sebitoane to look after his cattle while Sekeletu and Ma-mochisane were minors. Mpepe had decided kill the young chief and a plot was hastily prepared when news came of Sekeletu's imminent arrival. The plan was that when Sekeletu rose to speak, Mpepe would hamstring him so that his armed followers could then butcher him. However, Mpepe lost his nerve when Livingstone sat down between him and Sekeletu and the opportunity quickly passed. Later that night some of Mpepe's followers confessed that there was a conspiracy afoot and when Sekeletu heard all the details, he ordered Mpepe to be taken out of the village and slaughtered.[50]

The party proceeded to the river and Sekeletu, Livingstone and about 160 warriors clambered aboard thirty-three canoes and paddled up the Zambezi River through the Barotse floodplain. This floodplain, also known as the Zambezi Floodplain, is one of Africa's great wetlands and today lies mostly in the western province of Zambia. It is a large flat plateau about 1,000 metres about sea level. The Zambezi and its headwaters rise on the higher ground to the north and the plateau tilts very slightly to the south. This means any flood only slowly moves south.

The Mokololo subjugated the Barotse who inhabited a fertile country, that was an area roughly thirty miles wide and 100 miles long.[51] The only feasible method of transport is by water and they covered about 500 miles by canoe. The Zambezi is magnificent in this area, flowing north to south, and in many places the river is over a mile wide with islands up to three to four miles long in the middle.

They soon came to the first of many Barotse villages. In this part of the Zambezi, near modern day Sesheke in Zambia, the land is fertile and 'hunger is not known' although Livingstone noted that all the area had fever. At one village, they found Mpepe's father and mother hiding and since it was known that they had advised Ma-mochisane to kill Sekeletu and marry Mpepe, orders were given that they be bound and hurled into the river to the crocodiles. Livingstone would not have been impressed by these simple but barbaric solutions.

They proceeded along at a leisurely pace pushing up above the confluence of the Lungwebungu, or what Livingstone called the 'Leeambae or Leeamby', and on beyond the junction of the Zambezi with the Kabompo, where the Zambezi river becomes the Leeba. What really fired Livingstone's imagination was the fertility of the country and in a letter to Moffat you can hear his excitement about the agricultural possibilities:

> The valley [in the Borotse country] is extremely fertile, and so are the ridges. The latter are covered with gardens and people. Sugar cane grows luxuriantly, two sorts of manioc, the sweet potato, and two kinds of batata. Bananas too; these however we did not see. Caffre corn on short stalks and large pure white grain, & called lekoñka grows on flooded spots. Millet, beans, &c. &c. All declare it to be a land of plenty.[52]

Here was Livingstone's potential answer to combating the slave trade in this region.

Travelling in these craft could be quite perilous: the craft selected for Livingstone to travel in was about thirty four feet long and only twenty inches wide but manned by expert Barotse oarsmen. Six oarsmen stood in the boat and either punted or paddled the canoe, depending on how deep the river was. The men that accompanied Sekelutu were his 'Mopato', young men of the chief's age. They formed a type of presidential guard and it was considered to be a great honour to be a member.

The author witnessed the traditional Kuomboka festival at Mongu in 1991 when living in Zambia. This festival celebrates the annual migration of the Litunga, King of the Lozi people, from his compound at Lealui in the Barotse Floodplain to Limulunga on higher ground. The Kuomboka takes place at the end of the rainy season, when the upper Zambezi floods the plains of the Western Province of Zambia.

Waiting in Mongu for their King's household to arrive by canoe were thousands of his Lozi subjects. Heavy drumming of the royal Maoma drums preceded their spectacular arrival. The canoes, some holding up to 100 oarsmen, sped into view in full African pageantry. Smaller canoes, similar to what Livingstone may have used, also accompanied the larger canoes. The ability of these canoes to slip through the water at high speed and turn gracefully was the reason why Livingstone used them so extensively to travel around. He described how during his explorations of the Barotse Floodplain in a canoe with just six paddlers 'we passed through 44 miles of latitude, by one day's pull of 10½ hours: if we add the longitude to this, it must have been upwards of 50 miles' actual distance.'[53]

Livingstone enjoyed the expedition up the river: the wide lazy bends and broad stretches of water, up to a mile in width in places that were then, as they are today, framed by lofty Palmyra trees and dense green foliage.

Livingstone decided to leave Sekeletu's party when they arrived at the Barotsa capital of Naliele, near Katongo, and continue exploring further north. Sekeletu was determined that the Doctor should enter any village in a manner benefiting a good friend of a great chief and so he gave Livingstone a herald so that his arrival at any village could be properly announced. The man had been instructed to go before Livingstone and yell: 'Here comes the lord, the great lion'. Instead, the man whose pronunciation was poor would scream: 'Here comes the lord, the great sow'. Livingstone was not amused and silenced him.

Livingstone found the slave traders were back in the Borotse country, arriving from both the east and west. He was told one of the slave traders had rapidly departed when told an Englishman was arriving from the south.

The first trader Livingstone actually met was Caetano José Ferreira who appeared in Linyanti on 23 June 1853, accompanied by a large party of Mambari. His arrival electrified Livingstone; if this man could walk from St Philip de Benguela in six months, then so could Livingstone. The only problem for Livingstone was that he wanted to be the first 'white man' to explore central Africa, but this Portuguese trader threatened to usurp him. He therefore chose to describe Caetano Ferreira anonymously as a half-caste 'who resembled closely a real Portuguese'.[54] In fact the man was born in a suburb in Lisbon called Barreiro.[55]

The next trader he met in Linyanti was the celebrated Portuguese trader and explorer, António Francisco Ferreira de Silva. He arrived a month later on 13 July 1853.[56] Livingstone had not yet decided which way to go—east or west—and when Ferreira invited Livingstone to dinner it provided a valuable opportunity to talk through his ideas with someone with first-hand experience of travelling through the region. Livingstone described his encounter:

> He is rich. Has about 60 slaves to serve him. Has wine at his table, and swilled my share as well as his own. Sent two Dutch cheeses & some preserved pears, bread & cauliflower to me.[57]

It seems neither man liked each other. Livingstone called him *vulgar negrito*, writing Ferreira was a mere slaver but evidence suggests Ferreira was a respected trader who kept meticulous records of goods he traded.[58] Ferreira invited Livingstone to join his party but he refused, as he did not want to be associated with someone involved in the slave trade.[59] Then shortly before Livingstone left to go west, a group of traders, Arabs from Zanzibar, arrived also looking for slaves. Some of these Arabs could read and write and one wrote some Arabic in Livingstone's journal.[60]

Livingstone was interested to learn that Arabs of Zanzibar, who were subjects of Said bin Sultan, Sultan of Muscat and Oman,[61] did not like the Portuguese because they ate pork. Livingstone wryly noted in a letter to Moffat that, 'If they had seen me next day at a hippopotamous they would have been equally disgusted.'[62]

Livingstone was not surprised by the appearance of all these traders. After all, the Portuguese controlled most of the east and west coasts of sub Saharan Africa as they had established colonies in the sixteenth century that stretched right across Africa from modern day Angola in the west to Mozambique in the east. Their area of control had steadily increased and so by the time Livingstone was making his explorations, in East Africa, the Portuguese had established three large administrative centres, Tete, Sena and Quilimane, on the lower reaches of the Zambezi and on the coast. The Portuguese were active traders and explored up the Zambezi. This included trading for ivory and gold and increasingly slaves, despite slavery having been banned by the Portuguese Government in 1836. The Mozambique traders largely ignored this law and slaves were still exported from Mozambique as late as in the 1880s. Livingstone learned from the Makololo that the cotton clothing they wore had come from Portuguese Angola by way of intermediate native traders, the Mambari.

At about this time and unbeknown to Livingstone, the hardy Moffat, then aged fifty-nine years old and in occasional bad health, undertook a third journey to see Moselikatse, chief of the Matabele. One of the purposes of the trip was to see what had become of his son-in-law, as word had reached Kuruman that Livingstone had started for Linyanti.[63] Moffat eventually met Moselikatse on 22 July 1854 after an eighteen-day trek across desert country. Undaunted he then set out north-west in the direction of Victoria Falls but after several days, they could not progress any further with their wagons as the country was dry and the oxen were at risk of being killed by tsetse fly. Moffat was forced to turn back, but before leaving for Kuruman he asked Moselikatse to send a party of natives to carry supplies and letters for Livingstone. This was a brave decision as the Matabele were sworn enemies of the Makololo and it was very likely they could be killed when they entered into the Zambezi valley. It is testimony to the stature of Moffat that this party faithfully did as they were bid, eventually leaving the supplies on the banks of the Zambezi for the Makololo to collect. The Mokolo duly did find them and carefully stored them for Livingstone who picked them up on his return trip from St Paul de Loanda.[64] Meanwhile Moffat travelled back to Kuruman after an eventful seven-month trip[65] in which he had covered over 1,400 miles.[66]

His mother-in-law's anxiety about Livingstone is evident from a letter she wrote to Moffat when he was returning south:

> Livingstone's destiny being so involved in obscurity, you may turn back before you reach the Zambesi. The extract I now enclose with this to Frédoux[67] was taken from last week's papers, and gave me great joy to see that he was alive in April last, and that this information, having come through the Portuguese, there was no fear of their doing him any harm… It is a great tax on my strength to have to talk so much; to tell over and over again all about you and your journey as well as my own, with all the whys and wherefores. With a few more intelligent I have to expatiate on the probable reasons of your journey, and Livingstone's reasons for adopting the course he has done.[68]

5.4 Trip To St Paul de Loanda

Ferreira de Silva was planning to go west back to his trading station, which was based in Kuito in the central Angolan province of Bié[69] while Caetano Ferreira planned to continue down to Mozambique. That left only one other possible option if Livingstone did not want it to seem that he was following in the footsteps of either of these Portuguese; to go west but follow the course of the Zambezi which initially went due north. Besides, the distance to the west coast was shorter and he already had proof that it could be done. The next question was how? That was easy enough since he was fascinated by the Zambezi and he was interested to follow river, wherever it lead him.

Livingstone's ability to converse in the local dialect meant he was able to ask the locals about the geography and he had constructed a reasonably detailed map of the upper Zambezi before he left Linyanti. But where should he head for on the coast? The nearest place where he knew there were British stationed was at Benguela. The other alternative was to head for Loanda, or modern-day Luanda, although this was much further north, where there were both English and French people resident there. He decided in the end to first go northwards and then strike westwards to Loanda, mainly because the other shorter route lay through tsetse fly country.

Livingstone had secured letters of introduction from the Portuguese Consul in Cape Town, Chevalier Alfredo Duprat. These letters proved to be very useful to Livingstone on a number of occasions while travelling in Angola.[70] He also had a French brother-in-law, Frédoux, and he requested him to forward a thank you note that Livingstone had prepared to the Geographical Society of Paris who had awarded both Livingstone and Oswell with silver medals for their discovery of

Lake Ngami on 2 April 1852.[71] He also asked Frédoux to write to any members of the same society he might know requesting them to write to the French Consul in 'West of Africa' so that they might be on the look-out for him and offer assistance should Livingstone need it.[72]

When Livingstone broached the idea of travelling out to the west coast to Sekeletu, the chief was initially interested in accompanying him, especially as Livingstone said that he wanted to open up a trade route for the Makololo. At that stage the Mokololo conducted their trade mostly with slaving parties and the prices they received were not very high. Sekeletu quickly saw that if a trade route could be opened up to the west, then this would be of great advantage to them since they would have a choice of where they could sell their goods. Sekeletu eventually decided not to go but instead he selected two important Makololo and Barotse men and their attendants to 'form a party of about a dozen.'[73] There were others that joined this core group so that twenty-seven men actually accompanied Livingstone when he departed.[74] The balance was a mixture drawn from other conquered tribes such as the Batoka, Bashubia, and Ambonda. Their mission was to investigate what type of trade could be organised.

The route that Livingstone had decided on meant his wagons would have to be left behind, as they could not traverse through the numerous rivers and forests that lay ahead. This suited Livingstone as he liked to travel light—so light in fact that a number of people criticised him for being foolhardy. But he already knew that provisions only excited cupidity in the natives and he decided to carry only the following: three muskets which were to be distributed between the men; a rifle and a shotgun for himself; ammunition broken into small portions and given to his men; twenty pounds of beads for gifts; a few pounds of biscuits, tea, sugar and about twenty pounds of coffee. Four small tin trunks were also carried: filled with spare shirting, trousers and shoes; medicines; three books: a Nautical Almanac, Thomson's Logarithm Tables and a Bible; a 'magic lantern', and navigational instruments: a sextant, artificial horizon and a compass; and thermometer for measuring the altitude. His only indulgences were a tent, a sheepskin mantle that served as a blanket and a horse-rug as a bed. Four elephant tusks were also carried with the purpose of seeing how much they would fetch in Portuguese territory.

As far as posterity is concerned the other important item he carried was a 'lined journal' in which Livingstone recorded all that he saw and much of what he thought about. This particular journal is a leather-bound, quarto book of more than eight hundred pages, which could be locked. The penmanship is neat and it reads well. His high level of prose was due to Livingstone's habit of scribbling his observations into pocket-sized notebooks and later, when he had time, rewriting them laboriously into his journal.

Livingstone had one task to complete before he left and this was to decide what to do with the group that had accompanied him up to Linyanti. He wrote to Moffat to explain that he had decided to get them to make the hazardous return trip to

Kuruman. There were three principal reasons; they were scared of travelling on water and Livingstone intended using the river as his main passageway. Secondly, he could not afford to have them remain in Linyanti, as he felt obligated to pay them. Finally, one of his natives, a driver, had committed adultery with the wife of one of Sekeletu's principal men, Mahale.[75] Mahale was a Kolo sub-chief, and it seemed only a matter of time before the husband took revenge and killed him.[76]

On the 11 November 1853, the great journey that was to last nearly two years and result in the first 'known' trans-African crossing, begun. They had two canoes; one was forty feet by twenty-seven inches at the broadest part and the other was slightly smaller at thirty-four feet by twenty inches.[77]

They quickly settled down into a routine: up at five a.m. for a quick breakfast and then into the boats to paddle their way upstream. At about eleven o'clock, they would land and have a good meal. Then, after an hour's rest, they would again board their canoes and continue their journey. Their progress would slow as the day drew out and became hotter. They would normally continue until about two hours before sunset and then put into a suitable spot and prepare themselves for the night.

Each man knew his place and what was required of him. This was most clearly illustrated in the sleeping arrangements: the two Makololo, being members of the chief tribe, slept on each side of Livingstone; his head boatman made his bed at the foot of Livingstone's tent; and the rest divided themselves into small tribal groups and spread out around the fire.

Livingstone started to suffer from incessant attacks of fever and malaria that had begun after his arrival in Linyanti. Soon after beginning his trip, he wearily wrote in his journal, 'but as I am already getting tired of quoting my fevers, I shall henceforth say little about them.'

On 17 December 1853, the small party arrived in Libonta. This was the most distant town in the Makololo Empire and it was important to spend some time here to stock up on their provisions before departing into the unknown. Sekeletu had ordered that they should collect a stock of fat and butter as a present for the Balonda chiefs of the country they would next be travelling through. As soon as this was done, they pushed on up the Zambezi.

Livingstone enjoyed exploring this part of the Zambezi. He wrote:

Rains had now fallen, and the woods had put on their gayest hue. Flowers of great beauty and curious forms grow everywhere. Many of the forest trees are palmated and largely developed. The trunks are covered in lichens, and abundance of ferns shows that we are now in a more humid climate. The ground swarms with insect life, and in the cool mornings the welkin rings with the singing of birds ... the notes strike the mind by their boldness and variety as the wellings forth from joyous hearts of praises to Him who fills them with overflowing gladness.[78]

Livingstone noted the people of Balonda were: 'a prodigiously large tribe of woolly-headed negroes.' The women were nearly naked, wearing in their front a small strip about fifteen inches long by five inches wide. 'Yet they laughed at our men because their behinds were naked.'[79]

The next village that they arrived at had a chief called Manenko who, they soon found out, was a woman. Livingstone's party paused there as was customary, to introduce themselves and to explain why they were passing through her country. However, the chief was away and messengers had to be dispatched to find her. They returned two days later with the chief's request that they remain there until she could come. More messengers were dispatched and after another two days of waiting for her while the rain poured down, the messengers arrived back with instructions that Livingstone and his party should now go to her. Being ordered about by a woman was too much for Livingstone who was by now thoroughly wet and frustrated and so he ignored the order and decided to proceed upstream to a place called Makondo.

Five days later, on 6 January 1854, he came across a village where another woman ruled. Her name was Nyamoana, who was reputed to be the mother of Manenko and sister of Shinte, the 'greatest Balonda chief in this part of the country'. The usual parlay commenced with Livingstone explaining his purpose in travelling up through her lands and his intention to get to the coast. But it was a difficult meeting since everything had to be repeated twice: what Livingstone said was repeated by his appointed spokesman to the chief's husband who then repeated the message verbatim to his wife. Her response was also communicated by the same tortuous method. She prevailed on Livingstone to travel inland to meet Shinte but he refused. Soon after the authoritarian chief Maneko caught the party up and she immediately set to work on the intransigent Livingstone to persuade him to go and see Shinte. The argument dragged on until the two female chiefs changed their strategy and began to tell Livingstone's companions of all the dangers they would face, urging them to go and see Shinte and seek his protection. Very soon the wily women had terrified all his men—Livingstone alone remained adamant. Livingstone could see he was losing control of the situation and he suddenly lost his patience, telling his men to load the canoes in preparation for casting off. But Manenko came gliding up and:

> with her hand on my shoulder, put on a motherly look and said: 'Now, my little man, just do as the rest have done.' My feelings of annoyance, of course, vanished and I went out to hunt for some meat.[80]

It is the only incident we know of where Livingstone's plans were thwarted by an African woman. Manenko had a forceful personality and although Livingstone was annoyed at her interference in his plans, he clearly admired her. The sight of her also amazed Livingstone: she was a tall woman of about twenty years of age. Her body was smeared with a mixture of red ochre and fat, which provided some measure of protection against the elements. She was also adorned with a number of ornaments and medicines and a thin strip of leather that barely covered her private parts. Otherwise she was 'in a state of frightful nudity.'

Manenko decided to lead them to Shinte's town with her husband and a drummer. The young Amazonian set a tremendous pace with her drummer hammering away incessantly—Livingstone was riding on an ox and he was barely able to keep up. His men straggled behind, floundering in the mud, occasionally grunting their approval at her progress: 'Manenko is a soldier.' Six days later, soaked, hungry and tired, they arrived at the place where Shinte lived.

The visitors were lead into the chief's 'Kgotla', or place of audience. It was immediately obvious just how powerful Shinte was for there were about a thousand people assembled there. These included his numerous wives, musicians and about three hundred soldiers. There also happened to be two Portuguese slave traders present with a group of Mambari and a number of female slaves. All eyes were, however, focused on Shinte who made an impressive sight in his mixture of European and native dress. He wore a checked jacket and a scarlet kilt edged with green. He had many large beads strung around his neck while his arms and legs were clad in iron and copper armlets and bracelets. The outfit was topped off with an enormous arrangement of goose feathers.

Their welcome was frightening: a large group of soldiers with their weapons drawn suddenly ran screaming at Livingstone and his party. Livingstone, always cool in these types of situations, stood rock still and at the last minute, the soldiers stopped and after saluting Shinte, returned to their places. It was clearly a test of the mettle of the visitors.

Livingstone was summoned for an audience with Shinte during that first night but because he was suffering from another attack of fever, he decided not to do so. It was a dangerous thing to do because it could have been construed as a personal slight to the chief who could have reacted savagely. It also indicates just how debilitating the attacks of fever were becoming. Messengers were again sent next day and Livingstone was led into see Shinte. Livingstone quietly explained why he was travelling through the area and as he did so, the old chief clapped his hands in approval. Livingstone then asked him if he had seen a white man before: 'No, never. You are the first I have ever seen with white skin and straight hair.' Livingstone later presented Shinte with an ox when he heard that the chief's mouth was 'bitter for want of ox flesh'. However, when the pugnacious Manenko heard that Shinte had been given an animal, she was annoyed and flounced up to Shinte claiming the ox as hers, giving the reason that 'this white man belonged to her, therefore the ox was hers'. She then sent her men to retrieve the animal and immediately had it slaughtered, presenting her uncle with just a leg. Shinte must have known her well since he did not seem to be upset by what had happened. Livingstone's 'magic lantern' also generated much interest when he moved the biblical pictures. A large crowd had gathered to look at the images in the instrument but unfortunately the first picture they looked at was that of Abraham about to murder his son Isaac.

When Livingstone made the dagger move, the audience thought it was meant for them and immediately ran away, screaming loudly. Only Shinte remained, sitting impassively in his chair.

Livingstone was curious why nearly all the houses in the area had stockades. He was then dismayed to find out that this type of protection was necessary because slavery was prevalent in these parts, as evidenced by the presence of the two 'Portuguese bastards' and their Mambari. While Livingstone was staying there, two children aged about seven and eight-years of age, were stolen while collecting firewood. Thefts of this type normally took place under the cover of darkness by those who, unwilling to sell their own children or servants, captured others to sell to the slave traders. There would be little hope of recovery and the parents or the owners of the people that disappeared usually had no means of redress. It was a measure of the corrosive impact slavery had on a culture that is centred on the family—and an index of the poverty of the region. The Portuguese half-castes were purchasing them and they erected large huts to conceal the captives in an effort to disguise the success they had. At night the hapless victims would be led out quietly to feed and do their ablutions under strict guard.

Livingstone was embarrassed by Shinte when he tried to give him a ten-year-old slave-girl. When it was explained that Livingstone abhorred slavery, Shinte thought he was unhappy with the girl and immediately ordered another older girl be fetched. Livingstone again told Shinte that he thought it was cruel to take a child away from her parents and again politely rejected her. Shinte thought the white man had strange ideas.

When the time came to leave Shinte, he stole into Livingstone's tent and gave the Doctor a conical shell as a sign of his friendship. The shell had great value since it had been carried so far from the sea. Livingstone was touched by the sincerity with which the gift was given.

Livingstone and his party left Shinte's town on 26 January 1854. The chief had provided Livingstone with eight men to act as guides and porters and they immediately struck out in a north-westerly direction. But it was slow progress for in every village his guides made all sorts of excuses to delay while they enjoyed the hospitality that was being given to representatives of the great chief, Shinte. Livingstone was also having trouble in getting his men, particularly the Makololo, accustomed to the idea that the purpose of their explorations was peaceful, and not to plunder and murder. Accordingly: 'they either spoke too imperiously to strangers or, when reproved for that, were disposed to follow the dictation of everyone they met.' Also their habit of lying infuriated Livingstone: 'they care nothing for the truth if a lie will serve their purpose.'

The country they first passed through was flat and heavily forested. The villages were normally surrounded by gardens of manioc, which formed their stable food. It was normally eaten as porridge. The diet was also supplemented by sweet potatoes and maize. The countryside seemed to be generally devoid of game, however, which meant that they had to purchase most of their food from the people they met.

They were still travelling in the wet season and the constant rain became depressing: Livingstone's thin gipsy tent was little protection against the heavy showers during the night. Soon everything 'became rotten & everything mouldy.'[81] His only consolation was that he noticed that the local people were just as miserable since their huts were also not very effective at keeping the rain out. The inclement weather meant that in places the country was flooded and this required them to swim the oxen they had bought with them across rivers as well as helping them across oozing bogs. His native companions were soon suffering from sores on their unclad feet from being continually in water. Livingstone noted that '24 hours never passed without rain, and when we move it was in water usually ankle deep.'[82]

A messenger from another powerful chief called Katema met them one day. The messenger was a 'Shakatwala' whose job it was to give advice to his chief. Nearly all the chiefs had such a person and although normally of humble birth, they were usually very powerful due to their position. This man had been sent to find out if Livingstone's intention was peaceful and if so, he was to welcome them into Katema's town.

When the messenger brought Livingstone before his master, the chief grandly introduced himself as:

> I am the great Moene (Lord) Katema, the fellow of Matiamvo. There is no one in this country equal to Matiamvo and me. I have always lived here, and my forefathers too. You have found no human skulls near the place where you are encamped. I never killed any traders.[83]

He laughed continuously during his conversation with his visitors, which Livingstone interpreted as a good sign 'for a man who shakes his sides with mirth is seldom difficult to deal with.' But while his initial impression was favourable, Livingstone was angered when he subsequently found out about the extent of the chief's involvement in the slave trade. This usually involved the chief callously selecting a suitable village or family and ordering the execution of the headman or husband while the remainder would be sold off as slaves.

Livingstone was required to stay with Katema for a number of days and as so often happened when he was forced to stay in a place, he had another attack of fever. He made the following entry into his diary:

> Sunday 19th. (February) Sick all Sunday, and unable to move. Several of the people were ill too, so I could do nothing but roll from side [to side] in my miserable little tent, in which, with all the shade we could give it, the thermometer stood upwards of 90°.[84]

During his convalescence, he had plenty of time to observe the people. Their appearance was distorted by their custom of pushing a straw or reed through the cartilage of the nose. This was done to make them look more attractive. One man he observed had a piece that measured a half an inch in diameter.

Enquiries revealed the Leeba River flowed out to the coast and so he decided to follow its westerly course. As soon as Livingstone was strong enough they pushed on but they were frustrated at the interminable delays they had to suffer as a consequence of having to hire local guides. Their path led them into swampy plains that formed the watershed of the Zambezi and Congo river systems. This slowed their progress down even further since the thick and glutinous bogs hindered their movements and sapped their strength. Livingstone was also becoming increasingly concerned that they would not have enough money—beads and other tradeable goods—to buy supplies as they were being forced to purchase all their food, often at exorbitant prices as they went along.

The stinginess on the part of the tribes about supplying travellers with food, as was customary, was a direct consequence of the impact of slavery. This is because the slave traders needed the permission of the chiefs to pass through their lands and since there was a tremendous profit to be made, the traders were willing to pay handsomely to ensure they maintained this right. The other result of this policy was that in time, the locals grew contemptuous of the 'white' traders. It was also inevitable that the closer Livingstone and his companions came to the coast the more that was going to be demanded from them. Very soon payment was demanded just for the right for them to pass through the country, over a bridge or along a trail. It became very wearing for Livingstone since the demands were often outrageous and it took hours to negotiate a 'fair' bargain. Frequently the demand was for 'a man, a tusk, beads, copper rings, or a shell'.

One of the most perilous moments they faced on this journey was when a certain Chiboque chief refused a gift of meat. Instead a message was sent demanding 'a man, a gun, an ox, powder, cloth, or a shell'. They were also threatened that if a present was not immediately given, then they would be attacked. Very soon the small party was surrounded. Livingstone sat calmly on a campstool with a shotgun laid across his knees while his men formed a defensive circle around him with their spears at the ready. The Chiboque leapt around them, yelling and brandishing swords. Their appearance was not improved by their practice of filing their teeth to points. The chief and his counsellors arrived and were invited to sit down with Livingstone to discuss the problem. It transpired that one of Livingstone's men had accidentally spat on a leg of one of the Chiboque, which was considered to be a terrible slight. The chief demanded a man as recompense but Livingstone staunchly informed him that they would all rather die than surrender one of their companions. A counter demand for a gun was then made but it was pointed out that such a gift would only make it easier for the Chiboque to attack them. As these negotiations dragged on it seemed the Chiboque were becoming increasingly resolved on attacking them. At one point one of their warriors rushed up behind Livingstone to strike him down but he quickly turned and pointed his gun at his assailant's face and the man retired. His own men were strengthened by the presence of the Makololo who were well trained to withstand attack and to drive off any assailants but Livingstone knew that if a blow was struck then a bloodbath would result. He was therefore anxious to avoid any actual conflict. His men had also craftily surrounded the chief and his counsellors who had sat down near Livingstone and they too soon realised their own predicament. A stalemate was reached and Livingstone explained to the chief that he wanted to pass peacefully through their country while it was the Chiboque that appeared anxious to attack them. Livingstone then told the chief and his counsellors that they must strike the first blow 'so that they would be guilty before God'. All was quiet while this was considered. Livingstone sat impassively, quite aware of the danger that he faced: 'It was rather trying for me because I knew that the Chiboque would aim at the white man first, but I was careful not to appear flurried, and having four barrels ready for instant action, looked quietly at the savage scene around.' The chief finally conceded to Livingstone's point and a bargain was struck with Livingstone agreeing to give them one of his shirts, some beads and a large handkerchief.

The prevalence of slavery forced Livingstone to bear away again from his westerly path since the tribes his party would have to pass through were 'all familiar with the visits of the slave-trader and, we were informed, would strip us bare. The only one who should reach Loanda would be myself alone.'[85] He decided that it would be better to head in north-westerly direction towards the Portuguese settlement of Cassange.

The constant strain of the journey combined with frequent fevers and malarial attacks took a toll on Livingstone and he was forced to ride an ox. Livingstone's favourite animal seems to have been a bad-tempered ox called Sinbad:

> He had a softer back than the others, but a much more intractable temper. His horns were bent downwards and hung loosely, so that he could do no harm with them; but as he went slowly along the narrow paths he would suddenly dart aside. A string tied to a stick put through the cartilage of his nose serves as a bridle. If you jerk this back it makes him go faster, if you pull it to one side he allows his nose and head to go, but keeps the other eye on the forbidden spot and goes in spite of you. The only way in which he can be brought to a stand is by a stroke of a wand across the nose. Once when he ran in below a climber stretched across the path, so low that I could not stoop under it, I was dragged off and came down on the crown of my head. He never allowed a chance of this sort to pass without trying to inflict a kick, as if I neither had nor deserved his love.[86]

The other problem was the party was reduced to eating just manioc. When Livingstone had fever, he would eat nothing for days, then he would become ravenous for food but there was only the unsatisfying manioc available. Livingstone maintained that within two hours of eating all he could, he felt like he had an empty stomach.

The party battled on, besieged by the usual tribute demands:

> [The] natives became great hindrances. They would not let us pass without paying. Surrounding us, they would point their guns and brandish other weapons, demanding either a man, or an ox or a gun &c. &c., and always when we yielded they asked the more.

In response they adopted the stratagem of sitting down as a group and inviting the tribe that was preventing them from proceeding striking the first blow. It worked, as they 'made much noise, threatened more, and though we often expected them to maul us every moment, we passed among or by the very worse without harm.'[87]

Livingstone had become terribly thin but he was encouraged when they entered Portuguese territory on 26 March 1854 as he hoped their desperate situation would improve as they neared civilisation. He was, however, surprised by the lack of infrastructure in the country. One of the obvious ways to open up the interior and encourage trade was to build roads and Livingstone wondered why the Portuguese had not bothered to do so since it was in their own interest. In the end he decided that it was just another example of the slothfulness of the Portuguese colonisers who Livingstone considered degraded and dissipated.

Another surprising thing happened as they progressed towards the coast; the number of freed slaves they encountered. Livingstone was interested to find out from these people whether they felt they had been badly disadvantaged since they had been forced into slavery. He was surprised when they told him that their situation was better when they were slaves because it meant that they did not have to go hungry so often.

5.5 Contact with the Portuguese

Livingstone and his companions entered onto a high table land and at length, they reached the edge of a precipice that overlooked the Quango Valley. The difficulties they had experienced on their march were compensated by the glorious spectacle of the valley spread out below them. The sides of the valley dropped away sharply and the vista that greeted them was a valley that varied between fifty and a hundred miles in width, covered in luscious greenery. A passing thunderstorm, silhouetted by brilliant sunshine, added to the poetry of the scene.

Their joy was short lived for upon descending about 2,000 feet into the Quango Valley, their progress was again slowed by the continued demands for tribute.

On they battled but Livingstone's health was now becoming a major concern to his companions, particularly as he had become so weak that had to be assisted by his men. They were starving and so in desperation Livingstone ordered their remaining spare oxen be slaughtered at a point several hundred miles from their final objective. But help was at hand for a half-caste Portuguese militia sergeant[88] heard that there was a white man in the area and found them on the 4 April 1854. Seeing the desperate straits that they were in, the sergeant immediately offered to lead them to the nearest Portuguese settlement. This was Cassange and it was about three day's journey away. But if they thought their troubles were over, they were mistaken since their path took them through long grass that towered over them all, including Livingstone mounted on Sinbad. They were also drenched by continual rain and so it was a bedraggled and exhausted party that arrived at a small militia outpost late one afternoon.

On reaching Cassange, they were hosted by the Portuguese. Captain Neves[89] commanded the outpost, the most distant inland Portuguese station that lay about 325 miles east of Loanda. Neves generously received and fed the travellers and Livingstone was clearly grateful for the captain's hospitality. They stayed there for about ten days with Livingstone feasting at gatherings with the captain and other whites living in Cassange.

They also sold a remaining tusk in Cassange that they had faithfully carried with them all the way from Linyanti to pay for new clothing. A small profit was made in the transaction and this opened the eyes of Livingstone's native companions to the possibilities of trade. Livingstone noted the prices were in most cases much less than missionaries were paying for comparable goods in Kuruman.[90]

One of the interesting things that Livingstone immediately noticed was that many of the Portuguese posted to these outlying stations had families by native wives. There appeared to be no racial prejudice and half-caste offspring were rarely spurned, as was the case in most other places in southern Africa. Livingstone noted that many people could read and write in the Ambaca area, but there was a general lethargy that hung over this part of Angola, or as he described it, a lack of stimulus. There was also no evidence of any missionary endeavour; 'Not a Bible in the country.'[91]

They travelled from Cassange over well-beaten footpaths towards Loanda. An African militia corporal guided them, carried in a hammock by three slaves. The bounce appeared again in their step for they knew that the worse of their troubles lay safely behind them. However, another problem now manifested itself— Livingstone's companions feared that he meant to take them to Loanda so 'that they would be taken on board a ship, fattened, and eaten by white men, who were cannibals.' The closer they got to the sea, the more terrified they became at this awful prospect. It took all of Livingstone's persuasive powers to dispel their fears.

They entered another small military outpost in Ambaca. It was commanded by the impressively named Senor Arsenio Pompilio Pompeo De Carpo, district commandant.[92] This man had a colourful background: convicted of the manslaughter of his father; banished to Angola for being involved in revolutionary activities; he also had a dangerous reputation for making and then ruining friends. But he treated Livingstone most courteously. He could speak a little English and it was the first time that Livingstone had spoken in his mother tongue in about eight months and it felt strange. De Carpo thought so too: he 'thought I spoke it like a German.'

Livingstone was given a little wine because it was thought to be useful antidote against fever. Livingstone hated physical weakness in any man, particularly himself, and it is therefore surprising how frank he was in his first book, *Missionary Tales* about how he had suffered:

> The weakening effects of fever were most extraordinary. For instance, in taking lunar observations I could not avoid confusion of time and distance. I could not hold the instrument steady nor perform a simple calculation. I forgot the days of the week and names of my companions, and, had I been asked, probably could not have told my own.[93]

The will power that he must have possessed to keep moving, although frequently he was reduced to riding on his ox, is astounding. It also illustrates why so many other explorers succumbed to these types of illnesses in unknown parts of Africa.

Livingstone and his party left Ambaca on 12 May 1854 and entered the plains that stretched out to the west coast. The next place they passed through was Golungo Alto, which they reached on 16 May 1854, about thirty miles from Ambaca. His host was Lieutenant Antonio Castro.[94] Livingstone was still suffering from both fever and dysentery and was at the point of collapsing but the end was in sight and so he did not pause for long—just long enough to write letters to Mary, Moffat and his brother Charles. They soon departed for the coast and on 31 May 1854 Livingstone and his fellow travellers staggered up to the residence of the British commissioner of Loanda, Mr Edmund Gabriel. They had reached the coast and the first part of this great journey was over. Livingstone's constitution had suffered badly and Gabriel immediately saw how ill Livingstone was and had him taken to his own bed, as he looked like he might die.

He was soon receiving medical attention from the Portuguese authorities and from a surgeon from the HMS *Polyphemus,* a British frigate blockading the coast. Frigates were stationed outside Loanda, as the place had once been the biggest distribution point for slaves on the western side of the continent.

Livingstone's recovery was slow, especially as he suffered from recurring attacks of fever during the four months that he stayed in Loanda. When he was able to, he took the opportunity to write up his journal and to mail despatches to his family, the London Missionary Society and friends to let them know that he was alive. Unfortunately, there were no letters waiting for him but he was not surprised, as he knew people did not know which route he may take to the coast. It did not lessen the disappointment, however, as it was 27 months since he had waved goodbye to his family when their ship had departed from the Cape for England. He did not even known if they had safely arrived back in England and he was understandably anxious to hear news of them.

5.6 Mary in Britain

Mary was meanwhile desperately in need of support. She had spent a miserable time in Britain, struggling to bring up their family, short of money and continually worrying whether she would ever see her husband again. It was a time of great loneliness because she was removed from Africa, without her own family and friends, and without a home, in a foreign country. She had at first taken her family to stay with her parents-in-law at their Ulva Cottage in Burnbank Road in Hamilton but they were different type of people and the relationship soon broke down. Mary may have found the deeply religious, tee-totalling Livingstone family stifling and for the Livingstones, their daughter-in-law may have appeared strange with her African ways. Perhaps the children also upset the household with their unruly ways. It is unclear what caused the split and for a time it was deep and unforgiving. The estrangement forced Mary to find other lodgings, first when she moved to a one-bedroom apartment at 46 Almada Street in Hamilton. Later, gipsy-like, she moved to a number of places in England and Scotland.

These moves forced Mary to fall back on her own meagre resources and it was not long before she had to write to Arthur Tidman of the London Missionary Society, in mid-1852, requesting financial assistance. It was the beginning of a pattern of increasingly anxious letters to the London Missionary Society requesting support, as is evident from the fifteen surviving letters she wrote to the society.

> My health has been very poor since my arrival in Scotland, but I am now a little better. We are in lodgings at fifteen pounds the quarter independent of food and other expenses. Now that will never do for me.

She went on to add:

> I shall at present give you an account of the 30 pounds I received from you; first I paid five pounds for custom house dues. The journey from London to Manchester and Scotland including luggage twelve pounds, and five pounds for house rent. £2 for other expenses, now there is only five pounds left, this will be sufficient for me until October[95]

Mary received another payment from the London Missionary Society later in 1852 but she was clearly having trouble managing her money as she requested another £20 in January 1853 and then again in February 1853 despite assuring Tidman she would not need to draw further funds until April 1853. Mary must have made life difficult for Tidman, particularly as her letters were peppered with comments like 'I trust you will not refuse, as I have no one else to look to.'[96] However, she was honest and this comes through when she later wrote to the secretary:

> I would now beg of you to be lenient with me, I don't attempt to justify myself. I may not have [been] so discreet in the use of money.[97]

Mary's restlessness is evident when in February 1853, at about the same time as Livingstone was exploring the Zambezi, Mary abruptly moved her family away from Hamilton. Nobody seemed to know where she had gone, least of all her in-laws. In June 1853 Tidman received a disturbing letter from Livingstone's father:

> Mrs L does not write to us, nor are we anxious that she should, neither do we wish her to know that we are enquiring about them, yet we love the children very much.[98]

Next day Neil Livingstone penned another letter to Tidman:

> I addressed a note to you yesterday enquiring about our grandchildren, having no other way of getting any word about them, as their mother Mrs. L. was pleased to forbid all communication with us no less than three different times. We received a note from her this morning, which I enclose, but owing to her remarkably strange conduct ever since we became acquainted with her, we have resolved to have no more intercourse with her until there is evidence that she is a changed person.[99]

Mary had in fact moved to Hackney, soon after to London and then in October 1853, she shifted to Winton Bridge, near Manchester. Just what was happening to Mary is unclear but this manic moving around may have been evidence of the beginning of her gradual decline into depression, drink and questioning of her faith.

Her daughter, Anna Mary, later recalled an incident from this time when she needed someone to repair her ripped doll:

> I don't think it could have been my mother, as I have a curious remembrance of strangeness in this person, unlike what I was used to & I can remember her making some remark such as one would make to a baby.[100]

There is a further glimpse into her state of mind when she informed Tidman in a letter written in December 1853 that she was again moving to stay with the kindly Braithwaite's in Kendal. 'I feel extremely anxious on Mr Livingstone's account, have you heard any news from Africa. He has not written since last January.'[101] Fortunately a letter from Livingstone arrived soon after and she decided to return to Africa. She wrote to the London Missionary Society to advise them that her health had much improved and she could travel. 'I have had no return of paralises since the commencement of last year.' The letter from Livingstone suggested he was going to return to the Cape following his explorations and Mary reasoned that if she wanted to see her husband, she would have to take a voyage to South Africa.

> If nothing unforeseen prevents, Mr. L will be at the Cape to meet me in August [1854]. I have asked him to come to England, but he sternly refuses to do so, on account of his throat, which would be aggravated by the damp weather in this country. Therefore I beg and intreat of you to grant my request. I have had much to try me in every respect.[102]

Sadly she had another three years to wait until she saw her husband again.

CHAPTER 6

The Trans-African Crossing

'I shall open a path into the Interior or perish'[1]

6.1 Loanda

Livingstone was surprised to find the British Commissioner was the only Englishmen living in Loanda. Gabriel's job was to suppress the slave trade and in Livingstone he had the perfect guest and their friendship quickly grew. He later wrote to the directors of the London Missionary Society to tell them of his own impressions about their Scottish missionary:

> I consult, therefore the impulse of my own mind alone, when I declare that in no respect was my intercourse more gratifying to me than in the opportunities afforded to me of observing his earnest, active, and unwearied solicitude for the advancement of Christianity. Few, perhaps, have had better opportunities than myself of estimating the benefit the Christian cause in this country has derived from Dr. Livingstone's exertions. It is indeed fortunate for that sacred cause, and highly honourable to the London Missionary Society when qualities and dispositions like his are employed in propagating its blessings among men. Irrespective, moreover, of his laudable and single-minded conduct as a minister of the Gospel, and his attainments in making observations which have determined the true geography of the interior, the Directors, I am sure, will not have failed to perceive how interesting and valuable are all the communications they receive from him—as sketches of the social conditions of the people, and the material, fabrics, and produce of these lands.[2]

After reading this letter the London Missionary Society directors must have wondered what had come over their wayward missionary in the time since he left Kuruman and arrived in Loanda.

If Livingstone's companions had been anxious about their own safety on reaching the coast, they were also fascinated by the idea of 'a river that had no end'. And so, when they first laid eyes on the Atlantic Ocean, they were overawed. It was an exciting time for them because everything was new and wonderful. They marvelled at the stone houses, wondered at all the activities going on at the port, and stared at all the strange looking people. They soon found jobs at the port unloading 'stones that burned'—coal—for which they were paid a sixpence a day, a veritable fortune.

Livingstone later took them on board the frigate HMS *Pluto*. They were astonished and exclaimed: 'This is not a canoe at all; it is a town!' They looked upon the decks and masts as being, 'A town upon a town.' It is not hard to imagine the scene; brown bodies moving through the ranks of blue with laughter ringing through the rigging and the curiosity evident on their faces as they examined everything while Livingstone stood by getting obvious enjoyment from the occasion. They were also very impressed by the cannons that the ship carried. It was the enormous firepower of the British warships that was the most effective weapon that the British Government had to control the slave trade. One of Livingstone's men was allowed to fire a cannon and the resulting noise terrified them. However, they immediately saw the possibilities from possessing such a weapon and they asked if they could take one back with them to use on their old enemies, the Matabele.

Perhaps what would have made Livingstone most proud that day was the treatment accorded to the natives; the Makololo later told Livingstone: 'We see they are your countrymen, for they have hearts like you.'

On board HMS *Pluto* was a young Lieutenant, Norman Bedingfeld, and he immediately impressed Livingstone. Some years later Livingstone was to agree to have him accompany him on another expedition, which, sadly, was to end in an acrimonious parting of ways between the two men.

The offer of a passage back to England was made to Livingstone but it was rejected. Livingstone had promised Sekeletu to bring his 'black men' back safely to their families. It was a noble sentiment and was seized upon by the British public, as an illustration of Livingstone's faithfulness to his friends. It was one of the reasons why he was given such a tumultuous welcome when he did eventually return to Britain. But it was in fact a nurtured perception that had little in common with reality for Livingstone later showed little concern about abandoning them when he reached the other side of the continent and returned to Britain.

When the news of his arrival in Loanda reached Britain, it created a stir. He was hailed as a great explorer and details of his journey were carried in the press. The Royal Geographical Society saw fit to award him with its blue ribbon, the gold medal. There is little doubt that a letter that Maclear, the Astronomer-Royal at the Cape, had sent to the Royal Geographical Society helped in their deliberations. Maclear had been receiving regular reports from Livingstone about his astronomical observations. The letter included the comment: 'Such a man deserves every encouragement in the power of his country to give. He has done that which few other travellers in Africa can boast of—he has fixed his geographical points with very great accuracy, and yet he is only a poor missionary.'[3] The University of Glasgow also recognised his achievements by honouring him with a bachelor of divinity. However, Livingstone was oblivious to his growing fame and popularity back in Britain as he was busy preparing himself for the next stage in his explorations.

He wrote two letters to Mary after he had left Loanda and was making his way back to Linyanti. In the latter one he mentioned that he had lingered on the coast nearly four months, longer than expected or necessary, in the vain hope that he might receive some mail. It was all he could do but write:

> Give my love to all the children, they will reap the advantage of your remaining longer at home longer than we anticipated… How happy I shall be to meet them and you again! I hope a letter from you may be waiting for me at Zambezi. Love to all the children. How tall is Zouga? Accept the assurance of unabated love.[4]

6.2 Return to Linyanti

Livingstone had quickly decided that he was going back to the Zambezi after a short rest in Loanda. Uttering the stirring words, 'I will open a way to the interior or perish', Livingstone and his party left Loanda on the 20 September 1854 to begin the return journey to distant Linyanti. The party still comprised the same twenty-seven people who had accompanied Livingstone on the first part of the trip. An Austrian botanist who worked for the Portuguese authorities, Dr Walweitch, had asked to join them but Livingstone refused his offer for he was always mean about sharing the praise for his discoveries with others. He also thought there would be little point in having the botanist accompany him since he now felt much more confident about the return journey as he would be simply retracing his steps.

There was certainly something remarkable about him deciding to once more disappear into the interior of Africa when so many explorers would have been satisfied with this major accomplishment. After all, the man had just covered over one thousand three hundred miles traversing punishing terrain, constantly facing treachery and deceitfulness and barely surviving the effects of constant fever and malaria attacks. His decision meant deliberately spurning the opportunity to return to Britain where he would be hailed as a hero. There was also the powerful call of his family. So why did he make this decision?

The best place to start is to examine why Livingstone made the journey in the first place. Livingstone had always been very sensitive to the accusation that he had apparently given up dreary missionary work to win acclaim as an explorer. While there was certainly an element of truth in this statement that even Livingstone could not deny, he did gladly suffer all the privations because he was motivated by his christian duty to save the African tribes from the ravages of slavery, and to bring the benefits of 'civilisation' to this part of the world. He thought this could be best achieved by him opening up trade routes into the interior. But as he also well knew, the path that he had just followed was quite unsuitable for this purpose—there would be too few European traders who would be prepared to take the stupendous risks of penetrating into 'dark Africa' when there were other easier trading options. Therefore, Livingstone thought it was necessary for him to comprehensively demonstrate that crossing Africa could be done. This meant retracing his steps to Linyanti and from there, proceeding down the Zambezi to the other side of the continent to see what opportunities lay there.

There is, however, no denying that it was a very heroic decision for which he was later rightly acclaimed for as success was by no means assured.

Livingstone's intention to open up trade routes excited the commercial instincts of the Bishop of Angola and Congo and acting governor. This man, the Right Reverend Joaquim Moreira Reis, prevailed upon the Board of Public Works to entrust Livingstone with a horse, saddlery and a colonel's dress uniform so that Livingstone could present them to Sekeletu as a sign of friendship. The Board also gave clothes and blankets to each of Livingstone's men. Reis also instructed all commandants to furnish Livingstone's party with whatever he needed until he left Portuguese territory.[5] With an eye to the future, the local merchants quickly chipped in by giving him samples of their produce for him to show to all the tribes and two donkeys to help carry the loads. The donkeys were a valuable present as this animal is normally immune to the effect of a tsetse fly bite. Another merchant, a Dutchman, Mr Schut of Loanda,[6] gave him ten oxen for provisions and Livingstone collected these when passing through Ambaca. He also collected a number of letters of recommendation to the Portuguese authorities in eastern Africa.

Livingstone was touched by their generosity and he later wrote to Mary, 'The Portuguese have all been extremely kind.'[7] It was surprising that the Portuguese treated Livingstone so well, as he was already well known as an outspoken proponent for the abolishment of slavery and it hardly suited their purposes to have such a man looking around their territory.

His party was now well equipped, including new clothes and a new tent for Livingstone, which was a gift from his friends from the frigate, HMS *Philomel*, well-armed and well rested. Livingstone had also been able to purchase ten English muskets, four 20-pound barrels of powder and thirty pounds of lead.[8] This last purchase was particularly important, as a show of arms would help speed their passage back to Linyanti—weapons were a language that all the avaricious tribes understood. Finally and most importantly, they knew what to expect.

Livingstone had the company of his new friend, Gabriel, for the first thirty miles of the journey.[9] They initially followed the Bengo River back into the interior. The Bishop of Angola had provided him with twenty porters to carry his supplies, as Livingstone's own men were carrying huge bundles of goods that they had brought with their savings. It was therefore not surprising that at first they made good progress.

Livingstone generally liked to travel about twenty days in each month and rest for the remainder of the time. His party averaged about ten geographical miles per day or about two hundred miles in a month. Of course, as it was necessary to zigzag and occasionally retrace their steps, the actual miles covered were much more. By way of contrast, he observed that traders normally only spent about ten days in each month travelling and only covered about seven miles per day, or about seventy miles in a month.

Despite their good start their return journey was slower than the outward one due to their continuing sickness and the heavy rains that slowed their progress.

Livingstone was able to appreciate the landscape more than when he had first passed through the country. He was continually amazed at the beauty of the countryside. The luscious growth and broad river valleys, alive with birdsong, made their exertions that much easier to bear. However, the countryside was denuded of game. Just how devoid was evident when one day he observed the care with which a native had wrapped a field mouse in leaves to carry home. But pretty as the scenery was, it in no way compensated for degradation of the people; he thought that the effect of the Portuguese settling among them had only contributed to the problem since many of these settlers had adopted local customs. Polygamy was common among them: for if one of these settlers saw a beautiful native girl, he would simply purchase her as his concubine to satisfy his lust. Children would be produced and if in time he tired of her, he could simply cast about for another that attracted his eye. Livingstone knew that the development of Africa depended on the emancipation of its people; until that happened the prosperity of this great continent would remain a dream.

One action that Livingstone could be positive about was the effect of the British blockade on the slave trade. In a letter to Mary he described the change in the slave routes:

Formerly the trade went from the interior into the Portuguese territory; now it goes the opposite way. This is the effect of the Portuguese love of the trade: they cannot send them abroad on account of our ships of war on the coast, yet will sell them to the best advantage. These women are decent-looking, as much so as the general run of Kuruman ladies, and were caught lately in a skirmish the Portuguese had with their tribe; and they will be sold for about three tusks each. Each has an iron ring round the wrist, and that is attached to the chain, which she carries in the hand to prevent it jerking and hurting the wrist. How would Nannie like to be thus treated? and yet it is only by the goodness of God in appointing our lot in different circumstances that we are not similarly degraded, for we have the same evil nature, which is so degraded in them as to allow of men treating them as beasts.[10]

Livingstone's missionary curiosity about the old Jesuit missionaries led him to visit a number of their former missions. One lay only three miles north of Golungo Alto at a place called Bango. The church and surrounding buildings were largely derelict as all the books, gold and silver had been removed to Loanda. The Jesuits had been very active in the region until they were forced to leave in 1759 following the order to expel them from all Portuguese territories. One of their legacies was the high level of literacy of the local people.[11]

He also visited Massangano, which is situated to the south of Golungo Alto, and at the confluence of the rivers Lucalla and Coanza. There they saw the ruins of a massive iron foundry that was built in 1768. Spanish and Swedish workers were brought in to show the locals how to make iron, but the exercise failed when all the Europeans eventually succumbed to disease. There was a small party of native miners and smiths still smelting some 500 bars of good malleable iron every month.[12]

Their route led Livingstone through the Cazengo district that was famous for the mocha coffee that was grown there from seeds first brought by the early Jesuit priests. He was amazed at the size of the extensive coffee plantations that covered the surrounding hills.

Livingstone also paid particular interest in observing the local customs. He noted that the Portuguese tended to rule through the native hierarchy. A chief still retained his counsellors and maintained more or less the same position that his forefathers had enjoyed before the arrival of the Portuguese. But *noblesse oblige* meant that if, for example, one of his tribesmen was guilty of thieving, the chief would be expected to either replace the goods or compensate the aggrieved party out of his own pocket. He would then turn to the guilty party and attempt to reimburse himself from those responsible. The transaction would normally result in a profit for the chief for the insult and nuisance caused. Beneath the chief and his counsellors were various strata of society: from the village headmen down to the lowly porters. Privileges would be accorded based on an individual's station. For instance, Livingstone noticed that in some villages, one group of people would be allowed to wear shoes while the class below could not. In other villages some of the people would be called 'gentlemen', others 'little gentlemen'; and finally another way of making a differentiation between those of rank and others was for the upper classes to be called 'white men' while lower classes would be known as 'blacks'—although they were all of the same colour. It is sad that as early as the mid-nineteenth century the locals were already beginning to ape their European masters.

It was not very long until Livingstone began to suffer from various illnesses. In addition to the usual attacks of fever and malaria, Livingstone also suffered from a severe attack of rheumatic fever that was accompanied by him losing a great deal of blood. It was the first time that he suffered from this additional complication but it was ominous because from then on he suffered increasingly from bleeding from the bowels.

He decided to visit the famous huge Black Rocks at Pungo Andongo[13] formed at a time 'when the morning stars sang together, and all the sons of God shouted for joy.' It was while staying at Pungo Andongo that word reached Livingstone on 23 December 1854 that the mail ship, the *Forerunner,* had gone down off Maderia with the loss of all hands except one.[14] Livingstone would have been a passenger on this boat if he had chosen to return to England. He was also knew all his dispatches went down with the *Forerunner* and he therefore set to work to replicate his letters.

Livingstone and his party left Pungo Andongo on 1 January 1855. They followed the banks of the Coanza river until they joined up with the path they had followed on their outward journey. It was one of the trade routes and daily they met long caravans of porters bearing elephant tusks and beeswax heading towards the coast. Two weeks later they descended into the Cassenge valley. When they had previously passed through the area, Livingstone had been so sick that he did not have the energy to enquire about the people living in that area. Outwardly it seemed a pretty place and the valley was place of great beauty:

> I have often thought, in travelling through this land, that it presents pictures of beauty, which angels might enjoy. How often have I beheld, in still mornings, scenes the very essence of beauty, and all bathed in an atmosphere of delicious warmth, to which the soft breeze imparts a pleasing sensation of coolness, as from a fan.[15]

However, the place hid a local secret; the Cassange river was a mysterious place for the locals. People accused of being witches would come to prove their innocence by drinking a potion made from a poisonous tree that grew on the banks of the river. The result was usually fatal. Livingstone was saddened by the senseless loss of life and from the fact that the Portuguese authorities made no effort to stop it. 'How painful is the contrast between this inward gloom and the brightness of the outer world, between the undefined terrors of the spirit and the peace and beauty that pervade the scenes around us.'[16]

It was also very wet. The rain poured down continuously and soon they were trekking through flooded countryside. At night they would pile up earth 'somewhat like graves in a church yard' and covering it with grass, lie down to sleep. However, Livingstone became so cold that he was forced to rest for eight days during which he suffered from a most violent pain in his head. For most of the time he floated in and out of consciousness, much to the anxiety of his attendants. It was the worst attack of fever that he had endured to date. In desperation his men collected leeches and placed them on his neck and groin which gave him some relief. But his rest was interrupted when one of his men struck a headman of a small village who had been annoying them for meat and other goods. This affront could not go unpunished and in an effort to placate the man, he was given a gun and pieces of cloth. This had the opposite of the desired effect and the chief began to make increasingly exorbitant demands. The situation began to get ugly when the chief sent runners to the surrounding villages to send support and Livingstone, thinking that discretion was the better side of valour, immediately ordered that his party move. However, they did not get far when an armed body of men attacked them from the rear. Livingstone was up the front and when he heard the sounds of the attack he swung off his oxen and still weak from his fever, staggered back down the track. He was clutching his six-barrelled revolver and when he ran straight into the headman, the sight of Livingstone's haggard features and the awesome looking weapon aimed at his stomach completely unnerved the man for he blurted out: 'Oh, I have only come to speak to you and wish peace only.'[17] Livingstone saw the whole miserable incident as proof of the cowardly nature of the local inhabitants.

Their rate of progress slowed dramatically from this time on. At one point they only travelled about ten days in each month. The main reasons were sickness and the protracted time that it took to buy provisions. Livingstone had also deteriorated physically; he was terribly weak and had become deaf which was one of the side effects of all the quinine that he had been taking. His pallor was an awful yellowish colour.

After leaving the Kasai and passing over the Lotembwa River, Livingstone noticed a curious thing. On the north-westerly side of Lake Dilolo the river ran east whereas he had earlier noticed that the river flowing out the southern side went in the opposite direction. What he had found was a watershed; rivers flowing north from that point went into the Congo basin and eventually ended up in the Atlantic whereas the rivers flowing from the southern side fed the Zambezi that finally discourses into the Indian Ocean. It was a remarkable observation that helped shed light on the topography and hydrology of southern Africa.

They had by then reached Balonda country where they began to be met with hospitality rather than demands for tribute. But it was not until mid-June 1855 that they really felt they were among old friends—the Barotse. They received a warm welcome from old Shinte who was given a small pot that contained 'orange- and cashew-trees, custard apple-trees and a fig-tree.' These had survived portage all the way from Angola, another remarkable achievement.

With the end in sight, they were keen to push on but soon after a swarm of tsetse fly attacked Livingstone's temperamental but favourite oxen, Sinbad. Livingstone knew the animal would weaken and die, but he could not bring himself to order that the beast be slaughtered for meat.

They reached the town of Libonta on 27 July 1855. The sudden arrival had a tremendous impact and the townsfolk went crazy with excitement. It took some time before a 'Kgotla' was formed where the men sat in respectful decorum. One of Livingstone's men, Pitsane, delivered the first of many long speeches about their travels and how their 'father' had looked after them so well. Livingstone held two thanks-giving sermons on the Sunday. He described the scene in his journal:

> The men decked themselves out in their best, for all had managed to preserve their suits of European clothing, which, with their white and red caps, gave them a rather dashing appearance. They tried to walk like soldiers, and called themselves 'my braves.' Having been again saluted with salvos from the women, we met the whole population, and having given an address on divine things, I told them we had come that day to thank God before them all for His mercy in preserving us from dangers, from strange tribes and sicknesses. We had another service in the afternoon. They gave us two fine oxen to slaughter, and the women have supplied us abundantly with milk and meal. This is all gratuitous, and I feel ashamed that I can make no return. My men explain the whole expenditure on the way hither, and they remark gratefully: 'It does not matter, you have opened a path for us, and we shall have sleep.' Strangers from a distance come flocking to see me, and seldom come empty-handed. I distribute all presents among my men.[18]

Some of the men that had accompanied him left off here, the beginning of the end of a long and eventful journey. The remainder, including the Makololo, were eager to reach their homes and so Livingstone collected them up and they set off down the Barotse valley. However, because word had rapidly spread, visitors continually delayed them and it was not until 11 September 1855 that they eventually walked into Linyanti. The full trip of just over two thousand six hundred miles, had taken nearly twenty-three months to complete. It was a marvellous achievement.

The homecoming was rowdy and the celebrations long for here was a band of brave men who had travelled a seemingly impossible distance, seen unbelievable sights and had confronted and triumphed over adversity and frustration. The tribesman danced on the brown, dusty earth between the grass huts in the gathering gloom, celebrating the arrival of those they never expected to return. The local beer, or bombe, was passed from person to person to the sounds of much merriment. Despite this joyful occasion Livingstone would have reflected that there was no one waiting to greet him with open arms and a kiss but he would also have been4 proud and justifiably so, especially when he heard his men describing what they encountered:

> On reaching the sea, they thought that they had come to the end of the world. They said, 'We marched along with our father, thinking the world

was a large plain without limit; but all at once the land said 'I am finished, there is no more of me;' and they called themselves the true old men—the true ancients—having gone to the end of the world.[19]

Many of his men were disappointed to find that their wives had remarried in their absence. Some woman even came forward carrying babies fathered by new husbands and while they tried to shrug it off by saying: 'Wives are as plentiful as the grass' the men were obviously hurt. Livingstone was also annoyed to find out that in his absence, Sekeletu had reverted to his tribe's old marauding 'bad, bad' ways. Livingstone tackled him about it but only got an inconclusive answer: Livingstone had been away too long and his hold over the chief had yet to be re-established. What Sekeletu was more interested in was what presents had the missionary brought him? He was thrilled with the magnificent colonel's dress uniform and thereafter, wore it on every major occasion, including church services until it fell apart. The excited whispers of the congregation discussing the magnificence of the uniform must have stretched Livingstone's patience.

The presents helped to cement Livingstone's friendship with Sekeletu. This was going to be very important as Livingstone considered the next stage in his trans-African journey. He had been preoccupied by the thought of how this could be accomplished: what route should he take; how many men would he need; and would he be able to get provisions from both Sekeletu and the tribes that he must pass through in order to reach the Mozambique coast. He also knew that he had been lucky to survive the passage to Loanda. His return journey had been made considerably easier for one reason: they were well armed. He realized that his party, in whatever form it eventually constituted, must carry weapons—but would Sekeletu allow them to take away these most cherished of possessions?

The route that he settled on was to follow the path of the Zambezi. This was not a surprising decision as Livingstone wanted to follow the course of this most promising of rivers to evaluate its suitability as a river highway. There was also another added attraction, initially at least: he had been told about a large waterfall on the Zambezi. He and Oswell had decided not investigate it when visiting Sebitoane in 1851, but Livingstone was not going to miss another opportunity.

Livingstone also collected the stores that Moffat had arranged through Moselikatse to be sent to him. They were still sitting on the island where the Matabele had left them, near the falls of Mosi-oa-tunya but covered by a hut that Sekeletu had ordered be built. Most of the food was spoilt but there were welcome letters, books and:

Two portraits, of whom I could for some time form no conjecture, were enclosed, until I remembered having been told that a minister had drawn my father and mother's pictures for me. They are of singular artistic excellence, for they might pass for the likenesses of a few millions of people in England as well as for those of the worthy old couple.[20]

It was time to take stock of things when he reached Linyanti. The strain on him had been severe and the deterioration of his health rapid. He admitted in a letter to Moffat that their progress back to Linyanti had been much slower than planned and this was largely due to illness. Livingstone noted he had twenty-seven severe bouts of fever, including meningitis that laid him up for twenty-five days and nearly left him blind and deaf. 'I can treat it pretty well now, but a sudden check to the perspiration brings on distressing vomiting of large mouthfuls of pure blood.' Interestingly, for all that, he seemed to be in better condition than when he was last in Kuruman and happily concluded to Moffat that 'I have been made out of a piece of as good tough clay as Mamary was.'[21]

Livingstone also penned a long letter to his mother-in-law in response to a note that she had enclosed with the parcels that the Matabele had delivered to the Zambezi. While the stores were appreciated, the note was not. In his reply, Livingstone sets out to explain his reasons for his undertakings. It is clear that he is frustrated with Mary Moffat who he felt had not tried to understand the importance of what he was doing and instead was judgemental and critical. 'I am sorry to see you so much distressed on my account, and the more so as you appear perplexed at 'not knowing my plans'.' Livingstone continued by stating that everyone else seem to know, including the directors of the London Missionary Society who published the proposition of Livingstone going into the 'Interior of this country, endeavour to find a healthy locality for a mission, and to open up a way to it from either the East or West, on condition that my family be supported during my absence.'[22] Mary Moffat had also complained about the delays in finding a mission that seemed to have afflicted all of Livingstone's plans but all he could do was wearily recount the problems of the Boers in the south, fever in the country of the Makololo and his own long and serious illnesses both *en route* and after his arrival in Loanda.[23]

The underlying issue for Livingstone was that he felt his mother-in-law was attempting to undermine what he was trying to achieve, when there were already enough detractors questioning the purpose and validity of his explorations. Livingstone had never enjoyed a close relationship with Mary Moffat, and probably decided the best course of action after this was to minimise contact with her. It may have also been the start of Livingstone really questioning the value of him remaining part of the London Missionary Society. The comments made by his mother-in-law, who was deeply engrained in the London Missionary Society, provided some proof that Livingstone was unlikely to receive full recognition from his peers within the London Missionary Society.

Mary Moffat also expressed fears about his safety, being primarily driven by her concern about Mary being left in England with the children with no husband to support them. Livingstone responded:

As for the fears you express about my life, I believe that is not my 'look out' … 'Go ye all the world' and, '*Lo I am with you always, even until the end of the world.*' … I imagine there remains not the shadow of a doubt as to being in the path of duty in trying to open this immense and populous region to the gospel. As far as I am concerned, I have no dubiety, but while free to offer myself for the service I am far from clear as to bringing my family into an unhealthy region. Mary would come without hesitation, but I question whether it be right to expose our offspring without their own self-devotion.[24]

Livingstone also wrote to Mary to let her know that he intended to canoe down the Zambezi to Quelimane and then catch a ship back to England and that the end was in sight. He was of course worried about his wife and children, in particular Thomas who seemed to be having learning difficulties. He also apologised about his delay, which was unavoidable because of illness and the difficulty of travel. In good humour he wrote to Mary:

Don't know what apology to make you for a delay I could not shorten. But as you are a merciful kind-hearted dame, I expect you will write out an apology in proper form, and I shall read it before you with as long a face as I can exhibit.[25]

Livingstone was clearly missing Mary.

Livingstone planned to stay in Linyanti for about a month and then pass on down to the east coast to Quilimane by canoe. While resting there a familiar Arab from Zanzibar walked into his camp. His name was Syde bin Habib[26] who Livingstone had first met during his visit to Naliele with Sekeletu. He provided Livingstone with letters of introduction, written in Arabic and more importantly, took Livingstone's correspondence to Loanda for mailing.

6.3 Sekeletu's Gift and Departure from Linyanti

Livingstone was given 114 men to accompany him to the east coast. This was a significant increase on the twenty-seven men that accompanied him on his first journey to Loanda.

Sekeletu chose two men, Sekwebu and Kanyata, to lead his party. The most important person for Livingstone in trying to canoe down the Zambezi was Sekwebu. This man knew the river and was known by the people living on its banks and Livingstone was to rely heavily on his judgement and advice in the months ahead. Of the rest, the Makololo formed an important part of the team. They were normally treated with respect as members of the chief tribe in the area. They were also treated with care because their neighbours justly regarded them as incurable marauders. The party also included people from other tribes and they soon settled down into an effective unit. The fact that they were strangers in a dangerous land did, of course, have an immediate settling effect. This was never more clearly demonstrated than when they were faced with mortal danger. On several occasions, 'when before the enemy' they showed themselves to be a courageous and cohesive team.

The rains that heralded the beginning of the wet season first fell on the 27 October 1855. It was a cue to Livingstone to make haste since travelling during the rainy season, although cool, slowed his progress, especially when passing through flooded areas. It also meant the traveller was being constantly drenched—there is no effective protection against the force of a tropical downpour.

On the 3 November 1855, they bid goodbye to the inhabitants of Linyanti and headed into the great unknown. Sekeletu and about two hundred followers escorted them to the banks of the Zambezi, a journey of about ten days, as it was customary to escort honoured guests a short way to ensure that they began their trip safely. There Livingstone and some of his party boarded canoes while the rest drove the oxen along the banks of the Zambezi.

They initially travelled on the Zambezi and their fragile craft floated along in mid-stream. They carefully observed hippo wallowing in the still waters and quietly and carefully slipped around them when they were fighting and playing in deeper waters. They also passed countless crocodiles sunning themselves on sandy banks: the smaller ones slipping into the water while the large ones would remain where they were, observing the people in the canoes with hungry eyes.[27] The biggest fear they would have had was from lone hippopotamus—normally bulls that have been cast out of a group—who are bad tempered and unpredictable. These are likely to attack any boat that gets between them and the deep water. The sight of a charging hippo bull is an awesome one, once experienced by the author, for they are capable of great bursts of speed over short distances. The animals also have fearsome teeth which are easily capable of splintering a boat in half should they seize a craft with their powerful jaws.

The land rose and they left the river to pass over an elevated plain. The Batoka lived in this area and they were not a tribe that Livingstone liked. They were addicted to 'mutokwane' or cannabis, and he abhorred their customs, especially their manner of greeting strangers:

> They throw themselves on their backs on the ground, rolling from side to side, and slap themselves on their thighs as expressions of thankfulness, uttering the words, 'Kina Bomba.' This method of salutation I disliked, and asked them to stop, but they imagined that I was dissatisfied and only tumbled about more furiously. The men being totally unclothed, this performance gave me a sense of their extreme degradation.[28]

On 21 November 1855, nearly three weeks after leaving Linyanti, Livingstone was confronted with one of the natural wonders of the world, Mosi-oa-tunya or 'The Smoke that Thunders.' It is difficult to fully appreciate the size of this waterfall simply because it is so large; the river is nearly nineteen hundred yards wide at the point where it plunges up to three hundred yards to the 'boiling pot.' Over one million litres of water falls into this chasm every minute and this causes huge pillars of vapour to rise high into the sky; it can be seen from over five miles away.[29] Livingstone was flabbergasted: the Makololo had told him that it was large but he was not expecting the magnificent sight that stretched out before him. He wrote poignantly in his journal:

> It had never been seen before by European eyes; but scenes so lovely must have been gazed upon by angels in their flight.[30]

He decided to give the waterfall an English name and so he named it the Victoria Falls in honour of Her Majesty, Queen Victoria. It was the first time that he had named a geographical feature and it was both 'proof of his loyalty'[31] and indicated how impressed he was by this natural wonder.

While exploring around Mosi-oa-tunya, Livingstone found what he thought would make a suitable missionary site. He had started thinking about settling down with the Makololo on the Batoka Plateau, in an area immediately north east of the Victoria Falls.[32] In preparation for this he established a small nursery near the edge of the actual falls on a place that is today called Livingstone Island, although he worried about the hippopotamus destroying the garden. Livingstone later enthusiastically wrote to Moffat to start arranging for a smith, books, ploughs and mills to be sent north to the Zambezi.[33] He also carved his name in a Baobab tree it was not the only recorded instance of Livingstone resorting to this little vanity.

Livingstone thought the central African plateau would be very suitable for establishing a number of missions and developing trading operations as the land rises up to over five thousand feet. He was certain that the land was healthy and suitable for white settlers. But there was a problem—the Batoka lived in permanent fear of the Matabele who occupied the area south of the Zambezi. Indeed, Sebitoane and his favourite Makololo had been driven out of this fertile area and into the unhealthy land that they now occupied by this tribe. Livingstone chose later to ignore this important fact, perhaps hoping the presence of well-armed traders would deter any attacks from the Matabele.

6.4 Matabele Country

One month after leaving Linyanti, Livingstone and his party reached the edge of the area under control of the Makololo. It was a land of changing allegiance and it was necessary to proceed with caution. The normal procedure when arriving at any village was to camp some way off and send messengers to explain to the locals that their purpose was peaceful and they wished to travel through their country. On the 4 November 1855, they came to a village and just on dusk, they suddenly found themselves surrounded. When one of Livingstone's men went to get water, they attempted to spear him. Then, suddenly, out of the gathering gloom, rushed a warrior with his battle-axe raised to confront them. The bloodcurdling scream that he made and his crazed appearance was frightening: 'His eyes were shot out, his lips covered in foam, and every muscle of his frame quivered.' The natural reaction of his men was to leap up and kill the man but Livingstone had warned them against this. Sekwebu, his boatman causally picked up his spear as if to piece a piece of leather that he held, but was tensed and ready to hurl it at the man to protect his master. The seconds passed slowly as all eyes were riveted on the dancing, shouting form. Then, after some minutes, the man drew back. It was clearly a test of Livingstone's courage and as always, he had reacted coolly and with great fortitude.

On another occasion, they were again surrounded by a large group of armed men who looked them over. They voiced their contempt: 'They have wandered in order to be destroyed. What can they do without shields?' Sekeletu had ordered that they were not to take their shields because he thought it might make the group seem like a war party. Livingstone's answer was to have all his men discharge their weapons later to discourage a night attack. They were not molested.

This was example of Livingstone's heroism. With quiet courage and an unshakeable faith in his God, he outwardly faced danger resolutely and calmly. It is only when you read his diaries that you get a measure of his distress:

> 14th January 1856.—At the confluence of the Loangwa and the Zambezi. Thank God for His great mercies thus far. How soon I may be called to stand before Him, my righteous judge, I know not. All hearts are in His hands, and merciful and gracious is the Lord our God. O Jesus, grant me resignation to Thy will, and entire reliance on Thy powerful hand. On Thy Word alone I lean. But wilt Thou permit me to plead for Africa? The cause is Thine ... I leave my cause and all my concerns in the hands of God, my gracious Saviour, the Friend of sinners.
>
> Evening.—Felt much turmoil of spirit in view of having all my plans for the welfare of this great region and teeming population knocked on the head by savages to-morrow ... I will not cross furtively by night as I intended. It would appear as flight, and should such a man as I flee? Nay, verily, I shall take observations for latitude and longitude to-night, though they may be the last. I feel quite calm now, thank God.[34]

The further that they progressed east, the more populated the country became. Livingstone made a point of treating the sick—to the frustration of his men—and whenever he stopped word soon spread of his skill. At that time a whooping-cough epidemic was sweeping through the land. The benefit of this kindness soon became clear—his party started to be provided with food in great abundance.

The Batoka plateau they travelled through was fertile and was covered in game of all sorts. 'The number of animals was quite astonishing, and made me think that here I could realize an image of the time when megatheria fed undisturbed in the primeval forests.' This was in contrast to the first leg of his trans-African crossing to Loanda where Livingstone had placed too much reliance on the generosity of the tribes to sell him food and his ability to hunt. Despite the large size of his party he was able to regularly provide them with meat as the country 'had more game on it than anywhere I had seen in Africa'. The natives did not normally hunt the bigger game and so it was not difficult for him to stalk to within shooting distance although he did not enjoy the role of hunter. Livingstone was also limited in his ability to fire and had to use an adapted gun as he was unable to raise his arm as a result of the mauling in the lion attack.

They soon left the flat country and after several days of crossing over a range of hills, they came across the ruins of ten stone houses with a small fort and church that overlooked the area. This was Zumbo, the most distant colony that the Portuguese had established in the interior of Mozambique. The place had long since been abandoned which was illustrative of the economic decay of this Portuguese colony that had been built up on the extraction of precious metals and gems, slavery, ivory and coffee.

Soon after leaving Zumbo, they met a black man in European clothes; his attire was complete with jacket and a hat. This man had come from Tete, an important Portuguese settlement located further down on the banks of the Zambezi. He warned them that Mpende, a local chief, had given orders to his men that no white men should be allowed to pass through his land. It was a serious situation, particularly as armed men starting gathering around them at dawn on the next day, screaming strange cries and throwing powder at them. They then lit a fire into which they threw various charms. They were clearly trying to use magic to 'render us powerless, and probably to frighten us.' Soon it was obvious that they meant to attack and so Livingstone had his men prepare for battle. As a way of boosting his men's courage, he ordered an ox be slaughtered and roasted. One of his men came up to Livingstone and grimly told him: 'You have seen us with elephants, but you do not yet know what we can do with men.' However, this roasting of meat proved to be the key for when two of Mpende's men came forward, they were handed a leg as a present for Mpende. Two old men were later dispatched to find out who this strange white man was. Livingstone told them: 'I am a Lekoa' (an Englishman) but this puzzled them because they did not know this tribe for they had taken him to be Portuguese. To convince them, Livingstone showed them his hair and his chest and asking them if the Portuguese looked like him, and they replied: 'No, we never saw skin as white as that', adding: 'You must be one of that tribe that loves the black men.'[35] It was a proud moment for Livingstone—and the British nation. Mpende was persuaded to let Livingstone and his party pass through. Later, when the chief saw Livingstone treating one of his men who was ill, he remarked, 'That white man is truly our friend, see how he lets us know his afflictions.' It was actions like these that did so much to make the English name respected across Africa.

They moved from there down to Pangura where Livingstone was to make a decision that he was to regret for the rest of his life. Mpende had told him that the Zambezi continued to flow for about seventy miles in an easterly direction before turning sharply to the southeast. It therefore occurred to him that he could make his journey quicker if he was to proceed straight to Tete over a route that was about fifty miles shorter than following the course of the river. He was also told that the path alongside the Zambezi was treacherous in places, as they would have to pass through a rocky pass. By this time many of Livingstone's men were sick and with rotting clothes, the prospect of a shorter route settled the matter for Livingstone and he elected to go straight to Tete.

The result of this decision meant that Livingstone did not see the Kebrabassa Rapids. While they are modestly called rapids, they are in fact made up of a number of cataracts that stretch thirty miles down the river in a magnificent, but awesome display of the power of the Zambezi. 'Kebrabassa' is aptly named as it means 'where the work cannot go on', presumably because of the rapids in the gorge. A cursory look would have been enough to dispel any notion that the Zambezi could be used a river highway. That would have been galling to the ever-hopeful Livingstone but it was nothing in comparison with his later ignominious admission that he had been deceived.

Livingstone later wrote weakly in his *Missionary Travels* that he had attempted to find out what lay in this stretch of the river:

> I was informed about of the existence of a small rapid in the river near Chicova; had I known of this previously, I certainly would not have left the river without examining it. It is called Kebrabassa and is described as a number of rocks which jut out across the stream.[36]

Livingstone had been measuring the height of the Zambezi River as he travelled along its course and it is therefore surprising that for a man who was unusually thorough in his geographical observations not to have picked up on the fact that the Zambezi lay at over 3,700 feet at Linyanti and fell slowly to a little over 1,500 feet at a point one hundred miles west of Zumbo. The river then falls about 600 feet in the relatively short distance of five hundred miles to Tete. This is clearly a substantial fall. He had also been alerted to the fact that 'the only impediments I know of being one or two rapids, not cataracts'[37] and so he should have guessed that the Kebrabassa Rapids could pose a significant barrier to boats moving up and down the river. Perhaps he was just too tired to worry about it.

His journey from Pangura was relatively smooth and although they were starved and weakened, they finally reached Tete on the 3 March 1856. This was a large Portuguese settlement on the banks of the Zambezi with about thirty European houses there although it was a shadow of the very large settlement that it had once been— the ruins that littered the landscape were depressing. The commandant, Major Tito Augusto d'Araujo Sicard looked after him most kindly, serving him with a 'civilised breakfast' and Livingstone was grateful to him for helping 'to restore me from my emaciated condition.'[38] Tete was also the effective end of his momentous journey since he decided to leave his men there while he returned to Britain. The Major helped out by generously giving these natives some land to grow their crops and the right to hunt elephants. He also allowed them to purchase goods with ivory and dried meat so that they might be able to take something back with them when they eventually left.

Livingstone was able to proudly write to the London Missionary Society directors while he was in Tete:

It will be gratifying for you to hear that I have been able to follow without serving from my original plan of opening a way to the sea, on either the East or West coast, from healthy locality in the Interior of the continent.[39]

He was, sadly, in for a rude shock when he received a letter from the directors when he reached Quelimane.

6.5 Arrival at Quelimane

Livingstone did not leave Tete until 22 April 1856 as he suffered another debilitating attack of fever. Livingstone had to make this last stage on foot because all his oxen had died from tsetse fly. He was accompanied by Sekwebu and they took nearly a month to walk over rough stony country.[40]

Livingstone finally reached the end at the village of Quelimane on 20 May 1856. It was but a few days short of four years since he started from Cape Town. He had faced seven life-and-death situations at the hands of natives and he had starred them all down. He was tired, thin and ill.

Livingstone also seemed oddly unimpressed with his achievement on the completion of this long and difficult journey: the challenge was in the doing; and on its completion, his task no longer appeared interesting. Perhaps he knew the trip had been made before and this detracted from his pleasure in finally completing a journey that no other 'white man' had done, let alone attempted. In this sombre mood he wrote:

I do not feel so much elated by the prospect of accomplishing this feat. I feel most thankful to God for preserving my life, where so many, who by superior intelligence would have done more good, have been cut off.

If Mary had known what he was writing, she would have cried out in her loneliness:

But it does not look as if I had reached my goal. Viewed in relation to my calling, the end of the geographical feat is only the beginning of the enterprise ... We are all engaged in very much the same cause. Geographers, astronomers, and mechanicians, labouring to make men better acquainted with each other: sanitary reformers, prison reformers, promoters of ragged schools and Niger Expeditions: soldiers fighting for right against oppression, and sailors rescuing captives in deadly climes, as well as missionaries, are all abiding in hastening on a glorious consummation to all God's dealings with our race.[41]

His eloquent message is as pertinent today as it was in 1856.

He had mail waiting for him in Quelimane and there was a letter from his brother John, then living in Canada. He had the sorrowful duty to tell Livingstone that his namesake and nephew, David Livingstone, aged eleven, had drowned.

Among the letters was official notification that the Royal Geographical Society had at their annual meeting in May 1855 awarded Livingstone the Patron's Gold Medal for 1854. The citation recorded that the award was made 'for his explorations in Central Africa.'[42] The gold medal accompanied the chronometer-watch that the Royal Geographical Society had awarded to 'the Reverend David Livingston, of Kolobeng, for his successful explorations in South Africa.' in 1849.[43]

This medal was quickly followed by another award; the University of Glasgow had conferred on Livingstone the honorary degree of LL.D in 1854.[44]

Livingstone sailed from Quelimane on 12 July 1856 and reached Mauritius on 12 August 1856.[45] Before he left, he wrote to Moffat that he intended to stay a month or two in England as wanted to get back into his missionary work on the Zambezi.[46] Little did Livingstone know what was in store for him when he reached English shores.

CHAPTER 7

Return to Civilisation

7.1 The Bitter Sweet Homecoming

When Livingstone reached the coast he was greeted with the news that a Brigantine, HMS *Dart*, had been patrolling the coast but had recently returned to Britain. While this was disappointing, worse was to come when he was later told that a Lieutenant and five seamen had been lost at sea when they attempted to row a boat across a treacherous bar in the river mouth. They were a search party looking for him and Livingstone was understandably upset for he felt he was responsible for this tragedy. It was all that the tired explorer could do to write 'this sad event threw a cold shade over all the joy.' A melancholy Livingstone later wrote:

> I never felt more poignant sorrow. It seemed as if it would have been easier for me to have died for them, than that they should all be cut off from the joys of life in generously attempting to render me a service.[1]

The delay in waiting for another ship to arrive meant that Livingstone had plenty of time to reflect on this sad incident.

He also had time to mull over a letter from the Secretary of the London Missionary Society which he found waiting for him in Quelimane. The carefully worded letter, written by Tidman, set out the position of the London Missionary Society with regard to establishing more missions within Africa:

> The Directors, while yielding to none in their appreciation of the objects upon which, for some years past, your energies have been concentrated, or in admiration of the zeal, intrepidity, and success with which they have been carried out, are nevertheless restricted in their power of aiding plans connected only remotely with the spread of the Gospel.[2]

It was a sensible letter, for its purpose was to state clearly that the London Missionary Society could not afford to expand their operations and that

Livingstone should be under no illusion about this. The Society's financial position was indeed serious. They had just announced a financial loss of over £5,400 in their 1854–55 accounts and this amount, together with previous losses meant, the London Missionary Society was in debt for nearly £13,000—a huge amount.[3] It was the intimation that Livingstone's achievements, while significant, had little to do with missionary work that struck a raw nerve and Livingstone was first shocked and then angry at what had been written. He was stung into writing an acid reply to the directors:

> I was pleased to find a silence of more than four years broken by your letter of the 24th August 1855 … I find the intimation that the Directors are restricted in their power of aiding plans connected only remotely with the spread of the Gospel. And it is added also that even though certain very formidable obstacles should prove surmountable, 'the financial circumstances of the Society are not such as to afford any ground for hope that it would be, within any definite period, in a position to enter upon untried, remote, and difficult, fields of labour.'

Livingstone reacted badly to the news. How could the financial effort required to establish new missions be too great and the potential rewards too little to justify the attempt? It made his Highland blood boil. He continued:

> If I am not mistaken, these statements imply a resolution on the part of the gentlemen now in the Direction to devote the decreasing income of the Society committed to their charge to parts of the world of easy access, and in which the missionaries may devote their entire time and energies to the dissemination of the truths of the gospel with reasonable hopes of speedy success … I feel constrained to view 'the untried, remote, and difficult fields', to which I humbly yet firmly believe God has directed my steps, with a resolution widely different from that which their words imply. As our aims and purposes will now appear in some degree divergent—on their part from a sort of paralysis caused by financial decay, and on mine from the simple continuance of an old determination to devote my life and my all to the service of Christ in whatever way he may lead me in Intertropical Africa.[4]

This later part was an ultimatum to the directors: give him the support to follow his chosen path or face the consequences. More importantly, the uneasy relationship that he had maintained with them now crystallised into disrespect about the financial management of the London Missionary Society and his decision to later leave them can be traced back to this unfortunate letter. As it happened, the directors dithered in what they should do with him and in the end Livingstone made the decision for them.

The brigantine HMS *Frolic* arrived at Quelimane to Livingstone's immense joy. He was soon on board bound for Mauritius and to his surprise realised he was famous. However, his enjoyment was suddenly shattered when his faithful servant, Sekwebu,[5] in a fit of insanity, threw himself overboard. It seems that the man was completely overwhelmed by what was happening and the fact that he may never see his native land again. It was made worse when Sekwebu, who was a strong swimmer, deliberately pulled himself underwater using the anchor chain in order to drown himself. It was a sad crew that sailed away as Sekwebu had been popular among the ratings.

Livingstone had plenty of time for reflection on his trip back to England. He had spent fifteen years as a missionary, earning only £100 per annum and as a result was 'as poor as a church mouse.'[6]

In Mauritius the governor, Major-General Charles Hay, generously hosted Livingstone and while there he was treated for an infection of the spleen, the result of frequent attacks of fever. He was lucky to be in a place where he could receive good medical treatment for in his weakened condition, he took quite some time to get over the complaint. As soon as he was well, he boarded a ship bound for Britain. But his journey was not meant to be easy. First, the ship that he was travelling on was nearly shipwrecked on leaving Malta. The engine broke down and for a while they watched anxiously as they were swept helplessly towards some treacherous rocks until an offshore wind sprung up and fortuitously blew the ship clear of the impending disaster. Livingstone immediately wrote to Mary his long-suffering wife to say that he had been unavoidably delayed. He told her not to get upset: 'I'm only sorry for your sake, but patience is a great virtue, you know. Captain Tregear has been six years away from his family, I only four and a half.'[7]

His journey was further spoilt when he received the tragic news in Cairo that his father would not see his son's triumphant homecoming. His last words about Livingstone with whom he had always enjoyed a special relationship with were: 'I think I'll know whatever is worth knowing about him. When you see him, tell him I think so.' Livingstone felt the loss keenly, saying: 'that there is no one left to whom I should [have] liked better to have narrated my toils & adventures than to him'.[8] It was a great personal blow.

7.2 Mobbed in Britain

Mary had spent a miserable four years, struggling to bring up their young family and continually worrying about money and whether she would ever see her husband again. It was a time of great loneliness because she was without her own family and friends, and without a home in a foreign country. After she had abruptly left Hamilton in January 1853 she moved to Hackney, a village near London. She remained there over the summer then had a temporary stay in

Lancashire until the end of 1853 when she next moved her family to Kendal in Westmoreland. The move to Kendal followed Mary's dramatic decision to send Agnes to stay with a Quaker family, the Braithwaite's. The rest of them arrived soon after and for a short period, enjoyed a settled family life. Unfortunately it was not to last as Mary's wanderlust reasserted itself and Mary, Tom and Oswell moved to Epsom some months later. Robert and Agnes remained behind with the Braithwaites and they continued to attend the local Quaker school.

As Julie Anderson has described in *Looking for Mrs Livingstone*,[9] sometime in 1853, Mary received a graphic letter from Livingstone describing how their home in Kolobeng had been ransacked and defiled by a Boer commando, following their armed assault on the place. This had resulted in death and subsequent capture of 124 native children. It is easy to imagine that to a lonely, dispirited and removed Mary, the news came as a real shock for not only had she taught many of the captured children, her daughter Elizabeth was buried in the garden.

Livingstone wrote regularly to Mary and children after they returned to England in April 1852. He made a point of writing letters to his children, either individually or as a group, whenever he could. The letters are tender with him always urging his children to place their faith in God, be kind to each and to Mamma (Mary). He also attempted to explain to his children his reasons for staying in Africa. 'I have separated myself from you all, my dear children, & from Mamma whom I love very much too, in order to please Jesus and tell sinners who never hear of him about his love.'[10]

It was during his stay at Linyanti before he set off to Loanda that Livingstone had time to send his children another letter setting out what he thought was useful advice for his children. There is no doubt that he must have wondered about his chances of survival. 'Here is another letter for you all. I should like to see you much more than write to you, and speak with my tongue rather than with my pen; but we are far from each other—very, very far.' He then went on to exhort them to follow Jesus, 'when I think of you I remember, though I am far off, Jesus, our good and gracious Jesus, is ever near both you and me, and then I pray to Him to bless you and make you good.' The need to work hard to read, write and work is continually reinforced, but he went on to say, 'you must play too in order to make your bodies strong and be able to serve Jesus.' The urging to get a good education is a consistent message in all his letters to his children as Livingstone was all too aware that it was only through his own faith, hard work and perseverance that he had escaped the cotton mill on the River Clyde.[11]

He certainly had the usual parent worry about whether their children will make a success of themselves. One telling comment appeared in a letter to Dr Kirk in 1863 when the later was returning to Britain at the conclusion the Zambezi Expedition. 'If you see my boy Robert say a kind word to him and advise him to work, for I fear he may turn out a "Ne'er do weel."'[12]

Mary was soon regularly requesting money from the London Missionary Society. She pitifully wrote to Tidman in February 1853 requesting money and adding 'I trust you will not refuse as I have no one else to look to.'[13]

Mary must have felt intense anxiety during his long period of absence—with no messages or official word on Livingstone's whereabouts—and rumours circulating occasionally about his presumed disappearance or death. The continuing strain resulted in her health deteriorating; it was whispered that she had taken to drink and she may later have become an alcoholic. No doubt the pressures of raising children during the many absences of her husband contributed to her poor health and psychological well-being. When her financial troubles began to grow, she was forced to turn to the London Missionary Society for help. After some time, she decided that it would be best to return to Africa where at least she would be with her own family, but she could not even raise the money for the fare. She had, in effect, become trapped, and with constant problems about money, she became depressed. It was in this mood that Livingstone returned to find her.

Mary had written a sad little poem to greet her husband with:

> A hundred thousand welcomes, and it's time for you to come
> From the far land of the foreigner, to your country and your home.
> Oh, long as we were parted, ever since you went away,
> I never passed a dreamless night, or knew an easy day.
> Do you think I would reproach you with the sorrows that I bore?
> Since the sorrow is all over, now I have you here once more,
> And there's nothing but the gladness, and the love within my heart,
> And the hope so sweet and certain that again we'll never part.
> A hundred thousand welcomes! how my heart is gushing o'er
> With the love and joy and wonder thus to see your face once more.
> How did I live without you these long long years of woe?
> It seems as if t'would kill me to be parted from you now.
> You'll never part me, darling, there's a promise in your eye;
> I may tend you while I'm living, you will watch me when I die;
> And if death but kindly lead me to the blessed home on high,
> What a hundred thousand welcomes will await you in the sky!

Mary'[14]

Livingstone finally set foot back in 'Mother England' on 9 December 1856, saddened by the recent news of his father and angry with the directors of the London Missionary Society. It was almost exactly sixteen years to the day since he had left. But if he was wondering whether his explorations had been worth the pain and suffering, he was soon under no illusions about just how popular he was.

His ship had unexpectedly berthed in Dover and he was welcomed home a hero by an adoring crowd. However, his immediate concern was his family and they were waiting in Southampton where they expected the ship to dock. Livingstone quickly boarded a train there where he met his 'spoke in the wheel'. For three short, precious days, the Livingstone family shared a house together. Livingstone found he had to provide much needed solace to Mary and re-acquaint himself with his children who he had last seen four years earlier.

Livingstone's slow return to England had enabled him to recover from the physical effects of his travels so that when he landed back in England he looked healthy and strong. But if physically recovered he needed the love of his wife and family and the companionship of his friends and supporters.

For Mary, having Livingstone suddenly back in her life after such a long absence must have been both gratifying as well as overwhelming.

Livingstone was to spend fifteen months in England and soon after arriving in London they began what turned out to be a long tortuous routine of meetings, parties and banquets. During this time he was fêted and praised wherever he went. The adulation for this 'humble missionary' was extraordinary and needs to be seen in its historical context. Britain had recently finished the somewhat inconclusive Crimean war with Russia and the dreadful stories of slaughter of the Indian Mutiny made grim reading in the newspapers. The anti-slavery policy was spluttering along with no dramatic reduction in the numbers being sold into slavery all over the world. In some ways the feeling within the country was epitomised by the Prime Minister, William Gladstone who was a colourless but able politician. And then suddenly a hero stepped forward into the brilliance of the Victorian age, symbolising all that the period yearned for: humbleness, a Christian cause, and a fight against the odds. Here was a man, figuratively still covered in the dust of Africa, who could stand tall as he had shown what strength of character, a sense of purpose and a refusal to give in could achieve. The heart of the nation opened up to him, they clambered and fought to hear him, touch him and soak up something from him.

One of his first public engagements was at the Royal Geographical Society on 15 December 1856. Here he was presented with the Patron's Gold Medal that had been awarded after he reached Loanda in 1855. He made a striking impression: his face worn by the African elements, his manner awkward and his language halting. Even his excuse for speaking English so badly—that he had hardly spoken it in the last fifteen years—seemed extraordinary. Livingstone, however, cautioned his admiring audiences—although they saw his comment as another illustration of his modestly—'I cannot pretend to a single note of triumph', continuing: 'a man may boast when he is putting off his armour, but I am just putting mine on ... my future may not come up to the expectations of the present.'[15] It was a wise statement since it brought back to mind the disastrous Niger Expedition that took place ten years earlier, and other false hopes that can be raised by courageous words.

At this and subsequent meetings, audiences vied with each other in their efforts to laud Livingstone until it became ridiculous. At one point he was being described as 'Traveller, geographer, zoologist, astronomer, missionary, physician, and mercantile director, did ever man sustain so many characters at once? Or did ever man perform the duties of each with such painstaking accuracy and so great success?'[16]

Another reason for his immense popularity can be attributed to the fact there were a number of interested parties who wanted him to be famous for their own purposes. Not the least was the London Missionary Society whose finances were groaning under the burden of debt. His fund-raising activities could be the salvation to their financial problems.

The public went wild about him. After a time he became so well recognised that he was in danger of getting mobbed—on one occasion he had to take refuge in a cab on Regent Street from the clamorous crowd. On another occasion he was recognised when attending a church service and after the service, people leapt over pews in their eagerness to shake his hand and congratulate him.[17]

Mary, as always, remained in the background, looking after her children. One ray of official acknowledgement of the important role that she played in their marriage, and in supporting Livingstone's 'noble' work, came from the Chair of the London Missionary Society, Lord Shaftesbury, soon after Livingstone's return to London. The august and eloquent Shaftesbury spoke about how Mary had 'exchanged one great name for another, born a Moffat she had become a Livingstone.'[18] He went on to record how Mary had first supported Livingstone in their early years of marriage, supporting him in his missionary endeavours and raising a family, and in the period after her return to England in 1852, stoically and uncomplainingly allowing Livingstone to continue spreading civilisation and Christianity through unexplored parts of Africa. It was a generous comment from such an eminent person. Many must have wondered how she could have done it.

Livingstone soon made his intentions clear that he wanted to return to Africa. In a letter he wrote to Sir Roderick Murchison[19] on 22 December 1856, barely two weeks after arriving back in the country, he stated that he did not intend 'giving up working for the amelioration of Africa.' He also expressed an interest in an idea put forward by Murchison of adopting 'the plan of a roving commission'.[20] Livingstone thought he should try and secure such a post.

Livingstone took his family to Hamilton over Christmas where they stayed in a cottage owned by his two sisters who had established a growing millinery business. He did take time out to give a speech to the Blantyre Works and Literary and Scientific Institute in the mill's schoolroom where he had attended as a child. On 2 January 1857 he was awarded the Freedom of Hamilton. This award was followed by the Freedom of Glasgow and £2,000 in September 1857.

It was an important family holiday, but too short as Livingstone was soon back in London and staying with a friend from the days when he was studying medicine, Sir Risdon Bennett.

7.3 Missionary Travels

The publisher, John Murray, had already been in contact with Livingstone to see if he would like to write a book. Livingstone had in fact been thinking about it for some time for as early as 1852, he had written to his brother Charles[21] that:

> I admire the wonderful works of God, and the wisdom he had displayed in the animal kingdom; and as I have already some facts not known in works of natural history, I think a work written after the manner of White [*The Natural History of Selborne*], with neither tawdry sentimental reflections or idolatrous spouting about Nature, but with a manly acknowledgement of the Divine wisdom and special operations in all the developments of instinct and adaptation.[22]

After his successful journey from Linyanti to Loanda, the far-sighted publisher, John Murray, met with Sir Roderick Murchison to discuss the possibility of getting Livingstone to write about his travels in Africa. Murchison agreed and wrote to Livingstone about the suggestion although it appears that the letter missed Livingstone. However, the shrewd Murray approached Livingstone just before Christmas when he returned to Britain to follow up on the idea. Negotiations ensued and it was quickly settled that Livingstone would receive two-thirds of the profits. A few days later the promise of thousand guineas as the first instalment of the royalties that the book was expected to earn was added as a further inducement when other publishers started calling on Livingstone. It was a remarkably generous offer and is testimony to the level of interest Livingstone was creating about Africa.

Livingstone was not one to prevaricate and in late January 1857 he moved his family to 57 Sloane Street, London to start writing his book. It was a slow job for Livingstone who was unaccustomed to being shut up for days at a time, wearily re-working his journals into a narrative suitable for a book. What he did enjoy was writing about his scientific observations, something that he had been interested in since his childhood. Also, the extensive notes that he had made ensured that whatever was produced was going to be full of interesting anecdotes that he recorded during his many years in Africa.

Livingstone settled into a routine with his characteristic perseverance and determination and within six months had produced a manuscript of over three hundred thousand words—a significant achievement.

Livingstone was demanding both on himself, and his publisher, to ensure the narrative, maps, and pictures were properly done. Murray engaged the services of a well-known cartographer to draw a map for the book, John Arrowsmith.[23] Livingstone was not impressed when the man seemed to be taking a long time to complete his task. Livingstone was roused enough to write to Murray complaining, 'That ruffian Arrowsmith is putting all the blame for his delays on me.'[24]

Meanwhile trouble with the London Missionary Society was quietly percolating beneath all the laudatory statements. *The Times* carried a report stating that Livingstone had said that the:

> L.M.S. had given him a free commission to open up those paths, and he wished to acknowledge the great kindness with which they had always treated him, so that for sixteen years he had never had a word of difference with them.[25]

But Livingstone was being less than honest when he said this. Certainly the letter that he had received from Tidman when in Quelimane still rankled, and for a man that rarely forgave others, it is obvious that it was only a matter of time before he terminated his contract with them. Indeed, the seeds of discontent had been sown when Livingstone first stepped ashore onto African soil sixteen years earlier as an outspoken missionary when he was left waiting for his instructions at Kuruman. The continuing failure of his missionary work combined with the gradual realisation that he could not be content living in one place 'tending his flock' meant that his usefulness as a missionary appeared to be diminishing year by year.

It was the manner in which Livingstone terminated his contract with the London Missionary Society that has preoccupied many of his biographers. Indeed, the circumstances surrounding the whole unhappy episode are clouded in a subterfuge that Livingstone employed. He did not want to leave them until he had been offered something better. At the time of the rupture the society was reluctantly agreeing to re-consider establishing missions amongst the Makololo and Matabele, while Livingstone was writing to Lord Clarendon with the proposal that he should lead an expedition to open up the Zambezi to 'Christianity and commerce'. He suggested that the best way would be to try and establish some industries, particularly cotton growing, which Livingstone thought had tremendous potential in that region. Implicit in these plans was the assumption that the Portuguese would be willing to help a British expedition to carry out such an ambitious task.

The Missionary Society held meetings on 12 and 22 January 1857 where the topic of establishing the missions was discussed. It was decided that a committee would be formed to study and make recommendations about the feasibility of the missions and their positive recommendation was confirmed at a board meeting on 26 January 1857. Essentially, their plan was that another missionary should be found be help Livingstone to found a mission among his favourite Makololo while Moffat would be asked to establish one among the Matabele since he had strong relations with that tribe. It was a wise choice of men, but for Livingstone, it was not a course of action that he would end up following. Tidman also seems to have been tardy in informing Moffat of his very important role as he did not get around to writing to him until early April 1857. It is hard to know the reason for this. One reason could be that Tidman was less than enthusiastic about the project.

During the society's deliberations, Livingstone kept quiet about his plans for a roving commission from the Government, as he was worried about the reaction of the public to his intended course of action. He even wrote to Murchison again in April 1857, privately expressing his concern. 'I fear if I got it now, my friends of the Mission House will make use of the fact to damage my character in the public estimation by saying I have forsaken the Mission for higher pay.'[26] In fact Livingstone did not have to wait long before he got what he was after: a consulship was offered about the first week of May 1857. Murchison wrote to Lord Clarendon on 6 May 1857 suggesting a salary of five hundred pounds per annum for Livingstone. This meant that he now had an official reason to leave the society, but he hesitated, asking the Government to postpone the official announcement.

Livingstone moved with his family to a house kept by Jane Moffat, Mary's sister that overlooked Hadley Green in London.[27] It was quieter than the place that they had been renting in Sloane Street and the change was welcomed given his busy schedule of public meetings and convoluted discussions he was having with both the Mission House and Whitehall. Here Livingstone got some peace to finish his book. He also took time out to be admitted to the Honorary Freedom of the City of London at a reception on 21 May 1857.

The manuscript was completed in July 1857, and that meant that Livingstone was able to concentrate on meeting a number of public speaking engagements. He was an outstanding success as his oratory style was most effective. It is surprising since his speech lacked fluidity and he was not animated when talking. And yet his practical message was appealing because it was underlined by his understated and humble manner. He patiently explained to his audience the positive contribution they could make and his quiet-speaking and homely expressions touched a nerve with his audiences. Soon huge crowds were flocking to hear the man from Africa. People were caught up in the excitement of hearing about his explorations and began to feel that they too could play a part in supporting Britain's important role of developing a part of Africa.

The book appeared on the shelves on Tuesday, 10 November 1857 and was immediately acclaimed. The interest in exploration had grown significantly, due in no small way to Livingstone's own achievements, and that meant that the demand for the book was going to be high. However, it exceeded even Murray's expectations as the book immediately sold out. Further editions were printed until eventually there were eight editions of the book. The literary success resulted in Livingstone earning a substantial amount of money: by 1859 he had received over £12,000 in royalties.

The society had meanwhile commenced an appeal to raise funds to meet the costs of establishing the proposed Matabele and Mokololo missions. A target of £5,000 had been set and the money was steadily being collected following the sensational interest in Livingstone. But the board of the London Missionary Society was to get a shock when Livingstone's letter to them was read out at a meeting on the 27 October 1857. In that letter he stated that he was not available to help establish a mission, but that he would give them all the assistance he could. He also told them that he 'would probably in future sustain some relation to the British Government.'[28] It was the first formal announcement of his intention to leave the society and while it probably did not come as much of a surprise to Tidman, it certainly would have been unexpected news to the majority of the board.

The severing of his ties with the London Missionary Society did not mean that he was no longer interested in missionary work but had more to do with Livingstone realising he needed more freedom to do what he wanted. Despite the gentle way that this severing was done, predictably there was some criticism from people who felt that he owed the society his continuing loyalty and membership.

Meanwhile money continued to pour into the society's fund—and helping to reduce the society's large overdraft.

Livingstone was still interested in the plans for the new missions as he felt he had been largely responsible for galvanising the directors into action. He wrote to the board in late February 1858 asking them when they proposed sending out the missionaries as he clearly thought they had been dilatory:

> Abundant funds having been furnished for all that is needed … I should be glad to be assured that the intentions of the friends in subscribing so liberally are likely soon to be realised.

Livingstone was making the point that unless the London Missionary Society carried out their publicly stated intention. Livingstone would ensure that the matter did not die quietly. Tidman must have cursed his former missionary colleague. However, he wrote back to him in a friendly manner stating that a party would be leaving in May 1858. Livingstone in turn blandly assured the directors that 'his companions will readily lend them their aid in crossing the river.' It was a weak offer of assistance, particularly as he suggested that it 'might be better to go by Lake Ngami', a route that if taken was far from where Livingstone would be able to provide assistance.

The casualness of Livingstone's offer of assistance was surprising. At the first meeting of the society when the issue of establishing the two missions was discussed, it was agreed that having Livingstone lead the mission was vital to its success and Livingstone would have been aware of this. To have then coerced the London Missionary Society into undertaking this ambitious project into a region that had only just been 'opened up', without proper planning and support, bordered on negligence. Livingstone later wrote that 'I never felt a single pang at having left the Missionary Society'[29] but he would subsequently be deeply chastised for his cavalier involvement in their future missionary activities on the Zambezi.

7.4 The Next Step

Livingstone kept hammering home a simple message during his lectures:

> My desire is to open a path to this district [the Zambezi and the Eastern highlands], that civilisation, commerce, and Christianity might find their way there … A prospect is now before us of opening Africa for commerce and the Gospel.

The opportunity to help christianise Africa combined with the prospect of making money for those that dared to run the risk, resonated throughout the country. It came at a time when the middle class of industrial Britain was burgeoning and it provided a balm to their wealth creating, god fearing consciousness—help the savage and God will help you. So successful was the cry that those 'two pioneers of civilisation—Christianity and commerce—should ever be inseparable…' that there were few who thought of the ramifications of such a policy—and even less who spoke out against it. In some respects, the message is still relevant today as evidenced by the giving of aid to many third world countries where conditions relating to democracy and human rights are often attached.

Livingstone kept repeating his message, and eventually the reluctant Prime Minister, Lord Palmerston and the Foreign Secretary, Earl of Clarendon had to listen, since the attention Livingstone was getting meant that the Government had to be seen to be actively responding to public pressure to support Livingstone's lofty aims. At that time their attention was preoccupied with the problems in the Far East and India and the 'problem' of Africa received minimal attention.

The catalyst for how the Government might give effect to their support was again the President of the Royal Geographical Society, Sir Roderick Murchison, who encouraged Livingstone to write to Lord Clarendon, to request the Government to investigate the ways in which it might assist. The idea of an expedition was then raised with the purpose to explore the Zambezi to see if 'God's Highway' could be used to open up highlands to commerce. The interest of the Government was piqued by the opportunity to get access to new resources and markets for British industry.

After much procrastinating and dithering, the Government grandly announced just before Christmas in 1857 that it was to fund an expedition to the Zambezi and that a grant of £5,000 had been approved to underwrite the cost.

In February 1858 the Government formally appointed Livingstone Her Majesty's Consul at Quelimane 'for the East Coast of Africa to the south of the dominions of Zanzibar, and for the independent districts in the interior, as well as commander of an expedition to explore Eastern and Central Africa.' Not only would he have official status, it also meant that he would receive a salary of £500 per annum.

The ramifications of these developments were significant. First and foremost, it meant that Livingstone now had official sanction to do what he had always wanted—promoting commerce, eliminating slavery and encouraging Christian families to colonise Africa. But first he had to prove the Zambezi was navigable and that would be the first objective of the expedition.

When all the preparations had been done, Livingstone prepared to make a triumphal tour of Britain. There have been some marvellous and inspiring speeches in British history but there are only a few that have significantly change the way people think. Livingstone made such a speech in the Senate House at Cambridge University on Friday, 4 December 1857. The scene was ideal; dark brooding skies, an almost reverent, packed audience coming to hear this strange looking man talk about a distant land. Livingstone, in his halting and at times, barely audible voice, carefully worked up the enthusiasm of the crowd, ending his lecture with these piecing words:

> I beg to direct your attention to Africa;—I know that in a few years I shall be cut off in that country, which is now open; do not let it be shut again! I go back to Africa to try to make an open path for commerce and Christianity; do you carry out the work, which I have begun? I leave it with you![30]

It is easy to imagine the wild cheers that followed the speech; the look of rapture on the eager faces of the young students. What a challenge this presented. And yet, sadly, so rarely have words been taken so literally and carried out for so little gain and with so much tragedy and incrimination.

The Earl of Clarendon decided to appoint an experienced naval officer, Captain John Washington,[31] to draw up expedition plans for consideration by Whitehall. Two alternatives were finally presented at the end of December 1857. Washington had ambitiously decided that in each case a large party of about two hundred people would be required. When Livingstone heard about these plans he became alarmed for his expedition was taking on a whole new complexion. He therefore drew up his own plan that was much less ambitious and quietly submitted it in early January 1858. It called for just seven Britons and ten natives; a small steamer and an iron house with the proviso that these last two items were to be collapsible. Clarendon was attracted to the simplicity of Livingstone's proposal since there was much less political risk—and cost—associated with an expedition of this size and promptly accepted it. Livingstone was given clearance to start selecting the men that he thought would be suitable.

The planning for the expedition initially fell under the jurisdiction of the British Foreign Office but it was soon transferred to the Admiralty as the best organisation to prepare and support such an undertaking. Livingstone acknowledged that Captain Washington was very useful in getting anything required for his expedition, but that he liked to be 'acknowledged'.[32]

His first choice for the post of expedition second-in-command and officer in charge of naval operations was a man who Livingstone had met on one of the cruisers in Loanda in 1854: Commander Norman Bedingfeld, RN.

The Government had quickly realised that the expedition needed a strong scientific focus and a letter was sent by the Foreign Office to the Royal Society, the Royal Geographical Society and to Kew Gardens requesting their help. A small team advised the Government on appointments and as a result a young Scot, Dr John Kirk was chosen primarily for the post of botanist and zoologist, but also filled a useful role as the medical officer of the expedition.[33] Another young man of science, Richard Thornton, was selected for the position of geologist. Thomas Baines was posted as the expedition's artist and storekeeper while the important task of keeping the paddle steamer going was given to a Scottish engineer by the name of George Rae. A final choice for the unusual post of 'moral agent' was given to Livingstone's own brother Charles who had returned to England in April 1857.[34] Livingstone obviously created this post just for Charles since he thought it would be useful to have a member of his family to support him in any difficulties he might have with any other member of the expedition. Charles also had some knowledge of cotton growing and this was important, as Livingstone was keen to promote its production so that a new source for British cotton mills could be developed. For Charles it controversially meant leaving his family and his pastor flock in the United States.

The exploration of the Zambezi required a suitable ship with sufficient power and size to carry enough men and supplies up the river. Livingstone and Bedingfeld threw themselves enthusiastically into the project and a shallow draught paddle steamer was procured for the navigation of the Zambezi. The paddle steamer was called *Ma-Robert*, after Mary, as the natives, in accordance with their custom, always named a mother after her first-born son's name. Mr John Laird built *Ma-Robert* at his new shipbuilding works in Birkenhead. It was built in three sections using a steel plate construction to keep the ship light, but strong. It had a 12-horsepower engine.

It was a large vessel at about seventy-five feet in length, had a breath of eight feet and a three foot draught. Bedingfeld, with Rae assisting, oversaw the construction. Unfortunately, harmlessly noted by *The Illustrated News of the World*, was the fact that in completely uncharted river-ways in central Africa, the Zambezi Expedition would be relying on 'the first application of this cheap steel to boat-building purposes.'[35]

When Kirk was being informally sounded out about the expedition he was told by Livingstone that the 'contemplated length of the expedition is two years but there is a possibility of its being prolonged beyond that period by circumstances of which we are not at present aware.' As it turned out the expedition was to last from 1858 to 1863. Kirk was offered an annual salary of £350 and told he would need to 'rough it'.[36] It was the beginning of a long and profound relationship with Livingstone as it seems that the two doctors got along well together right from the beginning. Their amount of correspondence was significant and wide reaching and did not stop until 1872, when it appeared that Livingstone had been lost in Africa.

On his appointment Kirk was instructed to prepare a list of medicines for the expedition. He was told fever would be the common complaint and that he could spend 'about £15'. When Kirk pointed out that this figure was inadequate, Livingstone quickly amended the amount to £50, also increasing some of the quantities of medical supplies. Livingstone's medical knowledge and experience would help Kirk immensely, especially in the early days:

> Allow me to suggest a good stock of the Resin of Jalap. I found a pill composed of that with calomel & quinine an excellent remedy in fever—also Fowlers solution of arsenic—a larger quantity of soda as it is very useful in allaying obstinate vomiting—& a decided increase in Epsom salts for the natives. The Quinine is not a whit too large. Increase that too. It will be advisable to give quinine wine to all the Europeans before entering and while in the Delta.[37]

Another member of the Zambezi Expedition was Thomas Baines[38] who was an English artist and explorer of British colonial southern Africa and Australia. Before he met Livingstone he worked for a while in Cape Town as a scenic and portrait artist, and as official British army war artist during the so-called Eighth Frontier War. He came highly recommended due in part for his role in Augustus Gregory's 1855–1857 Royal Geographical Society sponsored expedition across northern Australia as both official artist and storekeeper.

During the final hurried preparations before their departure Livingstone received a formal invitation to meet Queen Victoria. On the morning of 13 February 1858 Livingstone arrived in his trademark black coat and blue trousers, and his consular cap made by Sarkey's of Bond Street. The cap was surrounded with a stripe of gold lace and particularly favoured by Royal Navy officers because of the protection it provided against the sun. His cap was to become closely associated with Livingstone as he was rarely without it after this time.

They discussed his travels during their half hour meeting and Livingstone told Queen Victoria that he could now say he had met his chief. Apparently this was always a surprise to the natives, particularly as open access to their own chiefs was a normal thing. Livingstone entertained the Queen about her wealth as he:

> mentioned to Her Majesty also that the people were in the habit of inquiring whether his chief were wealthy; and that when he assured them she was very wealthy, they would ask how many cows she had got, a question at which the Queen laughed heartily.[39]

That evening Livingstone attended one of his last formal functions before departing. It was a banquet in the Freemason's Tavern in London. It had been intended to limit it to 250 guests, but in the end there were nearly 350 people at the private dinner, including the Ministers of Sweden and Norway, and of Denmark; Dukes of Argyll and Wellington; Earl of Shaftesbury and Earl Grey; bishops of Oxford and St David's. A drawing and an accompanying article about the farewell banquet later appeared in *The Illustrated News of the World*, such was the popular demand for news about Livingstone.[40]

Sir Roderick Murchison presided at this august occasion and telling his audience:

that notwithstanding eighteen months of laudation, so justly bestowed on him by all classes of his countrymen, and after receiving all the honours which the Universities and cities of our country could shower upon him, he is still the same honest, true-hearted David Livingstone as when he issued from the wilds of Africa.

Livingstone took the opportunity to thank everyone for their support and kindness, and then did something quite unusual for that time; he publicly thanked his wife who was also preparing to accompany him back to Africa:

It is scarcely fair to ask a man to praise his own wife, but I can only say that when I parted from her at the Cape, telling her that I should return in two years, and when it happened that I was absent four years and a half, I supposed that I should appear before her with a damaged character. I was, however, forgiven. My wife, who has always been the main spoke in my wheel, will accompany me in this expedition, and will be most useful to me. She is familiar with the languages of South Africa. She is able to work. She is willing to endure, and she well knows that in that country one must put one's hand to everything. In the country to which I am about to proceed she knows that at the missionary's station the wife must be the maid-of-all-work within, while the husband must be the jack-of-all-trades without, and glad am I indeed that I am to be accompanied by my guardian angel.[41]

It had been quite a day for the Scotsman.

CHAPTER 8

The Zambezi Expedition

'I am prepared to go anywhere, provided it be forward.'

8.1 Early Successes

Livingstone was pleased to finally leave England and return to Africa, just sixteen months after his triumphal return. The adulation of the crowds had become hard for him to bear and the constant demands for his time and speeches, or 'public spouting' as he referred to it, was very taxing for a man who had just spent four-and-a-half isolated years in deepest Africa. He now had a new purpose in life; he would lead 'the development of African trade and the promotion of civilisation.'[1]

The Zambezi Expedition left Birkenhead, on 10 March 1858, on SS *Pearl*. On board were the staff of the expedition: Commander Bedingfield, RN, naval officer, expedition second-in-command; John Kirk, MD, botanist and physician; Charles Livingstone, brother of Livingstone, moral agent, general assistant and secretary; Richard Thornton, practical mining geologist; Thomas Baines, artist and storekeeper and a Scotsman George Rae, ship engineer. Mary and their youngest child, William, also accompanied the expedition party as she was resolved not to be parted from Livingstone again. The other children remained in care back in Scotland.

They arrived in Cape Town in mid April 1858. A few days before landing Livingstone presented all members of the expedition with instructions on what each of them was to do as a member of the expedition. In Kirk's case it was a lengthy but carefully worded document and in the first paragraph Livingstone set out the ambitious purpose of the expedition.

The main objective of the Expedition to which you are appointed Economic Botanist and Medical Officer is to extend the knowledge already attained of the geography and mineral and agricultural resources of Eastern and Central Africa, to improve our acquaintances with the inhabitants and to engage them to apply their energies to industrial pursuits and to the cultivation of their lands with a view to the production of raw material to be exported to England in return for British manufactures; and it may be hoped that by encouraging the natives to occupy themselves in the development of the resources of their country a considerable advance may be made towards the extinction of the slave trade, as the natives will not be long in discovering that the former will eventually become a more certain sources of profit than the latter.

The letter went on to carefully explain how Livingstone proposed to run the Zambezi Expedition and the role that Kirk was to play.[2] Two other letters accompanied Livingstone's letter, one from Doctor Joseph Hooker of the British Museum on the duties of a botanist and a letter from Professor Richard Owen, containing 'Instructions to the Zoologist of the Zambezi Expedition'. Kirk and the others must have felt a little overwhelmed by all these detailed instructions and requests.[3]

The Moffats heard about the Zambezi Expedition and that the party, including Livingstone and Mary, would call in to the Cape *en route* to the mouth of the Zambezi. For Moffat it was an opportunity to see if Livingstone could help other missionaries in their efforts among the Makololo. Moffat was well aware that the London Missionary Society was planning to establish a mission at Linyanti as he was planning his own trip to see Mosilikatse with a view to establishing a mission to the Matabele.

Livingstone did still want to support missionary work and he made a private arrangement with Moffat's younger son, John, to become a missionary to the Makololo.[4] Furthermore Livingstone was prepared to pay John out of his consular salary. It was agreed that John[5] would receive £500 for outfit and supplies and £150 a year for five years as a salary. Other expenses would be met as appropriate. In total it amounted to a pledge of at least £1,250 and represented two-and-a-half years of Livingstone's own salary.

Mary arrived in Cape Town in poor health, having looked after William, then six years old, after a difficult voyage. She was also two months pregnant and it was decided that it would be best for her and William to go back to Kuruman with her parents and then later join the Zambezi Expedition, possibly by travelling overland from Kuruman. Meanwhile Livingstone and rest of the party would sail up the coast to begin unpacking the expedition.

It must have been a tearful reunion and a tearful farewell in the Cape. For Livingstone it was to be the final time he met his in-laws and for Mary, it would be another four years before she saw her husband again.

Before departing Livingstone called on the Cape governor, Sir George Grey, with whom he had developed a good relationship. One of the reasons for meeting Grey was to discuss Moffat's Sichuana dictionary, or 'vocabularies' as Livingstone described them, with Grey, including Livingstone own translation of Sichuana into the Barotse language.[7]

The Moffats soon departed for Kuruman and Mary remained with her parents and sister Bess for much longer than expected, eventually staying nearly fourteen months. On 16 November 1858 she gave birth to Anna Mary Livingstone in Kuruman, and she was the last of Livingstone's six children. Anna Mary later recalled that she had a black nurse-man and was told he tenderly cared for her like a mother, feeding her and keeping the flies off her face while she slept.[6]

Mary had hoped that she would be able to travel overland to the mouth of the Zambezi, but this was not feasible due to the difficult terrain and risk of fever and so in 1859, reluctantly, she returned to England where she could provide proper care for Anna Mary and the rest of her children who had remained in school in the care of Livingstone's aunts.

8.2 The Expedition Gets Underway

The expedition left Simon Bay on 21 April 1858 and arrived at the lower Zambezi on the 14 May 1858 on board the SS *Pearl*. The Zambezi delta is braided and posed a considerable navigational challenge. They had hoped to sail the SS *Pearl* into the Luabo,[8] one of the channels in the Zambezi delta but the river was too shallow for the 12-foot draught of this ship.[9] Instead they anchored and began ferrying the stores to Expedition Island which lay about forty miles upstream. Livingstone had decided that this island was a good stepping off area. Rae, the ship engineer was immediately put to work assembling the *Ma-Robert*, which had been transported in sections in the hold of the SS *Pearl*. This they did on the banks of the Zambezi with the SS *Pearl* remaining on hand to provide manpower and equipment to complete this task.

Livingstone was wise in his choice of Expedition Island, as he knew just how unhealthy the country is with mosquito-borne fevers and malaria. For the others they too quickly realised that they were in a race against time as a fever was raging through the countryside: to spend any longer than necessary in the delta area would eventually mean death. And so the team was thrown immediately into transferring stores and materials over treacherous sand banks, mangrove swamps and weeds. The next step after Expedition Island would be Tete as Livingstone thought this would be the best place to establish a secure base for the next stage: the exploration of the Zambezi.

Livingstone and Bedingfeld had jointly determined the specifications for the *Ma-Robert*. The main requirement for river work was a vessel that had a shallow draught, was highly manoeuvrable and powerful. In reality, when the boat was trialled on the river they realised they had ended up with a boat that was nearly everything that it was not meant to be.

They had also brought a pinnace as it was thought it would be useful to have a small light boat to make quick trips in. Unfortunately this also was too heavy for the engine to move along quickly, particularly in low water.[10] It showed just how inexperienced they were about river transport.

In a situation of unfamiliarity, frustration and heat tempers flared, firstly between the ship's Captain, Duncan, and Bedingfield about how they should proceed. Commander Bedingfield also started to disagree with Livingstone about the landing of stores on Expedition Island.

The seventy-five-foot steamboat *Ma-Robert* was assembled under the watchful eye of Rae and when the water trials started the disagreements quickly grew. Bedingfield's job was to command all things relating to river movement on the Zambezi and in this he had a number of assistants; George Rae, ship engineer, and Tom Jumbo, leading crew member. But Bedingfield quickly realised he was going to have to play second fiddle to Livingstone and as a proud naval commander, this was difficult for he had a substantial ego. In due course Bedingfield resigned before the expedition had really got underway, and he returned to England on the SS *Pearl* when it came time for that ship to depart. At the time it was distressing, but there could only be one boss of the expedition—and Livingstone was not a person to surrender control of that.

The resignation of the expedition second-in-command was no small thing and Livingstone prepared a report on the circumstances leading to Bedingfield's resignation.[11] Livingstone later told Oswell he did not like the fellow, describing him as 'an awful bore from extra ostentatious piety—associated with a terrible forgetfulness of statement.'[12] Nevertheless it was a poor start to the expedition.

The resignation of Bedingfield meant Livingstone now had to also assume responsibility for sailing the *Ma-Robert* as well as the expedition, which placed more pressure and responsibility on him. The additional responsibility was no small thing as the number of people employed as part of the expedition grew. After Bedingfield's departure Livingstone persuaded two British sailors, John Walker, ship quartermaster, William Rowe, leading stoker to join his enterprise. In time over a 100 additional British sailors, natives from Comoros Islands and Sierra Leone as well as locals from along the Zambezi River were variously employed as crew, guides, canoe men, specimen collectors and porters.

On 17 August 1858 they clambered aboard the *Ma-Robert* on her maiden voyage and headed for the Portuguese settlement at Tete. If the trials had shown the ship to be unsatisfactory, actual use on the fast flowing Zambezi demonstrated that she was a dog.[13] Livingstone described her as 'an awful botch of a job.'[14]

Livingstone had actually had his doubts when they were conducting trials on the Mersey, but Bedingfield had reassured him that she would meet their requirements. The main problem was her furnaces as they were inefficient because of poor workmanship. It took between four and five hours to get up steam, which meant she used excessive amounts of fuel. Livingstone estimated it took them a day-and-a-half to cut sufficient wood to keep her boilers going for a day. It was no wonder she was quickly nicknamed the *Asthmatic*.[15] Compounding this problem was the fact that the *Ma-Robert* immediately began to leak.

Livingstone was deeply disappointed with the whole affair and wrote to Captain Washington to inform him the ship was not fit for purpose.

> The vessel is altogether an ill-planned affair. She drew more than 18 inches at her first trial in the Mersey. We shall make the most of a bad & shabby bargain, but it is mortifying to be obliged to spend precious time which otherwise would have been devoted to the exploration & civilisation of Africa, in tinkering a vessel—a mere punt—for which we paid such an enormous price—£1200 (extras all paid for besides) was pretty fair for twelve months very slow work with-out any whine of 'doing it all for the good of the cause.' If I ever hear the phrase after this, I shall ask if the 'cause' at the bankers is meant or what.[16]

Livingstone drove his team hard to get the *Ma-Robert* up the river. They were in the heart of malarial country; dysentery contributed to their discomfort and the blazing sun made all but the strongest of men lethargic. They were subjected to drenching tropical downpours; soon after they would be sweating in the heat pulling on ropes; rigging up pulleys and cutting firewood. It was exhausting and a brutal introduction to Africa.

Malaria, otherwise known as 'African fever', was the major concern for their urgency as Livingstone had seen many people succumb to it. He had by now significant experience in treating it having experimented with different remedies, largely on himself, over many years. Livingstone's favoured remedy at the time of the Zambezi Expedition was a combination of quinine and purgatives. The mixture contained:

> four grains of quinine were added, resin of jalap eight grains, calomel eight grains, and rhubarb four grains, the whole mixed well together, made into pills with spirit of cardamoms and given when required in a dose of ten to twenty grains. Following the discharge of bile, quinine was given until the ears were ringing.

This remedy apparently relieved headaches and pain within four to six hours, and Livingstone maintained it was 'successful in every case'. The members of the expedition quickly started calling it the 'Zambezi rouser'.[17]

While a new base was being established in Tete, Livingstone was keen to immediately start exploring the upper Zambezi and they soon set off upstream in the *Ma-Robert*. Due to the low river level the crew was forced out of the boat to haul the paddle steamer through endless shallows. Kirk recorded in his journal just how hard and difficult it was; when they were not spending long days of cutting wood for its voracious boiler, they were pulling on ropes and shouting themselves hoarse over the sounds of the river. It was a terrible start to their expeditionary endeavours.

Later in June 1858 Kirk returned to Expedition Island to start his botanical research while Livingstone took a small party on up the Zambezi to Senna. *Enroute* they arrived at Mazaro, south of Shupanga[18] in late July 1858, and were horrified to see numerous headless and mutilated bodies floating in the river. They had arrived in the middle of a local uprising and the Portuguese militia asked them to help them remove the Portuguese governor to safety. While they waited for the ill governor to board the *Ma-Robert* further fighting broke out. Eventually the governor arrived and they immediately set out on a four-day voyage to Senna.[19]

Livingstone returned to Expedition Island at the end of July 1858 to pick up Kirk and on 2 August 1858 they set off to see how far up the river they could get the *Ma-Robert*. This time they battled their way up to Shupanga, before returning again to Expedition Island. Livingstone was encouraged by their progress and he set off once again a few days later with Kirk and Baines to return to Shupanga, where he had decided to establish a forward logistics base. They made their base next to the headquarters of the Portuguese commandant, Colonel Nuñez. Kirk remained in Shupanga while Livingstone and others took stores further up the Zambezi to Island of Pita, which lay above Senna.

They reached Pita on 25 August 1858. They immediately started shipping their supplies to shore but in the process they capsized the pinnace and were lucky only to lose some equipment and iron pieces. It was not the first time they had found the pinnace difficult to use and Livingstone decided to leave it with Baines at Pita, while they went further up the Zambezi.

While at Pita, Livingstone wrote to Kirk on 25 August 1858 about the difficulty of navigating the river. In this same letter Livingstone asked Kirk for his support in the way that he had handled the dispute with Bedingfeld, particularly as he needed to send a letter on the matter to the Foreign Office.[20]

Livingstone also wrote to Thornton on the same day asking him to prepare a statement about Bedingfeld. He was specific about what he wanted Thornton to address.

I shall require from you for the use of that minister your evidence as to what you heard when I requested Bd [Bedingfield] to adopt some system in the expenditure of the Kroomen's provisions—that 'he would have nothing to do with it'—'that I ought to have got a lighterman instead of a man of his standing' etc. or words to that effect, and as it is on such evidence as yours that the Foreign Secretary places great reliance you might state any opinion you may have formed as whether the expedition could have gone on efficiently in the state of insubordination into which Bedingfeld was drawing it.[21]

Both Kirk and Thornton duly replied to Livingstone's request. Livingstone sent a full report to London and his conduct in handling the matter was later established to the satisfaction of the Admiralty and the Earl of Clarendon.

The weather and rough river conditions would test the resolve and unity of the toughest of groups. It would also challenge the leadership skills of any man to the extreme.

Livingstone was not a natural leader. An idea of the level of micro-management he exercised can be gleaned from one of his letters:

> I forgot to say, before I was leaving, that you ought to make fresh bread for yourselves. The flour is under my boxes … May I suggest a short morning prayer again. We have been unable to attend to this for some time past.[22]

His poor management skills should not have been unexpected, as he was a missionary who had no experience in leading men, except natives. He was also known to be difficult to work with, as evidenced by his interactions with other missionaries.

The expedition members, Kirk among them, all realised that Livingstone was an inept leader incapable of managing a large complex project. Perhaps Bedingfield was the first to recognise it. It also did not help that Livingstone could be secretive, self-righteous and moody. He certainly could not tolerate criticism. Kirk famously noted in 1862: 'I can come to no other conclusion than that Dr Livingstone is out of his mind and a most unsafe leader.'[23]

Despite the obvious failings of their leader, they finally reached Tete on 8 September 1858 where Livingstone had left his Makololo; they were patiently awaiting his return from England. It had been a hard slog, but the enthusiastic welcome that the expedition members received from them uplifted their spirits.

Kirk joined Livingstone and with the others they set off to explore the upper reaches of Zambezi. Their plan was to continue to work their way up the river to the Bakota Plateau.

Livingstone had always thought the Zambezi was navigable along its full length. He had been told about rapids on the Zambezi, but had no idea about the size of them and he had confidently written to a Sir Morton Peto, a Member of Parliament and supporter of Christian causes that: 'the rapid above Tete is, I am informed, not a waterfall, but a series of rocks jutting out of the stream, if they can be blasted, as there is a deep channel among them.'[24] This proved to be completely wrong. As it transpired, during the six years that the Zambezi Expedition was in existence most of the time was spent along the last 250 miles of the Zambezi and the lower 130 miles of the lower reaches of its northern tributary, the Shire River.

On 9 November 1858 they arrived at the Kebrabassa Rapids,[25] and saw for the first time what a major obstacle they represented—a series of major cataracts and rapids that were impassable by any type of boat at any time of the year. It was a bitter blow and Livingstone must have felt the implied criticism from his crew keenly. After all he was the one who had publicly called for the establishment of a system of river transport on the Zambezi, but the Kebrabassa Rapids clearly showed the folly of his idea.

After the initial shock, they had no option but to return back down the river and explore the other major tributary that they had passed on their way to the Kebrabassa Rapids. This river, which they called the Shire River, headed north. Livingstone had heard a report that at its source was a great lake. The lake was in fact Lake Nyassa, now known as Lake Malawi.

Livingstone and Kirk headed up the Shire River in early 1859 in the *Ma-Robert* and made good progress on this large river for about 200 miles, in the process rising about 1,200 feet. At one point they entered a great marsh where there were no trees. The ship burnt prodigious amounts of wood and soon they ran perilously low on fuel. The crew feared the worst, but the resourceful Livingstone had seen a great mass of bones where a large herd of elephants had been slaughtered and the bleached bones were soon being used as supplement firewood.[26] Onward they continued until they reached a place called Katunga, near Tshibisa where they came upon some more impassable rapids. Again Livingstone's plans for opening up the interior had been dashed by cataracts and rapids. He must have raged against nature's obstructions.

Livingstone decided to name the most southernmost and finest of these cataracts the Murchison Cataracts in honour of his friend Sir Roderick Murchison. Disappointed, Livingstone and his crew returned to Tete.

While Livingstone was busy exploring the Shire River, Charles Livingstone and Thomas Baines had been tasked to go back up to the Kebrabassa Rapids to see if they became passable when the Zambezi became flooded in the rainy season. They reported that while it helped, the river remained un-navigable to any large boats.

Livingstone decided they should next explore the area around the Shire River and he set out with Kirk, Charles Livingstone and Rae, together with thirty-six Makololo porters and two native guides. Livingstone meant to find the great lake that he had heard about. They started out on 4 March 1859 on the *Ma-Robert* and continued until they found a secure place to leave the vessel near Katunga. They then departed on foot and heading into the eastern part of the Shire Highlands they soon saw Mount Zomba. They crossed over one of the mountain spurs and discovered Lake Shirwa, a salt lake on 14 April 1859 lying about 2,000 feet above sea level. It took them four days to reach the shoreline as the terrain was difficult. It was only when they arrived that they were able to see clearly how large the lake was—they thought it was twenty to thirty miles wide and fifty or sixty miles long.[27] Buoyed by their discovery they then continued to circle around Lake Shirwa, noting the rich well watered land where there was an abundance of cotton and sugar growing,. They returned to the *Ma-Robert* before sailing back down the river to Tete, arriving on 3 June 1859.

Livingstone was well pleased with their explorations. He was well aware that other explorers were moving south, including Richard Francis Burton and John Hanning Speke, two intrepid British explorers who were trekking down towards Livingstone. It was Speke who became the first European to sight Lake Victoria in 1858.

Livingstone was fiercely competitive and the discovery of Lake Shirwa meant he had notched up another success. This is evident in a letter he immediately wrote to Oswell:

> We could not hear a word of Burton—I have had no news from home—if he has discovered [lake] Nyassa first, thanks to my naval donkey [Bedingfeld]—I would have done all this last year—but we have got a lake of our own and a short cut to his.[28]

Soon after he had arrived back at the *Ma-Robert* Livingstone wrote to governor Grey to tell him about their discovery. 'We have lately discovered a very fine Lake by going up this river [Shire] in the steam launch about one hundred miles and then marching some fifty more on foot. It is called Shirwa, and Lake Ngami is a mere pond in comparison.'[29]

Livingstone was indefatigable and not content with this minor exploration, he decided that they needed to undertake another major expedition to explore parts of the Shire Highlands that they did not cover. The natives had told Livingstone that Lake Nyinyesi [Lake Nyassa]—'Lake of the Stars'—lay close by and this was the lake that Burton had set out to find. Had Burton succeeded in his quest? Livingstone did not know and was anxious to find the lake first if he could. He was also aware the Portuguese would lay claim to the area if they knew the river was so easily navigable and he wrote to Grey:

> We go back to Shirwa in July [1859] and may make a push for Nyinyesi, but say nothing at present about it. We have not told the Portuguese how near Shirwa is to them. We let that come to them from our own Government, but they mean to claim all by setting up a station forthwith at the mouth of this river![30]

Setting out again from Tete in August 1859, they headed to their familiar anchorage place near Kutunga. Accompanying Livingstone this time were Kirk, Charles Livingstone and Rae, together with thirty-six Makololo porters and two native guides. They quickly pushed up into the Shire highlands and then traversed Mount Zomba and Lake Shirwa before heading out to the Shire River. After hitting the river they then turned north and following the left bank they soon came across a small lake called Pamalombwe.

Lake Pamalombwe was a teaser to the big prize and they knew they were getting close to a large lake from the repeated reports they got from the local natives. The people that they encountered had in most cases never seen a white man and were naturally curious to know if they were the same as themselves. On aspect about the white men that astonished them were their ablutions, particularly brushing teeth. Despite this the natives were generally friendly. However, the party all recognised the need to treat them carefully as they could quickly turn hostile if threatened.

The party diligently followed the course of the Shire River, trekking through hard, broken country. Then on 16 September 1859 their efforts were rewarded when they suddenly emerged onto the southern shores of Lake Nyassa [Lake Malawi] —before them lay a huge expanse of simmering water.[31]

Livingstone thought they were possibly the first Europeans to visit Lake Nyassa but in fact a Portuguese trader Candido José da Costa Cardoso claimed to have visited the lake in 1846,[32] but Livingstone strongly disputed the facts around this Portuguese's claim.[33] The issue was resolved when Livingstone later made the first map of the lake, which he named Lake Nyassa and the British claim was upheld. This name survived because in 1891 the British expanded the Shire Highlands Protectorate to include Nyasaland, under the new name of the Nyasaland Districts Protectorate.[34] Their claim was further strengthened when the Universities' Mission to Central Africa, UMCA, established a mission station on the island of Likoma in Lake Nyassa.

Livingstone explored the southern end of Lake Nyassa, but it was too large to try and circumnavigate; that would have to wait for the next time they visited the lake. Meanwhile, unbeknown to the party in the south there was a young German explorer, Dr Albrecht Roscher, nearing the lake from the northern end. He had disguised himself as an Arab to make his passage easier and reached a small town on the southern part of Lake Nyassa, two months after Livingstone had made his discovery.[35] Unfortunately Roscher's success was short-lived; natives murdered him on his journey back to the coast.[36]

They did not have long to savour their success as Livingstone wanted to re-join the men who they had left on the *Ma-Robert* to protect the boat. They quickly travelled back, no doubt buoyed by their success, and reached the ship on 6 October 1859.

Livingstone immediately recognised the huge potential agricultural, fishing and trading opportunities—but only if only British merchants and farmers could be persuaded to come. He was not worried about the Portuguese, as they seemed more concerned about shutting down opportunities rather than opening up new ones. Livingstone by now had lost any respect he may have previously felt towards the Portuguese on account of their behaviour. 'Nothing can be done with the Portuguese—they are an utterly effete, worn out, used up, syphilitic race: their establishments are not colonies, but very small penal settlements.'[37]

On his arrival back at the *Ma-Robert* in October 1859, he received disturbing news about Thornton and Baines, and Livingstone subsequently dismissed them both from the expedition. In the case of Thornton, he had been left back in camp for long periods to do his own work with little or supervision. In the heat and suffering from the usual malaria, fever and dysentery the young man, then only twenty years old, had become discouraged. When Livingstone heard about this he complained that while honest, Thornton had not performed the role of geologist, 'chiefly from ignorance and a want of energy.'[38] As will be seen by Thornton's subsequent explorations, Thornton's dismissal had more to do with Livingstone's poor management of him, rather than a serious flaw in Thornton's character.

Livingstone's relationship with Baines, the expedition artist and storekeeper, is more difficult to ascertain as he also spent long periods at Tete camp working quietly on this own. The charges made against Baines were serious as Livingstone alleged that Baines had taken large quantities of expedition property, including 'four barrels of loaf-sugar, butter, cheese, hams etc.'[39] Livingstone was highly observant and he knew that Baines had in his possession only three personal boxes when he disembarked from the SS *Pearl* but 'these are now increased by the appropriation of 'biscuit boxes' to which he has no right—no permission having been asked or granted.'[40] He later added that Baines had taken to drinking and debauchery.[41] On the face of it Livingstone's charges may have been exaggerated, but in the light of their precarious position, absolute trust among the expedition members was essential if the fabric of the team was to be maintained.

Livingstone formally wrote to Kirk, now appointed his second-in-command, instructing him to take Rae with him to escort Thornton and Baines overland to Kongone on the Zambezi delta. Livingstone wanted them to catch a ship back to England at the first opportunity. Kirk was further instructed to search Baines personal effects and to ask about the disappearance of five jars of butter and five barrels of loaf-sugar.[42] Kirk faithfully did as he was ordered but it cannot have been an easy task to undertake.

Baines later publicly asked for an apology from Livingstone, suggesting that his brother Charles had overly influenced him. There may have been some justification. Kirk certainly did not like Charles, particularly as he had concerns about his morals. Charles Livingstone was not a popular figure among the other expedition members as it seems he may have been a disruptive influence. One of the criticisms was that Charles was prone to holding grudges about trivial things and then inciting Livingstone to criticise the person involved. Thornton and Baines seemed to have come in for more than their fair share of this criticism. There is also a suggestion that it was Charles who first accused Baines of stealing the loaf-sugar and other supplies and then informed on him to Livingstone.

Baines never got a fair trial and despite his artistic talents his dismissal meant that he was unlikely to get another major commission. Baines chose to stay in Africa and continued to paint and explore, until his death in 1875.

By November 1859 the *Ma-Robert* was showing the effects of constant groundings and had begun slowly sinking. Small leaks had appeared in a number of places; the right-hand after hold, fore hold and stoke hold as well as in the cabin where the men slept. Livingstone had planned to go down to Expedition Island, but was still in Shupanga in early November 1859. By this stage the ship required constant pumping to keep her afloat. Finally, in desperation they beached the boat and repaired the hull.[43] It was a most trying time for all the members of the expedition.

When the repairs were completed—and they were no more than just temporary fixes—they set off for the Kongone mouth.[44] The reason for their urgency was because Livingstone had decided to send Rae back to England to advise the Admiralty on the construction of a replacement vessel and also to oversee the construction of another purpose-built vessel, later known as *Lady Nyassa*. Rae and Livingstone had agreed on the dimensions of a boat for use on Lake Nyassa. Livingstone was uncertain whether the Foreign Office and Admiralty would agree to pay for both boats, but if necessary he was prepared to finance the cost of *Lady Nyassa*, stating, 'The thing must be done.'[45]

It was a wise decision sending Rae back because he was an engineer and also knew intimately the problems with the design of *Ma-Robert* and the difficulties of river sailing.

After Rae had departed they stopped at Expedition Island and continued to improve the repairs to the *Ma-Robert*. They returned to Tete as there was something on Livingstone's mind; he had made a promise to Sekeletu to bring the Makololo back to their tribe.

They set off from Tete on 15 May 1860, taking those Makololo that wanted to return home. As it happened many chose not to as they had married local girls and settled in the area around Tete. Kirk and Charles also accompanied Livingstone. They took the *Ma-Robert* up as far as the Kebrabassa rapids where they left the vessel and headed over land towards Sesheke. But first they came across the magnificent Victoria Falls.

Kirk and Charles, like Livingstone before them, were filled with wonder at the awe-inspiring sight. They spent some time at the falls taking accurate measurements of the width and depth of the Victoria Falls, using plump lines. They then pushed on to Sesheke, in mounting excitement, particularly for the Makololo, and arrived there on 18 August 1860. The welcome was tumultuous—and colourful—for the tribe welcomed their warriors and greeted Livingstone and his friends in typical African style. The only sadness was discovering that Sekeletu was suffering from advanced leprosy. Livingstone and Kirk gave him what assistance they were able, but they could see the chief was doomed to die from the disease.

They spent about a month with Sekeletu. It is easy to imagine Livingstone and the elders talking about tribal politics, the impact of traders, womenfolk and all the other numerous things that get discussed around a camp fire between old friends. However, Livingstone was aware he had men waiting for him and an expedition to run and on 17 September 1860 he, Kirk and Charles left to return to Tete. The trip was made easier and faster as they travelled by canoes that they bought from the Batoka. In their agile canoes they were able to rapidly navigate their way past the Kariba rapids, but at the Karivua rapids they did so, but only with some difficulty. In the process all their supplies were soaked. However, the Kebrabassa rapids were an entirely different proposition. While carefully making their way near the confluence of the Loangwa River disaster suddenly struck. Kirk was thrown into the water and nearly drowned in the raging water before he struck out for the shore. Unfortunately Kirk lost some important notes and many scientific samples and valuable instruments. The party dragged themselves on shore and then set out on foot for Tete, arriving on 23 November 1860. They had been away six months.

Livingstone decided to once again head back down to the Zambezi delta as they were expecting a ship from England that was hopefully bringing a steamboat replacement for the *Ma-Robert*. They left Tete on 3 December 1860, but with the river lower than usual found they were constantly grounding the ship and this opened up the leaks again. Finally on 21 December 1860 she was grounded for the last time. It was an ignoble end for an inappropriate vessel. Livingstone and his party removed everything of value from the *Ma-Robert*, but without transport, they spent Christmas on the island of Tshimba, a short distance above Senna. Fortunately word spread of their predicament and the Portuguese sent canoes to collect the party and to ferry them down to the Kongone mouth. They arrived there on 4 January 1861 and stayed in the newly built Portuguese station.

Three British battle cruisers arrived off the Zambezi river mouth on 31 January 1861. In the hold one of the cruisers was their new boat, the HMS *Pioneer*. There was also new crew to join the expedition; Mr May, the new Commander of HMS *Pioneer* and Charles Mellei, who joined the expedition in the official capacity as the medical officer of the HMS *Pioneer*.[46]

There were also missionaries on board, led by Bishop Charles Mackenzie.[47] His party included Henry Burrup,[48] Horace Waller[49] and four others of the Universities' Mission to South Africa or the UMCA as it became known. The UMCA was formed by Oxford, Cambridge, Durham and Dublin universities in response to Livingstone's public challenge that he had made before he had left Britain to open a 'path for commerce and Christianity.' The newly consecrated bishop led the mission and their goal was to establish missions in central Africa, starting in the Shire Highlands.

The HMS *Pioneer* was eighty-feet by eight-feet.[50] Livingstone was initially pleased with the HMS *Pioneer*, noting with satisfaction that it had taken them a day and half to travel seventy miles upriver whereas previously it had taken them ten days in the light, slow wood burning paddle steamer, *Ma-Robert*.[51]

The Shire River was the obvious navigable route into the Shire Highland, once the Murchison Cataracts had been bypassed. But the problem was that the Portuguese controlled the Zambezi River and were unlikely to allow the English to have open access up this tributary. It would therefore be better if another route could be found. The one that had not been explored was the Rovuma River, well to the north of the Zambezi and out of Portuguese control. Livingstone had already received instructions that he should, when convenient, explore this river system.

The solution was to take that route. However, it was felt prudent that the exploring party should be kept small and Livingstone only took the bishop while the rest of the missionary party were taken to the Johanna, now called Anjouan that forms part of the Comoros Islands.

Livingstone and the bishop set out from the mouth of the Rovuma River on 11 March 1861, but were only able to get thirty miles up the river before the HMS *Pioneer* became stuck in shallow water. Unfortunately, like the *Ma-Robert* before her, it was soon apparent that the new boat still lacked sufficient power to get up the fast flowing Rovuma River, which was quickly receding after a recent flood. This forced a rethink and it was decided that Livingstone would take the full missionary party up the Zambezi River and into the Shire River. Despite the apparent failure, Livingstone was encouraged to think the Rovuma River was a possible entrance into eastern Africa as the river was three-quarters-of- a-mile wide at places with a sandy bottom.

They entered the Zambezi through the Kongone mouth and made good progress until they got into the Shire River where the continuing low river level caused them much delay. They persevered, frequently having to pull the HMS *Pioneer* off sand banks and dragging her through shallows and they eventually reached their preferred mooring spot at Katunga,[52] in the middle of July 1861. The natives had disturbing news that the Wa-Yao were on the warpath around Mañanja,[53] seeking to capture slaves for the Portuguese. It was always dangerous when this happened as Livingstone well knew from experience, and so it was agreed that Livingstone and the plucky bishop would continue on to locate a suitable site for the mission in the Shire highlands while the rest of the missionary party remained behind. Setting out they soon came across numerous Wa-Yao slave parties.

The sight of chained and yoked natives sickened both Livingstone and Mackenzie. The only good thing that happened was that they found a number of slaves who had escaped and when they recognized Livingstone, immediately attached themselves to his party.

If Livingstone's skill as a leader was questioned, his bravery was apparent to all. Kirk was moved to write in his diary, 'His absolute lack of any sense of fear amounted almost to a weakness. He would go into the most perilous situations without a tremor or a touch of hesitation.'

After much searching, they decided on a place called Magomero for the site of the new mission after the chief of the Mañanja invited the bishop to settle there. No doubt the chief was hoping the presence of the missionaries would reduce the amount of raiding by the slave traders.

They returned to the HMS *Pioneer* to collect the rest of the party and stores, and when loaded they set out for the missionaries' new home. But if the missionaries

1 Birthplace of Livingstone, south front of Shuttle Row, Blantyre, before restoration, date unknown. *Reproduced by kind permission of The National Trust for Scotland Photo Library*

2 Livingstone family room inside Shuttle Row, Blantyre. *Reproduced by kind permission of The National Trust for Scotland Photo Library, photographer Mike Bolam*

3 David Livingstone in his forties. *Reproduced by kind permission of The National Trust for Scotland Photo Library*

4 Mary Livingstone nee Moffat, in her late thirties. *Reproduced by kind permission of The National Trust for Scotland Photo Library*

5 Reception of the Livingstone Mission by Shinte, Chief of the Balonda, January 1854.
Reproduced by kind permission of the Royal Geographical Society

6 Livingstone's trademark consular cap. Made by Sarkey's of Bond Street, London.
Reproduced by kind permission of the Royal Geographical Society

7 Victoria Falls on the Zambezi river, also called Mosi-oa-tunya. *Reproduced by kind permission of the Royal Geographical Society*

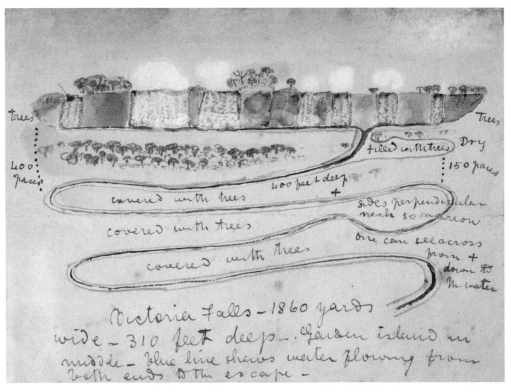

8 Sketch of the Victoria Falls by David Livingstone. *Reproduced by kind permission of the Royal Geographical Society*

9 Slave chains brought back from Africa by David Livingstone. *Reproduced by kind permission of the Royal Geographical Society*

10 Gang of captives met by David Livingstone at Mbame's on their way to Tete. *Reproduced by kind permission of the Royal Geographical Society*

11 Hypsometrical apparatus and thermometer used by Livingstone. *Reproduced by kind permission of the Royal Geographical Society*

12 Prismatic compass used by David Livingstone. *Reproduced by kind permission of the Royal Geographical Society*

13 The adventure with a hippopotamus. Engraving from *Missionary Travels*. *Reproduced by kind permission of the Royal Geographical Society*

14 The main stream came up to Susi's mouth. *Reproduced by kind permission of the Royal Geographical Society*

16 Mary Livingstone and
William Oswell Livingstone.
*Reproduced by kind
permission of the National
Trust for Scotland Photo
Library*

17 The Livingstone Family.
*Reproduced by kind
permission of the National
Trust for Scotland Photo
Library*

18 The *Ma Robert* and elephant in the shallows, Shire River, Lower Zambezi. Painting by Thomas Barnes. *Reproduced by kind permission of the Royal Geographical Society*

19 Shibadda or Two Channel Rapid above Kebrabasa on the Zambezi River. Painting by *Thomas Barnes. Reproduced by kind permission of the Royal Geographical Society*

20 Robert Livingstone, David and Mary Livingstone's eldest child, aged about fifteen. *Reproduced by kind permission of the National Trust for Scotland Photo Library*

21 Thomas Oswell Livingstone, David and Mary Livingstone's second son. *Reproduced by kind permission of the National Trust for Scotland Photo Library*

22 David Livingstone and Anna Mary during this second visit home 1864–1865. *Reproduced by kind permission of the National Trust for Scotland Photo Library*

23 Anna Mary as a young woman with her Aunt Agnes. *Reproduced by kind permission of the National Trust for Scotland Photo Library*

24 Dr Livingston,
Missionary and Explorer,
1813–1873, M. Stewart,
© *CSG CIC Glasgow
Museums Collection*

25 Livingstone's surviving children on his death; left to right: William, Agnes, Anna
Mary and Thomas. *Reproduced by kind permission of the National Trust for Scotland
Photo Library*

26 The meeting of Stanley and
Livingstone at Ujiji on shores of
Lake Tanganyika, October 1871.
*Reproduced by kind permission of
the Royal Geographical Society*

27 David Livingstone and Stanley on the Rusizi river, November 1871. *Reproduced by
kind permission of the Royal Geographical Society*

28 Mvula tree at Chitambo under which Livingstone's internal organs were buried. *Reproduced by kind permission of the National Trust for Scotland Photo Library*

29 Wainwright inscription on the mulva tree. This section of the tree with the carving is on display at the Royal Geographical Society. *Reproduced by kind permission of the National Trust for Scotland Photo Library*

30 Jacob Wainwright with David Livingstone's coffin on board the ship *Malwa*, 1873. *Reproduced by kind permission of the National Trust for Scotland Photo Library*

31 Livingstone's coffin lying in the Map Room at the Royal Geographical Society, Savile Row, London, April 1873. *Reproduced by kind permission of the Royal Geographical Society*

32 After Livingstone's death. At Newstead Abbey, 1873; from left to right: Agnes, William, Susi, Chuma and Thomas. *Reproduced by kind permission of the National Trust for Scotland Photo Library*

33 Susi and Chuma studio portrait, 1874. *Reproduced by kind permission of the National Trust for Scotland Photo Library*

needed any further introduction into just how wild and dangerous a place they were entering they soon received it when the Wa-Yao slave raiders attacked the party, firing poisoned arrows. They were forced to defend themselves and fired a rifle volley into the slave traders who then dispersed. Might had ruled on that particular day.

The only disappointment was that they knew the slave traders had captured a large number of Mañanja but as their party did not possess sufficient force they were unable to pursue and release the captives. However, they had more success when they meet other slave trading parties, mainly Portuguese, and on being challenged many of the slavers melted away into the forest leaving their slaves behind. Eventually Livingstone was able to hand over to the bishop about 140 former captives for schooling at his new mission.[54]

They arrived at Magomero after their eventful trip and immediately set to work to establish the mission. It had been a brutal introduction and the bishop resolved to actively oppose the slave trade wherever he encountered it, earning the enmity of the Wa-Yao.

After the seven-man mission was safely established, Livingstone decided to take a small team to explore the area up and around Lake Nyassa. The party was comprised of Livingstone, Kirk, Charles, a white sailor and twenty Makololo.[55] They returned to the HMS *Pioneer* at Tshibisa and rigged up a small four-oared gig that they had brought with them in which they planned to sail around Lake Nyassa. They set out on 6 August 1861 and the first job was to carry the gig about forty miles overland around the Murchison Cataracts. They then launched the gig and sailed up the Shire River for the remaining sixty miles until they reached Lake Nyassa on 2 September 1861.

They decided to explore the western coast first. There was a mountain promontory nearby which Livingstone decided to call Cape Maclear in honour of his friend, Thomas Maclear. By now Livingstone was enjoying naming features and rivers after his friends and patrons.

In sailing around they came to the conclusion that the lake was about 200 miles long and twenty to sixty miles wide[56] but a later measurement showed that Lake Nyassa is in fact much bigger at about 360 miles long, and over forty-five miles wide at its widest point.[57] Livingstone also referred to the lake as 'The Lake of Stars' due to the large number of lights from the lanterns hanging from the boats of men fishing at night.[58] When later they had to sit out a particularly bad storm, Livingstone nicknamed it 'The Lake of Storms'.

During their explorations of the Lake, they were, in most cases, hospitably treated except for when they got to an area where the slave trade was prevalent. Here the people were invariably unfriendly, sometimes refusing to sell them food and in one case, breaking into their camp to steal most of their stores. At the northern end of Lake Nyassa lived a tribe of Zulus known locally as the Angoni Zulus or as Livingstone called them, Mazitu.[59] They terrorised the area, regularly plundering the surrounding countryside, killing and carrying off people and animals. At one stage the Mazitu even chased the gig in canoes but fortunately a good breeze sprang up and the gig was able to pull away from the pursuers.

Livingstone noted how productive the surrounding land was and the extraordinary range of fish caught in the lake.[60] The stopped frequently in villages and what they found then would not be much different today: the pungent smell of drying cassava, ranks of bisected fish drying in the sun and chickens scratching around in the dust.

They spent nearly two months exploring the lake and it was a satisfying and fruitful trip but by the end of October 1861 they needed to return to the HMS *Pioneer* as their stores were running low, and they were concerned that if they delayed longer they would not be able to sail back down the river with the onset of the dry season.[61] They arrived back at HMS *Pioneer* on the 8 November 1861 in a weakened state as they had had become seriously starved.

A week later, while still recovering, Bishop Mackenzie arrived at the HMS *Pioneer*. He seemed happy about the state of his mission particularly as the Mañanja around his mission house at Magomero seemed safer from the deprecations of slave traders. It was a promising start for the mission.

Mackenzie and Livingstone were both keen to get back down to the coast to meet a ship that was heading up from the Cape bringing two important passengers; Livingstone's wife and the bishop's sister. However, the bishop wanted to do some more exploring and so it was agreed that Livingstone would meet the ship and then rendezvous with the bishop and other missionaries at the mouth of the Ruo, a tributary of the Shire River, around 1 January 1862.

Bidding farewell to the bishop, Livingstone set off in HMS *Pioneer,* eager to see Mary but with the river still low it was not long before they hit a sandbank. This time she was stuck fast and for five frustrating weeks they had to wait until the river rose high enough for them to be able to float HMS *Pioneer* off. Once free they then made their way swiftly down river and reached the coast on 11 January 1862.

During this period of forced inactivity waiting for the river to rise, Livingstone wrote to Sir George Grey about what they had seen during their three month expedition around Lake Nyassa. He described in detail the geography of the land, the people he encountered and problems navigating on Lake Nyassa, noting that there was an Arab dhow already operating on the lake, mostly to ferry slaves across to the eastern shore.[62] The land was ripe for commerce and Christianity.

8.3 The Death of Mary Livingstone

Mary returned to Britain in late 1859 and moved into a house in Glasgow. She had become reunited with Livingstone's family after his visit and following the death of her father-in-law. Livingstone's sisters began to play a more influential role in the lives of their nieces and nephews. Mary also had other people to support her, including

James Young who was a firm friend of the family. Another person was Reverend James Stewart, who was, in time, to cause Mary many problems.

Stewart was a tall, good-looking man who readily offered Mary support and provided a fatherly presence for 'poor misguided Robert', who was struggling in school and displaying his 'vagabond ways'. When George Rae arrived back in Scotland he quickly summed up the situation and mischievously intimated in letters to Livingstone about Mary's supposedly inappropriate relationship with the Reverend.

Livingstone conveniently ignored the letters of Rae and others that alluded to Mary's on-going problems, but when Lady Angela Burdett-Coutts, an expedition supporter, wrote to Livingstone to remind Livingstone of his duties to his wife, as well as to the expedition that Livingstone was suddenly stung into doing something about Mary's position. His response was to immediately write to her and instruct her to accompany Rae when the later brought out the *Lady Nyassa*. The command came as a surprise and Mary was both unsettled and undecided about what she should do. She wrote to Mary Fitch soon after telling her that 'I received a letter from Livingstone dated 28 March, 1861. In it he says "embrace the first opportunity to come out ..." So you see the orders have come.'

As Davidson has commented, it was the first time that Mary actively rebelled against the summons.[63] The dutiful, diligent wife suddenly seemed in no hurry to rally to the summons from her distant husband. Her main concern was her children; what was to come of them if she left? All of them concerned her; wild Robert, pubescent Agnes, sickly Thomas, child Oswell while her youngest, Anna Mary, was only two years old. What was their mother to do? As much as she wanted to be united with her husband she knew it meant abandoning her family to the care of her in-laws and friends. Livingstone had given Mary the devil's decision and so she did what any mother would do, she prevaricated. In the end Rae sailed back to South Africa alone, but soon after Mary decided she needed the emotional and physical support of her husband more than her children. She reluctantly booked herself on a Royal Mail ship, *Celt*, accompanied by her friend, the Reverend James Stewart. They departed on 6 July 1861 on what became her final passage.

Her youngest daughter Anna Mary later recalled her departure:

I have no recollection of her, I mean of seeing her, but I do remember Aunt Agnes holding me up to the window to wave goodbye to Mamma as she disappeared round the corner to the station. I was quite willing to do that, but a more absorbing interest to me was to lift a foot up to show Mamma my new red shoes.[64]

Rae, Mary and others met up in South Africa and together they transferred to two ships that were sailing up the coast and arrived three weeks later on 31 January 1862 at the entrance to the Luabo river channel. In the holds of the HMS *Gorgon* was precious cargo—Livingstone's new steamer, *Lady Nyassa*, that he had paid for. The ship had been constructed by the Glasgow shipyard of Messrs Tod and McGregor under the watchful eye of George Rae.

Accompanying the HMS Gorgon was a square-rigged brig, *Hetty Ellen*, carrying equally important cargo. Livingstone was waiting anxiously onshore and was delighted when Captain John Wilson[65] signalled 'Wife Aboard'.[66] Also on board were four other women; Miss Anne Mackenzie, the elder spinster sister of Bishop Mackenzie, accompanied by her housekeeper, Jessie Lennox and a maid, Sarah, and Mrs Elizabeth Burrup, the newly married wife of an UMCA missionary, Henry Burrup from Oxford.

Stewart had accompanied the group, as he wanted to investigate the feasibility of establishing a Free Kirk Industrial Mission somewhere around Lake Nyassa. Despite his obvious closeness to Mary, members of the Zambezi Expedition regarded him with suspicion. Rae suspected that Stewart was a 'trader in disguise', while Charles Livingstone immediately disliked him, writing in a letter:

> What is the Mr Stewart? None of us like him. Is he a humbug, or does he really mean to be a missionary? Dr. K. [Kirk] says that he was very rude and insulting to his [Kirk's] mother in Edinburgh before he left.[67]

Miss Mackenzie had come at the urging of her brother who wanted someone to keep house for him in Magomero. Livingstone described her as having a 'rather loose tongue' and while considered prudish and stiff, she showed courage and conviction to undertake such a dramatic venture. In contrast Mrs Burrup was vivacious and young—just twenty-one—and popular with her travelling companions and crew. She had married Burrup two days before they had sailed and enthusiastically agreed to join her missionary husband. Kirk described her as 'full of life, talked nautical and jumped about.'

The Livingstones were quickly reunited after their nearly four-year separation and it was a loving and joyous reunion—although it was to be short lived. Livingstone was anxious to hear about their children, particularly Anna Mary, their youngest who he had not yet seen.

For Mary it was a time of great joy to be reunited with her husband. Her return to Scotland after accompanying Livingstone and the other original members of the Zambezi Expedition as far as Cape Town, before leaving because of her untimely and probably unwanted pregnancy, had been a great disappointment for her. After staying in Kuruman she found herself once more back in Scotland—remote, lonely and invariably short of money.

Unfortunately Mary was well aware of the salacious rumours circulating about her inappropriate relationship with Stewart. To his credit Livingstone did not believe infidelity was a possibility and immediately dismissed the suggestion. He clearly held to that view as in 1865 Livingstone sought Stewart's assistance in treating his dying mother, who was suffering with bronchitis.[68]

Soon after Mary's arrival Livingstone wrote to one of his trustees, James Young[69] about care of their children. Mary and Livingstone had obviously been discussing their future. It was decided to keep William in Brighton because of concerns about his chest. Thomas was now at Kendall school where Robert had also attended. They were pleased with the progress Thomas was making at school but it was a different story with Robert. He complained that he was not learning anything at St Andrews school and had in fact run away at one stage. Livingstone described his temperament as excitable:

> I suppose he has some of my nature and judging from myself placing him in a quiet family for lodging and allowing him to pursue his best in studies according to the advice of Dr Playfair will prove more beneficial than he could be with Mr Hall as a cramming master.

Robert was also reputed to have fallen in with bad company, which was clearly due to a lack of parental attention.[70] Within twelve months Robert had boarded a ship and arrived unexpectedly in the Cape with most unfortunate consequences.

The enlarged party, together with Captain Wilson of HMS *Gorgon*, set off in the overloaded HMS *Pioneer* for the rendezvous with the bishop. Livingstone was in good spirits and at night would entertain his guests by relating stories about his African adventures. Livingstone's pet dog also contributed to the entertainment one evening when he fell through a skylight and landed in the middle of the supper table, scattering dishes and food, causing much hilarity. Livingstone also found time to go off for quiet walks with Mary where they could share intimate moments together.

Livingstone had taken longer than he had planned to pack up the missionaries and their mountains of baggage and consequently they were well behind schedule to make the rendezvous on New Year's Day. It was in the third week of February before the HMS *Pioneer* slowly chugged into Shupanga. The delays and problems encountered on this trip brutally revealed Livingstone's inadequacies as a leader. One of the naval personnel, Devereux, the Paymaster noted in his diary, 'I never saw such constant vacillations, blunders, delays, and want of common thought and foresight as is displayed on board the *Pioneer*.'[71]

If the veneer of goodwill had survived it was suddenly shattered when they arrived at the confluence and the bishop was not to be found. They continued up the river to Tshibisa, worried, where they received the shocking news that the bishop and Burrup had died of the fever. Later it became known that Mackenzie's drugs were all destroyed when his canoe had capsized and he had no means of treating himself or his party for malaria and other illnesses.[72] It was a terrible tragedy for both Miss Mackenzie and Mrs Burrup who had come so far only to be deprived of their loved ones at the last minute. Livingstone had to take his sad party back down the river to the delta and they returned to Britain. Later

Livingstone visited the site of Mackenzie's death and erected a cross over his grave.

Livingstone knew the death of the bishop and his companion missionary would reflect badly on the Zambezi Expedition and was heard to murmur 'this will hurt us all'. Later he wrote in his diary, 'I will not swerve a hair's-breadth from my work while life is spared.' Despite this sentiment he knew they had to rethink the wisdom of siting the mission at Magomero, as it was difficult to resupply. A decision was made, reluctantly, to downsize the mission and just two of the missionaries, Horace Waller and Dr Hugh Rowley, remained to continue their good work. This meant that over the ensuing few weeks Livingstone and his party were busy ferrying the missionaries and their supplies back to the HMS *Gorgon*. The HMS *Gorgon* sailed on 4 April 1862 and with it went the dashed hopes of Livingstone and the UMCA of establishing a number of missions throughout the Shire Highlands.

Meanwhile Mary had thrown herself into helping load stores and working alongside the men. Her energy and capacity for work both surprised and horrified the other women and for the menfolk, showed up what a 'common woman' Mary was. What exactly was the wife of the great explorer doing getting muddy, heaving boxes and such like? But to Livingstone, this was part of the reason why he loved his 'rib'. This is what his faithful missionary wife was born to do and to sit idly by would be both an anathema to her as much as it would have surprised her husband. It certainly did surprise Kirk who wrote meanly that she was 'a coarse, vulgar women' and a 'queer piece of furniture'. It showed just how little Kirk and others knew this African woman and how little they appreciated her endeavours.

Livingstone was keen to get Mary and the rest of his party away from the delta area because of the risk of exposure to malaria and other fevers. They left for Shupanga on 11 April 1862 on HMS *Pioneer*, carrying sections of the *Lady Nyassa* in her hold. Unfortunately it was not quick enough and tragedy struck for a third time; by about the middle of the month Mary was prostrated with fever, probably cerebral malaria. Livingstone and Kirk did everything they could to nurse her but the problem for them in trying to treat Mary was her constant vomiting.

The phlegmatic Kirk recorded their attempts to combat the malaria. '

I was sent for at 3.00 a.m. Found her in a half comatose state. It was impossible to get medicine taken. Blisters would not rise and injections proved unavailing. Steadily coma deepened into perfect insensibility and the skin tinged of a deep yellow.[73]

Despite all their attentions she quickly succumbed to the effects of the fever and died on 27 April 1862. She was just 41 years old.

George Rae, the mischievous but practical Scot, built a makeshift coffin. Livingstone, too distraught to conduct a service, asked Reverend James Stewart to do the honours. She was quickly buried in Shupanga, under a large Baobab tree in the garden of the Portuguese Commandant's house.[74]

Livingstone was shattered by it. He wrote in his journal, 'For the first time in my life I feel willing to die.'[75] He also wrote to Young, lamenting, 'I cannot tell you how greatly I feel the loss. It feels as if heart and strength were taken out of me—my horizon is all dark. I am distressed for the children.'[76]

The Moffat's got to hear about the death of Mary some months later. The news did not come as a great surprise for her mother who, according to Mary's brother John, had a strong belief that if her daughter went to the fever-stricken Zambezi region she would not return, describing it as 'a sacrifice ready offered up.'[77] Her mother's intuition was right.

Dr James McNair, editor of David Livingstone's *Travels*[78] subsequently wrote that 'Livingstone has frequently been censured for lack of consideration for his wife and children … He could not have done the magnificent work he did without a formidable share of the burden falling on his family. Mary Livingstone, on her part, accepted her fate proudly.' The nature of Mary's relationship with her husband has been much discussed by historians, both in the light of his tough, independent nature, and from the feminist perspective. But it is clear that they were extremely close partners, and that she was just as tough in her way. Certainly, she accepted her fate, but whether she did so as a willing partner to Livingstone's increasingly ambitious plans to discover Africa is not clear.

Later, long after the death of Mary and when he was looking for the source of the Nile, Livingstone confided to Kirk that 'I have but one regret in looking back to my stationary missionary life and that is that I did not play more with my children but I worked so hard physically and mentally that in the evenings there was seldom any fun left in me.' It was a sad admission to make.

After her death a Mary Moffat Museum was established in Griquatown in the former London Missionary Station house. It is believed the house was built in the late 1820s and so is not the house that Mary was born in. Somewhat incongruously Barclays Bank acquired the House directly from the London Missionary Society and used it until 1952. The pulpit that Moffat used to give his sermons is now on display.

8.4 Expedition Failure

The death of Mary greatly affected Livingstone and to get over his grief, he threw himself into prosecuting the aims of the expedition.

The priority was to get the forty-foot steamer, *Lady Nyassa*, assembled as soon as possible. Rae and his team were soon all busy constructing the boat but it was slow work. Among the many natives employed to help was a young native called Susi who would turn out to be one of Livingstone's most loyal servants.

Livingstone hoped to use the *Lady Nyassa* to stop the slave trade around Lake

Nyassa as he estimated 20,000 people were annually being taken out to the coast as slaves.[79] He had already seen the dhows in operation on the lake and Livingstone meant to stop them, as well as in time transporting trading goods. This would include ivory as Livingstone realised that the sale of ivory made the slave trade profitable as the profit offset the cost of providing food—and the losses—on transporting slaves to the coast for eventual sale.[80]

The launching of the *Lady Nyassa* on 23 June 1862 meant he could get back to exploring the rivers. Unfortunately the *Lady Nyassa* could not be immediately used as it was the dry season and the river was too low. He did have on hand the HMS *Pioneer* with its shallower draught and Livingstone decided to explore the Rovuma again. His exploration party left Kongone Harbour on 6 August 1862 and ascended up the river for 160 miles until the low water forced them to turn back. It was an eventful trip as the locals were frightened and restless, particularly as there were many slave raiding parties ranging across the countryside and these could appear at any time. At one point Livingstone and his party passed through two villages near Ntandé. The women casually came out to look at the passing expedition while their menfolk rapidly departed to prepare an ambush further up the river. Suddenly shots rang out and four bullet holes appeared in HMS *Pioneer's* sail. The unprovoked attack was quickly met with accurate fire and two natives, a father and son, were stuck down with gunfire. The attacking party quickly melted away into the forest, frightened by the rapid and deadly response. The action, while momentarily terrifying, was a good thing in that it established a reputation that these white men were not to be trifled with. Livingstone passed through these villages in 1866 on his way to Lake Tanganyika and noted both had long since been abandoned.[81]

They arrived back in Shupanga on 19 December 1862. Livingstone, restless and doggedly determined as ever, set out again on 10 January 1863 but this time with the HMS *Pioneer* towing the *Lady Nyassa*.

As they travelled up the Shire River they were horrified to see large numbers of floating bodies in the river. They were the victims of slave traders. Indeed there were so many bodies that at one stage *Lady Nyassa's* paddle wheels became fouled. It was a sickening job hauling out the rotting remains jammed in the paddle wheels.

Livingstone was ever mindful of the health of his crew and made a point of mooring the *Lady Nyassa* in mid-stream at night so they could enjoy the evening breeze. It was also a safety measure as a boat moored in the river was more difficult to attack. Unfortunately it was to have a fatal outcome for one of the natives from the Johanna Island working for Livingstone. One morning the fellow, a brother-in-law of another Johanna man, Musa Kammaals who was later to cause Livingstone many difficulties, stepped off the bank to swim out to the ship. A crocodile immediately took him. The man screamed out, holding his hand out of the water but Musa and the other Johanna men made no move to go to his assistance. When Livingstone remonstrated with him, Musa replied simply and brutally, 'Well, no one tell him to go in there.'[82]

They arrived at the Murchison Cataracts and started dismantling the *Lady Nyassa* so she could be transported over land around them. Given the size of her sections this required a road to be built over the forty miles of rough ground. It was a huge undertaking and it taxed the strength and resolve of everyone. The main problem was in trying to hire sufficient native labour and in ensuring they had enough supplies to feed everyone. It was a losing battle and their efforts slowly petered out.

In January 1863 during all this work Thornton suddenly reappeared with an amazing story of what he had done since Livingstone had dismissed him and Thomas Baines from the expedition in October 1859. He recounted how on making his way to the coast he met with Baron Karl von der Decken,[83] a German nobleman who at the age of 27 had devoted himself to exploring east Africa. Von der Decken had just made an unsuccessful attempt to reach Lake Nyassa and was then planning to climb Mount Kilimanjaro.

A German missionary Johann Rebmann had first reported the existence of a snow-capped mountain close to the equator in 1848, called Mount Kilimanjaro. His guide had spoken of it being very cold on the mountain and that others from his tribe had been sent to collect the silver on the mountain, but returned carrying only water. Rebmann's report initiated much debate about whether a mountain could have snow at this latitude. In Victorian Britain people scoffed at the notion and dismissed the missionary as mad.

Von der Decken and Thornton agreed to jointly solve Rebmann's paradox. Their caravan set out from Mombasa on 29 June 1861 and by the time they had climbed to nearly 8,000 feet all their porters had deserted them and they were forced to turned back, but not before confirming the presence of snow and ice. Thornton was also able to identify the composition of the volcanic rocks and make a very accurate estimate of the height of the mountain as well as recording in his diary detailed descriptions of 'local culture, society, agricultural practices, vegetation, geography and geology.'[84] Livingstone was suitably impressed. Thornton agreed to re-join the expedition and immediately volunteered to take goats and sheep to the UMCA at Magomero that was in need of resupply.

Thornton's reappearance was curious although this may be put down to Thornton wanting to redeem himself for his previous 'ignorance and a want of energy'. It was to prove a fateful decision as the resupply required Thornton to trek 150 miles overland to buy supplies at Tete. He then set out to return with sixty goats and forty sheep. It was an arduous journey and he arrived back sick with fever and dysentery. The three medical doctors, Livingstone, Kirk and Meller all provided medical attention but ten days later he died on 21 April 1863.[85] Thornton was buried the next day under a large baobab tree just 1,500 feet from the bottom of the Murchison Cataracts. He was just twenty-five years old.

There were many others at Murchison Cataracts also suffering from sickness. Dysentery was a particular problem and the attacks suffered by Kirk and Charles Livingstone was serious enough for Livingstone to order them to leave the expedition.[86] Charles made his way to the coast and returned to the United States to join his family. He arrived back in America in 1864, after a nearly seven-year absence.

Kirk was about to start out for the Zambezi delta when Livingstone fell seriously ill. Kirk chose to stay and nurse him and he did not finally leave until 9 May 1863. During Livingstone's illness, many of his native helpers lost enthusiasm and either slipped away or fell ill and died from fevers. Livingstone was undeterred and determined as ever to continue, announcing, 'I am prepared to go anywhere, provided it be forward.'

Livingstone later sent Kirk a letter while he was still at Murchison Cataracts requesting him to settle some accounts. He also provided news that the two UMCA missionaries, Lovell Proctor and Horace Waller, were both surviving at Magomero. He also had news about James Stewart who was pursuing his Scottish Free Kirk plans. Livingstone had become unimpressed with his fellow Scot after Rae had told him that Stewart had said he had only seen five cotton bushes in the whole country and no indigo bushes. Writing to Kirk, Livingstone lamented, 'if the saying is true, he did not know either the one from the other'. In the same letter he touchingly told Kirk, 'You were always a right hand to me and I never trusted you in vain. God bless and prosper you.'[87]

Rae re-joined the expedition and Livingstone decided that they would leave the team carving out the road around the Murchison Cataracts and go and see if the gig was still secure on the banks of the upper Shire. Unfortunately they were too late, as they only found the burnt remains of the boat. It had apparently burned by the Mañanja three months before.

Livingstone and Rae returned to HMS *Pioneer* on 2 July 1863 and soon after he received a despatch from Lord Russell[88] of the Foreign Office recalling the Zambezi Expedition and advising him that he and his party should be at the mouth of the Zambezi by the end of July 1863 in order to be picked up and returned to England. He was further advised that all salaries would cease to be paid after 31 December 1863.

It had been a good run and the expedition had gone on much longer than anyone had initially conceived. For Livingstone, he was not personally surprised as he confided in a letter to Kirk the next day.[89] The only thing that upset Livingstone was that Lord Russell mentioned that the government had as yet, received 'scanty information about the resources of the country',[90] a comment that annoyed Livingstone, particularly as he and Kirk had ensured that numerous plant samples and information had been furnished to Kew Gardens in London. He encouraged Kirk to continue his work to complete 'a magnificent botanical work, economical and everything else, at Government expense.' It would be one important and demonstrative way of proving the value of the expedition to all concerned.[91]

In the letter to Livingstone the Government praised the zeal and perseverance of the expedition members but the real reason for the decision to recall the expedition was because of the increasing cost and demonstrable failure to find a navigable route into the interior. The Government had shown much forbearance in allowing the expedition to continue for as long as it did.[92] Livingstone had been fortunate that in the early days of the expedition the ambitious Sir George Grey had been a strong supporter of the Zambezi Expedition and had supplied funding and supplies when requested by Livingstone. However, he had been replaced in 1861.[93]

Livingstone also wrote to Horace Waller of the UMCA to let him know about the recall of the expedition. He noted, 'I don't know whether I am to go on the shelf or not. If I do, I make Africa the shelf.'

Charles Meller was down stream and he decided it was easier to make his way straight out to the coast. He left the expedition on 17 July 1863, heading for Kongone mouth. He had been upset by the death of young Thornton and according to Livingstone had been acting strangely since then, a 'busybody and the tale-bearer' and so Livingstone did not consider him to be a loss to the expedition when he left.[94]

Livingstone's low opinion of Meller would explain why Livingstone later never actively supported Meller in securing Government posts in the way that he continued to urge and support Kirk's career. Livingstone knew Meller was being considered for the post of consul for Madagascar at the time; Livingstone's response was to strenuously urge Kirk to apply for the position of consul for Zanzibar.[95]

Livingstone soon after had a visit from Bishop William Tozer[96] who had replaced Bishop Mackenzie as head of the UMCA after a hiatus following the death of the latter. Bishop Tozer was appointed to the position following his consecration in February 1863 and his first volunteers were two Lincolnshire clergy, the Reverend C. A. Alington, and Dr Steere. Alington would later meet Livingstone back in England to ask if he could accompany him on his return trip to Africa.

When Livingstone met Tozer, the bishop was contemplating how to progress his fledgling UMCA work. Magomero, the spot originally selected, had proved to be disastrously unhealthy and a famine had meant most of Mañanja had relocated away from the mission area. Tozer decided to re-establish the mission on Morambala Heights, but at 4,000 feet but it was too isolated and he later moved the mission back to Zanzibar.[97]

The move to Zanzibar was a step too far for many people, including Livingstone, who felt the bishop was abandoning this important part of Africa to the Portuguese and slavery. Livingstone described Tozer in a letter to Kirk as 'very cautious and no courage, but seems not too old to learn.'[98]

In retrospect Livingstone and others had under-estimated the difficulty of Europeans living in this area. Bishop Tozer went on to establish a vibrant centre in Zanzibar that in time grew to support missionary work throughout much a central Africa, including the establishment of a training college to develop a native ministry. This practical step was consistent with Livingstone's own earlier view about the need to educate natives so that they could become missionaries. Again Tozer seems to have been wise when in less than forty years the Mission lost six bishops, twenty-seven clergy, and forty-six lay workers to fever. A gift of five black slave boys from the Sultan of Zanzibar were the first pupils of the training college, and soon after British cruisers began to bring in freed slaves. Bishop Tozer devoted most of his energies to the founding of the school and a establishing a Wells-Tozer Fund. By 1899, thirty-six years after first meeting Livingstone, Tozer's work in laying down the foundations for these changes had resulted in a native staff of thirteen clergy and 105 other teachers.[99]

It was not possible for HMS *Pioneer* to get down to the Zambezi river mouth at that time of year and it meant that they would have to wait for the rainy season to commence in December 1863. Livingstone also had the *Lady Nyassa* screwed together again for the impending trip back to the coast as he was keen for HMS *Pioneer* and *Lady Nyassa* to both be removed so that they could not fall into the hands of the Portuguese or Arabs and be used for slave trading.

Livingstone received word that his eldest son Robert was in Natal in South Africa. He had been robbed on the ship and had arrived with no money and was idling his time away and running up debts. Livingstone was relieved to hear that Maclear had stepped in and got him to come down to the Cape where he was put into proper lodgings and encouraged to find a job.[100] Livingstone toyed with the idea of bringing Robert up to the Shire to help him sail the *Lady Nyassa*, but the problem was how to get him up to Shupanga. It was too difficult and in the end Livingstone decided that Robert 'must work his own way in Natal.'[101] Kirk was about to return to England and Livingstone was hoping that Kirk would call into Cape Town and possibly see Robert *en route*, but this did not happen. Livingstone asked Kirk to 'Give him a kind word if you see him.'[102] Livingstone could not have foreseen the consequences of Robert failing to join him and was forever saddened about what transpired.

Livingstone also wrote to Kirk to ask if he could find a skipper for the *Lady Nyassa* as he had started to think that if he could not sell her in Zanzibar, he may be forced to sail the boat to India.

8.5 Journey to Lake Nyassa

The decision of the British Government to recall the Zambezi Expedition in 1863 provided an opportunity for Livingstone to explore the area up and around the northern end of Lake Nyassa before he too went back to England.

Livingstone had decided to take his remaining Makololo with him and they set off in August 1863. They carried a small sailing boat with them around the Murchison Cataracts and on reaching the river, five natives jumped into the boat and it promptly sank, much to Livingstone's chagrin.[103] Setting out on foot they headed in a north-westerly direction until they ran into a high range that towered over 2,000 feet above them. They continued pushing up through the valley, over beautiful clean streams until they suddenly ran into a slaver's stockade, with rotting bodies scattered round. Unwilling to get involved in local troubles Livingstone took his party north-east and they came out onto the shores of Lake Nyassa at a place called Chitanda. They found more slave traders operating in the area, including one engaged in building another dhow to ferry captured slaves across Lake Nyassa to secure stockades. Livingstone noticed with mounting alarm and disgust how the Arabs were furiously buying slaves from all the surrounding villages, at a fathom[104] for a boy and two for a girl.'[105]

Livingstone took his party west along the great slave route to Katanga. These routes are visible today as the Arabs had a habit of planting palm trees on ridge lines and prominent features that marked the routes into the interior.[106] They proceeded in a westerly direction, plodded up on to the Zambian plateau over a distance of about 90 miles before trekking north until they reached a place called Tshimanga, near the Loangwa River. Temptingly it was here that Livingstone was told that he was only ten days journey from a large lake called Bangweulu. However, Livingstone needed to return if they were to be back on the Shire River, ready for when the river level rose with the onset of the rainy season. He was also concerned about his natives, particularly the Shupanga men who, while impervious to malaria, could not handle travelling on the colder plateau. It was so cold at times that one man died of exposure. 'They complained of pains all over—cut themselves everywhere, I never saw anything like it.'[107] The other issue was that he knew the British Government would stop their pay on 31 December 1863 and it was wrong to continue knowing the men would not get paid.

They returned to Lake Nyassa, reaching its shores on 8 October 1863. They passed Morambala where they picked up the remaining members of the UMCA, including forty former slaves, and then made good progress to rejoin the rest of the expedition on HMS *Pioneer* on 1 November 1873.[108]

Livingstone was well pleased with his journey as he was able to better understand the water system, including what rivers fed Lake Nyassa, and how the water flowed back into the Zambezi. As always, he made careful notes, observations and maps of this area, which were published later in his book, *Narrative of an Expedition to the Zambesi and its Tributaries.*

Livingstone's intention of immediately heading to the coast was thwarted when the rainy season was late. There was nothing to be done, but wait patiently for the river to rise. Eventually, on 19 January 1864 the river level was high enough to allow both boats to float free and they set off down the Shire. *En route* they ran HMS *Pioneer* over a sandbank and broke her rudder, and because of this delay they only arrived in Shupanga on 10 February 1864. It was while there making repairs that Livingstone read about his apparent death from a report published in a British paper in 1863. He was amused but also hoped that his children had not read the same report. He also learnt that Robert had signed on to a mail ship as a common sailor that sailed regularly between the Cape and New York.

The party reached the mouth of the Zambezi on 13 February 1864 and to their delight found anchored in the bay two British warships, HMS *Orestes* and *Ariel*, which were patrolling the area.

The *Lady Nyassa* and the HMS *Pioneer* were immediately taken in tow and they headed to Mozambique, *en route* encountering a huge hurricane. On reaching Mozambique the Zambezi Expedition came to a formal conclusion. It was decided that Waller and other mission members would sail HMS *Pioneer* to the Cape while Livingstone would take the *Lady Nyassa* to Zanzibar.

Livingstone set out for Zanzibar with Rae with the intention of selling *Lady Nyassa* there. However, he could not find a buyer so at short notice he determined on the risky plan of sailing the boat to Bombay.

CHAPTER 9

Return to Britain

'I have kept the faith.'
St Paul, Second Epistle to Timothy

9.1 The Slow Boat Home

Livingstone's plan to sail the *Lady Nyassa* to Bombay quickly became more complicated when his faithful engineer Rae decided to leave Livingstone in Zanzibar and go and seek his fortune in the local sugar fields. The loss of the only engineer on the ship made the 2,500 nautical mile trip across the Indian Ocean a risky proposition, particularly as the monsoon season was due to start in May. Undaunted Livingstone set out with three Europeans, a stoker, carpenter and sailor and seven native men and two boys.[1] All of Livingstone's companions were totally unfamiliar with sailing *Lady Nyassa*.[2]

They sailed from Zanzibar on 30 April 1864 and the voyage took forty-five days rather than the expected eighteen days. They arrived in Bombay harbour unnoticed on 13 June 1864, with only a small amount of coal left.[3] In that time they were becalmed, encountered storms, high winds and drenching rain. The monsoon fortuitously broke the same day they arrived in Bombay. The courage that Livingstone displayed is characteristic, but even Livingstone knew he had been lucky when he later wrote that he could have 'left Zanzibar on 30 April, 1864, and never more heard of.' The author sailed from Jakarta to the Seychelles in an eighteen-metre wooden boat and has a good understanding of the risks involved in sailing a ship like the *Lady Nyassa*.[4]

In Bombay, Livingstone was generously received by the governor, Sir Bartle Frere.[5] Despite Livingstone's best intentions and the obvious seaworthiness of the boat he was unable to sell the *Lady Nyassa* for a fair price and he was forced to leave the boat in the care of a Captain Young while he returned to Britain. One advantage was that he could possibly use the *Lady Nyassa* when he went back to Africa.[6]

His immediate worry was money as he had most of his financial capital tied up in the ship. Furthermore Livingstone had spent all his available cash in outfitting her for the voyage and he did not have enough money left to pay for the passage money for himself and one of his men, and he was forced to borrow it. He embarked for England without fanfare and arrived on 23 July 1864.

The reception Livingstone received from the Government was very different from the wild public and private acclamation he had received on his first trip back to England. The Government's position had changed significantly; having spent about £30,000 supporting the Zambezi Expedition they were disappointed with the lack of scientific and economic success and embarrassed by Livingstone's public comments on the activities of the Portuguese in central Africa. Portugal was at that time an ally of Britain and the Government wanted to keep relations friendly. When Livingstone in due course met the Foreign Secretary, Lord John Russell, he specifically asked Livingstone to refrain from making further public remarks about the Portuguese. He was reminded that it was a sensitive matter for Queen Victoria as she was related to King Luís I of Portugal by marriage for her husband and King Luís were both members of the House of Saxe-Coburg and Gotha.[7]

Livingstone also had to endure uncomfortable comments about the Zambezi Expedition, which had been castigated as a failure in many newspapers of the time. One of the anonymous letters published by *The Times* in 1863 summed up the public feeling of the time.[8] 'We were promised cotton, sugar, and indigo, commodities which savages never produced; and of course we got none. We were promised trade, and there is no trade, although we have a consul at £500 a year. We were promised converts to the Gospel, and not one has been made. We were told the climate was salubrious, and a bishop and some of the best missionaries of the temperate region of South Africa, with their wives and children, have perished in the malarious swamps of the Zambezi. In a word, the thousands subscribed by the Universities and the thousands contributed by the Government have been productive only of the most fatal results.'

There was debate and discussion about the fate of the UMCA and the needless deaths of Bishop Mackenzie and Burrup. Livingstone was deeply implicated in both of these events and his reputation suffered significant damage. It was unsurprising that Livingstone consequently experienced difficulty in raising funds to cover the costs of making further explorations in Africa.

In time the Government and the public would recognise that some of the people appointed to the Zambezi Expedition, including the zoologists John Kirk and Charles Meller, and geologist Richard Thornton did contribute large collections of botanic, ecological, geological and ethnographic material to scientific institutions across Britain.[9]

Livingstone was chastened after the cool reception he got from Lord Russell and he only stayed in London for a week before heading to Glasgow, first to meet one of his trustees, the redoubtable James Young, and then to Hamilton for a welcome reunion with his family.

It was in Hamilton that he met for the first time his youngest child Anna Mary, then five-years old. It must have been both an awkward and sad meeting for them both with Mary dead and with nothing to link them except kinship. Agnes was also there and as a young woman of eighteen she was able to help smooth things. Both Thomas and William were away at school. Livingstone found his sisters were in good health but his mother was ailing.

Livingstone received the news from Agnes that Robert had caught a ship to Boston and joined up with the Union Army in January 1864. He told her he enrolled as Rupert Vincent of Company H, Third New Hampshire Regiment, 10th Army Corps, giving his age as twenty-one although he was in fact only seventeen. Livingstone received a letter from Robert in October 1864 where he suggested that he had been kidnapped after going to bed one night on ship when they were in Boston port and woke up to find himself enlisted into the Union Army. He also stated that he had changed his name to protect his father from any embarrassment. His enlistment documents actually show he was enlisted on 22 January 1864, in New Hampshire, as Rupert Vincent. At the time of enlisting his documents show that he was conscious and sober, five feet seven inches high with a dark complexion and hazel eyes.

For a Christian the thought of his son actively engaged in taking life was a complete anathema to Livingstone's belief and faith. He wrote to Kirk saying, 'My heart is rather sore—that bad boy (Robert) has got into the American Army and will be made manure of, for those bloody fields.'[10] Livingstone's comment was only too prescient.

Livingstone was also worried about his other son Thomas who lived with his ageing aunts in Hamilton. Thomas had caught measles and this was complicated by his liver failing so that, 'he passed frightful quantities of blood as if mixed with soot.'[11] However, these concerns did not stop Livingstone accepting an invitation from the Duke of Argyll[12] to visit the Highlands in August 1864. Together they visited Staffa, Iona, Mull and Livingstone's ancestral home on the Island of Ulva in the Hebrides, as the Duke owned it. It was a happy and pleasant trip and the traditional Scottish hospitality did much to revive Livingstone after his cold reception in London. He arrived back in Hamilton at the beginning of September 1864 reinvigorated. He was pleased to find young Thomas recovered from his measles and had gone off with Anna Mary to stay with the family of James Young.[13]

Despite the apparent failure of the Zambezi Expedition, Livingstone was still sought after company. His continued to promulgate his message about the need to actively stamp out slavery and his message resonated at the highest levels of Government. Livingstone later met the Prime Minister, the elderly Lord Palmerston and his wife and he found them greatly interested in his work and thoughts on how best to abolish slavery. At this stage of his political career, Lord Palmerston had firmly taken the political course that slavery in all its forms must be stopped.[14]

Livingstone gave a public address to 2,500 people to the British Association for the Advancement of Science at their annual meeting in Bath on 16 September 1864. It was one of the few public addresses that he gave during his time back in Britain and he later described it to Oswell as a 'dreadful ordeal'.[15] What was interesting about this event was the fact he was not the main act as Burton and Speke were programmed to debate the source of the Nile. Unfortunately Speke died the day before in what promised to be a bitter debate, in tragic circumstances after he shot himself in a hunting accident. The interest in both the source of the Nile and the two protagonists—and not Livingstone—in what *The Times* referred to as 'a gladiatorial exhibition'[16] had attracted nearly 1,500 fee-paying attendees to the meeting. Despite his warning from the Foreign Secretary, Livingstone took the opportunity to once more criticise the Portuguese activities in Central Africa.

9.2 Newstead Abbey

Livingstone had received a number of invitations to stay at Newstead Abbey in Nottinghamshire as the guest of Mr and Mrs William Frederick Webb. Livingstone had first met Webb when he had come to South Africa on a hunting trip during Livingstone's missionary days. After turning down the invitation several times Livingstone eventually agreed and in September 1864 he and his daughter Agnes moved to Newstead Abbey where they spent eight enjoyable months. During that time his other children Thomas and William also visited. Livingstone found the Webbs generous and kind hosts, describing them as 'uncommonly nice people.'[17]

Livingstone had intended to write a pamphlet on Portuguese policies and activities in central Africa and what Britain could do to stop the slave trade by establishing profitable trading enterprises. He turned down an 'immense' number of invitations to start on this project.[18] As he slowly started to develop the pamphlet he realised it would be better if he turned it into another book and it was during his stay at Newstead Abbey that Livingstone found time and the peace to write, *Narrative of an Expedition to the Zambesi and its Tributaries*.[19]

Livingstone did not enjoy writing and had to apply himself laboriously to the task each day. Indeed, after the publication of his first book and bestseller, he had colourfully declared that he would rather walk across Africa again than write another. He had his own journals to base his new book and he also had access to Charles Livingstone's journals. Charles had found being a pastor in Massachusetts unfulfilling and had returned to England to assist Livingstone write his book. Charles was subsequently named as a co-author although the work was mainly Livingstone's. The ownership of the publishing rights was split to reflect this relative effort; a memorandum of agreement was signed between Livingstone and Charles whereby the latter was given full and sole publishing rights within the United States and entitled to all profits derived only in that country, while

Livingstone and his publisher, John Murray, had the right to determine the title, and how best to secure copyright in both the United Kingdom and the United States.[20]

Livingstone had both his daughter Agnes and Mrs Webb to assist him by undertaking secretarial duties. From Livingstone's letters it seems he found Agnes to have been a very capable assistant. He was also fortunate that he had a patient and capable publisher in John Murray and other friends, such as Oswell and Kirk, to review his book, confirm details and make additions. In the case of Kirk, Livingstone often sought his confirmation on minutiae. Livingstone's grasp of botany, as in many other fields, was at times extraordinary. For example in March 1865 he wrote to Kirk. 'What do you call the tree from which the bark cloth is made?—and the Molompi—would it be sufficient to say a *Ptero carpus*—the *vallis nerid*? For the Lake plant of which they make salt and is the *Sarsaparilla* of the hills known.'[21] With this kind of support Livingstone was able to complete his 600-page book in five months.

Webb's daughter Alice had the opportunity to closely observe Livingstone during his extended stay and in 1913 she published an account of Livingstone writing 'he was always extremely neat and careful in his appearance although even apart from his predilection for his gold banded cap, there was nothing in the least clerical about his dress.'[22]

Notwithstanding his discussions with the Prime Minister, Livingstone continued to be preoccupied with the controversy about his discoveries and the role of missionary work in Africa. Livingstone had already refuted the Portuguese claims about who made the first discovery of the Zambezi and other lakes and rivers in the Shire area in 1862. Livingstone's widely reported attack on the Portuguese at the British Association for the Advancement of Science stirred the Portuguese up again and they responded by publishing a pamphlet in English refuting his specific claim to have been the first European to have made a trans-African crossing and discovery of Lake Nyassa. To make things worse, Burton chimed in and supported the Portuguese claim. Burton also launched his own attack on the value of missionary endeavour in Africa—it was quickly getting nasty.

Amongst all the controversies one irritating incident did annoy Livingstone and that was Thomas Baines's public demand that Livingstone admit that he had been dismissed unfairly from the Zambezi Expedition. Baines claimed, with some justification, that Charles Livingstone had overly influenced his brother. Livingstone would not countenance a public statement much less an apology, but was sufficiently concerned to write to Kirk seeking his support. In his letter Livingstone reiterated the reasons for the dismissal of Baines.

Baines demands that I should say that I dismissed him without hearing and was led by the evidence of my brother alone. As that is not true, I shall not tell a lie. I myself saw that the goods were gone and asked him whither. He offered to pay for them and begged to be allowed to stay with us without salary—this was to myself.[23]

In October 1864 Charles Livingstone was appointed Her Majesty's Consul at Fernando Po to replace Burton who had left to take up another Government position. Murchison had initially encouraged Livingstone to apply for the consulship, but Livingstone had proposed Charles instead.[24] In 1867 Lord Stanley added to Charles's area of responsibility 'the Bights of Benin and Biafra', including 'the mouths of the Niger'.[25] That left only Kirk to secure a meaningful role and Livingstone proved that he was loyal friend of Kirk by continuing to encourage him to apply for consulate positions for which he thought Kirk was eminently suited.

In November 1864, during a visit to Newstead Abbey, Murchison raised the possibility with Livingstone that he might be asked to determine the watershed of the Nile. The true source of the Nile remained unresolved in many people's minds, particularly following the cancellation of the debate between Burton and Speke. Livingstone was interested, but prevaricated. Discussions continued and in early 1865 Murchison, in his capacity as President of the Royal Geographic Society, formally wrote to Livingstone to request him to undertake the task. To make it more attractive he offered Livingstone £500 to help underwrite the cost of the expedition.

Livingstone was interested to take the role, but he was worried about the focus on proving a single geographical feature. He did want to solve the mystery, but he also wanted to make a lasting improvement to the tribes around Lake Nyassa by continuing to look for ways to open up the territory.[26] In another letter to James Young he offers further insight into his thinking at this time. The first point he makes is that he still saw himself as needing to complete important missionary work. He also did not want to be the leader of another large expedition as he recognised he was ill-suited to the task. 'It was a great affliction to be a "skipper" but I had to be or let B [Bedingfeld] ride roughshod over us all.'[27] Livingstone was happy to explore with just his Africans as his companions.

It was in December 1864 that the Government first reached out to Livingstone to see what could be done for him and his family. The Prime Minister dispatched Mr Haywood QC to Newstead Abbey to meet Livingstone. Livingstone responded by asking that free access to the African highlands by the Zambezi and Shire rivers be formally ratified by treaty with Portugal. He characteristically chose not to ask for any favours for himself, or more importantly, his family. It was a decision that he and his family later regretted.[28]

In January 1865 Livingstone received word from the Adjutant of Robert's Regiment in the United States that Robert was not left either dead or wounded on 7 October during a skirmish the day before the Battle of Richmond. The Adjutant advised that they were negotiating to have him exchanged for a Confederate prisoner.[29] Robert was in fact wounded and had been captured in the Battle of Darbytown and New Market Roads and was in a prisoner-of-war camp at Salisbury, North Carolina.[30] Livingstone was even then thinking of taking Robert with him on his next trip if his release could be secured.[31]

On 18 May 1865 Livingstone was given an opportunity to be interviewed by a House of Commons select committee investigating the British policy of supporting the establishment of trading posts and missions on the west coast of Africa. The key question was whether the idea that Christianity, commerce and civilisation really did work? Livingstone, the great explorer, 'was rather nervous and confused'[32] and he thought he had performed poorly in front of the committee,[33] but in the event the Government did continue to support these colonising efforts. However, it was also clear that the abolishment of slavery was not a universally held view across Government as some senior civil servants thought it was the wrong policy. Clearly the work of eradicating slavery, in all forms, was destined to take some time.

By this time Livingstone had decided to accept Murchison's challenge to resolve the issue of the source of the Nile. Murchison was delighted and keen for Livingstone to also explore the Rovuma river as part of this next expedition.

He was also offered a new consulship by the Foreign Office. This time he would be honorary consul 'to the Territories of the African Kings and chiefs in the Interior of Africa.' Being an honorary position he received a one off payment of £500 but would receive no salary or pension. He was further requested that his new expedition keep clear of any territory that either was or was claimed by Portugal.[34]

9.3 Preparations for a Return to Africa

Speke was the first European to sight Lake Victoria when in 1858 he reached its southern shore. He and Burton had together set out to explore central Africa and locate the great Lakes. Burton was not with Speke when he stumbled upon Lake Victoria, as Burton was ill and slowly recovering well to the south on the banks of Lake Tanganyika. When Speke saw a 'vast expanse of open water' he immediately thought he had at long last found the true source of the Nile. In celebration Speke named the lake after Queen Victoria. However, when Burton received news of Speke's discovery and heard of his subsequent declaration of Lake Victoria as being the source of the Nile, he was outraged. Burton, a brittle and antagonistic character, regarded this as still unproven.

One of the reasons for the debate was Speke's inability to confirm Lake Victoria as the source. This was because most of Burton and Speke's survey equipment had been lost by the time Speke made his 'discovery'. This resulted in Speke being unable to take vital observations about the height, and other important geographical observations. A very public quarrel ensued between Speke and Burton that not only resulted in intense debate within the scientific community, but also increased the interest of other explorers to confirm—or refute—Speke's claim.

Speke was subsequently commissioned by the Royal Geographical Society to lead another expedition, this time with James Augustus Grant, to prove conclusively the Nile's source. Speke had to leave Grant behind *enroute* to the lake because he was incapable of marching due to a buruli ulcer[35] on his leg that laid him up for several months. Speke reached Lake Victoria on 28 July 1862. He then travelled around the west side of the lake and followed it to the north side and stumbled upon a large river, later identified as the White Nile, flowing out Lake Victoria. The river flowed over some major falls, which he named Ripon Falls after George Robinson, 1st Marquis of Ripon. Speke subsequently travelled overland to Gondokoro in Southern Sudan, where he met Samuel Baker and his wife. Together they continued on to Khartoum, from where in 1863 Speke sent his famous telegram to the Royal Geographical Society: 'The Nile is settled.'[36] However, the controversy did not die as Burton claimed that Speke's expedition did not resolve the issue conclusively, because he had not followed the White Nile from the place it flowed out of Lake Victoria to Gondokoro, so that they could not be sure they were the same river.

The debate around the source continued to rage. Burton, Speke and Baker[37] had between them identified either Lake Albert or Lake Victoria as the source of the Nile and this formed the background to Livingstone's own Royal Geographic Society supported expedition. Livingstone firmly believed the source of the Nile was further south. This is not as unreasonable as it sounds as Livingstone had as good an understanding of the topography and water systems in that part of Africa as anyone. He would have no doubt been aware that all lakes need tributaries, even if he had not visited Lake Victoria. In fact Lake Victoria receives most of its water from numerous streams and rivers and the largest is the Kagera river, the mouth of which lies on the lake's western shore. The Kagera River is formed by the confluence of the Ruvuvu and the Nyabarongo, close to the northern-most point of Lake Tanganyika and although Livingstone did not know it at the time, it was an area that Livingstone had already visited. It did not help that Speke, when travelling around the western side of Lake Victoria, spent most of the time inland out of sight of the lake. This is an important fact that should have been noted more carefully by Speke and his sponsors, for if Speke had followed the shoreline, he would have seen the sizeable Kagera River, which is now estimated to provide twenty-eight per cent of Lake Victoria's net outflow.[38] With the benefit of hindsight, Speke's failure to recognise the Kagera River as a major tributary was as big a mistake as Livingstone made in not following the course of the Zambezi River and missing the discovery the Kebrabassa Rapids on his way to Quelimane in 1856. Today, the exact source of the Nile is still being determined.[39]

Another appealing aspect of this expedition for Livingstone was that he would continue to be involved in opening up the area around Lake Nyassa, accessing the region by either the Zambezi or Rovuma rivers. He saw the establishment of a settlement in central Africa, out of the jurisdiction of the Portuguese, as the only effective way of ending the East African slave trade. The thought of achieving both these goals for Livingstone was too tempting.

Livingstone returned to London in April 1865 to start preparations for the printing of *The Zambesi and its Tributaries*. He also worked feverishly to check facts, incorporate comments and agree punctuation in his book from Oswell, Kirk, Charles Livingstone and others and to finalise maps and illustrations with Arrowsmith and other people from Murray & Co. who were involved in publishing his book.

Finally, on 13 May 1865 a relieved Livingstone wrote to Kirk and informed him that he planned to take his draft manuscript to Murray in the following week.[40] While the draft was ready for printing the maps and illustrations could not be engraved in time and James Murray made a commercial decision to put off publishing the book until November 1865 as there was a general election looming and the canny publisher wanted to launch the book after the election.[41] It was disappointing for everyone involved who had been working to a tight deadline, but it did give Livingstone some quiet moments that he enjoyed with his children. He also joked with Oswell that he was ageing—grey and wrinkled. When a barber offered to dye his hair for 10s. 6d., he told Oswell 'I must be very good tempered for I did not fight him.'[42] But beneath the levity, Livingstone was anxious to get on with his explorations, as he knew he would not always have the strength and energy to undertake these tasks.

In May 1865 two UMCA missionaries, Waller and Alington, called on Livingstone while he was in London. Alington had been one of Bishop Tozer's first volunteers for his UMCA mission and was familiar with the country around Lake Nyassa that Livingstone was hoping to explore further on his next expedition. He was keen to join Livingstone so that he might be able to continue his missionary work; he pressed his case telling him that he spoke some Zulu and he was prepared to pay his own expenses. However, Livingstone was wary—the unpleasant experience of dealing with Captain Bedingfeld and other Europeans during the Zambezi Expedition was still too raw and in the end Livingstone thought that Alington was a good person, but still too inexperienced. He wrote afterwards to Kirk saying, 'I would rather go alone than take anyone untried.'[43]

In May 1865 Livingstone's mother had a bad attack of bronchitis that caused her to lose her strength and her mind started wandering. She finally succumbed peacefully to her illness on 18 June 1865.[44] Livingstone had returned to Hamilton to be on hand, but on the day of her death he was in Oxford to give a lecture. On hearing the news he raced back to Hamilton to organise her funeral. With this tie now cut, Livingstone only had his children to care for and he focused on trying to be a good father to them.

In regard to Robert, having heard that he had been taken prisoner, Livingstone was gloomy about his prospects. 'We hear nothing of poor Bob and I fear never will. I think that it cannot be denied that the Confederates treated their prisoners cruelly. They had not rations enough for their soldiers, and we cannot wonder that they starved their prisoners.'[45] In fact Robert had died six months earlier on 5 December 1864 in Salisbury, North Carolina. His was a wasted life.

With regard to Agnes, Livingstone decided that he would place her in a Protestant English finishing school in Paris. The school was run by relations of French Protestant missionaries that Livingstone had got to know in South Africa. He also signed over care of her to his trusted friend Oswell to ensure that Agnes would be cared for in the event of his death.

Thomas and William were still in school. Thomas's illness still worried Livingstone, as it seemed his illness reappeared if he over-exerted himself. However, he was proud of the way Thomas was developing, particularly as he had shown artistic merit and won a school prize for drawing. Livingstone was thinking of setting him up in India as a tea planter where it was thought the warmer weather would suit him better. William was also doing well at school, achieving dux in six subjects, including German, French, Latin, geography and Scriptural knowledge.[46] Finally, there was his youngest child, Anna Mary, aged six, to think about. It was decided that she would remain in the care of his ageing aunts in Hamilton. Anna Mary later recorded her memories of her father.

> I remember once his taking me to a lovely wood where there is a cold, clear well far down in the shade. In and out among the crevices of that lovely spot grew common ferns in abundance. Papa took his walking-stick & dug up one & gave it to me. It was planted at home & flourishes luxuriantly to this day, & I am now fifteen years of age. And then I remember seeing Papa off for altogether & nodding to him as the train moved away. Little did I think as I retraced my steps from the station, that I had seen my noble father for the last time.[47]

Livingstone finally left the Webb family on 9 August 1865. They had grown very close in the months that Livingstone had stayed with them. Mrs Webb cried and Mr Webb told Livingstone that we 'wish you were coming instead of going away'. Livingstone himself was emotional at their parting.[48] He also said his goodbyes to his old friend Oswell and following a dinner with John Murray, Livingstone left London on 13 August 1865 before his book had been published even though he knew it contained some errors.[49] He and Agnes headed to Paris where Livingstone left her in the hands of his protestant missionary friends. It was another tearful parting for both Agnes and Livingstone. Hardening his heart he then continued overland to Marseilles and sailed for Africa via Bombay on 20 August 1865 on his final, deadly, explorations.[50]

CHAPTER 10

In Search of the Source
of the Nile

'The future is purchased by the present.'

Samuel Johnson

10.1 Honorary Government Consul

Livingstone was pleased to be away again at last, for he was a man with a country, but not a home. Ageing and with a family that was quickly growing up, he realised that despite the public acclamation, he was out of place back in Britain.

He arrived in Bombay on 11 September 1865, and on his arrival he heard that Colonel Robert Playfair,[1] the British Consul at Zanzibar, was ill and on his way to convalesce in England. It was widely speculated that Playfair would not return to his post. Livingstone hurriedly wrote to Kirk urging him to apply for the role, but the shy Kirk again failed to act upon Livingstone's recommendation. Livingstone planned to remain in India until November, and during that time he heard about the sad death of Rae, who had faithfully served the Zambezi Expedition in the role of ship engineer. Rae had since married, but died very suddenly of a perforated stomach in Zanzibar.[2]

Livingstone subsequently wrote four more letters to Kirk on the subject of securing a good post in Africa. His intentions in urging Kirk to apply were motivated both from an honourable purpose of wanting to see Kirk recognised by an appointment to a prestigious post, and also because he wanted to have Kirk based somewhere in Africa where he would be certain of his strong support. On 31 December 1865 Kirk was finally appointed to the position of Assistant Political Agent in Zanzibar. Livingstone was delighted.[3]

One of the first jobs Livingstone had to do in Bombay was to sell the *Lady Nyassa* to raise funds for his forthcoming expedition. Livingstone had paid £6,000 for the *Lady Nyassa* out of his own resources. Despite her obvious seaworthiness he was only able to sell it for paltry £2,300.[4] It was a loss that he could ill-afford and it was made worse when he invested some of this money in shares in an Indian bank that failed within a couple of years.

In November 1865 Oswell wrote to Livingstone to tell him about the response to the publication of *Narrative of an Expedition to the Zambesi and its Tributaries, etc.* by David & Charles Livingstone. Livingstone obtained copies of the *Saturday Review* and *Athenaeum Review* (published on 18 November 1865) and was generally pleased with the comments. As it transpired the book was not nearly as successful as *Missionary Travels,* which was a best seller, but it provided a much-needed additional source of income from royalties.

Livingstone had expected to stay in India until November 1865, but he did not leave until 2 January 1866.[5] By all accounts it was a pleasant stay, although Livingstone did get frustrated about the delay. During his time there he got to know Sir Bartle Frere, the Governor of Bombay well. Frere reciprocated the friendship by providing Livingstone with a free berth on the HMS *Thule* to Zanzibar. The HMS *Thule* was a Government vessel and Frere commissioned Livingstone to formally present the ship to the Sultan of Zanzibar as a gift from the Bombay Government and also to impress the Sultan about the importance of Livingstone's work. Frere's aim was to induce the Sultan to directly support Livingstone's expedition.[6]

Livingstone arrived in Zanzibar on 28 January 1866. The Sultan was delighted by the gift and gave Livingstone a very friendly reception, and as hoped, provided Livingstone with letters of recommendation to carry to the Arabs of the interior. The Sultan also provided Livingstone with a house. The building is still standing today; a three-storied building made of plastered brick, as was the fashion at the time. It is about a ten-minute walk from the old town and has a commanding view of the harbour. In short, it was an ideal place from which Livingstone could plan his expedition and during the period while he was stationed there, it was a hive of activity.

Livingstone's first task was to select a team to take with him. He had brought with him from Bombay nine African natives from the Nassick Christian Mission of the Church Missionary Society, and thirteen Indian sepoys,[7] comprising twelve soldiers and their leader, a Havildar.[8]

The Nassick Mission was located near Bombay to educate former African slave children. They were bought up as Christians and trained in useful industrial occupations such as carpentry, smithing, and brick-laying and as servants, so they could find work in India. Livingstone visited the mission and offered to take them home to their tribes, but most did not want to return to Africa. In the event nine Nassick children accompanied Livingstone. They were chosen both for their ability to speak the languages of areas he intended to pass through and their skills in carpentry and smith work that Livingstone thought would be useful if they had to build a boat to sail on lakes Nyassa and Tanganyika.[9]

Governor Frere was also instrumental in getting Indian sepoys to join his expedition. They were from the Bombay Marine Battalion and were chosen because they 'had roughed it already and can manage buffaloes.' Both groups were to turn out to be a huge disappointment to Livingstone.[10]

In December 1865 Livingstone wrote to William Sunley,[11] a sugar plantation owner and the British Consul of the Comoros, to ask for Johanna men; 'six good boatmen at Five dollars per month the sixth being headman to have more.'[12] The choice of the Johanna men from the Comoros Islands was something that Livingstone first pondered while in Britain because of their boating skills although he knew 'they are a poor lot to trust to.' His first experience of dealing with them was during the Zambezi Expedition and had been disappointing.[13] Sunley eventually recruited ten Johanna men and the HMS *Wasp* put into the Comoros and picked them up *en route* for Zanzibar. Livingstone knew three of these men; Musa had been a sailor on *Lady Nyassa* and Susi and Amoda had been employed to cut wood for HMS *Pioneer* in Shupanga, on the Zambezi.[14]

Livingstone also picked two Wa-Yao boys, Wekatani and Tshuma, later called Chuma, who were two freed slaves from the UMCA, and who had sailed with him on *Lady Nyassa* on the perilous voyage to Bombay. These two boys joined Susi and Amoda and twenty-four local Negroes.[15] Susi and Chuma were to earn international recognition for the loyalty and dedication they showed to Livingstone on this, his final journey.

The next task was to outfit and provision the expedition. As always, finances for this expedition were minimal. The Foreign Office and the Royal Geographical Society each provided £500 and he received a further £1,000 from a private friend.[16] These finances were supplemented by £2,300 from the sale of the *Lady Nyassa*. This meant that he had available, at most, £4,300 to outfit his expedition. It was not enough.

He also realised that he needed a good logistics base if he was to be successful in his mission. One of the depots he decided to establish in advance was at Ujiji, located on the shores of Lake Tanganyika. He had not been to Ujiji, but it was clearly an important trading town and so it was arranged that an Arab living in Ujiji, Thani bin Suelim, would look after Livingstone's supplies that included beads, cloth, flour, tea, coffee and very importantly, sugar.[17] Ujiji was to be frequently re-supplied over the next seven years that Livingstone was to remain in central Africa.

Livingstone wanted to see how different animals reacted to the bite of the tsetse fly and he bought six camels, three Indian buffaloes and a calf, two mules, and four donkeys,[18] to determine their respective levels of resistance. He also hoped to demonstrate that these animals might prove to be efficient beasts of burden. The decision to take these animals shows how progressive Livingstone's thinking was at this time, in comparison with other explorers who were largely focused on just making new discoveries—and surviving—in this harsh continent. Finally, for company, Livingstone bought along as a pet, a poodle dog called Chitané.

Livingstone was able to see first-hand in Stonetown, Zanzibar, what happened to the slaves that survived the march to the coast. Nearly all the slaves came to Zanzibar by way of Bagamoyo, on the east African coast. The name Bagamoyo means 'lay down your heart' and got its name because it was the place where slaves would abandon all hope of freedom when they left the mainland, crammed onto dhows bound for Zanzibar.

Some slaves, particularly the weaker ones, or if there was a glut of slaves as happened occasionally, would not be shipped to Zanzibar. In these cases the Arabs simply handed over their worthless surplus to the Doe tribe north of Bagamoyo who enjoyed eating 'excess supplies'.

The Omani Arabs controlled the Zanzibar slave market and it was a busy place. It became a major market in 1811 and did not close until 1873. During this time it was the hub of the slave trade for all of East Africa and it has been estimated that more than one million slaves passed through this market. Visiting the slave market Livingstone noted that between 70 and 300 slaves were sold on a market day. The main buyers were 'Northern Arabs and Persians'[19] from the Seychelles, Mauritius, Oman and Persia although there were also Europeans buyers wanting slaves to work on their plantations in the Indian Ocean islands. They paid between seven to twenty dollars per slave. Livingstone could see that the slaves were largely Mañanja but also included people from other tribes from the Lake Nyassa area and he felt 'sick at heart to think of it, and raises bitter regret that we did not work out our experiment of cutting up slaving at its source.'[20]

When Livingstone was resident in Zanzibar, the dhows would sail straight into Stonetown and off-load their human cargo directly into fifteen underground chambers hewn out of the rock. The chambers were low, dark, dank, and for the newly arrived slaves, it must have been a terrifying place. They huddled together for warmth and out of fear. Seawater was able to flow through the chambers at high tide and this washed out all the human excrement.

Slaves were separated on arrival; men were isolated from women and children, regardless of the fact they may be members of the same family. All were chained and in the cramped cells, many succumbed to illness, exhaustion or died from heartbreak. A 'strong' slave would still be in reasonable physical condition after three or more days of surviving these foul conditions.

When it came to market day, the surviving slaves were washed and often the men would have their skin oiled while the women would be dressed in attractive clothes, and may even be adorned with necklaces and bracelets, to increase their sale value. They would be lined up from the smallest to the tallest and paraded through the market, while the owners announced their price. A prospective buyer would be encouraged to physically inspect the slave, looking at teeth, eyes, ears and any other part of the anatomy they wanted to examine.

If the owner was more vicious he may order selected slaves to be tied up to a large tree in the centre of the market and whipped in a bestial display of the slave's strength and ability to withstand pain. If a slave did not cry out then the person would normally fetch a higher price on the basis that they could be worked harder. The whipping could be severe as whips were made out of cattle hide or a tail of a stingray and could result in awful wounds.

There was no room for any form of modesty as the slaves were paraded and inspected, just like cattle. Children were similarly treated and if a purchaser bought a number of adult slaves then the seller would frequently throw a number of children in for free. In this way the children would be separated from their families. After all this degradation the newly acquired slave would be loaded onto dhows and ships and transported to their new homes, in far-away places, to work on plantations or in the houses of their new owners.

It was heart-wrenching for a person like Livingstone to witness the callousness and brutality of slave market day.

On 19 March 1866, after a six-week stay in Zanzibar, Livingstone was ready to set out to discover the source of the Nile on his third and final African journey. For protection and status, he had been appointed British Consul and the Sultan of Zanzibar had further furnished him with a signed document calling on any subject of his to render any assistance that Livingstone might need. With him were a large party of sixty men and boys, including a number of porters recruited locally, and no Europeans.[21] He was fifty-two years old.

10.2 Back to Lake Nyassa

Livingstone knew that he would need to take careful notes of the geography and his route if he was to successfully determine the source of the Nile. The instruments that he took were surprisingly extensive for they included a prismatic compass, meridian instruments, poles clinometer, thermometer, universal sun-dial and compass, field glasses, telescope, brass microscope, mapping ruler, clock and a log book.

Livingstone's plan was to go up Rovuma River, north of the Portuguese area of influence, and travel to Lake Nyassa. One of his reasons for retracing his steps to Lake Nyassa was that he had not had time previously to properly explore the area to the north of the lake because the activities of the marauding Mazitu. A key question that he wanted to resolve was to see if a river linked Lake Nyassa and another lake that lay about 220 miles to the northwest—Lake Tanganyika.

To achieve this he planned to establish an initial supply depot at Ndonde near the coast and then head westwards from the Rovuma river[22] first to Bemba, and then continue west.[23] He clearly thought this is where he would find the source of the Nile.

Livingstone and his party and stores boarded the HMS *Penguin*, under command of Lieutenant Garforth, and they arrived off the mouth of the Rovuma River on 22 March 1866. They immediately ran into difficulties entering the river mouth as the bar and shoals had moved since Livingstone was last there. They also realised the surrounding country was too broken and thick with vegetation for the camels to pass and it was decided it was safer to sail twenty-five miles north to Mikindani Bay,[24] a very small settlement, and unload there. Livingstone hired a house there at a cost of four dollars per month while he prepared for his departure into the interior.[25] His animals had been transported on an Arab dhow and had suffered on the voyage. It was not until 4 April 1866 that they were all landed, packed and ready to depart into the interior.

Livingstone had given the responsibility of looking after the animals to the Indian Sepoys but it was immediately obvious they had had no idea of animal husbandry as they soon began maltreating them. Livingstone found them ill-fed, under watered and overloaded with stores. As often happens in a new and unfamiliar situation, in the *mêlée* of loading up animals, a buffalo got free and immediately gored one of the donkeys so badly that it had to be destroyed.[26] It was a sobering start to the journey.

They set out for the Rovuma River in the south and then headed north towards Mtarika, in the Wa-Yao country. Chuma and Wekatani were both Wa-Yao and this may have influenced Livingstone in deciding to take this route. He wrote of his exhilaration of being once more back in Africa exploring. 'The mere animal pleasure of travelling in a wild unexplored country is very great. When on lands of a couple of thousand feet elevation, brisk exercise imparts elasticity to the muscles, fresh and healthy blood circulates through the brain, the mind works well, the eye is clear, the step is firm, and a day's exertion always makes the evening's repose thoroughly enjoyable.'[27] Unfortunately all too soon Livingstone's legendary health and robustness would begin to fade.

On reaching the river they turned and followed its course in a north-westerly direction. They soon plunged into thick, dripping forests, and began to gradually climb on a continual basis until they got to within fifty miles of Lake Nyassa. The trees were spaced closely together, it was damp and rough underfoot and creepers hung down catching any protruding objects. In the dim light they blundered along small trails until occasionally they happened upon a small village hacked out of the forest. Livingstone made a practice of treating the natives fairly on being invited to enter a village and normally presented a fathom, or six feet of calico to the headman, who usually reciprocated with chickens and a basket of rice or maize.[28]

They marched for eighty miles through this dark forest until it slowly became less dense as they climbed higher. After two hundred miles the land opened up into undulating country that offered views of the surrounding hills and mountains.[29] But it was slow progress and Livingstone estimated they were only averaging four miles a day, in a straight line. One reason was his guide, Ali, would lead the party on a zigzag course, often just so he could meet his friends in different villages. The other reason was the sepoy's who dawdled along and would, when given a chance, sit down to smoke and eat.[30]

One of the delights of this early stage of the journey was the presence of Livingstone's poodle dog Chitané that he had brought along as company. He loved the little fellow, and wrote, 'He had more go in him than a hundred dogs of the country, took charge of the whole line of march, ran to see the first man in the line, and then back to the last, and barked to hasten him up'.[31] Unfortunately, much to Livingstone's sadness, his pet was later drowned in a river when they were travelling between lakes Nyassa and Tanganyika.

Livingstone noticed that animals seemed to be able to survive the incessant tsetse fly attacks. The donkeys and the mules did not seem to get bitten often whereas the camels and buffaloes where constantly bitten, but remained unaffected. However, he noted with increasing alarm that the Sepoys continued to overload the animals and cruelly prodded them with sharp sticks until they gouged bloody holes in their bodies. They also frequently failed to feed or water them and within a month of setting out two camels and one buffalo were dead. The ill treatment continued and despite Livingstone's continued protestations to the sepoys, on the 8 May 1866, it was all that Livingstone could do but note, 'One mule is very ill, one buffalo drowsy and exhausted, one camel a mere skeleton from bad sores, and another has a small hole at the point of the pelvis which sticks out at the side. I suspect that this was made maliciously, for he came from the field bleeding profusely.'[32]

Livingstone then made a further mistake. They were passing through land afflicted with drought and food was becoming scarce. He decided to leave the animals with the sepoys and the Nassick boys under command of the Havildar so that they might give the animals a rest while he and the remainder of the party, comprising the Johanna men and his twenty-four carriers, made a forced march to Mtarika in order to obtain food. He made this decision based on his kindness towards animals, but it was most unfortunate. The Havildar simply could not control the sepoys or the Nassick boys without Livingstone around.

When one of the Nassick boys, Abraham, later caught up with Livingstone he told him that a second buffalo was dead, and a camel and a mule had been left behind ill.[33] The truth about the animals was much worse as Livingstone later discovered; the camel had been bludgeoned to death by the sepoys using the butt-end of their muskets. This was followed in short order by the death of a third buffalo and its calf.

Abraham also told Livingstone that the sepoys had resolved to come no further. The maltreatment of the animals incensed Livingstone who hated seeing cruelty inflicted, be it on man or beast and this threatened mutiny forced Livingstone into sending a strongly worded message back to the Havildar that he was aware of 'their disobedience, unwillingness, and skulking' and that he would release them after he received formal evidence from the Havildar about the actions of him and his sepoys.[34] The prospect of being charged with disobedience spurred an immediate response and the sepoys and some of the Nassick negroes progressively caught up with Livingstone's party as they marched slowly towards Mtarika. However, the shortage of food was becoming a very real problem and many of the carriers could only walk for an hour and half, before having to take long rests because they were so weak with hunger. Livingstone remonstrated with the carriers, warning them that they would not receive their wages—about two feet of calico per day—if they made no progress. Such was the seriousness of the situation that one Nassick boy, Richard, became ill and fell behind and later died.

To make matters worse they had to march past horrific sights from the slave trade; prostrated women who had been bayonetted because they could not keep up or emaciated and sick slaves left to die for lack of food, still tied together with their slave collars—or slave taming sticks—as they were otherwise known. Livingstone described how each of these sticks was six or seven feet long and had an iron rod that was riveted at each end around the throat of a slave. These taming sticks weighted between thirty and forty pounds and often the slaves were required to carry a load on their heads as well. Occasionally they came across slaves wearing crude iron masks with a gag. This brutal treatment was reserved for the most recalcitrant of slaves who had offended the slave master.

It was sobering for all of them. Often Livingstone's party stumbled upon slaving parties and when they heard there was an Englishman present they would abruptly turn away in order to avoid meeting him. It depressed Livingstone to see how denuded the countryside was of people; one Arab party he met had about 800 slaves that were being driven to the coast.[35]

The other threat was the Mazitu who continually ranged across the country murdering and stealing. They had become so feared that few would venture far from their village without adequate protection. In several cases, Livingstone came across villages fully barricaded and would only be admitted after much parlay and careful consideration by the natives.

On 11 June 1866 while still about two week's march to Mtarika, Livingstone's native carriers suddenly announced they would go no further. The reason was they believed they were at risk of being captured for slaves when Livingstone later released them, and they tried to return to their villages. Livingstone duly paid them off and put the word out to the locals that he would pay them to transport his supplies and equipment.

Despite all of these difficulties Livingstone was continuing take lunar observations and observing fauna and flora, customs and practices. He wrote about everything; the widespread practice of filing of teeth into points, the strong resemblance of the tattoos of the people of the Upper Makondé area to old Egyptian drawings, and how fire was made with sticks from wild fig-trees and how natives transported coals in dried balls of elephant dung.

The party straggled on. One sepoy was robbed of all his clothes when he lay down for a rest and promptly fell asleep while a Nassick boy had his bundle containing about 240 yards of cloth stolen while he too slumbered. Livingstone patiently put up with these setbacks warning his party not to straggle, as there were many murderers, slavers and thieves about. Eventually, on 1 July 1866, they reached Mtarika. This was a Wa-Yao market town on the banks of the Rovuma. Here they were able to buy food, but it was at vastly inflated prices. The reason was the townsfolk were wealthy from trading with the slavers who passed through this area.

On 5 July 1866 Livingstone turned his party to the south-west and headed for the town of Mataka, a march of about eight days. It was tough going and Livingstone recorded crossing fifteen streams, varying in width from one to ten yards, in one day's march of six hours.[36] Food continued to be in short supply because of the widespread drought and as they progressed the party became increasing strung out, with the sepoys, as usual, lagging. When Livingstone heard that two sepoys had deliberately hung back after leaving Mtarika so that they could cajole strangers into carrying their loads, he waited for them to come up and then gave them a good thrashing with his cane.[37] As satisfying as it was, Livingstone later wrote that he felt he had degraded himself by his actions.

They continued their weary march and on the outskirts of Mataka on 14 July 1866, Livingstone met a large slaving party owned by an Arab slaver, Sef Rupia, who generously presented Livingstone with an ox, a bag of flour and some cooked meat. He had heard of the impending arrival of this strange party and gently chided Livingstone about his efforts to end slaving.[38] Livingstone gladly accepted the gifts and his offer to escort him into Mataka, which was duly accomplished with much gunfire to signal their arrival. His acceptance of their offer showed how dire his situation had become.

The town was situated in a high valley, some 2,700 feet above sea level. There were over 1,000 houses and the town was surrounded by a number of neighbouring villages. Next morning Livingstone met the Wa-Yao chief who treated Livingstone and his party generously, providing them with a house and making sure they were able to buy food, and frequently supplying them with cooked food. The sudden supply of rich food caused some illness among his party with Livingstone noting he had not eaten any meat in over two months except a chicken and some turtle-doves and guinea fowl that he had shot.[39]

It was while they were in Mataka that Livingstone finally decided to dispense with the services of the sepoys as they 'have neither the spirit nor pluck as compared with the Africans.'[40] On 20 May 1866, he ordered the Havildar to formally report to him about the disobedience of the sepoys as he intended sending a report to Frere, Governor of Bombay so that they would be charged with insubordination on their return to India. Livingstone noted that they 'left their duty whenever I was out of sight, sat down and smoked and ate in the march. Their sickness was not fever but eating too much, and vomiting'.[41] They were paid off and sent back to Zanzibar with the exception of the Havildar who wanted to stay on, evidently fearing the consequences of returning to India. It had been a failure of culture and understanding.

After two weeks rest they set off again on 29 July 1866 for Lake Nyassa and continued to climb up through rich mountainous country that was sparsely covered with small trees. Livingstone noted with interest that there was no tsetse fly over 1,600 feet above sea. They were soon passing through villages at 3,400 feet above sea level. They travelled without haste or difficulty, although the ground was broken with mica schist and other igneous rocks and they were constantly wet from having to forge numerous mountain streams. It was cold and Livingstone had to wear his thickest flannels. Eventually they reached the shores of Lake Nyassa on 8 August 1866 and took in the inspiring view of the surrounding mountains, rising up to 4,000 feet above sea level. These mountains provided the watershed for the lake and the Rovuma River.[42]

Livingstone was delighted to be back on the shores of the lake and wrote in his journal. 'It was as if I had come back to an old home I never expected to see again; and pleasant to bathe in the delicious waters again, hear the roar of the sea, and dash in the rollers.'[43] It had been a difficult, trying trip, but well worth the effort.

Livingstone's next task was to arrange passage across to the western side of the lake, hopefully on an Arab dhow, but the Arabs were all too afraid that he had come there to put a stop to their slave trade. They were also worried that Livingstone would burn their boats. They quickly disappeared, taking with them the only two dhows that were used for ferrying slaves across the lake. The native chiefs suggested that the best path was for Livingstone to lead his party around the south end of the Lake Nyassa to Marenga. This settlement had been established by an influential Mohammedanised chief called Mponda.

The party set off in a leisurely fashion and were entertained and provided for at many villages as food was plentiful and their hosts generous. However, if they thought they could sit back and relax, they were quickly reminded of the dangers when a leopard entered a house next to theirs and killed a dog. The same leopard had previously attacked a man.

Livingstone took the opportunity during his rests to write letters and to update his large journal. Not for the first time he had to make up ink using the juice of berries and a fruit from a local creeper.[44] He normally used iron gall ink, and wrote on a small writing table that formed part of his baggage. When the iron gall ink ran out he experimented with making inks from various plants. One extract he found useful was derived from the seeds of the achiote tree. It now has a botanical name of *Bixa orellama* and is commonly used today in making products like lipsticks, margarine and popcorn.

On 13 September 1866, near Mount Gomé, Livingstone was able to glimpse the Shire, where he, Kirk and others had five years previously, battled in during the Zambezi Expedition. It had been for little apparent success. He rued the fact that his plans to open up the region around the lake to legitimate commerce had been cruelly thwarted by the Murchison Cataracts. He wrote bitterly:

Many hopes have been disappointed here. Far down on the right bank of the Zambezi lies her [Mary] whose death changed all my future prospects; and now, instead of a check being given to the slave-trade by lawful commerce on the Lake, slave-dhows prosper![45]

By mid-September 1866 they had progressed to a known slaving area and Livingstone visited the villages of first Mukate and then later Mponda, as they were two of three Wa-Yao chiefs who were conducting slave raids on a large scale. At each of these villages Livingstone quietly spread the word against slaving although he knew the intoxicating prospect of obtaining highly prized European goods from the Arabs meant nothing was likely to change in the short term.

They reached Lake Pamalombwe and Livingstone and his party boarded eight canoes and on 20 September 1866 they entered Mponda. One of Livingstone's Wa-Yao boys, Wikatani, a favourite of Bishop Mackenzie, soon recognised his brother and discovered he had another brother and one or two sisters living nearby. His father was dead and this was fortunate as it was his father who had sold Wikatani into slavery in 1861. Livingstone was pleased to allow him to stay, both for the obvious pleasure in helping reunite a family, but also to show the natives that the British treated people kindly.[46]

Livingstone set off westwards, with the purpose of crossing around Cape Maclear on Lake Nyassa and heading further inland. The Havildar continued to be useless, complaining of sore feet and at one stage standing by while two Wa-Yao porters helped themselves to the contents of their loads before disappearing into the forest with their stolen goods. Livingstone decided to search the Havildar's gun belt and pouch and discovered that the Havildar had been selling the ammunition, evidently to get some money to pay a slave trader to take him back to the coast. He was left behind in the next village to fend for himself.

They continued to push inland, across hills that rose above Lake Nyassa. This was Machinga country. While camped at a small village, the natives, curious to meet the Englishman, soon surrounded them. The chief, a one eyed man, was also there among the crowd although he did not announce himself. Livingstone, suspecting that the chief was incognito, asked loudly if the chief 'were an old woman, afraid to look at and welcome a stranger?'[47] This question was met with much laughter and the embarrassed chief stepped forward. His gentle and often humorous approach in situations like this did much to endear Livingstone to the natives. There were many instances of natives who recognised him from his previous visit to Lake Nyassa who came up and offered him food and presents as a mark of their friendship and respect.

Livingstone was soon approached by a brother of a chief, Marenga, located in a nearby village to ask him if he would go to his village so that Livingstone could treat the chief of a disfiguring and painful skin disease. Livingstone's medical skills became well known and he was frequently asked to help heal people as the word spread that he was a powerful medicine man. They reached the village of Marenga, which was situated at the eastern edge of the bottom of Lake Nyassa, after first forcing their way through a large bog, where black ooze rose over their boots. The chief came out to meet them, elegantly dressed in a 'red-figured silk shawl, attended by about ten court beauties'.[48] Livingstone was taken into a hut and treated the chief as best he could, using the medicines he carried around in a large medicine chest. Livingstone's skill as a doctor helped him to gain the confidence of the natives, which in turn made it easier to get access to tradable goods and food.

Unfortunately it was while the party was stationed at Marenga that Livingstone's first major troubles began. An Arab passed through the village and told one of Livingstone's Johanna men, Musa, that a marauding Mazitu party had slaughtered a slaving party of forty-four Arabs and their attendants. The Johanna men became increasingly scared by rumours that Mazitu were patrolling the country in front of them. Livingstone took Musa to speak to the chief who advised them that they would not pass any Mazitu in the direction they were taking, but the Johanna man was clearly spooked. He told Livingstone, 'I no can believe that man.' When Livingstone asked why Musa believed the Arab, but not the chief, he replied, 'I ask him to tell me true, and he say true, true.'[49]

Soon after, in their fear, they deserted Livingstone and made their way back to Zanzibar, taking their loads with them. Realising the seriousness of their actions, the Johanna men later used the story of the Mazitu raiding parties, embellishing it by describing how Livingstone and the others had been involved in a fight with the Mazitu and were subsequently slain.

Livingstone was never one to get too depressed by these types of occurrences—he had seen it all before—and he resolved to continue on with his plans. One of the benefits of not having the Johanna men around was that they were inveterate thieves, stealing from the natives with impunity and without remorse. Among the goods stolen from Livingstone he recorded that one man stole 'fifteen pounds of fine powder, another seven, another left with six table-cloths of about twenty-four'. It seemed that their leader, Musa Kammaals, was involved in all these connivances and consistently lied to Livingstone, saying 'I every day tell Johanna men no steal Doctor's things.'[50]

Livingstone did realise that without the boating skills of the cowardly Johanna men, he would not be able to build a boat to sail around the top end of Lake Nyassa, nor could he be able to cross over the middle of the lake. Instead he procured canoes while at Marenga and he and his diminished party, now consisting of Susi, Chumah, Simon and a few other Nassick boys, carefully paddled around the southern shores of Lake Nyassa to the village of Kimsusa, arriving there on 28 September 1866.

Livingstone was well received at Kimsusa, as he had visited the place previously. It was while resting and feasting on sheep and goat that an old woman approached Chumah and told him she was his aunt. Chuma was happy to meet her, but elected to remain with Livingstone.

The chief was particularly fond of beer and Livingstone was expected, and did partake, although he found the strong African drink difficult to digest because of its acidity.

On 6 October 1866 they departed Kimsusa, escorted by the chief and his vigorous young wives as he headed in a westerly direction towards Kirk's Range, which

Livingstone had named in his honour on their previous visit to Lake Nyassa.⁵¹ His escort party led him to another friendly chief after climbing about 2,200 feet above the lake, or about 4,000 feet above sea level.⁵² Rich, rolling country spread out before them and although it was the hottest time of the year, the air was 'delightfully clear, and delicious.'⁵³ The area had been largely denuded of trees and replaced with large patches of cultivated land. Livingstone thought that it only needed some hedgerows for the vista to look like somewhere in England.

This was Manganja land and they passed through many villages. Livingstone thought the people were more primitive; the men were dressed in ill-fitting goatskins and carried large knives made of iron and bows made out of bamboo. Some of these bows were unusually long and Livingstone measured one along the bowstring and discovered it was six feet four inches long. Many of the women were tattooed with a crisscross pattern on their chests and arms, and in some cases, had cuts all over their bodies. Despite their appearances, they were generous with their food. As usual, Livingstone took the opportunity to talk about teachings from the Bible, the power of the Christian God and the evils of slavery. He was listened to patiently but without reward.

By mid-October 1866 he decided they needed to move north, but because of his men's fear of the Mazitu, he struck out in a north-westerly direction so that they would avoid any chance of coming into contact with them. They soon crossed over the Lilongwe and entered a forest, with the majority of it being comprised of gum-copal⁵⁴ and bark-cloth trees and rhododendrons. They came across a herd of elephants knocking down trees. They also saw eland, buffalo and Livingstone shot a hartebeest. It was while they were roasting it that they heard a nearby village was in full flight from a Mazitu war party. Soon after another large crowd of panic stricken villagers came surging by, seeking to hide themselves in the nearby ranges. Livingstone coolly decided to follow them, but only after they had finished eating and they took up a defensive position on the bottom slopes of the range and waited for the Mazitu to arrive, determined to beat them off if they could. Fortunately a trial of strength was not required as the marauding Mazitu headed south.

They continued picking their way north, passing from one village to the next. There was always something for Livingstone to comment on in his diary, whether it was the peculiarity of the language, descriptions of teeth filing or social customs, such as the respectful clapping of hands when wanting to pass someone or to thank them. As always Livingstone and his party were a curiosity. They were also surprised at the industriousness of the people, who carefully cultivated large areas, hoeing, and burning weeds and long grasses to fertilise the land. He noticed that fig trees were usually planted around the villages as they provided shade and medicine was made from the tender roots. Livingstone continued taking his detailed measurements. For example, on 29 October 1866, he recorded, 'The first rain—a thunder shower—fell in the afternoon, air in shade before it 92°; wet bulb 74°. At noon the soil in the sun was 140°, perhaps more, but I was afraid of bursting the thermometer, as it was graduated only a few degrees above that.'[55]

On the 30 October 1866, while staying in the village of Makosa, black slave traders from Tete on the east African coast appeared wanting to buy slaves. Livingstone dryly noted that their return signalled the return of vermin, particularly human ticks that seemed to always accompany all Arab and Swahili slaving parties.

By early November 1866 they had passed into land that was being continually ravished by the Mazitu. Headmen warned Livingstone about proceeding, but he was indefatigable. However, they quickly saw the effects of fear—villages surrounded by large stockades. In one ruined village he noted that the stockade was made of stout trees that had enabled the villages to successfully defend themselves from a Mazitu siege but had later been destroyed by elephants when the inhabitants had temporarily abandoned the village. Elephants were a real pest and one old fellow they met had twenty-seven rings of elephant skin tied around his arm, signifying that he killed them all single-handedly, using nothing but a spear.[56]

They pressed on, avoiding parties of Mazitu, and putting their faith in God. The rains began to come more frequently and they sewed up a large calico tent as protection. They also found it difficult to hire carriers, either because they were unwilling or in most cases, demanded exorbitant wages. Livingstone's practical response was normally to have his men ferry their supplies forward in packets to the next village, while leaving someone behind to guard what remained to be collected. It was slow, hot work but it was an effective solution to their problem.

Livingstone had a deep knowledge of geology and the land they were passing through piqued his interest. He described the land thus:

> The mountains on each side are gently rounded, and, as usual, covered over with tree foliage, except for where the red soil is exposed by recent grass-burnings. Quartz rocks jut out, and much drift of that material has been carried down by the gullies into the bottom. These gullies being in compact clay, the water has but little power of erosion, so they are worn deep but narrow. Some fragments of titaniferous iron ore, with haematite changed by heat, and magnetic, lay in the gully, which had worn itself a channel on the north side of the village.[57]

In this area of war, food was scarce and one of his weakened attendants, Simon, fell sick again, this time with blisters that erupted into pimples when goat's fat was rubbed onto the surface. This forced Livingstone to redistribute the supplies so that some of his other followers were each carrying up to fifty-pound loads. Despite their poor situation, Livingstone noted in this diary what pleasant country they were passing through:

> The scenery of the valley is lovely and rich in the extreme. All the foliage is fresh washed and clean; young herbage is bursting through the ground; the

air is deliciously cool, and the birds are singing joyfully: one, called Mzié, is a good songster, with a loud melodious voice. Large game abounds, but we do not meet with it.[58]

Soon they entered another forest where at first the trees were stunted, but progressively got larger as they penetrated further into it. As usual they had difficulty in hiring guides and continued to head north, sometimes following game paths across the undulating country. Their progress had slowed to a snail's pace, covering only eight miles a day as they searched for food and zigzagged to avoid the Mazitu marauding parties.[59] The rains were now falling regularly and even Livingstone was affected by illness, recording in his diary on 6 December 1866, 'Too ill to march.'[60] They finally reached the Loangwa on 16 December 1866.

10.3 Lake Tanganyika and beyond

The Loangwa river was seventy to hundred yards wide and is a large river that drains the high table land between lakes Bangweulu and Nyassa, called Chibalé country. The headwaters are about 7,000 feet above sea level. The Loangwa flows into the Zambezi and Livingstone had encountered it having passed across its confluence when traversing the Zambezi some years before.

Livingstone was mortified to find that there was very little food to be obtained despite the rich country as the constant raids by the Mazitu meant the locals were too afraid to cultivate the land. They were forced to go on, heading north towards Lake Tanganyika. By this stage they had no grain and lived only on meat from animals that Livingstone shot. Their path northwards meant they had to travel through the country of the Ba-bisa, themselves active in supplying slaves to the Arabs. The small party spent a very miserable Christmas Day in a village of Kavimba. In desperation Livingstone persuaded the chief to guide him to a herd of rhinoceros where he hoped to shoot one, but they could only find their spoor.

They pushed on up Mushing Mountains, which are comprised of pink and white dolomite rock at altitudes up to 6,000 feet. This country is part of the Lilongwe Plain, also known as the Central Region Plateau.[61] It is a vast tableland and the greater part of the plateau has poor, sandy soils supporting grasslands and little free-flowing water. It was difficult for them to survive in this lean country, as they found few animals to shoot. They had finished their salt and sugar and grain was roasted as a substitute for coffee.[62] He did not have his goats to provide them with much needed milk, as these had already been lost, or as he suspected, stolen by Kavimba. The gruelling travel and lack of food meant they were rapidly losing weight, and Livingstone noted laconically in his journal, 'I took my belt up three holes to relieve hunger.'[63]

Added to this were the incessant downpours as it was the height of the rainy season. Anyone experiencing an African downpour for the first time is often struck of the violence of it as it soaks you completely in a matter of minutes. Up on the cold plateau the effect of the rain and wind was at times severe, and the phlegmatic Livingstone noted in a letter from this time, 'Must add the rainy season as more potent than all except hunger ... The rains too are more copious than I ever saw them anywhere in Africa. But we shall get on in time.'[64] The only protection he had was a newly invented water proof fabric that Livingstone used as a type of tent and waterproof boots that he wore on the five hundred mile march into the interior. His only regret was that he had not taken more waterproof protection.[65] During one heavy downpour two of his men wandered from the path and another two remained behind, lost when the tracks were quickly washed out in the rain. It was not until next morning that they were found when they heard their rifle shots. Soon after they entered a village where some hunters were selling rotten elephant flesh but so great was their hunger that they paid an exorbitant price to satisfy their craving for food. They pushed on, even marching on a Sunday, which Livingstone strenuously avoided, in their desperation to find food. Soon after they crossed over the Chimbwé river, which was about a mile wide. Livingstone led his party across, but in the act of carefully fording the river, nobody remembered to carry Livingstone's pet dog Chitané who swam after them but must have drowned when his strength failed. Livingstone was despondent about his loss, writing that, 'He was so useful in keeping all the country curs off our huts; none dared to approach and steal, and he never stole himself.'[66]

They continued to climb, well over 5,000 feet above sea level. Livingstone noted in his journal, 'Nothing but famine and famine prices, the people living on mushrooms and leaves.'[67] If this was not enough, soon after occurred an event that had life threating consequences for Livingstone and his attendants. On 20 January 1867, near Lisunga, two Wa-Yao porters decided to desert and they did so, carrying off their loads. Livingstone's party immediately gave chase but they were in a dense forest and after the first drenching shower they could not follow them in the wet forest floor. The porters escaped with all their plates and dishes, two guns and some gunpowder. But what was even more important was in one of the loads was Livingstone's medicine chest with all the drugs. It was a calamity as it meant Livingstone was without any means of treating himself or his party, and could not offer assistance to native tribes who sought out his medical help. He was anxious and despondent and wrote in his journal, 'I felt as if I had received my death-sentence.'[68] This event marked a turning point in Livingstone's health and constitution, which had been much remarked upon. After this event the illnesses he suffered become more prolonged and serious and it really spelt the beginning of the end. In time he was forced out of desperation to try native medicines 'and trust in Him who has led me hitherto to help me still.'[69]

By this time they were just surviving, mainly by eating African maize. At night Livingstone dreamt of eating roast beef. 'The saliva runs from the mouth in these dreams, and the pillow is wet with it in the mornings.'[70] Soon after he shot a good-sized poku, or tsebula male. Ever the keen observer and despite his gnawing hunger he took the time to accurately measure his waiting dinner:

> It measured from snout to insertion of tail, five feet three inches; tail, 1 foot; height at withers, three feet; circumference of chest, five feet; face to insertion of horns, 9½ inches; horns measured on curve, sixteen inches. Twelve rings on horns, and one had a ridge behind, ½ inch broad, ½ inch high, and tapering up the horn; probably accidental. Colour: reddish-yellow, dark points in front of foot and on the ears, belly nearly white. The shell went through from behind the shoulder to the spleen, and burst on the other side, yet he ran 100 yards.'[71]

It would be interesting to know what his hungry attendants were thinking while Livingstone was taking his careful measurements. The next morning Livingstone changed his clothes and 'was frightened at my own emaciation.[72]

There was nothing for it but to push on and on 28 January 1867 they crossed the Tshambezi or Chambeze, which flows into Lake Bangweulu and entered an area that he described as 'almost trackless dripping forests and across oozing bogs.'[73] They managed to shirt around the numerous swamps and on 31 January 1867, exhausted and mudded, they entered the large stockaded village of Chitapangwa,[74] chief of the Ba-bemba. The chief accorded Livingstone a majestic welcome complete with drummers and dancers and gave him a cow and a huge elephant tusk. They stayed in Chitapangwa for about three weeks recovering from their long march and during this time Livingstone sent letters out to the coast with a party of Swahili slave-traders in which he asked for medicines and stores to be sent to him at Ujiji. He also sought the assistance from his friends in ensuring his children were properly educated and cared for, particularly Tom who was then sixteen and at Glasgow College and William, ten-years-old and attending a private school in Hamilton. He also sought information about scholarships. Clearly Livingstone, while battling deep in central Africa, was constantly thinking about his children. These letters were safely carried to Bagamoyo on the coast and in time back to England.

Livingstone was surprised to hear from the Swahili slave-traders about a slaving route out to Bagamoyo, which was a much shorter. Nobody in Zanzibar seemed to know about it—or were simply unwilling to talk about this particular route. He also discovered that amongst the slaving party was a person who had accompanied Speke and Burton on their journey to Lake Tanganyika and could still imitate the sound of a trumpet.

Livingstone fell ill with rheumatic fever while at Chitapangwa. It was the first time he had this illness and without medicines he only very slowly recovered.

Finally on 20 February 1867 Livingstone and his nine attendants set off again, heading to Ulunga country. Unfortunately within a day or two Livingstone had fallen ill again with fever and their pace was reduced to a crawl. With uncharacteristic openness, he described how 'every step I take jars in the chest, and I am very weak; I can scarcely keep up the march, though formerly I was always first, and had to hold in my pace not to leave the people altogether.'[75] They slowly plodded north. In one small village called Kasonso, they all woke up in the night covered in driver ants that had swarmed through the village covering everything in their path. Livingstone found his body covered and hair full of them and the ants bit furiously when they were disturbed, and only slowly moved off.

Three weeks later they emerged from the hills, forest and the mud and descended into a number of valleys. On 1 April 1867 they beheld the enormous Lake Tanganyika that had first been discovered by Burton and Speke. Livingstone was still very ill. 'I am excessively weak—cannot walk without tottering, and have constant singing in the head.'[76] After descending 2,000 feet they came to Pambete, near Niamkolo, at the south-eastern end of the lake where he rested up. Livingstone took his usual recordings and noted that Pambete lay 2,800 feet above sea level.

Livingstone was exhausted and his recovery was slow for without medicines he had to wait until nature took its course, but in the meantime he suffered terribly. For two weeks he lay prostrate, too sick and weak to move, delirious at times and for a period suffered from temporary paralysis. His men hung a blanket over the door to his hut, as they were afraid that the natives would see how feeble Livingstone was. It was evident to his men that he must receive medical supplies if they were to remain in the interior of Africa.

Livingstone was nothing if not tough, and when he recovered he set off westwards. He had planned to explore the north-western edge of Lake Tanganyika, but there was a party of marauding Mazitu, and so wisely he decided to do this at a later date. Tantalisingly, Livingstone was told of how Lake Tanganyika was dammed up at the north-western point and there was a huge waterfall, two miles wide.[77]

His party soon came down into a valley of the Lofu River and arrived at Chitimba's village on 20 May 1867, still in Ulungu land. War had broken out between a tribe lead by a chief called Nsama[78] of the Itawa country and the Arab merchants. Nsama had started a war and had led a war party that had ravaged the surrounding countryside. It was a dangerous time to be in the area. All was bedlam as the Arabs soon responded and sent their own war parties out to kill and capture Nsama and his supporters, and this forced Livingstone to wait until the peace broke out. It was here that he met a party of Arab slavers who, to Livingstone's surprise, treated him with much kindness. It was fortunate that the Arabs were friendly, as he had to remain in the Lofu valley for over three months.

The Arabs that he got to know well were called Hamees Wodin Tagh,[79] the principal Arab in the region, and his brother Syde bin Ali. These brothers were both connected with a major Arab mercantile house in Zanzibar. Hamees was clearly impressed when Livingstone produced his letters from the Sultan of Zanzibar.

During the enforced delay Livingstone was able to recover his strength although as late as 2 August 1867 Livingstone still had 'constant singing in his ears'.[80] He also took the opportunity to talk with the Arabs about what they had seen in their travels and worked out that it was 440 miles to Bagamoyo on the coast.

Time dragged on. Livingstone wrote to Maclear and described Lake Tanganyika in detail. He was now resolved to continue pushing to the west in order discover Lake Mweru and whether this lake was the watershed for either the Congo or the Nile. In the meantime he had to be patient as the Arabs and Nsama would eventually sort out their differences. Despite it being the start of the hot season, they shivered away in the elevated village. 'Minimum temperature is as low as 46°; sometimes 33°'.[81] He also had time to observe nature, agricultural practices and the people. He was interested in how the Arab's regular native porters who carried out heavy loads to the coast often formed callouses across their shoulders, sometime up to one-and-a-half inches thick. One old man was pointed out to Livingstone as he had reputedly carried 175 pounds of ivory all the way out to the coast.

Hamees decided he would initiate the peace process and departed with 300 followers to meet Nsama in his heavily fortified village. It turned out the chief was a huge, bloated old man, who could only move if he was carried and was waited on continuously by his wives. He quickly agreed peace terms, but needed time to collect together all the supplies taken from the Arabs, and to supply thirty tusks as part of the reparations. Livingstone's way to Lake Mweru looked like it was opening up again.

These types of setbacks best show Livingstone's wise and phlegmatic side of his character that made him so successful in traversing Africa; others may have tried to force a passage or have elected to take a different route but Livingstone knew better. As he well knew, it would just take time and money, in the form of trading goods for the situation to be resolved.[82]

On 29 July 1867, while still waiting for all the reparations to be paid, Livingstone walked to another village of Ponda, two-and-a-half hours west of Chitimba. Here he met another Arab slave trader that he was in time to get to know well, called Hamidi bill Muhammad, who was later nicknamed Tipo Tipo.[83] This Arab had borne the brunt of Nsama's attack and had defeated the natives with only twenty guns. He presented Livingstone with gifts although he had lost most of his goods during the war. He himself was recovering from two arrow wounds.

Finally, after a delay of three months and ten days, Livingstone departed for Lake Mweru. Tipo Tipo's slave party had already departed westwards, but Livingstone's party soon caught up with and remained with them. Soon after Baraka, one of Livingstone's men, deserted and headed back to Ponda. Livingstone was unconcerned as the man was lazy and he thought it was inevitable that Baraka would in time himself become a slave.

Their party passed by Nsama's village and Livingstone went to meet the chief, who wanted to feel his woollen clothes and hair. While staying close by in a village called Hara, some traders arrived on 10 September 1867 from Ujiji and told Livingstone that his supplies had arrived there and were in safekeeping. A relieved Livingstone sent out a box, containing papers, books and some clothes with these same traders who were soon to return to Ujiji, obviously with the intent to lighten his load so they could make a quick trip around Lake Mweru before heading to Ujiji.

Livingstone and his party started out on 22 September 1867 for Lake Mweru and he accompanied Tipo Tipo's large Arab slave trading caravan as they trekked through Itawa country. Most of the natives were too frightened to come near the Arabs as they had heard of the power of Tipo Tipo's guns in defeating the great chief Nsama.

Livingstone fell ill with fever again and soon could not walk. Tipo Tipo's men responded by building a hut for him and they treated him with medicines. After a few days of care he was ready to move on. They headed to the Choma river, but unfortunately, all the villages were empty as they had heard of the approaching Arabs and they could not buy food. The Arabs decided to stop at a village of Kabwabwata and send out trading parties. However, Livingstone was keen to continue and he decided to push on to his objective and his small party of just nine arrived on the shores of Lake Mweru on 8 November 1867. They could see it was a large lake, some twelve or more miles wide, and that on both the east and west sides it was flanked by forest-covered mountains. They moved around the northern edge before heading south with Livingstone carefully checking the rivers to see if they were tributaries or distributaries of the lake. He was surprised to learn the lake was abundant with fish and noted the natives could name thirty-nine species.

They moved south and on 18 November 1867, on the banks of the Chungu river, Livingstone identified the place where Dr Lacerda, a Governor of Tete and man of some scientific achievement, had died. Lacerda was Portuguese and had attempted to establish an overland communication post between the Portuguese eastern and western possessions. His people had become involved in fighting with people from Ujiji who were staying in chief Kazembe's village at the time. In order to placate the warring parties Chief Kazembe[84] gave both sides slaves, but Lacerda died soon after. It was here that Livingstone bravely decided to go to Kazembe, which lay in known cannibal country.

10.4 Mission to Find Livingstone

The Johanna men had meantime made their way back to Zanzibar arriving there on 6 December 1866. One of the extraordinary aspects of their journey was that they passed through an area where slavers were active. It may have been good luck, or the fact that the Johanna men were known to be part of Livingstone's party, or both, that enabled these men to successfully traverse such dangerous country, unmolested.

The Johanna men knew that on their arrival back at Zanzibar they would be questioned closely about why they had deserted Livingstone and so they concocted a story about the death of Livingstone and his party. The story was centred on Livingstone suddenly meeting a marauding party of Mazitu[85] and after a brief bloody fight the Mazitu overwhelmed and killed Livingstone and others.

Kirk initially did not believe the men, but so convincingly did their spokesman Musa Kammaals present the story, which was collaborated by the other Johanna men on a number of occasions, that Kirk was eventually inclined to believe the story. The British flag was flown at half-mast and the acting British Consul, Dr Edwin Seward wrote to the British secretary of state for foreign affairs, Lord Stanley[86] to inform him about the death of Livingstone.

When the news filtered back to England there were a number of people who refused to believe that Mazitu could have killed Livingstone and they resolved to confirm the story. While Murchison hoped that the story was untrue, Edward Young, the former Gunner on the HMS *Pioneer* did not believe the story. He had met the Johanna men, including the silvery tongued Musa when the latter had been a sailor on *Lady Nyassa* and knew them to be untrustworthy.

Murchison wanted the matter confirmed and was instrumental in getting the Royal Geographical Society to fund another expedition and Young was approached to lead the search party to Lake Nyassa to establish the truth. He readily agreed and no time was lost as the search party sailed from England in May 1867 and reached the mouth of the Zambezi on 25 July 1867. They had brought a steel boat with them, appropriately named *Search*, and after assembling the boat ascended the Zambezi and the Shire rivers until they reached the Murchison Cataracts. They then disassembled the boat and carried it around the Cataracts, reassembled it for a second time and then continued up the Shire River heading for Mponda.

Soon after Young's search party had disappeared into the rivers and forests of central Africa, a Swahili slave arrived in Zanzibar in September 1867 and provided a hopeful report of seeing a white man in the interior. Could it be Livingstone? This was followed by other reports about a white man, including one from a native saying he saw Livingstone give letters to an Arab slave trader. This was encouraging news, but it was not until 24 January 1868 that the final proof was established; the Arab slave trader arrived in Zanzibar carrying letters from Livingstone. The new British Consul, H. A. Churchill quickly passed the news on to London and the lying Musa Kammaals was put into prison for eight months. Unfortunately for Livingstone, this was not the last encounter he had with Musa Kammaals.

Meanwhile the search party was battling their way further into the interior and when they arrived at Mponda they received the first word that Livingstone may be alive and was continuing his search into the interior, reportedly heading in a north-westerly direction.[87]

Mponda was the place where Wikatani, one of Livingstone's Wa-Yao boys had been reunited with his family and decided to stay. It was therefore not surprising that the chief, who was under Wikatani's influence, hospitably received Young and his party.[88]

The conclusive proof for Young came from a Swahili slave who told the party that he had seen a white man north of Lake Nyassa, 'the great 'M'Sungu' and confirmed that Livingstone had avoided the Mazitu tribe during their murderous sorties into the area.[89] An important clue for his searchers was the observation that the white man was alone and was not engaged in trading goods.[90] Young was satisfied and decided that he did not need to try and follow after Livingstone as he had fulfilled his duty and he needed to report on the situation. They returned back down the Zambezi and reached England in early 1868.

Livingstone only got to hear of Young's search party in February 1870 and in November 1870 while in Banbarre he sent an official letter of thanks to Her Majesty's Government thanking all who were involved.[91]

10.5 Cannibal Country and Lake Bangweulu

Livingstone moved south towards Kazembe, in the province of Londa. His party arrived at Kazembe, named after the chief, on 21 November 1867. It was in fact a small town on the banks of the Lunde River. The chief's palace was fortified with reeds up to nine feet high and topped with human skulls; a cannon stood at the entrance.

An Arab slave trader, Mohammad bin Saleh, was the first person to meet Livingstone. Saleh was a long-term resident in the town and he gave Livingstone and his party quarters and food. Livingstone later found out he was in fact a prisoner of Kazembe, who had reduced Saleh to poverty.

Kazembe[92] was a powerful chief who had a fearsome reputation for cutting off the ears and hands of his people for trivial offences. One of the first people Livingstone saw had no ears or hands. However, the man that Livingstone met was intelligent, commanding and dressed in a crimson kilt.[93] Here the land was fertile, and Livingstone remained in Kazembe for a month resting up, although he continued to suffer from fever throughout his stay.

It was inevitable that Livingstone learnt more about Kazembe and it is clear that in any other society he would have been classified as a psychopath. Whole areas of his tribe had been denuded of people as Kazembe had them either killed or on a whim sold them into slavery. As an example of his madness, any person that Kazembe dreamt about more than two or three times was immediately put to death for allegedly practising secret arts against him. He was even rumoured to have killed his queen's mother to ensure there was no objection to Kazembe marrying her daughter.

Not long after Livingstone arrived, the chief's queen herself decided to visit the white man. She was a fine looking woman and arrived with her entourage, all carrying large spears, to add dignity to the occasion. Livingstone saluted her while some distance away and then beckoned her to him as if she was a child. In doing so it spoilt the solemnity of the occasion and Livingstone burst out laughing. The queen's entourage quickly picked up on Livingstone's infectious laughter until everybody was roaring with laughter. It is a good example of the way Livingstone was able to easily relate with the natives.[94]

Soon after their arrival in Kazembe, Livingstone heard that Mohammad bin Saleh would be released so he could return to Ujiji. Saleh delayed leaving, as he wanted Livingstone to accompany him. Livingstone wanted to join him, but he first wanted to explore that part of the eastern shore of Lake Mweru they had not covered. One thing that he did discover while waiting was that there was a large river that connected lakes Bangweulu and Mweru. The natives knew it as the Luapula although Livingstone later called it Webb's River. This meant that there were now three large rivers draining the region to the north; the Luapula, Lualaba and the Chambeze. Could these all flow into Lake Tanganyika?

His reason for not heading further south to Lake Bangweulu was clear from a draft letter that he wrote, but never sent to Earl of Clarendon:

> Since coming to Kasembe's, the testimony of natives and Arabs has been so united and consistent, that I am but ten days from Lake Bemba, or Bangweolu, that I cannot doubt its accuracy. I am so tired of exploration without a word from home or anywhere else for two years, that I must go to Ujiji on Tanganyika for letters before doing anything else. The banks and country adjacent to Lake Bangweolo are reported to be now very muddy and very unhealthy. I have no medicine. The inhabitants suffer greatly from swelled thyroid gland or Derbyshire neck and elephantiasis, and this is the rainy season and very unsafe for me.[95]

In that same letter Livingstone avoided providing a map of the region as he felt there were still too many areas that remained uncharted.

Kazembe provided three guides and on 22 December 1867 Livingstone's party joined the Arab slave-trading party and headed back to the Chungu river. The rainy season had started again and on crossing the Chungu Livingstone noted:

> Rain from above, and cold and wet to the waist below, as I do not lift my shirt, because the white skin makes all stare.[96]

Christmas came and went with them sitting in a bed of bracken in pouring rain, and Livingstone ill with fever again. Mohammad came to his aid and provided him with porridge and a fowl as Livingstone had been for some time only surviving on coarsely ground sorghum.[97]

On 1 January 1868, Livingstone wrote, 'Almighty Father, forgive the sins of the past year for Thy Son's sake. Help me to be more profitable during this year. If I am to die this year prepare me for it.' He was to become perilously close to dying later that year near Lake Bangweulu.

The large convoy slowly continued north and they soon reached the vicinity of Lake Mweru where Livingstone was able to see a large island in the lake called Kirwa. By 13 January 1868 they had walked the full length of the lake, where they had been forced to plunge into thick vegetation, waded through countless streams and forded many rivers. However, this had been relatively easy country in comparison to what came next when they entered a flooded plain north of the Lake Mweru. Here they had to force their way through foul smelling swamps, sinking deep into black mud. It is a continual source of wonder why his small band of companions trekked endlessly after Livingstone through this tortuous country, in the vain hope of finding the source of a river that none of them had heard of, or would ever see.

On the 16 January 1868 the exhausted convoy straggled into a village on the banks of the Kakoma river, called Kabwabwata where Saleh's son was living. The village put on a huge demonstration of welcome, with much clapping, firing of guns, lullilooing and shouting. The local women were smeared with clay and it made a great spectacle.

Lake Tanganyika lay just thirteen days march from the village, but Saleh was naturally keen to stay in Kabwabwata to see his son. It was also the wet season, and they knew the land they needed to cross over was muddy. Soon more Arabs arrived in the village and told them that in many places the land was flooded up to waist and chest deep. Despite Livingstone's desire to push on, he was in fact too ill. His Arab companions continued to look after him as Livingstone acknowledged, noting Saleh 'cooks small delicacies for me with the little he has, and tries to make me comfortable.'[98] Livingstone's increasing reliance on Arab slaver traders was a trend in these later years and although he records in his journals his continuing disgust about slavery, there is no doubt he would not have survived as long as he did without the help of these traders.

It was while they were waiting in Kabwabwata that people told him about the Rua Mountains on the western shore of Lake Mweru. He heard about a strange people who led a troglodyte existence living in naturally formed caves in the mountains. They were also told about rivers that flowed from the mountain further to the west. Livingstone resolved to explore the area as soon as he could.

During this time he spent a lot of time with Saleh and he became a close friend. 'No better authority for what has been done or left undone by Mohamadans in this country can be found than Mohammad bin Saleh, for he is very intelligent, and takes an interest in all that happens.'[99] Religion was obviously a big topic of conversation. Livingstone was interested to learn, despite the huge numbers of Arabs moving through the country, why they had such little social or religious impact, despite living among them, as Saleh had done for over twenty-two years. They agreed it was because the Arabs did not proselytize nor did they print the Koran in local languages. Livingstone maintained this was one of the reasons why the British, led by a few Christian missionaries, were well regarded, as they readily imparted knowledge, not only about Christian love, but also useful knowledge that improved the lives of the natives that they came into contact with.[100]

On 16 March 1868 Livingstone left Saleh, and took his party due west to the Lualaba, a large river that flowed out from the top end of Lake Mweru. Livingstone thought the Lualaba might lead into the Nile, but in fact it feeds into the Congo river system. They arrived at a village called Mpweto and were immediately taken to a house owned by Syde bin Habib. Livingstone had first met Syde in Naliele and later in Linyanti in 1855. Here they waited patiently for an audience with the chief because, as Livingstone put it in a message to him, 'we were nearly out of goods now, having been travelling two years, and were going to Ujiji to get more.'[101] However, the chief was offended when Livingstone only offered him one large piece of cloth and refused to help. After waiting eight days, Livingstone was forced leave empty handed and they re-joined the Arabs at Kabwabwata.

It soon become clear that the flooded country northward was impassable and it could be another two months before the floods receded. Livingstone was anxious as ever to get on and so he decided to head south to discover Lake Bangwuelu. Saleh strongly cautioned him about following his plan, not the least because he thought Kazembe would demand an extortionate payment to be able to pass through his village on his way to Lake Bangweulu, which lay about eighty miles south of Kazembe.

Livingstone uncharacteristically dithered as he knew how low his supplies were, but he was frustrated that they had lost three months waiting at Kabwabwata. What probably tipped the balance was news that he received from 'reliable sources' who suggested 'the springs of the Nile rise between 9° and 10° south latitude, or at least 400 or 500 miles south of the south end of Speke's Lake [Lake Victoria].' Lake Bangweulu lies at this latitude and Livingstone had been told about a river that flowed in a north-westerly direction from Lake Bangweulu into Lake Mweru. Was this a missing link that Livingstone needed to put the whole Nile river system together?

On 13 April 1868 Livingstone attempted to set out, but for the first time all his men mutinied. It was clear that Saleh had spoken to Livingstone's attendants and warned them not to follow him. They were exhausted and the thought of returning to Ujiji where they could rest and be resupplied was too tempting.

Livingstone remonstrated, but when he set out the next day for Lake Bangweulu only Susi, Chumah, Amoda, Gardner and one other servant accompanied him. The rest remained in Kabwabwata with the surplus luggage that Livingstone had left behind with Saleh to be carried to Ujiji.

Next day Amoda also fled back to Kabwabwata as he 'Wishes to stop with his brothers.'[102] If Livingstone was facing a real crisis it did not change his mind; in fact in a doughty Scots way, it probably only hardened his resolve to continue.

They plunged once more back into marsh, mud and misery. The mud was particularly horrible, for when the surface was broken it 'discharged foul air of frightful fæcal odour.'[103] They had to ford areas that were in places whole chest deep, requiring them to carrying their loads on their heads. On another occasion Livingstone became separated from the rest of the party in the long grass, and only fortuitously met up much later after firing his gun.

However, they realised that they were in mortal danger when the natives found out that he had come back into Kazembe's country without first getting permission. The problem was that he had become too closely associated with Saleh. For four days they waited, anxiously, for word to come from Kazembe. The seriousness of the situation is clear by the references in his journal constantly seeking God's help. His prayers were answered as Kazembe warmly welcomed them back.

They crossed over the still swollen Chungu and entered Kazembe on 4 May 1868. It had been quite a return trip.

They waited in Kazembe for guides that the chief had promised. Fortunately for Livingstone there was another Arab staying there, Mohammad Bogharib, and they kept each other company. Bogharib was there to buy ivory, but the hunting was poor that year and he waited months to buy only a few tusks. Livingstone pondered his decision to leave Kabwabwata while they continued to wait in Kazembe but it was not until 11 June 1868, a long vexatious delay, that they were finally able to depart. Passing beyond Kazembe's village they entered into hilly country further south. Livingstone passed a number of slaving parties, which always upset him. He recorded in his journal how he came across six male slaves singing lustily, seemingly oblivious to the weight of the slave taming sticks and their perilous position. On being questioned about their apparent happiness they told Livingstone, bitterly, the reason for their joy was the thought 'of coming back after death and haunting and killing those who had sold them.'[104]

They also found in the forest a neat rounded mound that was clearly a grave. It was covered in flour and beads had been thrown over it. Livingstone reflected that this is the type of grave he would prefer. He also noted how Mary, buried on the Shupanga, also had a similar grave. His increasing references about his death in his journals from this time were no doubt premised on the increasing possibility that he may very well die in his attempt to find the source of his Nile. His illnesses, and in time increasing frailty, made this an ever real possibility. Perhaps he welcomed the prospect of death.

On 28 June 1868 they arrived at a Banyamwezi[105] stockade at Kizinga, and built some accommodation while they did the usual thing and contacted the paramount chief of the area, Chikumbi of the Imbozhwa. Chikumbi promised to send them guides and while waiting Livingstone sat down to write to the consul at Zanzibar to order supplies to be sent to Ujiji. As usual he was very specific about the goods he ordered as he knew exactly what was valued as trading goods. The list included a range of beads and cloths of various types. He also ordered personal items and the list shows how frugally he lived when exploring. 'I ask for soap, coffee, sugar, candles, sardines, French preserved meats, a cheese in tin, Nautical Almanac for 1869 and 1870, shoes (two or four pairs), ruled paper, pencils, sealing-wax, ink, powder, flannel-serge'.[106]

Chikumbi eventually sent word that he could not now send guides that he had previously promised, and so Livingstone hired a Banyamwezi guide from Kombokombo's stockade instead and they set out on 10 July 1868. The reason for Chikumbi's change of mind later became apparent when he led an attack on the Kombokombo's stockade. The chief had realised that the Banyamwezi would kill any guides he gave Livingstone.

They continued to push on into succeeding valleys and the ground soon began to get marshy and they knew they were getting close when they once again entered vast swampland.

On 13 July 1868 they had a particularly frightening encounter with a group of armed, drunk natives in a deserted area of the forest. They suddenly surrounded Livingstone's small party and threatened them with their spears, bows and arrows and axes. Livingstone calmly pacified the war party and they were allowed to go on their way.

The journey had taken several weeks, but on 18 July 1868 their hard work was rewarded when they reached the shores of Lake Bangweulu and looked out over a vast expanse of water. In doing so Livingstone became the first European to discover Lake Bangweulu, entering from the northern end of the Lake Chifunabuli section.

Livingstone had by now expended almost all his stores and he had to rely on the kindness of the chiefs he encountered for help, food and guides. He was lucky to find one who was friendly and he ordered the fisherman to take Livingstone out as far as Mbabala Island.[107] It was a large canoe, forty-five feet long, four feet deep and four feet broad and propelled by five strong men. Unfortunately, despite having pre-paid wages to cover four days of travel around the lake, they were only away two days before the fishermen had to rapidly return. It seems the fishermen had stolen the canoe and during the trip they received word that the former owners were coming to take it back. However, it was long enough to enable Livingstone to estimate the lake to be 150 miles long by 80 miles wide. He also discovered that the Bangweulu swamps are fed mainly from the northeast by the Chambeze river,[108] and drain away to the south into the Luapula River.[109]

Livingstone still thought at this time the Chambeze fed the Nile, but in fact it is the most remote headstream of the Congo river.

In reading Livingstone's journals he makes little of his discovery of one of the largest central African lakes. It is a reflection on his state of mind and maturity that he does not boast about his accomplishments in his journals. His entries also showed how his passion waned as his health slowly deteriorated.

With his supplies in a critical state Livingstone was forced to head north again as soon as possible and they set out on 30 July 1868 after spending just twelve days exploring around the lake. They headed back to Chikumbi's village as quickly as possible as he thought Mohammad Bogharib might pass through there on his way to Katanga. Livingstone now hoped to accompany him onto Ujiji on the eastern shores of Lake Tanganyika. It was no easy route as Livingstone noted that in moving from Lake Bangweulu to Kizinga, a distance of thirty miles; they crossed through twenty-nine 'earthen sponges or oozes'.[110] These bogs varied in size from a quarter of a mile to a mile wide and from two to ten miles long. Floundering in the mud with their heavy loads and plunging up to their thighs in ooze while covered in leeches was a nightmare of an experience.

Livingstone arrived back in Kizinga and on 1 September 1868 two men came from Kazembe to formally tell him about his own death. This rumour had started when the Johanna men had arrived back to Zanzibar on 6 December 1866 and convincingly told their story about the death of Livingstone. For a second time Livingstone was amused by the thought that he was now dead.

While resting in Kinzinga Livingstone wondered if the lakes Mweru and Bangweulu could really be the source of the Nile. He felt confident enough about his idea to write to his old exploring friend, Oswell, to explain the location:

> I hope I am not premature in saying that the sources of the Nile arise from the 10° to 12 south—in fact where Ptolemy[111] had described it as starting from the Mountain of Moons. The Chambeze is like the Chobe 40 to 50 yards broad—but the country is not like that at all, it is full of fast flowing perennial burns[112]—we cross several every day—and crossed the Chambeze in 10° 34′ south. It runs west into Bangweolo—leaving that Lake it changes its name to Luapula—then into Lake Mweru. On leaving it the name Lualaba is assumed.[113]

His luck was in as he received word from a passing Arab party in Kizinga that Mohammad Bogharib had not moved from Kazembe because of the war between the Imbozhwa and Banyamwezi. Livingstone gave them some letters as they were heading for the coast. The Arabs thought the journey would take about five months.

Livingstone soon after met up with Mohammad Bogharib and learnt he was now planning to head to Manyuema.[114] This suited Livingstone as he thought he would take the opportunity to continue his explorations around the Lualaba, which flows into Lake Mweru further to the north. However, just as he was completing his preparations so that they could depart they received reports that a tribal war between chiefs wanting to usurp Nsama had now spread throughout the whole region. The situation was serious enough for the Arab traders in the area to agree to join up in order to safely retreat out of the war zone. For Livingstone, the best course seemed to be to wait until the situation became clearer. It was cold and on 29 August 1868 there was a remarkably heavy shower, heralding the start of the wet season.

Livingstone decided they needed to move and they arrived back in Mpweto's village in September 1868 where he was surprised to find Mohammad bin Saleh still there, seven months after Livingstone had left, together with Livingstone's attendants who had remained behind.

The good news was the men that refused to accompany Livingstone on his trip to Lake Bangweulu slowly approached him to see if they could once more join his party. Livingstone noted ruefully:

I have taken all the runaways back again; after trying the independent life they will behave better. Much of their ill conduct may be ascribed to seeing that after the flight of the Johanna men I was entirely dependent on them: more enlightened people often take advantage of men in similar circumstances; though I have seen pure Africans come out generously to aid one abandoned to their care.

He also noted, 'I have faults myself.'[115]

Livingstone's plan was if possible to still head to Manyuema, the country westwards of the northern part of Lake Tanganyika, to see if he could, once and for all, prove that the Lualaba River was the source of the Nile. This was despite admitting in a letter to Oswell that the 'tramp on foot is tiresome.'[116] However, the war continued, and on 23 September 1868 Livingstone and his party reluctantly joined the some Arabs and about 400 Banyamwezi and moved north to Kalongosi. Their passage over a small river was disputed by 400 of Kabanda's men. Predictably it was Livingstone who went over to parley with them and they were allowed to pass, but Livingstone noted that had they showed any sign of weakness Kabanda's men would have attacked. In Kalongosi Syde bin Habib left them to return to the coast.

On leaving the Kalongosi they needed to cross a ford, called Mosolo, which Livingstone paced out as being 240 yards wide, fast flowing and thigh deep. Their way north was blocked, this time by more than 500 of Nsama's people. Again Livingstone intervened and two fathoms of calico was sent over as a present. Livingstone and thirty men armed with guns then crossed the ford and provided protection while the rest of the Banyamwezi party waded through the treacherous water and crossed into Nsama country.

They marched on until they reached Kabwabwata on 22 October 1868. Here they waited while the war continued, which was further inflamed when Salem bin Habib was attacked and killed. The Arabs decided they needed to retaliate and Syde bin Habib changed his plans to go to the coast and returned. He set out on a violent war of vengeance, capturing slaves and seizing ivory from the Rua people. Meanwhile Livingstone nursed himself through another attack of fever. Eventually the war petered out and Syde bin Habib arrived back in Kabwabwata, bringing with him an enormous war booty that included about 5,250 pounds of ivory and 10,500 pounds of copper.[117]

Whilst waiting, Livingstone had time to reflect on the Nile. He wrote:

> The discovery of the sources of the Nile is somewhat akin in importance to the discovery of the North-West Passage, which called forth, though in a minor degree, the energy, the perseverance, and the pluck of Englishmen, and anything that does that is beneficial to the nation and its posterity.[118]

In acknowledging all the great explorers who had resolutely searched for the source of the Nile, Livingstone modestly noted, 'I call mine a contribution.'[119]

10.6 Lost Hope

Livingstone reluctantly decided to join Mohammad Bogharib's caravan that was planning to depart in late November 1868, to Ujiji. Livingstone had wanted to depart earlier as he was desperately hoping his letters may have resulted in supplies been sent there. Mohammad Bogharib continued to provide him with cooked dinners and 'I did not like to refuse his genuine hospitality.'[120] Then, just as they were about to depart on 22 November 1868, war broke out all around them again.

It started when one of Mohammad Bogharib's men, Bin Juma, went to a village close by and seized two women and two girls, in lieu of four slaves who had run away. The village chief shot an arrow into one of Bin Juma's men, and Bin Juma responded by shooting a woman. These actions ignited an immediate response among the Imbozhwa and at dawn the next day, their whole party, including Livingstone and the 400 Banyamwezi were attacked. Trees were cut down and a stockade built while the Imbozhwa were kept at bay with gunfire. The Imbozhwa kept up a number of concentrated and determined attacks and after three days fighting, a small party was sent out to contact Syde bin Habib, and they returned with four barrels of gunpowder and ten extra men. The Imbozhwa continued to besiege the stockade and on 3 December 1868 another reconnaissance party was sent out northwards, but were forced back into the stockade under attack. Next day the Arabs tried the same thing but this time parties were sent out in both an easterly and westerly direction to see if they could break through. In both cases their passage was blocked and on 5 December 1868 more work was put into strengthening the stockade. In the meantime, Livingstone took no active part in the fighting, but stayed close by his party and stores, protecting both.

Finally, sense prevailed and calm was restored when captives were returned and they were allowed to depart on 11 December 1868. Livingstone's party joined Mohammad Bogharib's motley crew that included some people wanting to leave the area and a large group of miserably yoked slaves.

It is surprising that Livingstone would attach himself to such a group, but it is an indication of both just how dangerous travelling in the area was, and how much Livingstone needed to return to Ujiji.

Mohammad Bogharib decided to head in a north-westerly direction towards the river mouth of the Lofuko on Lake Tanganyika, where he planned to pick up a boat or a dhow and sail to Ujiji. But it was forlorn party, particularly as Mohammad Bogharib continued to haemorrhage a large number of slaves that manage to escape, including eight in one night. The path was difficult and on 22 December 1868, while crossing the Lofunso, two people were washed away and drowned while wading the river that was neck deep. The crocodiles also came among them and attacked, biting one man before the men were able to drive the loathsome creature off. People fell ill with 'feebleness and purging'[121] from sleeping naked on the damp ground. On Christmas Day, 1868 they marched past Mount Katanga and feasted on a kid goat as their Christmas dinner. A passing trading party told them that they were but ten camps from reaching Lake Tanganyika. It could not come soon enough.

They continued their way, fording rivers and were continually wet. Normally this would not matter as Livingstone was tough, but he wrote ominously in his journal on 1 January 1869:

> I have been wet times without number, but the wetting of yesterday was once too often: I felt very ill, but fearing that the Lofuko might flood, I resolved to cross it. Cold up to the waist, which made me worst, but I went on for 2½ hours E.[122]

Livingstone quickly succumbed to pneumonia and became completely incapacitated. He faced a very real prospect of dying as he was coughing up blood night and day, and quickly weakened and at times became quite delirious. Another entry reads:

> *About 7ᵗʰ January.*—Cannot walk: pneumonia of right lung, and I cough all day and all night: sputa rust of iron and bloody: distressing weakness.[123]

He constantly thought of his family and friends, and lines of a poem continually rang through his head:

I shall look into your faces,
And listen to what you say,
And be often very near you
When you think I'm far away.

It was a very grave situation, but his Arab companions treated him with their medicines, fed and nursed him. When he was strong enough they rigged up a litter and carried him in that. Livingstone later described his suffering from pneumonia as being 'worse than ten fevers'[124]

They arrived on the west shore of Lake Tanganyika on 14 February 1869. Livingstone was still sick and weak. Syde bin Habib had three large canoes at Parra; the confluence of the Lofuko river and Lake Tanganyika, and Livingstone and his party boarded them and they left Parra on 26 February 1869. They followed the western shoreline and slowly made their way up Lake Tanganyika. The lake is large and the slaves paddling the canoe soon got tired as it was hard work propelling the large canoe through sometimes, rough seas. Livingstone was recovering although he never fully did. He was painfully thin and his cough had not improved.

On the 12 March 1869 they made a ten-hour canoe trip across Lake Tanganyika and finally entered Ujiji on 14 March 1869. Livingstone was desperately hoping he would find his stores and medicines waiting for him. Instead Haji Thani's agent only handed over a small amount of goods. Shocked he soon found out that the stores he had requested had been broken into and most of it stolen. This included sixty-two out of eighty bundles of cloth, each twenty-four yards long, and most of the best trading beads. His medicines, wine and cheese were also not available as they were blocked in Unyanyembe[125] by a Mazitu war. It was another bitter body blow. The only thing he was able to enjoy was coffee, sugar and some new clothes. He brought butter and four-year-old flour, from which he made bread.

At the end of May 1869, while still recovering in Ujiji, Livingstone wrote to both Kirk and Colonel Playfair (Livingstone was unaware that Playfair had been succeeded first by Seward and then soon after by H. A. Churchill as consuls in Zanzibar) about the slaving practices. He was well aware the slave traders were seeking to stop all his correspondence getting out to Zanzibar, as they feared Livingstone would expose their continuing illegal and brutal practice. In desperation, Livingstone was forced to entrust a letter with his former attendant Musa Kamaals who had unpleasantly reappeared in Ujiji.

The letter is typical Livingstone, complete with a note about Kammaals:

I could not employ him to carry my mail back nor can I say anything to him for he at once goes to the Ujijians and gives his own version of all he hears. He is untruthful and ill-conditioned and would hand off mail to anyone who wished to destroy it.[126]

Not only did Livingstone have to deal with a deserter, but he also knew Kamaals was a thief as 'he witnessed the plundering of my goods and got a share of them. I have given him beads and cloth sufficient to buy provisions for himself in the way back to Zanzibar. He has done nothing here.'[127] Livingstone also informed Kirk and Playfair that he had sent some forty letters, but he knew it was unlikely that they would have got through:

> A party was sent to the coast two months ago. One man volunteered to take a letter secretly but his master warned them all not to do so 'because I might write something he did not like'. He went out with the party and gave orders to the headman to destroy any letter he might detect in the way.[128]

What Livingstone really wanted was cloth, beads and other trading goods to be sent to him so he could continue with his explorations for the source of the Nile. He was still convinced that the Nile started some 500 to 700 miles south of Lake Victoria and he intended to follow this source. He knew there was an undiscovered lake west or south-west of Lake Tanganyika. He also needed to confirm whether the outflow from this lake fed the Congo or the Nile. He wryly noted in his letter to Kirk and Playfair:

> The people west of this, call Manyema, are cannibals if Arabs speak truly. I may have to go there first and down Tanganyika, if I come out uneaten and find my new squad from Zanzibar.[129]

Although this particular letter did reach the coast, Livingstone was correct in assuming that most of his letters from this time would not. The reason was the people of Ujiji were resentful of the British involvement in stopping slave trading as the sale of slaves could be very lucrative and consequently the slave traders were frightened of exposure by Livingstone. This meant couriers destroyed most of his letters and indeed only one of his forty-four letter dispatches made it to Zanzibar.[130] Livingstone was well aware of what was happening and it is not hard to imagine Livingstone's sense of loneliness and isolation, living amongst hostile hosts while trying to recover from exhaustion and sickness. [131]

What is interesting about the letter is the poor quality. By this time Livingstone had run out of writing paper and so was forced to tear pages from books and newspapers to write on. He had also run out of ink as he was using ink made from the seeds of a local berry.

On 26 May 1869 Livingstone finally met Thani bin Suelim, the person to whom all his supplies had been entrusted. He was a former slave who had earned his freedom and became very influential. Livingstone was unimpressed with his agent as 'he has a disagreeable outward squint of the right eye, teeth protruding from the averted lips, is light-coloured, and of the nervous type of African.'[132] He was also a thief and a scoundrel, charging Livingstone fourteen fathoms of cloth for bringing two boxes from Unyanyembe despite Livingstone having already paid for the portage while in Zanzibar. To add insult to injury, Livingstone discovered his agent had stolen a cloth in front of him by slipping it into the hands of a slave.

Livingstone hated his time in Ujiji. He described it as 'a den of the worst kind of slave-traders; those whom I met in Urungu and Itawa were gentlemen slavers: the Ujiji slavers, like the Kilwa and Portuguese, are the vilest of the vile. It is not a trade, but a system of consecutive murders; they go to plunder and kidnap, and every trading trip is nothing but a foray.'[133] He was forced to move house several times during the four months he spent there, recuperating and planning his next explorations. With nothing to hold Livingstone in Ujiji it was with much relief that he was finally well enough to leave, which they did on 10 July 1869 after hiring a boat and nine paddlers, to explore the area to the west of Lake Tanganyika.

They first headed south on Lake Tanganyika before crossing over the lake to the western shoreline at a place called Kasenge. It was here that he again met up with Mohammad Bogharib who wanted to start trading with the Manyuema. For safety reasons Livingstone decided to attach his small party to this large group of well-armed Arabs and Swahili slave traders.

It is unclear about the circumstances of this link-up, but it seems it must have been pre-arranged. Indeed, one of the hardest things for Livingstone during this time was whether to accept assistance from Arab slave traders. As a known abolitionist for slavery, it went against everything he knew to be right, and had argued so vehemently against, but given his pitiful circumstances, Livingstone knew he must either accept their assistance or die. Accept he did and he generously mentions how these Arabs were kind and caring in a number of his letters. It is interesting to surmise why these Arabs did provide help as it would have been much easier for them to let the old man die so that they could have more freedom to continue with their odious practice. But it is more likely they respected Livingstone and appreciated his pioneering and free spirit and his honesty and strength.

On 1 August 1869 and just before the party left Kasenge the Arabs prayed and feasted together as they normally did before undertaking a significant event. Livingstone was invited to participate with them in the feast. 'The cookery is of their very best, and I always get a share; I tell them that I like the cookery, but not the prayers, and it is taken in good part.'[134]

They departed soon after, but by 3 August 1869 Livingstone acknowledged that he was already very fatigued due to his weakness from pneumonia. He found that if they climbed at an incline of 45°, he would have to stop every 100 to 150 yards, as he would be panting in distress. It was very disturbing for his attendants to observe his weakness. It is also clear that the physical change in Livingstone was affecting his power of observation, as his journal entries from this time become increasingly cryptic and prosaic.

The group first headed down the west side of Lake Tanganyika before turning west to avoid crossing the mountains opposite Ujiji, and they set out in a north-westerly direction for the cannibal country of Manyuema. This area today is located in the eastern part of the Democratic Republic of the Congo. His aim was to properly explore the Lualaba river. The group moved through to Bambarré, which lay about 150 miles west of Ujiji. It was very hot and the heat affected everyone; even the strongest porters tired after three hours marching. They continued slowly, but fortunately they had good supply of meat as the elephants and buffaloes were abundant. Livingstone would eat the elephant heart if it was offered, as he liked it, particularly if it was well cooked.

They pushed on, perpetually fording rivers and going up and down hills. Livingstone saw many plants and surveyed gigantic trees, carefully measuring one with a circumference of twenty feet and branches that appeared only sixty to seventy feet above the ground.

The group came upon another trader, Dugumbé, who had 18,000 pounds of ivory that he brought very cheaply in Manyuema as no traders had yet entered into the country beyond Bambarré.

The fearsome man-eating reputation of the Manyuema ensured the slaves and porters were well behaved as many feared to leave the camp unless it was absolutely necessary. It was this same reputation that had ensured that the area had not been opened up to traders. Proof of the Manyuema martial skills came later when they learnt that one of Dugumbé people had stolen ten goats and ten slaves. The Manyuema's revenge was to kill four of Dugumbé's party.

It was a fearful trip with thick dark vegetation that they had to push through. Livingstone, the master of the understatement, was moved to write, 'My experience is Manyema has been trying—the vegetation is indescribably rank—the ills and rivulets innumerable and the mire or glaur grievous.'[135] At times it was so solid that they took turns to bodily throw themselves against the wall of vegetation in order to force a passage through. They were constantly wet from the deluges, soaking grasses and mud. Numerous leeches attached themselves to their bodies so that it was better to just let them have their fill of blood before harmlessly falling away. On top of all this Livingstone was also suffering terribly from ulcers that were painful in the extreme; 'a discharge of bloody itch with great pain each night may shew that they are allied to fever. Many slaves are killed by them.'[136]

Following well-worn paths, they finally arrived at Bambarré, the village of Chief Moenekuss[137] on 21 September 1869, land of the Manyuema. Here they found the renowned chief had just died and his two sons were ruling in his place. The brothers were suspicious and warned the group that they must not steal, as their own people did not. 'No stealing of fowls or of men.'[138] Mohammad Bogharib duplicitously agreed that his men would not steal and proceeded to perform a friendship ceremony, mixing their bloods with his own, while Livingstone responded in his own way by presenting the two brothers with two table cloths;

four bunches of beads, and a string of neck-beads. They seemed to be well satisfied with the gifts.

The wet season was upon them, and it made sense to shelter up. However, Livingstone's situation was pitiable as his party was completely reliant on the natives to supply them with food. They took advantage of his straightened circumstances and in return for providing him with food forced him to eat it in a roped off area for their entertainment. This was a difficult exercise for Livingstone as by now he had lost nearly all his teeth.

Livingstone had received letters while in Ujiji and had heard that Thomas had become partially blind after he was hit on the head by a roof slate. Livingstone confided to Oswell in a letter written in October 1869, 'while I feel that all my friends will wish me to make a complete work of the exploration I am at times distressed in thinking of my family'.[139] He also expressed his concern that he may well be wrong about the Lualaba:

> I was at a loss about the Lualaba for it was reported to enter a third lake and on coming out it flowed west no one knew whither. Its great size made me fear it was the Congo.[140]

He was in fact correct about the river flowing into the Congo Basin, although he was not destined to learn this.[141]

He also wrote to Playfair and Kirk in Zanzibar. This time the tone of his letter is much different as he was once more Livingstone the Explorer writing about the source of the Nile. His sweep of the geography is detailed, descriptive but ultimately wrong:

> This great lacustrine river Lualaba is the central line of drainage of the Great Nile Valley … This on emerging from the great Lake Bangweolo becomes the Luapula and that on coming out of Lake Mweru is Lualaba at first eight or ten miles broad and then holding a width of from two to six miles and always deep as far as known. West of this, two large rivers, each having the same native name Lualaba, unite and form a Lake before going North into, I suppose, the Nile.[142]

In fact the river does not flow into the Nile, but it was not until Henry Morton Stanley followed the river and determined the Lualaba flows north to eventually join the River Congo and then turns westerly to flow out to the Atlantic through Kinshasa during his epic journey in 1874-1877.

The letter was written in Livingstone's usual cordial manner, but just twenty-two days later when writing to Oswell Livingstone is full of bitterness towards Kirk, particularly as he thought that Kirk meant to take the credit for Livingstone's map sketches:

I see at a glance that the small geographers meant to exalt Kirk and soon his sketch appeared emblazoned on the walls in large letters 'Dr Kirk's sketch map of Nyassa', a simple falsehood.

He then went on to attack Arrowsmith and Baines in a most unusual and vehement way, referring to Baines's mother as an 'old hag'.[143] It was clear that Livingstone was starting to suffer from the isolation and loneliness of his great undertaking.

He was also badly affected by fever and without any effective medicines to treat his numerous complaints, had no choice but to lie up and hope to recover. This meant on numerous occasions he would be bedridden for long periods, waiting and hoping for assistance to come. This inactivity weighed heavily. He had only a few books, including his well-worn Bible, to read. These he re-read many times trying to fill in the long hours. The fevers also affected him badly, alternating from periods of great lucidity to hallucinating at other times. He also suffered terrible depths of despair and possibly depression, from being absent from his children while knowing that he had not yet completed his quest, and with it the possibility of failure always looming.

By the beginning of November 1869, Livingstone was feeling stronger as he had spent nearly six weeks in Bambarré resting up. He now decided it was time to strike out and explore the Lualaba as his accompanying Arab traders had settled down to trade. This meant heading west, and then south-west. The group travelled through the Binanga Hills[144] and Livingstone marvelled at the beauty of the landscape. He was once more writing lucidly, noting that they marched:

through a country surprisingly beautiful, mountainous, and villages perched on the talus of each great mass for the sake of quick drainage. The streets often run east to west, in order that the bright blazing sun may lick up the moisture quickly from off them.[145]

Despite the beauty, the one problem they had was in obtaining guides. Men would refuse to lead them to another village, saying, 'They were at war, and afraid of being killed and eaten.'[146] The fear the natives exhibited only underscores the bravery of the explorations that Livingstone and his party were undertaking.

Travelling through these villages was tiresome for Livingstone personally, as out of curiosity, native men and women would sit around his hut, staring, and then following his every step around the village. If he sought to take refuge in a hut the natives would on occasions knock down his door so that they could continue to stare at the white man.

They continued west, but by 15 November 1869, they had come into an area where Dugumbé's slave trading party had previously visited, and had maltreated, cheated and in some cases killed some natives. As a consequence these same natives were angry and spoiling for a fight. Livingstone's party hurriedly pushed on and soon they were just ten miles from the confluence of the Lualaba and Luamo rivers. Unfortunately here their journey stopped as the local chiefs resolutely refused him passage across the Luamo. They waited and Livingstone tried to get the chiefs to change their minds, but without success and so there was nothing to be done but turn around and leave the area. They were escorted by scores of men, fully armed with spears and large shields that drifted through the forest all around them. The group arrived back in Bambarré on the 19 December 1869. It had been a frightening experience.

In Bambarré they were greeted by a huge horde of Ujijians who had come up to plunder for ivory, as news of the success of Dugumbé's trading party quickly circulated among the other traders. The Ujijian party numbered 500 guns. They were aggressive and it was clear that a mistake by anyone could quickly start a war throughout the region.

Livingstone decided that they should leave the area and he and Mohammad Bogharib decided to try a more northerly route to the Lualaba River where Livingstone hoped to buy a canoe to explore the river while his Arab friend traded for ivory. Christmas Day was spent in Bambarré where Livingstone's party ate a goat that Mohammad Bogharib had presented them with. Livingstone made his final preparations for their departure next day, as he was anxious to move. 'We start immediately after Christmas: I must try with all my might to finish my exploration before next Christmas.'[147]

They initially made good progress. The only problem was members of the Arab party were petrified of the Manyuema; they imagined the Manyuema were going to kill and eat them at any time. One man got separated from his trading companions and in a blind panic was seen running as fast as he could into the trackless forest. They searched for him for several days in vain and he was given up for a murdered man who must have been eaten. They were very surprised when a Manyuema headman brought the fellow into their camp, fed and well cared for a few days later.

Their path forward slowly deteriorated. In one place, they had to struggle through paths carved out by elephants:

> The vegetation is indescribably rank. Through the grass—if grass it can be called, which is over half-an-inch in diameter in the stalk, and from ten to twelve feet high—nothing but elephants can walk. The leaves of this megatherium grass are armed with minute spikes which, as we worm our way along elephant walks, rub disagreeably on the side of the face where the gun is held, and the hand is made sore by fending it off the other side, for hours.[148]

Livingstone went on to describe their progress:

In places like this the leg goes into the elephant's holes up to the thigh and it is grievous; three hours of this slough tired the strongest; a brown stream ran through the centre, waist deep, and washed off a little of the adhesive mud.[149]

Livingstone was attacked by illnesses, including fever and choleric symptoms. In desperation he tried taking opium that Mohammad Bogharib gave him, but it had little effect. Livingstone noted that both he and others were 'greatly reduced in flesh.'[150] It was unhealthy country as Livingstone saw lepers; many of the natives were afflicted with syphilis, and curiously, there were large numbers of albinos.

By the end of January 1870, he was close to giving up in the wet and cold, as he realised how weak he was. It was only his incredible strength of will that made him continue, but after sleeping on a large rock during a thunderously heavy rain shower that he finally admitted he was 'quite knocked up and exhausted' and he decided to go into 'winter quarters'.[151] The place they decided upon was the village of a headman, Katomba. They arrived there on 7 February 1870, just six weeks after leaving Bambarré. Mohammad Bogharib and his party also stopped there, as they too were suffering. They had inadvertently picked the best, but also the worst of places to rest.

Over the next four months Livingstone and his party rested and waited out the wet season. His entries in his journal during this time are desultory. By late May he was thinking about moving, but fighting had broken out again, and he sent a message to Bambarré for the cloths and beads he had left there to be sent to him. It always seemed the fighting broke out for the smallest of reasons. On one occasion they heard Thani bin Suelim's trading party had killed forty Manyuema and burnt nine villages for the loss of four of their own over a string of beads. In June there was another outbreak of fighting and another forty Manyuema were killed and thirty-one captives taken as slaves together with sixty goats.

Livingstone was anxious to leave Katomba as the rainy season was coming to an end, although Livingstone had measured that in the first twenty-six days of June 1870 a massive fifty-eight inches of rain had fallen. Despite this, they left the next day, heading for the Lualaba. Unfortunately, not for the first time, some of his own party refused to accompany him and he only had Susi, Chumah and Edward Gardner as attendants.

It was immediately hard going, as the country was sodden. On the first day they crossed fourteen streams, some thigh deep. They passed through the nine destroyed villages, in silence, but their luck was in as they came across Mohammad Bogharib's party that was returning from trading on the Lualaba. He was able to tell Livingstone that the Lualaba did not flow in the north-westerly course that Livingstone had thought, but went in a west and south-westerly direction. They also told him they had gone a long way north without again encountering the Lualaba and that travelling was very difficult as they had to pass through thick forest and flooded paths.

Livingstone went on, but soon after had second thoughts and decided that he should heed the advice he had received and return as:

> For the first time in my life my feet failed me, and now having but three attendants it would have been unwise to go further in that direction. Instead of healing quietly as heretofore, when torn by hard travel, irritable-eating ulcers fastened on both feet; and I limped back to Bambarré on 22nd [July 1870].[152]

Meeting Mohammad Bogharib was a stroke of luck as Livingstone would no doubt have continued and possibly died at this point.

His feet were indeed in a bad way for he had three flesh eating ulcers and no medicine. When he put any pressure on them, they discharged a bloody ichor. They throbbed constantly which made sleep difficult. His agony reminded Livingstone of slave camps where:

> the wailing of the slaves tortured with these sores is one of the night sounds of a slave-camp; they eat through everything—muscle, tendon and bone, and often lame permanently if they do not kill the poor things.[153]

The ulcers that Livingstone suffered from were almost certainly a buruli ulcer, known after Buruli County in Uganda because of the many cases that occurred there in the 1960s[154]. It was first properly identified by Sir Albert Cook, a British physician, at Mengo Hospital in Kampala, Uganda in 1897. Ulcers were a common complaint. Another great explorer, James Augustus Grant, in his book *A Walk across Africa* (1864), describes how his leg became grossly swollen and stiff and later discharged copious amounts of pus and blood.

While recovering in Bambarré Livingstone heard gruesome stories about cannibalism. People were killed without warning, often if they were out tending their gardens or walking alone in the forest. If a wife argued too much with her husband it was not uncommon for her to be murdered by him who would then eat her heart, mixed with goat meat. Indeed the former chief, Moenekuss had also been eaten, and his sons kept his head, stripped of its flesh in a pot in his former hut. The sons communicated with the skull as if it was still alive.

With time on his hands, Livingstone ruminated on the news that Mohammad Bogharib had given him about the Lualaba. He speculated that the fountains of the Nile might lie south near Katanga based on new reports on the geography of the area that he received from natives and traders. This led him to postulate that water flowing from one of the fountains fed the Zambezi while the other one flowed north into the Nile. On and on he pondered, although it is not hard to believe his thinking was at times affected by his illness.

In August 1870 he was still laid up in Bambarré and clearly he was thinking about his own mortality when he confided in his journal, 'The severe pneumonia in Marunga, the choleric complaint in Manyuema, and now irritable ulcers warn me to retire while life lasts.'[155] If only he had taken his own advice.

When writing Livingstone's *Last Journals*, amongst the many scraps of paper that Waller found in Livingstone's journals was one on which Livingstone had written, 'Turn over and see a drop of comfort found when suffering from irritable eating ulcers on the feet in Manyuema, August 1870.'[156] It was snippet from a book review that he must have found among the supplies sent up from Zanzibar. Discovering and reading this review must have cheered up the ailing old man to a considerable extent.

Livingstone tried a number of medical treatments for his ulcers, but he only began to recover after he was advised to try the rubbings of Malachite applied gently using a feather. This seemed to have real healing effect and on 10 October 1870, Livingstone emerged from his hut having been confined to it since 22 July 1870, or eighty days. It would be a long time before the holes filled out. He was lucky that he had been isolated as a cholera epidemic had broken out in Bambarré and thirty people in the village died.

In the meantime Livingstone would eat on any occasion, in order to survive. On 3 November 1870, he shot 'a Kondohondo, the large double-billed Hornbill (the *Buceros cristata)*, Kakomira, of the Shire, and the Sassassa of Bambarré. It is good eating, and has fat of an orange tinge, like that of a zebra; I keep the bill to make a spoon of it.'[157]

As Livingstone lay hungry, Dr Kirk was trying his best to get much needed supplies to him. There was a re-supply for Livingstone that supposedly left Bagamoyo in November 1870, but Kirk became aware that the men and stores were still languishing in Bagamoyo in February 1871. He quickly crossed over from Zanzibar to Bagamoyo on the HMS *Columbine* and using his influence among the Arabs successfully persuaded the porters to leave. The diligent Kirk then accompanied them on a day's march into the interior. 'Once fairly off on the road, there is little to induce these people to delay.'[158] Unfortunately both for him and Livingstone, this group was to delay further and slowly consume most of Livingstone's supplies before they eventually met up with the explorer.

Kirk also noted the booming slave town had trebled in size since his visit to Bagamoyo four years previously, and stone buildings now replaced many native huts.

Livingstone waited on in Bambarré as he was expecting Syde bin Habib and Dugumbé to arrive from Ujiji, hopefully bearing goods and letters for him. He was by this time desperate for news from home.

The traders continued to be active, pushing out through the land in search of ivory. The Manyuema feared the Arabs and their slaves, but only because they had guns while the natives used spears and shields. This knowledge allowed the Arab trading parties to confidently swagger into villages and take over houses, help themselves to food, firewood, cooking pots without scruple or payment. The Arab traders would callously shoot anyone who tried to interfere or attempted to cause trouble. Unsurprisingly, the Manyuema grew increasingly sullen and dangerous.

The Arabs' own slaves were particularly cruel and cold-blooded to their former countrymen as they were encouraged to be so by their Arab masters. Livingstone's journal from this time is full of descriptions about murder, injustice and treachery. He simply could not understand why the Arabs prosecuted their trading in such a violent way, given the teachings of Islam. However, they did not have it all their own way as the Manyuema were slowly learning how to fight men with guns and the losses suffered by the trading parties steadily increased, for when given an opportunity, the Manyuema fought ferociously.

But if Livingstone loathed the practices of the Arabs, he also closely observed the degenerate Manyuema who also fought, stole and cheated each other:

> They are the lowest of the low, and especially in bloodiness: the man who killed a woman without cause goes free, he offered his grandmother to be killed in his stead, and after a great deal of talk nothing was done to him![159]

On another occasion he wrote about one custom of the people who he was living amongst:

> The Manyuema are the most bloody, callous savages I know; one puts a scarlet feather from a parrot's tail on the ground, and challenges those near to stick it in the hair: he who does so must kill a man or woman![160]

He longed to leave, but the prospect of receiving mail was stronger. November rolled into December 1870, and still he waited, but by then it was too late to leave, as the rains had come again. His frustration at the turn of events is evident in his writings and there is no doubt the delay and worries affected his constitution. On 10 December 1870, he wrote:

> I am sorely let and hindered in this Manyuema. Rain every day, and often at night; I could not travel now, even if I had men, but I could make some progress; this is the sorest delay I ever had. I look above for help and mercy.[161]

Finally, on 28 January 1871, the Arab caravan that Livingstone had long-expected arrived from the coast. They brought word of the death of Livingstone's 'brother' who he thought meant Dr Kirk, and news of a cholera outbreak that had killed 70,000 people on Zanzibar alone. Cholera was now spreading rapidly inland along the caravan routes into the African interior. More importantly for Livingstone, the Arabs told him his men and supplies that he ordered be sent up from Zanzibar had arrived in Ujiji. Livingstone hoped the porters would come on up to Bambarré and bring his needed goods and precious letters.

On the 4 February 1871, to Livingstone's great joy a rich Bamian trader arrived in Bambarré with ten former Bamian slaves carrying supplies organised by Kirk. One of porters, James, was soon after killed nearby when the Bamians went to buy food. They later heard a party had laid an ambush, killed and then feasted on his body.

The Bamians were to drive Livingstone to despair. During the sixteen-month period it had taken for them to travel from the coast to Bambarré they had helped themselves to his goods and then sold off the balance to buy slaves and ivory. Livingstone complained that it had cost him £500 to £600, money he could ill afford to lose. When Kirk later sent more supplies, again using former slaves, Livingstone was forced to travel 150 miles to find them. Livingstone was deeply upset at the perceived perfidious Kirk.[162]

Livingstone wrote another letter while waiting in Bambarré to Horace Waller.[163] His mood swing is obvious as the letter clearly shows the level of despondency that Livingstone had reached. 'I am terribly knocked up but this is for your own eye only.... Doubtful if I live to see you again.'[ ] His warning to Waller was prescient: he finally succumbed to another illness in May 1873.

After receiving his re-supply Livingstone wanted to leave immediately for the Lualaba river but his Bamians initially said they would not go, but then changed their minds when Livingstone offered to pay them six dollars per month. They were a sorry lot; Livingstone knew from experience that former slaves were unlikely to be faithful attendants. They told Livingstone that their job was to force him to return to Zanzibar, and they spread rumours in Bambarré that there was a letter from Kirk that ordered Livingstone to return home. In the end Mohammad Boughaib supported Livingstone and when the Bamians were threatened with being shot, they reluctantly agreed to accompany Livingstone. In the meantime, their two headmen, Shereef and Awathé had remained in Ujiji, purportedly looking after the rest of his supplies, but Livingstone was under no illusions. He knew that they would be helping themselves to his goods.

On 16 February 1871, nearly seven months after Livingstone had arrived back in Bambarré, they departed due west towards the Lualaba river. The people of the area that they initially passed through had not been spoilt by contact with the traders and were friendly and obliging with food. Livingstone's heart was once more light at being again on the road, doing what he loved best, exploring, particularly as they were travelling through beautiful, undulating countryside. On the way he met some Arabs, including Katomba, who gave him three letters; from Kirk, the Sultan of Zanzibar and Mohammad bin Nassib, all offering assistance. Livingstone was much cheered by this news. They also asked Livingstone if seven of their people could accompany his party and Livingstone gladly agreed, particularly as they knew a new shorter path to the river.

They continued on, but soon they entered an area where the traders had been; they encountered empty villages where the cooking fires were still smouldering from people too afraid to meet them in case they were Arab traders. But Livingstone's friendly approach soon won them over and the word spread that this was a different type of party and words of welcome would be called out loudly, 'Bolongo, Bolongo!' 'Friendship, Friendship!'[165] Livingstone was also privately pleased when he heard the Manyuema refer to him as the 'good one' and he felt sure that with proper missionary care, these people would respond well and freedom, peace and enjoyment would quickly be reasserted in their land.

By 6 March 1871 they arrived at the village of the Chief Kasonga and found out they were only six miles from the Lualaba river. They found some Arabs staying here and Livingstone was given a house to use by one of them.

Unfortunately his further progress was thwarted when Kosonga decided not to supply him with canoes to get his party across the river. One of the reasons was that there were more stories of killing coming in, including a report that Mohammad Bogharib's people had slaughtered a great number of people. Then the trading party attached to his own assaulted one of Kasongo's villages, killing three men and capturing a number of woman and children. Livingstone was despondent and his only entry on 20 March 1871 was, 'I am heartsore, and sick of human blood.'[166]

Deciding something must be done Livingstone left Kasonga with a goat and guide and headed north to buy a canoe. They soon met a large Arab trading party who had eight-two captives and twenty tusks. Apparently they had been fighting for ten days and Livingstone was keen to get well away from them.

Livingstone was unsuccessful in acquiring a canoe and returned to Kasonga. Here his Bamians continued to sorely test Livingstone, constantly trying to get him to return back to Zanzibar. They were also frightened as it was a dangerous area. Even Livingstone, who very rarely spoke of the risks, noted in his journal, 'I am greatly distressed because there is no law here; they [Manyuema] probably mean to create a disturbance at [Arab trader] Abed's place, to which we are near: the Lord look on it.'[167]

Livingstone decided to relocate to the banks of the Lualaba River and on 21 March 1871 they arrived at Nyangwé. It has his third attempt to reach the river and it was a magnificent sight to behold. It lay about 2,000 feet above sea level and was at least 3,000 yards wide and deep at that point. They carefully measured the current and found it flowed at about two miles an hour, to the north. Livingstone wondered if the river emptied into the Congo.

There was a huge market, or Chitoka, in Nyangwé, where up to 3,000 people, mostly women, would meet to barter and trade. Livingstone was surprised and pleased at the orderliness of the market although many were fearful when he and his party walked among them. There were also three Arabs already in Nyangwé, including Abed, together with their black half-caste Ujijian slaves. The Manyuema gave them wide berth because of their guns, but muttered ominously, 'If it were not for your guns, not one of you would ever return to your country.'[168]

He was keen to explore the river as he had done on the Zambezi, but obtaining canoes to cross the river was the problem. Offers were made, but nothing eventuated. Many of the locals thought he wanted canoes so he could make war on the people on the other side of the river.

While waiting Livingstone recorded descriptions of the geography of the land on the over side of the Lualaba. He also made ink out of the seeds of a plant that was used by the Manyuema for dying clothes and ornamenting their faces and hands.

He talked to the locals and they told him that they preferred all flesh rank. This included human flesh and they normally buried the body in a shallow grave for two to three days to make sure it was high before exhuming it and roasting it. They also told him 'human flesh is saltish, and needs but little condiment.'[169]

Time dragged on, and Livingstone grew increasingly impatient trying to obtain some canoes. He read the Bible and then reread it; he eventually read the Bible four times before he was to leave Nyangwé.[170] In the meantime, he continued to have trouble with his Bamians who mutinied three times. His situation was made more difficult as an Arab trader, Hassani, harboured them until Livingstone threatened the trader that he would have to pay him for them. However, it was clear the Bamians had no interest in going any further as they were completely unreliable. Abed later overheard the Bamians plotting to kill Livingstone if he took them on another expedition. Livingstone was thankful and described the Arab trader 'as a sincere friend, and I could not but take his words as well-meant and true.'[171]

This enforced inactivity weighed heavily on Livingstone. In his weakened state he had time to ruminate on his life's work and to think about his family. In a letter to Kirk, he painfully recalled his meeting with the Queens' Counsel, sent by the then Prime Minister Lord Palmerston, asking how the Government could aid him. He realised he had missed an opportunity to establish a secure financial future for his children; 'It never occurred to me that he [QC] meant ought for myself or children till I was out here and Lord Palmerston dead.'[172]

Livingstone was able to make friends with the locals, entering their vast markets alone to learn their language, customs and to find out about the fish and other produce that was being sold. The range of produce was staggering; vegetables, birds, animals and insects, cloth, metals, and pottery. He saw one fellow with a string of ten human jawbones tied about him and he told Livingstone with great relish that he had killed and eaten all of his victims. Despite their bloodthirstiness, he found the Manyuema much more pleasant to be amongst than his Bamians. His wanderings also helped in time to take away the fear the natives had of all newcomers.

On 1 May 1871, one of Katoma's trading parties returned to Nyangwé, carrying a huge load of ivory traded from a tribe known as the Ba-bisa. They found the Ba-bisa had an abundance of ivory, so plentiful in fact that they used it to build doorposts and house pillars. The trading party were able to buy an ivory tusk for just two iron rings and they were able to purchase so much ivory that it took three relays of porters to bring it all back to Nyangwé.

On 18 June 1871 Dugumbé arrived, and soon after presented Livingstone with four large pots of beads. The Arabs knew that Shereef was holding Livingstone's stores back in Ujiji and they sought to make life easier for him. Dugumbé had a huge trading party with him, numbering 500 guns. He also had his family as he was planning to remain in the area for six or seven years.

Livingstone finally decided enough was enough and made his preparations to leave Nyangwé sometime in July 1871. In desperation he offered Dugumbé £400 and his stores in Ujiji for ten men to replace his Bamian slaves. When the Bamians got to learn about this, surprisingly, they decided they wanted to accompany him, and despite his misgivings, Livingstone relented, so eager was he to complete his explorations. But he knew he was in perilous position and the continued stress and worries affected him. 'When baffled by untoward circumstances the bowels plague me too, and discharges of blood relieve the headache, and are as safety valves to the system.'[173]

Livingstone's plan was simple; accompany Dugumbé's trading party and head west and go to Katanga to see reputed underground dwellings, before heading further west to see the fountains that Herodotus had described as he was certain that is where they were situated. He then planned to return to Ujiji on Lake Tanganyika.

On 15 July 1871 shortly before his planned departure Livingstone witnessed the most harrowing incident he had seen in all his time in Africa. Livingstone had gone into the market on a hot, sunny morning and saw three Swahili men from Dugumbé's party, carrying guns. This was unusual. Livingstone estimated that there were up to fifteen hundred people crowded there, haggling, laughing and trading. Later, as he was leaving he heard two guns go off in the middle of the market. Livingstone knew immediately a massacre could be about to get underway. In the crowded atmosphere, the reaction was the same—panic. It soon became obvious that it was a premeditated attack because as the natives started to run to get to their canoes, another armed party opened up. The resulting confusion was dreadful to observe; the river was too small for the great number of canoes that the people were trying to launch and as shot after shot poured into the crowd, many jumped into the river and struck out for an island a mile away. The volley of shots continued and the slow and weak were cut down. Three canoes were, however, successfully launched, but when the paddlers stopped to help their friends, frantic swimmers grabbed the canoes until the combined weight dragged the boats under the water. Livingstone stood and watched helplessly as the heads of those in the water slowly disappeared until none were visible.

Fortunately, Livingstone was able to remain out of the fray and retreated back to his hut where he was able to save twenty terrified natives who came to him, seeking his protection.

It turned out Dugumbé's slave trading party were the main culprits. Livingstone was incandescent with rage and wanted to immediately kill them all, including their leader, a muslin called Tagamoio, but Dugumbé warned him not to start another fight and calmed him. Later Livingstone sat down and recorded his upset:

> As I write this I hear the loud wails on the left bank over those who are there slain, ignorant of their many friends now in the depths of the Lualaba. Oh, let Thy Kingdom come! No one will ever know the exact loss on this on this bright sultry summer morning, and it gave me the impression of being in Hell.[174]

Not happy with these killing, the slavers continued to rampage out of control and set fire to twenty-seven villages. Livingstone wrote that he personally counted seventeen villages in flames. Eventually the slavers quietened down and started feasting on goats, fowls and beer over the next two days. In the meanwhile Livingstone was so shocked by the scale and viciousness of the killing that he lay semi-comatose with a severe headache, which was only relieved by 'a copious discharge of blood.'[175]

The Arab slave-traders estimated that between three hundred and thirty to four hundred persons were slaughtered that day.

Livingstone's potentially deeper involvement in this tragedy has recently been uncovered through the use of spectral imaging technology[176] (2010). This process has revealed text that had been carefully removed from his journal, which shows Livingstone had concerns about the involvement of his own Bamians. He had written in his journals, 'I refused to send my slaves because they would only add to the confusion and murder. If they go anywhere I must go with them or murder is certain.'

Livingstone's highly emotional response to the tragedy is revealed in another note he made at the time of the massacre, 'I went over to Dugumbé and proposed to catch the bloodhounds who fired in the chitoba and on the canoes and put their heads on poles.' Livingstone subsequently toned down his bloodthirsty solution and wrote, 'I next proposed to Dugumbé to catch the murderers and hang them in the marketplace.'

Livingstone recovered, and sought to re-establish some form of peace, but it was an uneasy one. Many Manyuema came to Livingstone, seeking his assistance and he helped to mediate where he could. There were many blood mixing ceremonies between the headmen and the Arabs, as a way of re-establishing peace. However, the awful massacre of Manyuema by the slave traders effectively ended Livingstone plans. He realised that his association with the Arabs would cast a long shadow over his plans to travel west, and greatly disappointed, he gave up on his long cherished goal of finding the fountains of the Nile and of finding a fourth great lake that was rumoured to lie west. He had already named this fourth lake,

Lake Lincoln. It was with a very heavy heart that he left Nyangwé on 20 July 1871 to slowly make his way back to Ujiji. He had been three months in Nyangwé, and it had all been for nought.

Livingstone was fearful of reprisals and when one of his Bamians fell behind, he was left and the small compact party quickly pushed on. They were fortunate that in their party were natives from some of the villages they passed through. They had volunteered to help them carry their loads in return for some beads and this speeded up their progress. A few Manyuema came by and Livingstone was reassured to hear that they knew he had taken no part in the massacre. By 27 July 1871 they had reached Kasonga's village and some Arabs living there welcomed him.

These same Arabs politely asked Livingstone if some of their men could attach themselves to Livingstone's own party, as they needed to get resupplies from Ujiji. This request placed him in a difficult position, as the Arabs had been kind to him in his time of need. He felt he could not refuse the request although he was well aware of the risks of closely associating himself with them. Livingstone did eventually agree, thinking they would add strength and make their passage through the dangerous country to Bambarré safer. He knew that on their way they would pass through a land where the people would be burning with revenge. His party also included seventeen Manyuema who carried tusks for the traders.

On 4 August 1871, they passed through miles of destroyed villages. Suddenly and without warning they were attacked when an unseen assailant speared one of Livingstone's goats. Livingstone knew trouble was near as he had seen how unfriendly and suspicious the people were. They carefully moved on, armed and on alert. By the 7 August 1871 Livingstone had fallen ill and every step was taken in pain, but he knew he could not rest as the local Manyuema were clearly spoiling for a fight—they had seen the Arab slavers among Livingstone's party. Next day the attack came when they entered a carefully prepared ambush in thick forest. Suddenly the air was alive with spears hurtling through the undergrowth towards them. One grazed Livingstone's back as he quickly crouched over, missing, despite his attacker being only ten yards away, then soon after, another spear passed by him a foot to his front. Two of his men were killed and although they responded by firing into the dense forest, it was to no effect, as they could not clearly see their assailants. The Manyuema responded by jeering at their feeble efforts. This was only the beginning; for five long, terrible hours they ran the gauntlet of flying spears thrown by invisible enemies from the surrounding undergrowth. At one point, a tree was felled before them and the branches of the gigantic tree fell about Livingstone as he ran back away from the toppling danger.

This was Livingstone's third miraculous deliverance from death that day and his attendants began to cluster around him, thinking he was charmed, as they continued to push their way forward, cautiously peering into every dark space, expecting to see a spear come hurtling out. Livingstone later wrote that they got to a point of total exhaustion with the stress and that he no longer cared if he lived or died.

Hours later they broke out into cleared country and quietly rejoiced, as they knew they had survived. Soon after they met natives and it became clear the Manyuema had thought Livingstone was Mohammad Bogharib, as Livingstone had been seen earlier in the day wearing a red jacket similar to what the Arab wore. Livingstone's party were much relieved at surviving their brush with death although he was annoyed to learn one of his Bamian servants had thrown away his load containing all of Livingstone's remaining calico, a telescope, umbrella, and five spears he had collected.

By 12 August 1871, Livingstone was severely ill again, but he struggled on. He was bleeding from his bowels and when they arrived back in Katomba, he had to rest from his weaknesses. He was still not fully recovered when they set out on 30 August 1871, and it took him another week before he felt better, particularly as they had been able to buy Dura flour, *Holcus sorghum*, and this gave him strength. They headed towards the shores of Lake Tanganyika, climbing over mountain ranges, descending into deep gullies and fording fast flowing rivers before entering green undulating country as they approached the lake.

The stress and difficulty of their march told heavily on Livingstone. He was never one to exaggerate, but he wrote, 'In the latter part of it, I felt as if dying on my feet. Almost every step was in pain, the appetite failed, and a little bit of meat caused violent diarrhoea, whilst the mind, sorely depressed, reacted on the body.'[177] He was also deeply upset about his failure to end his quest for the source of the Nile, when even the traders had been successful. 'I alone had failed and experienced worry, thwarting, baffling, when almost in sight of the end towards which I strained.'[178]

On they stumbled, over sharp quartz rocks that made Livingstone's feet throb with pain as he had resorted to wearing ill-fitting French shoes. Much dust was thrown up in this dry rocky landscape and by the time he reached the lake he was suffering from ophthalmia. His cryptic entries in his journal attest to his continuing poor health.

They arrived on the shores of Lake Tanganyika on 9 October 1871 and immediately boarded canoes. They were exhausted and looking like walking skeletons, entered Ujiji on 23 October 1871.

Livingstone was desperately hoping that he had more supplies waiting for him in Ujiji but it was to be an unhappy place for when Livingstone arrived, he found that all the stores that had been sent to him had been sold off by Sherrif, an important Arab living in Ujiji. It was a large cache, 3,000 yards of calico and 700 pounds of beads—it was too tempting for the Arab trader. In his defence Sherrif said he believed Livingstone was dead and so had sold his goods for ivory, but he did not offer Livingstone either the ivory or other trading supplies.[179]

Over the next few days he lay about, dejected and with his spirits at their lowest ebb. Livingstone realised he was nearly destitute. Starvation and death loomed large in his thoughts.

Then on or about 28 October 1871, Livingstone's fortune changed dramatically when Susi, his faithful servant, came rushing up to him and gasped out, 'An Englishman! I see him!'[180] Susi immediately turned tail and darted back up track to meet the stranger. Henry Morton Stanley had arrived.

CHAPTER 11

An Encounter with Stanley

'Doctor Livingstone I presume.'

11.1 Poor Beginnings

Stanley was born in 1841 in Denbigh, North Wales. It was the same year that Livingstone first arrived in Africa. He was born to an unmarried eighteen-year-old woman who went on to have four other illegitimate children by at least two other men. Stanley's proper name was John Rowlands and he never knew his father. His mother left him in the care of his grandfather until he died when Stanley was just five years old. For a time he was lucky; another family took him in, but soon these guardians abandoned him at a local workhouse. Later in life Stanley would recall that he 'experienced for the first time the awful feeling of utter desolateness' after the guardian had fled and the workhouse door slammed shut.

It was the beginning of a lonely and hard life. By the time he was seventeen, he had escaped from the workhouses and got himself on a ship to the United States where he changed his name to Henry Morton Stanley. He energetically participated in the Civil War, first joining the Confederate Army and fighting in the Battle of Shiloh in 1862. After being taken prisoner he was recruited at Camp Douglas, Illinois by its commander, Col. James A. Mulligan, and joined the Union Army in June 1862, but was discharged 18 days later due to severe illness. Recovering, he served on several merchant ships before joining the Navy in July 1864. On board the *Minnesota* he became a record keeper, which led to freelance journalism. Stanley and a junior colleague jumped ship on 10 February 1865 in New Hampshire, in search of greater adventures. Stanley thus became possibly the only man to serve in the Confederate Army, the Union Army, and the Union Navy.

At the conclusion of hostilities, he realised he needed to urgently find himself a job. One skill he did have was in writing, and so he dedicated himself to becoming a successful journalist. His pacey style of writing was appealing, and particularly so when Stanley covered interesting stores emanating from the Wild West. After a succession of jobs he eventually ended up gaining a coveted position on the country's largest daily newspaper, the *New York Herald*.

Stanley was an inveterate liar, particularly about his early childhood. He allowed this account of himself to be published:

> Henry M. Stanley was born in the city of New York in the year 1843. It is related that he ran away from school while yet a boy, went to sea, and deserted his ship at Barcelona, by jumping overboard and swimming ashore. He lost his bundle of clothing, landed naked, was taken by a sentry and lodged in a castle. A captain of the garrison, taking compassion on him, re-clothed him, and guided him through the suburbs of Barcelonetta to the high road. The boy, nothing daunted, though in a strange land, started for France, with a view of going to the seaport of Marseilles. He had not a sou in his pocket, and, like Goldsmith, begged his living as he travelled.[1]

It was exciting stuff, but unfortunately, a complete fabrication, although it reveals the depth of his insecurities. His re-invention of himself into the 'gentleman' Henry Morton Stanley certainly made his progress in life, both at the *New York Herald* and during his triumphant tour of Britain much easier. It is hard to imagine he would have got anywhere near the level of attention in Britain had it been known he was just another abandoned, Welsh bastard.[2]

11.2 'Find Livingstone'

An equally flamboyant character, James Gordon Bennett Junior, was the proprietor of the *New York Herald*. Bennett had been carefully watching developments regarding Livingstone, aware that he had not been seen since 1866. He was a shrewd and successful businessman and knew there would be much to be gained from anyone finding Livingstone, and more so if it was someone from his own newspaper. He was well aware of Stanley from his work at the *New York Herald* and thought the pugnacious Welshman would be the right person to find Livingstone for him. When they met in Paris, his message to Stanley was simple, 'Do what you think best, but find Livingstone.'[3]

Stanley characteristically chose later to embellish his appointment:

> Urged by Mr. Bennett to undertake, single-handed, a task from which liberally equipped organisations, aided by the strong arm of England, had shrunk back in despair, Stanley unhesitatingly accepted the challenge to his pluck and perseverance, firmly resolved to find Dr. Livingstone, or perish in the effort.[4]

Stanley was given as much money as he needed to establish and provision an expedition. But he also knew Bennett was tough and while he had all the support he needed, he knew he had to succeed—or literally perish.

He was more than ready for the challenge, as he knew that it would make him as nearly famous as Livingstone himself. Stanley also hoped to make some new geographical discoveries. The opportunities for this aggressive and ambitious reporter lay open, enticingly, before him.

Stanley, at thirty years of age, was full of energy. He was a small man at just five feet six inches, but pictures taken after the trip show him to be a strongly built, tough-looking fellow brimming with confidence. He had blue-grey eyes and a typical Victorian moustache.

Stanley reached Zanzibar on 6 January 1871 and immediately started getting his expedition ready. But there was one major question that vexed him; where exactly should he start looking for Livingstone? The last report from Livingstone had him on the shores of Lake Tanganyika, and that is where Stanley chose to begin.

He took Bennett at his word to draw down as much money as necessary to outfit his expedition. The one thing Stanley did not do, when given the opportunity, was to stint on 'necessary' supplies to ensure an important expedition like his would be appropriately fitted out. In the end Stanley is reputed to have spent about £8,000.[5] Therefore, when he left Zanzibar bound for Lake Tanganyika, it was one of the most costly and resplendent expeditions ever to leave for the African interior.

They set off from Bagamoyo, in modern day Tanzania, on 21 March 1871. Stanley, as befitting the occasion, wore a white flannel suit and pith helmet, and was mounted on an Arab stallion. He had clearly not heard about the tsetse fly. He led a long procession of guards and porters, the latter carrying yards of cloth and brass wire for trade with tribes in the interior. They had forty guns, tons of ammunition, a mountain of battle-axes, swords and knives. Stanley was similarly outfitted and his personal baggage included a tin bath, a bearskin rug and a bottle of Worcestershire sauce. He took a dog, Omar, to guard his tent To cap off the magnificent sight, Stanley had an American flag carried at the front of the column.

Stanley had employed about 100 natives. He also brought two other Europeans; tough former British sailors—a Scot and a Cockney—to enforce discipline and ensure the expedition went as planned.

Stanley had never visited the southern parts of Africa before and everything was new, at times terrifying. The stallion quickly succumbed to the bite of the tsetse fly. They soon disappeared into swamps, bitten endlessly by fever bearing mosquitos, and the men soon started dying of malaria, fevers and dysentery. The Scot succumbed to suspected elephantiasis and the cockney sailor got malaria. This meant Stanley was the only white man left, and he in turn was gripped by fever. He lost three stones in weight and had 'insane visions' and 'frenetic brain-throbs'. But Stanley was made of stern stuff and despite his own sickness he continued to drive the expedition on. He was a fearsome disciplinarian and any infraction was quickly and severely punished.

As they stumbled northwest towards Lake Tanganyika they quickly ran into local tribes. These natives were unfriendly and threatening, demanding goods and payment for travelling through their lands. The situation became further complicated when he inadvertently wandered into a war between the Arabs of Tabora and the Nyamwezi chief, Mirambo.

The continued harassment soon started to tell on the expedition members; the scared and overworked porters began to slowly desert, and those left behind were forced to carry heavier and heavier loads. Soon morale within the group was low and dangerous, highlighted when some porters refused to carry the assigned loads. It was a moment when all could be lost, but Stanley, the only remaining European, was unfazed. He ordered the recalcitrant porters to be chained and whipped as an example to others. It had the desired effect and soon the expedition was underway again, although much diminished. By October 1871, some seven months after leaving, the number had fallen to just thirty-three unhappy members. By this time, they were deep into east Africa having travelled about seven hundred tough miles.

Stanley was not daunted by the difficulty of the terrain or the unfortunate turn of events, as he possessed tremendous will power. Much later the natives appropriately nicknamed him 'Bula Matari', 'Breaker of Rocks', for they soon appreciated—and respected—his indomitable will to persevere and conqueror.

An indication of his personal will can be gleaned from a letter he wrote in 1890 to *The Times*, explaining why he not only a survivor, but was successful in exploring hitherto unknown regions unlike most others:

> For myself I lay no claim to any exceptional fineness of nature; but I say, beginning life as a rough, ill-educated, impatient man, I have found my schooling in these very African experiences which are now said by some to be in themselves detrimental to European character.[6]

Things may have continued to worsen, but for some encouraging news that they received; there was a report of an old white man living in a place called Ujiji on the eastern side of Lake Tanganyika. This is where Stanley now headed hoping all the while that the rumour was true.

11.3 Arrival at Ujiji

Livingstone was meanwhile living in extreme circumstances after six long and difficult years in Africa. He was living on hand-outs from Arab slavers, without whose help he certainly would not have survived. His original fifty-nine followers had shrunk over time to his 'faithful's', Susi and Chumah and a small group of other men. He knew he was totally isolated, without writing paper. His chief source of comfort was his Bible, which he continued to read repeatedly.

Livingstone was in a very poor medical state as a result of losing his medical supplies. He was in constant pain and suffering the ill effects of a succession of debilitating diseases, such as malaria, dysentery and rheumatic fever. He also suffered dreadfully from haemorrhoids, which further weakened him and it is a matter of conjecture just how much longer he may have survived in Ujiji without medical supplies. Then suddenly an event took place that captured the imagination of the world. It all happened around about 28 October 1871, as both men had lost count of the date, when Stanley arrived in Ujiji.

A porter carrying the unfurled Stars and Stripes flag led Stanley's caravan into Ujiji. Livingstone's first thoughts as he viewed Stanley's vast baggage of 'Bales of goods, baths of tin, huge kettles, cooking pots, tents, &c., made me think "this must be a luxurious traveller", and not one at his wit's end like me.'[7]

Stanley was well aware of the importance of this historic meeting with Livingstone, particularly as he knew he would later write about it. Purportedly, in expectation of the meeting, he had his flannel suit pressed, his knee-high leather boots oiled and buffed and his Topee, a sun helmet, was freshly chalked. He mounted his last surviving donkey to ride into Ujiji. His men rose to the occasion and fired their rifles into the air. Quickly a crowd of natives assembled and slowly led Stanley into the village where an aged white man stood under a Mango tree, dressed in tweed trousers, a red shirt and the ubiquitous but somewhat faded blue-and-gold cap. Stanley reported that the natives welcomed his party into Ujiji by belting out 'monotonous tones' on their crude musical instruments.[8]

Whether this did occur as Stanley described them is difficult to know, as it would have required Stanley to be sure Livingstone was actually in Ujiji. In any event, for Livingstone, the arrival of the resplendent Stanley must had seemed like a godsend—and totally unexpected.

On seeing Livingstone Stanley later wrote that he wanted to express his delight by 'turning a somersault' and 'slashing at trees'. The great search was over and the prize was Stanley's. Dismounting from his donkey Stanley stepped forward and in a particularly Victorian fashion, politely raised his hat, and apparently said 'Dr. Livingstone, I Presume?'

No one will know exactly what was first said at the historical meeting between Livingstone and Stanley. 'Dr. Livingstone, I Presume?' is widely believed to be what Stanley said, but another version; 'Dr. Livingstone, I believe'[9] was printed in his American lectures as the form of salutation used. Stanley may have been trying to achieve a masterful level of understatement and to impart some sense of dignity to the occasion.[10] Unfortunately his words of introduction became the butt of many jokes in Britain and thereafter he sought to make his supposed greeting more believable. Then, as today, it seems a strange thing to say when meeting the only other white man in that part of Africa and for that reason was almost certainly made up later by Stanley.

Later, when they had both retired to Livingstone's hut, Livingstone told Stanley, 'You have brought me new life.' It was the honest truth.

When Livingstone had left England six years previously, he had dark hair and a moustache. Stanley was shocked to find an emaciated, grey-haired and bearded old man. By this time his teeth had largely fallen out and he was very deaf, a side effect of taking large doses of quinine over many years.

Livingstone's state of dress can only be imagined. One of the articles that is preserved in the David Livingstone Centre in Scotland is a shirt.[11] It is made of hard wearing rough cotton and the shirt was manufactured in the Glasgow region. What is striking is the colour, for it is still a deep rich red Turkey red, which has not faded.

The appearance of Stanley was an immediate tonic for Livingstone. Not only did he receive much needed food, medicines and other supplies,[12] but the unexpected arrival of another white man meant suddenly there was a person with whom Livingstone could converse with, hear news about the outside world and share his ideas and thoughts. In time this completely rejuvenated him.

Livingstone's appetite returned and instead of eating cold hard gruel, he luxuriated in eating good rich food, four times a day and within a week was beginning to feel strong again. He also had time to reflect on the miraculous appearance of Stanley. He confided in his journal.

> I am not of a demonstrative turn; as cold, indeed, as we islanders are usually reputed to be, but this disinterested kindness of Mr. Bennett, so nobly carried into effect by Mr. Stanley, was simply overwhelming. I really do feel extremely grateful, and at the same time I am a little ashamed at not being more worthy of the generosity.[13]

Three days later Livingstone wrote a letter to Earl of Clarendon in his capacity as the Foreign Secretary, to formally thank the Government for supporting a different search party to find him. He did not know Clarendon had died and had been replaced by Earl Granville:

> I became aware of Mr. Young's Search Expedition only in February last, and that by a private letter from Sir Roderick Murchison. Though late in expressing my thankfulness, I am not the less sincere in now saying that I feel extremely obliged to Her Majesty's Government, to the Admiralty, to Captain Richards, to Sir Roderick Murchison, and to Mr. Young, and all concerned in promoting the kind and rigorous inquiry after my fate.[14]

He could not resist adding:

Had the low tone of morality among the East African Mahometans been known, Musa's tale would have received but little attention. Musa is perhaps a shade better than the average low-class Moslem, but all are notorious for falsehood and heartlessness.

What is also interesting about this letter is that there is no mention of Stanley.

Livingstone was keen to continue his explorations and Stanley was keen to join him. Stanley helpfully offered to finance these explorations. On 16 November 1871, three weeks after Stanley's arrival, Livingstone was recovered enough for them to set out together to explore the northern part of Lake Tanganyika. The purpose was to finally determine if Lake Tanganyika did in fact flow into Albert Nyanza, or Baker Lake, as Livingstone had postulated.

They initially travelled by canoe. They put into shore one evening to eat and sleep but during the night they were disturbed by the sounds of men moving among the rocks around them. These natives were filtering into a position to attack them. Realising the danger, they quickly and quietly made off in their canoes just as the natives launched their attack.

By 27 November 1871 they reached the head of Lake Tanganyika and were able to confirm that the rivers flow into the lake, and not as previously postulated flowing into Albert Nyanza. This is the Rusizi River,[15] which enters the lake through a small delta at the northern end. Clearly Lake Tanganyika was not a source of the Nile.

They slowly and luxuriously returned back down the lake. *En route* they camped on the newly named New York Herald Islet. They were back in Ujiji on 15 December 1871, having filled in another important piece of the jigsaw with regard to the source of the Nile.

Stanley had been ill with fever during most of their trip and he had a relapse when he got back in Ujiji. Livingstone carefully nursed Stanley back to health. In the meantime Livingstone was preparing to leave Ujiji and go to Unyanyembe with Stanley to collect the rest of his goods that had been left there.

While in Ujiji he gave Stanley a large tin box of things he had collected, including spears and swords. He also left behind with Mohammad bin Saleh goods to pick up on his return. Chastened by his experience with other Arab traders, Livingstone carefully noted what he left behind in a journal entry on Christmas Day, 1871:

I leave here one bag of beads in a skin, 2 bags of Sungo mazi 746 and 756 blue. Gardner's bag of beads, soap 2 bars in three boxes (wood). 1st, tea and matunda; 2nd, wooden box, paper and shirts; 3rd, iron box, shoes, quinine, 1 bag of coffee, sextant stand, one long wooden box empty.

On 27 December 1871 they departed east for Unyanyembe, a journey that took nearly two months.[16] The trip started out well; they had bought with them goats and donkeys and the shooting was good. In his spare time Livingstone was busy copying his notes into his journals as he planned to give them to Stanley to take back to England.[17]

In early January 1872 Livingstone completed a letter to his old friend Oswell to ask him if he would mind if Livingstone named a 'fountain' after him. Livingstone supposed it was the source of both the Upper Zambezi and Kafue River. He had become convinced that this was one of the ancient fountains that Herodotus[18] had written about in *The Histories* as the fabled source of the Nile. One of the reasons why Livingstone chose to name this particular fountain after his friend was because they had both been told about this common source of the Zambezi and the Kafue when travelling together on the Upper Zambezi with Sebitoane's boatmen, the Mokantju.[19]

In reading his letter it appears that Livingstone was becoming increasingly addled and preoccupied with the existence of the 'Mountains of the Moon', describing them to Oswell in this fashion:

> I have heard of the earthen mound at which the four fountains rise so often—and I know pretty [well] the four rivers they form that I venture to say I wait another year to rediscover them. When we heard Mokantju's tale we were about 350 miles from the mound but Liambai whose fountain I call Palmerston's and Kafue whose fountain I call Oswell's do most certainly flow into Inner Ethiopia. The other two Bartle Frere's flows as R Lufira into lake Kamolondo and [James] Young's (I have been obliged to knight him to distinguish him from the gunner, as Sir Paraffin Young) goes through Lake Lincoln into Lualaba and North to Egypt. They thus [form] the central line of drainage, Webb's Lualaba into Petherick's branch.[20]

What Oswell made of this geographically incorrect and rambling letter nobody knows.

11.4 Like Father and Son

According to the pamphlet Stanley published for his American lecture circuit, he only remained with Livingstone for two-and-a-half months before he left to return to England.[21] However, this is incorrect, for they spent nearly four months together.

They made an odd couple—the grizzly old Scot, and the young, ambitious and troubled Welshman, but they had a common bond in that they both came from under privileged childhoods. They had achieved much through their own hard work and propensity to take risks, but both felt they were misunderstood by many of their peers. They were also conscious of their social disadvantage in a class-conscious Victorian Britain. It could be that during the time they spent together, Livingstone might have provided Stanley with an emotional compass, while Stanley certainly provided Livingstone with physical support. A tight father–son relationship certainly seems to have been forged during the short time they were together.

The reason for Stanley's haste in getting away was that he was a good journalist, and he was getting increasingly anxious to get his news released to the world before anyone else did.

They marched together through the rain-soaked, open undulating country, all the while conversing about all manner of things. They climbed steadily as they headed east, quickly rising to over 1,000 feet above Lake Tanganyika. The rainy season was in full force and they took their time. By 18 January 1872 Livingstone's feet were again troubling him, as his ill-fitting shoes greatly aggravated them. Then Stanley fell ill, and they rested up for three days until he was able to continue.

On a long march everyone settled down to plod their weary way forward. There was not much talking, as the porters sweated under their heavy loads. On 27 January 1872 Livingstone was peacefully riding along on a donkey that Stanley had bought for him, when suddenly both he and the animal were attacked by a large swarm of bees. The donkey did the unexpected; instead of running away, the animal fell to the ground and started rolling and rolling. Livingstone did the same and then got up and scampered into the forest, whisking a brush around his head as he did so. The old man must have made a funny sight as he set off on his skinny legs, but it was in fact no laughing matter as he was badly stung around his head. His donkey died two days later from all the bee stings.

Stanley fell ill again on 3 February 1872, 'with great pains in the back and loins: an emetic helped him a little, but resin of jalap would have cured him quickly.' He remained so ill that he had to be carried in a cot for a few days, as the party wearily splashed their way through muddy trails in cold, pouring rain. His recovery was short-lived as he was ill again with severe fever just ten days later, and so it was a tired and relieved group of men that marched into Unyanyembe on 18 February 1872. They had covered over 300 miles in fifty-four days.

Stanley urged Livingstone repeatedly to return to England with him, both because of his obvious frailty, but no doubt thinking that it would ensure a magnificent reception in that country for both Livingstone and himself. 'Mr. Stanley used some very strong arguments in favour of my going home, recruiting my strength, getting artificial teeth, and then returning to finish my task.'[22]

Unfortunately for Stanley his entreaties were unheeded as Livingstone continued to be fixated on finding the source of the Nile, no doubt thinking about his own immortality if he was successful in this regard. He was also comforted from a letter he had received from his daughter Agnes. 'Much as I wish you to come home, I would rather that you finished your work to your own satisfaction than return merely to gratify me.'[23]

Livingstone was now determined to find the legendary fountains of the Nile, 'four full-growing gushing fountains'.[24] He was certain they lay just eight days south of Katanga. He was also certain that two rivers sprung from two of these fountains and flowed north into Egypt and that two other rivers from the other two fountains flowed into Inner Ethiopia. While this all seems crazy now, it must be remembered that Livingstone carefully asked all the people that he came into contact with—Arab, Swahili or native—about the local geography and in doing so, was constantly cross-referencing the location of rivers, lakes and mountains. However, what is a mystery was why he was so certain about the location of the fountains and direction of the rivers. His recent foray to the top of Lake Tanganyika where he confirmed it did not flow in Albert Nyanza as he thought, was based on numerous, but ultimately wrong reports. This should have provided him with a timely reminder about not relying too much on local information. Perhaps, at the end of the day, he just simply wanted to believe that he had discovered, finally, the source of the Nile. It was a decision that was to cost him his life.

Livingstone resolved that after Stanley left he would travel back down and around the southern end of Lake Tanganyika, cross over the Chambeze river and march around the southern tip of Lake Bangweulu before heading due west for Katanga. It was to be a grand and glorious march and a fitting final testament to Livingstone's exploratory prowess as he noted in his journal:

> This route will serve to certify that no other sources of the Nile can come from the south without being seen by me. No one will cut me out after this exploration is accomplished; and may the good Lord of all help me to show myself one of His stout-hearted servants, an honour to my children, and, perhaps, to my country and race.[25]

However, before taking off on his final march, he and Stanley found to their anger and disgust that they had both been robbed of their supplies. Two headmen had been selected to look after their goods and had systematically helped themselves; one had since died of smallpox and the other was a whingeing, lying fellow. Fortunately Livingstone later searched the thief's premises and found some of Stanley's goods. It was most fortuitous as Stanley was then in a position to generously make good on almost all of Livingstone's missing supplies; calico, beads, brass wire, copper sheets, tent, a bath, cooking pots, tools, nails, books, paper, ammunition and most importantly, a medicine chest. It was a bounty and a boon to Livingstone, as he could not have set out again without receiving at least some calico and beads for trading.

Livingstone sat down to complete his journal and write a number of letters, including a thank you letter to Gordon Bennett and Earl Granville,[26] urging them to help end slavery. In his letter to Bennett, he wrote:

And if my disclosures regarding the terrible Ujijian slavery should lead to the suppression of the East Coast slave trade, I shall regard that as a greater matter by far than the discovery of all the Nile sources together.[27]

He also enjoined Earl Granville to encourage British settlement in this area of Africa. Stanley was keen to depart and Livingstone applied himself urgently to the task of completing all his writings and correspondence.[28]

Stanley left Unyanyembe on 14 March 1872. If Livingstone was emotional at first meeting Stanley in Ujiji, it was Stanley's turn to get emotional at their farewell. 'I looked back and watched his grey figure, fading dimmer in the distance...' Stanley wrote in his typically flamboyant way. 'I gulped down my great grief and turned away.' Stanley later wrote that during the period he spent with Livingstone 'he never found a fault in him, and that though himself a man of a quick temper, with Livingstone he never had cause for resentment, but each day's life with him added to his admiration of him.'

One of the important things that Livingstone entrusted to Stanley was his precious journal, a large Lett's Diary, sealed with five seals and with the instructions that they were not to be opened. Livingstone used his personal seal, '*David Livingstone*' and underneath, '*Christus Mihi Petra Vivens*', which translated means Christ is my living rock.

The journal was presented to Stanley in a canvas bag on which Livingstone had carefully written, 'Not to be opened. David Livingstone. Unjanyombo. March 13th 1872.' Later Stanley stencilled on the bag in his own hand above Livingstone's writing the word, 'POSITIVELY'. It shows how protective Stanley felt about Livingstone and his possessions.

Stanley faithfully carried the journal to England and gave it to Agnes Livingstone when he arrived later in the year. After Livingstone's death the journal was opened and it was found to contain notes of the period from when Livingstone arrived in Zanzibar up to the time just before he met Stanley in Ujiji.[29]

Stanley was bursting to depart but Livingstone had not had time to complete all his maps and so he immediately set about doing that. He carefully noted on his maps the routes he had taken, and observations he had made. Stanley left two men behind to wait patiently until Livingstone had finished his work with instructions that these men were to catch up Stanley's party as soon as they could. It took Livingstone two days to complete them and the men were soon on their way. Stanley's organisation and determination to leave gives a good indication about his character.

Stanley did not head straight for the coast, but decided to first circumnavigate Lake Victoria to see if he could conclusively prove Speke's claim that the lake was the source of the Nile. Whether Livingstone was aware that Stanley intended to do this is unknown—there would no doubt have been an interesting conversation had Stanley discussed his plans with him. Stanley doggedly pursued his course, and in doing so discovered the Ripon Falls on the lake's northern shore.

Unbeknown to Stanley and Livingstone, in 1870 Murchison raised the prospect of again trying to locate Livingstone in an address to the Royal Geographical Society, as he had last been seen in May 1869.[30] The information from Young had proven that the report of his death at the hands of the Mazitu tribe, as described by the Johanna men was false. However, there were subsequent reports received that Livingstone was at Ujiji, waiting for supplies to be sent to him. Sir Bartle Frere, the then President of the Royal Geographical Society took up the call and a public announcement was made that a relief expedition would be sent to find Livingstone. The public responded generously by donating over £5,000 while the composition of the expedition team was finalised. It was agreed that two Lieutenants, Dawson and Henn, would lead the relief expedition. Livingstone's twenty-year old son, William, also joined the newly named, 'Livingstone Search and Relief Expedition'.[31]

They made quick progress in outfitting their expedition and their ship landed in Zanzibar on 17 March 1872. They quickly moved to Bagamoyo, but on 27 April 1872, just as they were about to start out, three men entered their camp bringing extraordinary news; Livingstone had been found. They told the amazed team that an American, Henry Stanley, correspondent from the *New York Herald* had already been to Ujiji and found Livingstone. This news caused immediate consternation—what to do next? A meeting was held on 3 May 1872 and it was decided to cancel the expedition and instead send their expedition supplies on to Livingstone. Lieutenant Dawson resigned while Lieutenant Henn and William Livingstone resolved that they would continue to Ujiji, and were about to depart from Bagamoyo when Stanley arrived with full fanfare.

With an American flag flying, Stanley came triumphantly into their camp and was soon talking about all that he had seen and done. It was forerunner to what Stanley would steadily expand upon—and refine—during his tour of Britain. For the Livingstone Search Expedition, it was a moment of quiet disappointment as this brash American spoilt what clearly should have been a British success. For William it was an especially bitter disappointment, for it meant he would not get to see his father, and as it happened, he never saw him again.

Matters were made worst when Dr Kirk later alleged:

> Mr Stanley lost no time in assuring Lieut Henn that he and his party would be far from welcome and their presence only an incumbrance, as he, Mr. Stanley, held the Doctor's own orders for a gang of men and the special supplies he still required.[32]

It was the start of a lifetime enmity between Kirk and Stanley.

The expedition quietly packed up, and when the next ship called, they and Stanley and his party embarked and sailed back to England.

The Royal Geographical Society later conducted an investigation of the behaviour of Dawson and the other officers in abruptly terminating the expedition.

The investigating committee was critical of Lieutenant Dawson's behaviour and disappointed that there was a lost opportunity to support Livingstone. When Livingstone later heard of the break-up of the Relief Expedition in a letter from his son William, he, too, was disappointed, as he later made it clear he could have utilised the services of the officers.

In Zanzibar Stanley actively promoted the idea Kirk, now the British Consul in Zanzibar was to blame for many of the problems that Livingstone experienced. Stanley would have heard first-hand how disappointed Livingstone was that his precious supplies had been entrusted to former slaves. Indeed Livingstone had been incensed enough to write to Kirk, 'I feel inclined to relinquish hope of ever getting help from Zanzibar to finish the little work I have still to do ... I may wait twenty years and your slaves feast and fail.' To add insult to injury, Livingstone also reminded Kirk that it was against Government policy 'for its servants to employ slaves.'[33] Kirk was both mortified and hurt when he received this letter. Later when Stanley started making his allegations Kirk angrily fell out with him, particularly as he thought Stanley had poisoned Livingstone into thinking his office was not trying to do its best to halt slave trading in East Africa. Stanley later publicly attacked Kirk about his efforts to stop this practice. However, the allegations were unfounded, and Kirk went on to represent the British Government at the highest levels on the elimination of the slave trade.

Stanley got his despatch off to his newspaper when he arrived in Aden and on 2 July 1872 the *New York Herald* announced the news that Livingstone was alive. It was a major international scoop. The paper reported that:

> Preserving the calmness of exterior before the Arabs which was hard to simulate as he reached the group, Mr. Stanley said, 'Doctor Livingstone, I presume?' A smile lit up the features of the pale white man as he answered, 'YES, THAT IS MY NAME'.

If Stanley was wondering about his place in history then his fears of anonymity was immediately forgotten when he opened a cable message from Bennett, proprietor of the *New York Herald*. 'You are now just as famous as Livingstone, having discovered the discoverer. Accept my thanks and the whole world's.'[34]

In August 1872, Stanley arrived in England just five months since leaving Livingstone at Unyanyembe. He immediately went on a lecture circuit, describing the circumstances leading up to finding Livingstone 'a mere ruckle of bones',[35] and writing *How I Found Livingstone*. The Royal Geographical Society awarded Stanley its Gold Medal for services he gave to geography. He was on his way to becoming one of the most celebrated men on the planet.

When Stanley got back to New York he immediately started giving lectures on 'The Discovery of Livingstone'.[36] An entrance fee was charged, and this included a booklet that provided *Biographical sketches of Mr. H. M. Stanley and Dr. David*

Livingstone.[37] The booklet contained an engraving of Stanley, together with his boy Kalulu and interpreter Selim and a facsimile of a letter he had received from Livingstone. The letter is interesting for Livingstone intended Stanley to take it as proof from him that the ex-slaves had much stolen from him. The letter reads:

> I have been subjected to so much loss by the employment of slaves in caravans sent by the [unreadable] Consul that if Mr Stanley meets another party of the sort I beg him to turn them back but use his discretion in the whole matter.[38]

Stanley's ability for hyperbole was not diminished in writing his booklet. The opening passage reads breathlessly:

> The peculiarly novel mission whose successful accomplishment has imparted an imperishable lustre to the name of Henry M. Stanley, has also aroused a personal interest in him scarcely inferior to that which mankind feels towards its most cherished heroes.[39]

CHAPTER 12

The Final Chapter

'All the World's a stage
And all the men and women merely players:
They have their exits...'

'Seven Ages of Man', William Shakespeare

12.1 Livingstone Beaten

After the departure of Stanley, Livingstone was again alone, and for the last year of his life he was completely out of contact with the outside world. This did not worry him for he thought he was getting close to finally resolving the source of the Nile. He needed just one final effort to discover and map the rivers flowing into Egypt and when he had done so, would make his way to the coast and home to his family and friends. Or so he thought.

After the departure of Stanley, Livingstone began his careful preparations. He did not think it was necessary to follow the river all the way to Lake Albert as he was more interested in seeing whether its source was in fact in the Katanga highlands.

On 19 March 1872 he celebrated his sixtieth birthday—his last—in Unyanyembe. He was in a reflective and sombre mood when he wrote in his diary:

Birthday. My Jesus, my king, my life, my all; I again dedicate my whole self to Thee. Accept me, and grant, O Gracious Father, that ere this year is gone I may finish my task. In Jesus' name I ask it. Amen, so let it be.[1]

Livingstone knew he needed men to help him to undertake this final expedition and he waited patiently for fifty men that Stanley had promised to send him when he reached Zanzibar. Livingstone knew that these men were unlikely to reach Unyanyembe until about July 1872 so he had time to kill. One of the first things he did was to read the books that Stanley had given him. It was a rare pleasure and deeply satisfying. The books included one on the explorer Samuel Baker, *Mungo Park's Travels*, and Young's *Search for Livingstone*, and he was pleased with the kind words written about him. He also completed his final preparations; tarring his new tent to make it waterproof, making a sounding line and visiting Arabs and chiefs in the local area. He also made cheese, which he described as good, but sour as he did not have rennet, and had to allow the milk to coagulate over half a day. On reading his diary, it is clear he was carefully preparing everything, trying to remain strong and healthy while waiting for his new porters to arrive.

On 1 May 1872, exactly a year before he died, he concluded his daily diary's entry with a sentence about slavery that would later be immortalised on his funeral tablet in Westminster Abbey:

> All I can add in my loneliness is: May Heaven's rich blessing come down on everyone, American, English, or Turk, who will help to heal this open sore of the world.[2]

In the meantime continuing clashes between the Arabs and the local tribes swirled around Unyanyembe. It seemed that increasingly it was the Arabs and their slaving parties who were attacked and sometimes killed, including Mohammad Bogharib's chief slave, Othman. He died when a spear was thrust through him, the point coming out through his breast. Smallpox was also prevalent and caused a large number of deaths among the natives.

This caused Livingstone to reflect on missionary methods and what could be done for Africa. He mused:

> I would say to missionaries, Come on, brethren, to the real heathen. You have no idea how brave you are till you try. Leaving the coast tribes, and devoting yourselves heartily to the savages, as they are called, you will find, with some drawbacks and wickedness, a very great deal to admire and love.[3]

It was this capacity for love and kindness that made him such an appealing figure in Victorian Britain.

The land around Unyanyembe was rich and fertile, and Livingstone had plenty of time to explore it. He noted that the Arabs were clever cultivators and grew abundant crops of pomegranates, guavas, lemons and oranges, together with wheat and rice that they planted and tended. If only future Christian missionaries would follow the example of the Arabs and introduce new seeds and crops. He also mused how easy and inexpensive it would be to establish a mission in these parts. For example, he wore just four suits of strong woollen tweed during a five-year period. Why wouldn't the missionaries follow his example and come?

By late May 1872, he was ruminating on his future explorations. In a telling comment, he wrote:

I wish I had some of the assurance possessed by others, but I am oppressed with the apprehension that after all it may turn out that I have been following the Congo; and who would risk being put into a cannibal pot, and converted into a black man for it?[4]

His presentiment was correct; he was following the Congo river.

Livingstone also had time to do a little match making as he had good-looking woman called Ntaoéka, among his servants. He thought that it would be better for her if she was married and he proposed that she should marry one of favourite servants, Chumah, Gardner or Mabruki.[5] She eventually married Chumah.

At the end of June 1872, following Stanley's return to Zanzibar, some correspondence began to filter through to Livingstone. He got letters from Oswell that informed him that Sir Roderick Murchison had died, and he responded with letters to Kirk and sent a large packet of astronomical observations and a sketch map to Sir Thomas Maclear for checking. Still he waited and his diary entry on 5 July 1872 said simply, 'Weary! weary!'[6]

The men Stanley had organised finally started to arrive in Unyanyembe on 9 August 1872. Over the next few days, they trooped in until there were fifty-seven men and boys who Stanley had hired as porters, and some Nassick pupils who had been part of Lieutenant Dawson's expedition. Among the number were John and Jacob Wainwright.

This party joined Livingstone and his five followers. They included Susi, Chumah and Amoda who had joined Livingstone on the Zambezi River in 1864. There were also two Nassick boys, Mabruki and Gardner, who Livingstone had recruited when in India in 1866. Mabruki was to remain in Unyanyembe under the care of an Arab, Sultan bin Ali, as he had for a long time been troubled with illness.

It had taken the new arrivals seventy-four days to march from Bagamoyo. After his long delay Livingstone was keen to get underway. He had already calculated the distance to Katanga was some 750 to 900 miles, and he expected that they would not complete his explorations until March 1874.[7]

Livingstone carefully left behind some supplies to be picked up on his return to the coast. Among the stores that were inadvertently left behind was a box of desiccated milk, which he was to be in great need of in the coming months.

On 25 August 1872 they started out. Livingstone always made a short march on the first day as a way to shake out everybody and move his party away to a secluded area, free of camp followers and well-wishers. They headed first for the southern shores of Lake Tanganyika but it was an inauspicious start as two of the Nassick boys immediately lost one of ten cows in their care, and as always happens, she was the best milking cow in their small herd. The same two Nassick boys then promptly lost all the cows some days later. The herd was recovered but there was a missing cow. Susi gave the boys each ten cuts with his switch as a reminder not to be lazy.

Livingstone was eager as always to be out travelling, but it was not with the same level of vigour and strength. It was difficult to get water and food in the country they were travelling through. It was also hot and the men started falling ill with fever, and quickly become fatigued in the heat.

By the 19 September 1872 Livingstone was desperately ill again, having not eaten for eight days on account of dysentery, but he pushed on. On 27 September 1872 he noted in his diary that he was again eating and feeling better, but as Chumah and Susi later reported, Livingstone suffered a recurring pattern of illness from this time on until his death.

The hot weather and lack of food and water took its toll on the party, and there were numerous halts and delays. Some men had to be carried which slowed the march down considerably. Livingstone was secretly pleased. 'I feel it much internally, and am glad to move slowly.'[8] When they entered mountainous country he found he was suffering from shortness of breath, and soon after he was forced to ride a donkey to save his energy.

Meanwhile, far away in Scotland, Livingstone's youngest child, Anna Mary, was writing a touching letter to her father, unaware of the vicissitudes that he was dealing with. Stanley was about to visit Glasgow and the fourteen-year-old was excited. 'My dearest Papa, I am writing this letter at school, where I am a weekly boarder. I see from the papers that Mr Stanley is coming to Glasgow to lecture on the 23rd and 25th... I like Mr Stanley very much for having found you.'[9] She went on to write about Tom, her favourite brother:

> You will be sorry to hear that Tom has been so ill. He took Pleurusy the day we had to go to Lady Belhaven and has been very ill ever since, which is five weeks today. We hope now that the danger is over. I got such a fright when I went home last Saturday to see the bell wrapped up to prevent any one ringing, as it annoyed him.

It took nearly two months to reach Lake Tanganyika, arriving on 14 October 1872. Keeping to his plan of exploring south of Lake Bangweulu, he continued to follow Lake Tanganyika around the south-east edge and in doing so passed through the country of Fipa of the Ulungu. It continued to be hot and all were affected. Livingstone wrote, 'This heat makes me useless, and constrains me to lie like a log.' More ominously he added, 'Inwardly I feel tired too.'[10]

Livingstone led his party further south, following the winding bays of Lake Tanganyika before turning west. They had to cross a high pass and entered into an area called Lake Mountains that were full of steep climbs and difficult narrow tracks. On 1 November 1872 the first rains fell, signalling the start of the long wet season.

In the wet tempers frayed and on 3 November 1872, Livingstone recorded that he had to beat two of his porters, one of whom was an addicted bangé-smoker.[11] The fact that he did so is very unusual as he very infrequently resorted to violence, preferring to embarrass or stare down people that gave him trouble.

On 8 November 1872 they were still trapped in the Lake Mountains area and in desperation he sent out a reconnaissance party to see if they could find a path out of the hills. They were successful in determining a route out of the area and by the 10 November 1872 they were moving 'along high ridges of sandstone and dolomite.'[12] Livingstone was happy although he was again suffering from dysentery and losing a lot of blood. But it was steep and slippery; he noted in his journal: 'My third barometer (aneroid) is incurably injured by a fall, the man who carried it slipped upon a clayey path.'[13]

They then turned south-west. The land had seen many destructive raids by Tipo Tipo and other Arab traders and as a result the people had not been able to tend their crops. They were consequently unable and unwilling to sell food; in some cases the natives were themselves reduced to eating mushrooms and leaves to satisfy their hunger.

Livingstone was back in familiar country and they met the successor of Nsama of Itawa. Word soon spread that Livingstone was back in the area and an Arab party sent him some much needed food, and news that Kazembe had been killed by the Arabs and his head stuck on a pole.

Their progress started to slow as the rivers quickly began to swell in size and what were previously rivulets turned into fast flowing tea coloured streams that had to be forded. On more than one crossing their canoes were swamped with their heavy loads. On another occasion they had to bodily haul a cow across a stream and frequently they had to swim the donkeys across rivers, with a man on either side. Fortunately no one was lost.

They also had to deal with duplicitous guides who kept trying to guide them to villages where food was expensive to purchase and if a chief was given any opportunity, he would immediately demand a 'tax' to enable his party to move through the area. It was all very tiring, but Livingstone was an experienced explorer and was able, on most occasions, to deftly sidestep the obvious attempts to lead them away from his chosen course.

His new men had to learn about the difficulties of travelling across such rugged country carrying large loads. It took them some weeks to harden up and bear the difficulties stoically. Livingstone also had to teach them manners if they were to avoid any infractions with the natives:

My own men walk into houses where we pass the nights without asking any leave, and steal cassava without shame. I have to threaten and thrash to keep them honest, while if we are at a village where the natives are a little pugnacious they are as meek as sucking doves.[14]

By 18 December 1872 they had reached the banks of the Kalongosi River,[15] which flows into Lake Mweru. They weather was so wet and miserable that Livingstone was not able to take his observations for latitude and longitude. This was important enough for Livingstone to note it in his diary as he took observations, despite sickness, famine and threat, with an almost religious fervour, which explains why his maps and observations are so important. They crossed the river and passed into marshy, bracken-covered country.

Christmas Day 1872 was Livingstone's last and it was 'cold and wet, day and night' and they attempted to celebrate by slaughtering one of their oxen for a feast. 'The headman is gracious and generous, which is very pleasant compared with awe, awe, and refusing to sell, or stop to speak, or show the way.'[16]

Game was scarce although it would have been difficult to shoot given that the pouring rain, river crossings and floundering through the mud, soaked everything. They did see some buffalo, but they broke away from them and charged off through the forest, smashing down the undergrowth. The only thing Livingstone did kill was a seven-foot cobra snake that reared up before him in order to strike him.

On 29 December 1872, or 1 January 1873—Livingstone had now lost track of the days—one of his men died of exposure. This was soon followed by the death of their last cow that died of injuries received when crossing a river. On 5 January 1873 a woman in his party fell ill and had to be carried. It was no wonder as the spongy country they were travelling through was overflowing with water. Frequent halts were called when the rain and cold became just too miserable.

It must have been one continuing nightmare. To give an idea of the privation they were enduring, here is Livingstone's diary entry on 9 January 1873:

> Mosumba of Chungu. After an hour we crossed the rivulet and sponge of Nkulumuna, 100 feet of rivulet and 200 yards of flood, besides some 200 yards of sponge full and running off; we then, after another hour, crossed the large rivulet Lopopozi by a bridge which was 45 feet long, and showed the deep water; then 100 yards of flood thigh deep, and 200 or 300 yards of sponge. After this we crossed two rills called Liñkanda and their sponges, the rills in flood ten or twelve feet broad and thigh deep. After crossing the last we came near the Mosumba, and received a message to build our sheds in the forest, which we did.

The fact that a weakened Livingstone endured this while continuing to suffer from dysentery and hunger is a remarkable achievement. Not only did he have the will-power to continue, but he was able to effectively lead and motivate a large party through this most trying of periods.

They continued on and blundered into the large marshy area to the north of Lake Bangweulu. Livingstone noted that he had not experienced such a long spell of cold rainy weather since 1853. If they thought they had escaped from the morass, they were wrong, for they had just traded dreadful sucking bog for the swampy shores of Bangweulu, where they were continually tormented with swarms of mosquitoes, poisonous spiders, and stinging ants. Here Livingstone and his party foundered in the glutinous mud. It was difficult to obtain food and starvation was a very real threat. They tried to acquire canoes from the locals that would have made their passage easier and quicker, but could not.

The continued physical strain quickly began to tell on an enfeebled Livingstone, and as they continued to battle on, it became increasingly apparent to Livingstone's followers that the old man was failing. Many times he had to be carried across the rivers and sponges, mainly on the shoulders of Chumah, Susi or another servant, Chowpere. He was also suffering from excessive blood loss that he continued to believe acted as a valve for his system. They were in a terrible predicament, but there was no option but to continue on. To make matters worse they lost a week when a chief knowingly gave them wrong directions and they had to retrace their steps. Many leeches plagued them as they battled their way through the vegetation.

They had spent months in these terrible conditions, but finally they reached Lake Bangweulu on the 19 February 1873. The land around was frightfully flooded— Livingstone estimated that some twenty to thirty miles of the surrounding land was submerged. It was therefore essential that he obtain canoes as this was the only feasible means of transport. However, it was not until 1 March 1873 that they were able to obtain canoes to move his party onto some islands on the flooded plains that bordered Lake Bangweulu. Here they were able to rest, eat meat and fish and plan their next move. Livingstone also made bread from yeast that was carried in a bottle, as it was his habit to try and make bread every three days or so.

Livingstone really wanted to obtain a fleet of canoes so he could move all his party, including his donkey, at one time, as he was fearful about splitting his party up. This was difficult to organise and while waiting, he wrote a letter to Earl Granville, on 15 March 1873, his last known piece of correspondence. It was a trying time for him as he was keen to keep moving, but the natives had no sense of urgency. He lay around, fretted and was ill. The natives received word that Livingstone had some Arabs with him, and that their purpose was to attack the lake people. This meant further delays and complications until this misinformation could be sort out.

On his birthday, 19 March 1873, Livingstone showed his frustration when he wrote, 'Can I hope for ultimate success? So many obstacles have arisen. Let not Satan prevail over me, Oh! My good Lord Jesus.' Then later that morning when the local chief, Matipa, again failed to deliver canoes as promised, Livingstone uncharacteristically took over his village and house and fired a shot through the roof to demonstrate his seriousness about obtaining canoes. Within a few hours three canoes were brought up and he started embarking his party to head to the mouth of the Chambeze where Livingstone wanted to set up a camp.

It was a difficult crossing as it was bitterly cold, wet and windy in the canoes and all their goods were soaked. They stopped off on small islands *en route*. On 26 March 1873, when crossing a large stream one of the canoes sank and a young servant girl of Amoda was drowned. They cast around in the water and fished up two guns and three boxes of ruined cartridges. Livingstone's donkey saddle was among the items lost.

It took several days to get all his men, supplies and donkeys ferried across to their new camp and it was not until 3 April 1873 that they were all finally encamped on the left bank of the Chambeze River, ready for the next stage of explorations.

Unbeknown to Livingstone, his whereabouts was being constantly discussed across Europe and up and down the coast of Africa. Everyone seemed to be interested in hearing any news of Livingstone and if there were any further plans to relieve him. The King of Italy presented the President of the Royal Geographical Society, Sir Bartle Frere with a gold medal to be given to Livingstone on his return. The British Government also awarded Livingstone a pension:

> The Queen has been graciously pleased to approve, on the recommendation of Mr. Gladstone, of a grant of a pension of £300 per annum on the Civil List to Dr. Livingstone, in recognition of the value of his researches in Central Africa.[17]

He would remain unaware of these developments.

12.2 The last Trek

In 1950, Kittermaster, a South African, interviewed an old man, Headman Mumana, of the Ba-Bisa, who had met Livingstone as a boy. Livingstone's party stopped in his village for a week where Mumana's father was the chief when they were moving around Lake Bangweulu. Mumana recounted that when Livingstone's party first approached their village they were taken for Arab slave traders and all the villagers fled, only cautiously reappearing towards nightfall. They had first seen Livingstone in the distance riding a donkey, but as they moved closer they caught their first good look at a white man. They were struck by how different he was. 'Why that must be a freak for he was not as the Arabs are but red, like the sunset, with grey hair.'[18] The young Mumana and some other boys crept up and watched Livingstone have his dinner, eating with a knife and fork, and later pray outside his tent with his party. Next morning they followed him down to the stream where he proceeded to shave himself. However, when he spat into the water they could see blood. Mumana ran back to his father and reported that the red man was turning the water red. His father immediately cried out 'He is bewitching the water so that anyone who bathes there will turn red like himself' and ordered that they pack up and move the village. Much later they heard that 'the European has died.'[19]

The last few months of Livingstone's life was a misery; he was very much alone and the hopelessness of the situation weighed heavily upon him. It has often been asked; why did he not attempt to return to the coast, as it was clear that he was trying to do the impossible. The key reason why he was still in central Africa exploring when most people would have long since settled into retirement was his refusal to give up. Many of Livingstone's biographers have written about his 'heroic' struggle, but in truth, towards the end, it was probably just plain old pig-headedness that drove the man on. His diary entry on 25 March 1873 points to this. 'Nothing earthly will make me give up my work in despair. I encourage myself in the Lord my God, and go forward.'[20]

Then there would have quickly come a point when Livingstone was no longer capable of struggling back, even as far as Ujiji. Finally, there is the question whether the months of fatigue, sickness and lack of food could have affected his ability to think rationally about whether he could or should continue.

On 5 April 1873 Livingstone recorded an entry into his final pocket book, numbered XVII that he used as his diary. For the next few days he wrote in pen and ink, the later fabricated using local dyes. He then had to revert to using a pencil, attached to a piece of bamboo and protected in a steel penholder.[21]

They left their dry camp and headed around the southern shores of Lake Bangweulu. Livingstone had his stores punted alongside the lake's edge while a land party sploshed through the flooded countryside. Predictably the two groups quickly lost sight of each other in the driving rain. Livingstone remained with the canoes and for the next few days they struggled to punt and haul their heavily laden vessels through the shallows that were full of papyrus and reeds. It was exhausting work. It was also a period of continued anxiety for Livingstone as they had no idea where the land party was, and it was not until 9 April that they found sign of them.

On 9 April 1873 he took his last recorded observation of latitude. From then on Livingstone's health declined alarmingly; next day he was dangerously ill. Even Livingstone acknowledged his fragility. 'I am pale, bloodless, and weak from bleeding profusely ever since the 31st of March last: an artery gives off a copious stream, and takes away my strength.'[22] Livingstone was dying. He was so weak he allowed himself to be carried. Livingstone, in a remarkable piece of understatement, wrote, 'It is not all pleasure, this exploration.'[23]

He continued to bleed and on 18 April 1873 he tried taking a large dose of quinine as he thought that bleeding, as with most other African illnesses, was just another form of fever. Miraculously it did stop the bleeding, but only for a short time.

On 22 April 1873 his attendants built a wooden litter, known as a kitanga to carry him in, as he was so weak. The wooden base was covered in grass and a blanket and there was another blanket laid over the frame that kept the sun off his face. Any movement caused great pain for him. Consequently they were only able to make short marches for fear of killing him.

By this time they were steadily moving along the southern side of Lake Bangweulu. On 27 April 1873 he made his last entry in his diary. 'Knocked up quite, and remain—recover—sent to buy milch goats. We are on the banks of the Molilamo.'[24] It was as if the old man really just wanted to end it all; he had become immeasurably tired.

On 29 April 1873 they decided to move to a crossing point on the Molilamo River, but the great explorer was so weak that he could not move, so in desperation his attendants knocked down a side of his hut and lifted him directly into his kitanga, whereupon they gently carried him into Chitambo's[25] village near Ulala.[26]

Ulala is about 100 km south-east of the lake, near the edge of the floodplain that borders the great Bangweulu swamps of modern-day Zambia.[27] Livingstone was placed in a straw hut. Majwarra, a young boy that Stanley had given to Livingstone, was tasked to sleep just inside the door so he could be on hand to help his master during the night.

Livingstone by this time was floating in and out of consciousness, as he could not bear any pressure on the lumbar region of his back. When he was not delirious he asked Susi, 'How many days is it to the Luapula?' and when he was told three, he only answered, 'Oh dear! dear!'[28] He had come to the end of the road; he would travel no further as by now his health was too frail. Indeed, the situation had really become quite pathetic.

It is generally thought that Livingstone died from malaria and internal bleeding caused by amoebic dysentery.[29] Dysentery was known in those times as the flux or the bloody flux and is an inflammatory disorder of the intestine, especially of the colon, that results in severe diarrhoea containing mucus and blood in the faeces. It is accompanied by fever and abdominal pain. In the case of Livingstone, it was left untreated and became fatal. Dysentery can also cause rapid weight loss, and generalized muscle aches and this problem, together with his general breakdown in health, explains why Livingstone became so weak that he had to be carried in a litter by his attendants into Ulala.

12.3 The Final Hours

It was not until 30 April that the final chapter of this remarkable explorer came to an end. According to reports compiled afterwards from the faithful Susi and Chumah, this is what happened: at about 11.00 p.m. on that evening, Susi was summoned to go to the dying Doctor. At the time of entering into the dark hut where Livingstone was lying prostrate, there were loud shouts from nearby. Livingstone asked Susi if his men were making the noise? 'No' replied Susi, 'I can hear from the cries that the people are scaring away a buffalo from their dura fields.'[30]

Susi soon left the Doctor but about half-an-hour later Livingstone's boy, Majwarra came and told Susi that, 'Bwana wants you, Susi.' This time Livingstone wanted some hot water and so the servant set to work to boil some. When he returned, Livingstone asked him to carry his medicine chest over to him and to hold a candle so that he could see what he was looking for. Susi did as he was bid and standing over his master, holding the candle aloft in his rough hands. He became alarmed when he realised Livingstone could hardly see. After much fumbling, Livingstone selected a bottle of calomel and placed it next to him. Susi then poured some water into a cup and put that and an empty one near him. Livingstone then told his faithful servant in a feeble voice, 'All right; you can go out now.'[31] Susi left his bedside and these were apparently his last words.

It was not until about 4.00 a.m. on 1 May 1873 that Susi was again disturbed by Majwarra who feared that his master was dead. The obvious concern in his voice was enough to alarm Susi sufficiently that he first went and woke up Chumah, Chowpere, Matthew Wellington and Muanyasere. The five men and the boy then went to the Doctor's hut and cautiously entered.

They found Livingstone had got off his bed and was kneeling, seemingly in prayer. They immediately drew back out of respect, but Mujwarra stopped them, whispering, 'When I lay down he was just as he is now, and it is because I find that he does not move that I fear that he is dead.'[32] The boy had earlier fallen asleep. He did not know how long he had slept for, but he thought it had been for some time.

Summoning up their courage, they approached the Doctor—the flickering light of a candle cast his shadow against the wall of the hut. They saw that he was kneeling, his body pitched forward with his head placed in his hands upon the pillow. Watching him, his men immediately got the impression of someone at peace with himself and his God. Matthew was the first to move; stepping forward, he placed his hands against Livingstone's cheeks; they were quite cold.

Gently they lifted the body back onto the bed and covered it with a blanket.

12.4 Disembowelment and Burial

The actions that his men then took spoke of the affection and respect they had for Livingstone. Their actions have also become an inspiration to succeeding generations about the value of loyalty.

The rest of the party were quickly told the distressing news and at first light they all assembled. But what to do? Susi and Chumah had all the boxes brought out of Livingstone's hut and opened in front of everyone so that all knew what contents lay in them, in order that all would take responsibility for their care. Jacob Wainwright, who could write, carefully made a list of the contents. The next issue was what to do with Livingstone's body? They knew that many tribes had a deep superstitious fear of the dead and many of their party wondered if the tribes would attack them for releasing a departed spirit that would wander their lands causing trouble. Also there was the problem of where they were staying—would Chitambo fine them for having a dead body, as they feared, and force them to leave? In the confusion, Susi and Chumah were appointed joint leaders for the party.

They decided to keep Chitambo ignorant of Livingstone's death for the time being and, more importantly, they agreed that they would take the body back to Zanzibar so that his English friends could give Livingstone a proper burial. This meant preparing the body for the trip, and for this reason they immediately set to work to build a new place outside the village where they could make their preparations unobserved. However, native tongues soon wagged and the chief quickly learnt of their plans, but instead of being angry as they expected, he was supportive and in due course he and all the villagers attended a fitting African mourning ceremony for Livingstone.

As regards the preparation of the body, this required them to remove Livingstone's heart and other internal organs, as they would rot. Farijala, who had worked as a servant to a doctor in Zanzibar, undertook the task, using primarily salt and a bottle of Livingstone's brandy. He had a Nassick boy, Carras, as an assistant. Susi, Chumah, Muanyasere, Tofike and John Wainwright were also present.

The disembowelling of Livingstone was not difficult as he was more-or-less skin and bone at the time of his death. After removing the viscera, the body cavity was filled with salt. The people present immediately noted two strange things; Farijala pulled out a clot of coagulated blood, about the size of an orange from the left side of Livingstone's body[33] and that his lungs were dried up and had black and white patches over them.

His heart and other parts of the viscera were placed in a tin box and were buried nearby under a Mvula tree.[34] Jacob Wainwright then quietly read out the burial service using his own Prayer Book that he had brought for this purpose. Later Wainwright carved the inscription on the Mvula tree 'LIVINGSTONE MAY 4 1873' together with the names of the attendants on the tree.[35]

The body was left exposed for fourteen days to dry out and harden, with the position of the body occasionally changed to ensure every part of it was exposed to the air.

While this was taking place Susi, Chuma and others commenced to pack up his personal effects. Livingstone had two tin boxes he brought from England, and these had survived despite all the years of travel. They contained his treasured notebooks, letters, his well-thumbed copy of *Webster's Dictionary* and other papers and much care was taken in sealing them up. They carefully packed up everything, including his instruments, clothes and books.

Chief Chitambo was also presented with a biscuit box and some newspapers as evidence that Livingstone had been there and asked that he would look after and honour the place where Livingstone had died.

At the end of the drying-out period they carefully wrapped the body in calico, after first bending the legs at the knees to make the package smaller. The package was then wrapped in bark and disguised in sailcloth and later, given a thick coating of tar to protect it against water infiltration. It was lashed to a pole so that two men could carry it. This was important as the natives objected to bodies being carried through their lands as it could bring bad luck and ruin on a tribe.

With that all done they then set off the coast. It was to be a long and arduous journey, and they ended up carrying Livingstone's remains more than 1,000 miles until they reached the Indian Ocean. So successfully had the team disguised the body that they were able to travel unmolested through the various tribal areas. It was a brave task to undertake, as discovery would have meant the body would have immediately been disposed of and the faithful few subjected to retribution. It was be the final epic act of loyalty by his faithful followers.

They first headed away to south-west, and in doing so completed the circumnavigation of Lake Bangweulu, as their plan was to then head north-west and hit the Luapula River, some 120 to 150 miles away. This would then enable them to get their bearings so that they could then strike out for the southern end of Lake Tanganyika. Or so they planned. By the end of three days marching half their number was too ill to continue and for a whole month they had to rest while they recovered and the rains stopped. It seemed all the country around them was similarly affected by ill health.

About this time, unaware of the death of his father, Thomas Livingstone wrote a letter to his favourite sister, Anna Mary from Alexandria in Egypt where he had moved to recover his health:

The weather here is very hot and we won't have rain till November. Think of that you folks in wet Scotland. It is so hot that one perspires easily sitting still and it rolls down ones hands & face in big drops. The Nile has begun to rise and all day long there are big white clouds rushing overhead away to the south. They run in an endless race till they reach somewhere where perhaps Papa is, then they come back again in the Nile as sweet water, but never as clouds. The south wind brings no clouds here but Oh! Such heat.[36]

After resting Livingstone's party continued until they reached the banks of the Luapula River and to their surprise found it even wider than the Zambezi, perhaps over four miles wide. After passing over in canoes, they struck out through country where the news of Livingstone's death had already arrived. Fortunately, his name and kindness were well remembered and the party was mostly well received. There was only one act of hostility at a village called Chawende's. Here they were turned out and after much bickering between the villagers and members of the party, Susi and Chumah responded by leading them in attacking the village, swarming over the stockade, and firing on the people. So sudden was their attack that they successfully routed the enemy, but fearing another attack from the surrounding villages, they then went on to sack and burn six other villages. It is not hard to imagine what Livingstone would have thought of this aggressive action had he been alive.

The next river they reached was the Kalongwesi and from here on Susi and Chumah knew where they were and it was with confidence that they led their party in a north-easterly direction towards Lake Tanganyika. While on the way, they received word from some passing Arabs that Livingstone's son was leading an expedition to find Livingstone, and had last been seen in Bagamoyo some months previously. This was heartening news.

They circled the bottom edge of the Lake Tanganyika, this time well to the south so as not to re-experience all the difficulties they had when they came through the area with Livingstone. The country was rolling with good hunting. It was while moving through this country that they met a party of elephant hunters who had recently left Unyanyembe. They were able to confirm that news of Livingstone's death had already reached Unyanyembe and that Livingstone's son and party had arrived there.

It was decided that contact should be made with the Englishmen as soon as possible and Jacob Wainwright was tasked to write an account of the circumstances leading up to, and the death of Livingstone. Chumah and three others took the letter and then hurried on ahead of the main party, and about 16 October 1873, arrived in Unyanyembe. Waiting there was not Livingstone's son, William, but the Livingstone Relief Expedition, also known as the Livingstone East Coast Expedition, led by a Royal Navy Lieutenant, V. Lovett Cameron[37]. This was a second Livingstone search expedition that had been sent out by the Royal Geographical Society to find Livingstone, and to see what could be done for him.

This expedition had started from the east coast and had encountered numerable delays and frustrations. However, these were overshadowed by the death of Moffat's grandson and namesake, Robert Moffat, who died soon after the expedition arrived on the mainland. Robert Moffat had joined the Livingstone Relief Expedition in Zanzibar having received permission from his mother to leave his sugar plantation in Natal, South Africa, to help find Livingstone. It was a heartfelt loss by all who had come to know young Robert.

There was another expedition to find Livingstone that had left England at the same time as Cameron's, alternatively titled the Livingstone West Coast

Expedition or the Livingstone Congo Expedition. This expedition landed at Loanda on the west coast of Africa. Under command of Lieutenant Grandy, RN, the party headed up the River Congo. They explored the region, but returned when the Royal Geographical Society recalled them when they received reports that Livingstone was not in the area, and had possibly died. Livingstone's friend and Trustee, Sir James Young, underwrote the cost of this second expedition, later estimated at over £3,000—a large sum in those days.

On meeting Chumah and reading the letter prepared by Jacob Wainwright it was clear that Livingstone had finally succumbed to disease. Cameron immediately sat down and wrote to the Royal Geographical Society:

> It is with extreme regret I write to announce to you the melancholy news of the death of Dr. Livingstone, of which we received news from Chumoi [Chumah], his servant, who came in advance of his caravan, in order to get some stores, as he says they are utterly destitute.[38]

The appearance of the native party carrying Livingstone's bound-up remains caused some consternation about what was the best thing to do. There were a number among the Search Expedition who argued that the body should be buried immediately, but Livingstone's 'faithful's' were resolved that their master's body should be sent to England, despite the risk of travelling through Ugogo country. Cameron soon agreed to their wishes. The members of the search party were naturally curious to see what was in all of Livingstone's boxes and many of Livingstone's articles were taken out for examination. As normally happens in these situations, a number of the articles were not replaced, but kept as personal mementos.

Cameron wanted to take up where Livingstone had left off and follow the Lualaba to discover where it flowed. He took a small party and first they retraced their route to Ujiji to recover Livingstone's journals and stores and Cameron arranged for them to be sent back to Zanzibar. The papers were essential in piecing the last years of Livingstone's life. Cameron then went on to prove Lake Tanganyika flowed into the Lualaba River.

Livingstone's native party joined those members of the expedition wanting to return to the coast, under the command of Lieutenant Murphy R.A. who had resigned, saying he thought the purpose of the mission had been achieved. Many of the expedition members also joined Murphy as they were suffering from ill health and wanted to return to the coast. Cameron himself 'had eight fevers and a bad attack of inflammation of the eyes, which for some time rendered me quite blind; and even now I am unable to use them for long, and my sight is hazy and indistinct.'[39] When all was ready, the enlarged party set off with the body of Livingstone still being carried by his native party. It was not a happy marriage as there were disagreements about when to start marching in the mornings.

Livingstone's party were used to leaving early before it got hot whereas the expeditionary people would follow later in the day. Sickness affected many of them and the only other Englishman, Doctor Dillon sadly shot himself in a state of delirium a few days after their departure.

They decided to try and bypass the villainous Ugogo's and instead try to pass through the forests undetected. Unfortunately as they advanced, word preceded them about the body and this made the villagers hostile. Livingstone's native party then hit on a subterfuge; they repacked the body in calico to make it look like any other bale of calico. When they entered a village they cleverly told the villagers that the body had been sent to Unyanyembe for burial. In the meantime Livingstone's body would be deposited among all the other bales of goods.

After their long and eventful trek the party proudly marched into Bagamoyo, the mainland departure point for so many African slaves, where they were met by Her Majesty's Acting Consul-General from Zanzibar, Captain W. F. Prideaux. The consul, in true Victorian style immediately took charge of the body and arranged for it to be transported the thirty nautical miles to Zanzibar on board a British cruiser. Prideaux made it clear that the job of Livingstone's faithful's was now complete and from that point they were largely excluded from the proceedings. They had received no thanks for the noble act that they had done and it may well have ended there as none of them had been invited to sail to Zanzibar. Fortunately when Livingstone's Trustee, James Young, heard what had happened, he generously paid for Jacob Wainwright to accompany the body back to England and then later for Susi and Chumah to join him in England.

There were just five servants that carried Livingstone's body into Bagamoyo from the group that had set out with Livingstone from Zanzibar in 1866. They were Abdullah Susi, James Chumah, Amoda who had joined Livingstone on the Zambezi Expedition in 1864, and two Nassick boys, Gardner and Mabruki, who had joined Livingstone in 1865.

The Acting Consul-General duly sent a despatch to Earl Granville of the Foreign Office reporting the death of Livingstone and this arrived on 27 January 1874. When the story broke in the newspapers about the death of the 'King of African pioneers',[40] the public reacted with astonishment, and in some cases, outright disbelief.[41] Among them was Moffat who was back in England when he received the news about the demise of his famous son-in-law. Moffat was at the time grieving for his grandson and namesake, Robert, who had died only a few months before.

Livingstone's family received the news when Agnes, Livingstone's sister, was reading the paper one morning. Anna Mary recalled the moment:

> When Stanley came home, he told us he expected Papa in 1874. And he did come home then but alas! Only to his last resting place. On the 28th January 1874 I was preparing for school. Aunt Agnes who had been looking over

the papers glanced hurriedly at me, saying, 'O hinnie here is a report of your father's death. She read on that Papa's body was on its way home embalmed in salt. We were terribly stunned at first, but on careful consideration the story seemed so improbable that we dismissed it at once.[42]

Unfortunately the newspaper report was accurate and confirmed later that day when her school head teacher informed Anna Mary about the death of her father.

The Peninsular and Oriental Company's steamship *Malwa*, carried Livingstone's withered remains back to England. When the ship docked at Southampton, General C. P. Rigby and Colonel J. A. Grant formally accepted the body on behalf of the Royal Geographical Society and in accordance with the directions of the Foreign office. Moffat was also on hand to assist and to thank the shipping company.[43] In front of a large, silent crowd, the body was carefully removed and placed in a special train provided by the South-Western Railway Company and the accompanying cortège quickly departed for London. They arrived in London at 3.00 p.m. on 15 April 1874.

The first job was to confirm the eviscerated eleven-month old remains were Livingstone's. Sir William Fergusson, a noted surgeon and former friend of Livingstone was given the task, assisted by Livingstone's old Zambezi colleague, Dr James Kirk and Dr Loudon, the family surgeon from Hamilton in Lanarkshire. Livingstone's father-in-law, old Moffat, was also present. They set to work later that day in the Royal Geographical Society's Council Room to make their examination. It was no easy task as what was left was so withered as to make the job extremely difficult. The features of his face could not be recognised and Fergusson was only convinced after he was able to examine the fracture in his left arm bone that the lion had mangled all those years previously.

Livingstone's burial began on a Saturday morning, 18 April 1874. It took place in the Map Room of the Royal Geographical Society offices at 1 Savile Row, Burlington Gardens, London where the chief mourners, key Government and learned society representatives gathered around. It was a most fitting place to start the funeral proceedings as Livingstone had been much favoured by the Royal Geographical Society during his lifetime, with some suggesting that he was their most favoured explorer.

After a short service his hearse set out for the magnificent Westminster Abbey followed by twelve mourning coaches and a line of private carriages. Thousands lined the street and thousands more of ordinary people stood outside the ancient church, many of them in tears. After the service, Livingstone's body was interred in the nave of Westminster Abbey, London. A black slab marks his resting place in the centre of the nave in the Abbey. It seemed fitting that Livingstone's heart was buried in Africa, among the people he most cared for, while his body was buried at the very heart of the British Empire where only the Empire's most illustrious lie.

Livingstone's family attended the funeral and Moffat was among them. The event greatly affected the old man, then aged seventy-nine. The pallbearers included General Sir Thomas Steele, who had accompanied Livingstone and Edwards on their trip to Mabotsa in 1843, Henry Morton Stanley, the 'workhouse bastard' who Livingstone had thought of as a son and William Webb[44] who had become a close friend during Livingstone's stay at Newstead Abbey. The other pallbearers included Dr Kirk, Jacob Wainwright, Reverend Horace Waller of the UMCA, William Oswell, Livingstone's co-explorer and famous hunter and James Young, life-long friend, trustee and the funder of the West Coast Expedition.

Moffat, together with Thomas and Oswell Livingstone followed the coffin while their sisters Agnes and Anna Mary waited in Westminster Abbey with Livingstone's two surviving sisters, Janet and Agnes. The only other native present was Livingstone's African boy, Kalulu.

Susi and Chumah arrived after the funeral and would later quietly visit their former Master's grave. Livingstone's servants were later generously recognised by the Royal Geographical Society in 1875 when fifty-nine of them were awarded with specially minted silver medals. Thirty-three of these servants later accompanied Stanley on his subsequent explorations.

Livingstone's youngest daughter, Anna Mary, poignantly recorded the succession of events in her diary:

> I am fifteen years of age & have only seen Papa once on account of his being in Africa, & that was when five years old. The heavy weight of bereavement is now overwhelming us for my noble father died on the 4th of May 1873 at Ilala, Central Africa. We heard nothing of it till 26th January 1874 when he had been several months on his journey home in a rude native coffin. Terribly sad it all was, & what honours could be done for him when the coffin was solemnly lowered at Southampton, amid the half-mast high vessels, & mourners was done. Among the chief mourners were Grandpa [Dr Moffat], my brothers Mr. Stanley, Papa's noble discoverer, & Jacob Wainwright Papa's servant. Then in the Geographic rooms, London, which were hung with, I think it was, Union Jacks, there was a Scotch service here ere he was carried to his last resting place in Westminster Abbey. And yet not even when the solemn procession marched up the long resounding aisle to soothing strains of music did I realise what I was losing. But when the wreath-covered coffin was lowered & the beautiful anthem was struck up by the little choristers, then, only then I realised I was an orphan. It was singularly solemn, I can never forget it.[45]

The newspapers all carried detailed descriptions and illustrations of the proceedings including how wreaths were laid from Queen Victoria and Benjamin Disraeli, the Prime Minister. In a spirit of the occasion the Government generously paid £500 to cover the cost of the funeral.

Sir Bartle Frere, President of the Royal Geographical Society and active leader in organizing two society funded Livingstone Search Expeditions said in his obituary of Livingstone: 'As a whole, the work of his life will surely be held up in ages to come as one of singular nobleness of design and of unflinching energy and self-sacrifice in execution.'[46] Frere would also write, 'I never met a man who fulfilled more completely my idea of a perfect Christian gentleman, actuated in what he thought and said and did by the highest and most chivalrous spirit, modelled on the precepts of his great Master and Exemplar.' It was a wonderful obituary for a humble born former cotton piecer.

CHAPTER 13

Livingstone's Legacy

'The whole earth is the sepulchre of famous men; they are honoured not only by columns and inscriptions in their own land, but in foreign nations on memorials graven not on stone but in the hearts and minds of men.'

Thucydides, Greek historian

13.1 The Immediate Response

Livingstone was immediately lionised across Britain, and nowhere more so than in his native Scotland. Forgotten were questions about why he had not properly warned people about the dangers of living in central Africa due to disease and climate. One example was—with some justification—the dreadful hardship and loss of life suffered by the UMCA as a result of his urgings, and that it had not been properly prepared or supported by Livingstone.

Forgotten also was the apparent failure of the Zambezi Expedition. In retrospect many people questioned why a former missionary who had no experience in leading a team should have been chosen to undertake an ambitious task of exploring and opening up a passageway into central Africa. However, in time the apparent failure of Zambezi Expedition was re-examined, and by 1866 the new bishop of the UMCA, Bishop Steel, had resolved to re-occupy in the area where Bishop Mackenzie had founded his first mission, and there were other plans to establish more missions in the Lake Nyassa region. Livingstone would also have been pleased to learn about commercial plans to establish a regular boat service both above and below the cataracts on the River Shire.[1]

Livingstone became, arguably, one of the first modern celebrities, particularly during his first return to England in 1856. He was frequently mobbed walking down Regent Street, London and there were reports of 'chaos, with people clambering over the pews to try and shake his hand' when he attended church services.[2] But it was the circumstances of Livingstone's dramatic death and subsequent burial that regenerated a huge interest and reappraisal of what he was trying to achieve in Africa. Even his attempted discovery of the source of the Nile took on heroic proportions despite the issue seemingly to have been comprehensively answered when the scientific establishment accepted Speke's claim.

The impression the public had of Livingstone; one of deep faith, a dogged passion to discover new things, and an abiding enmity towards the evils of slavery, was brought sharply into focus with news of the loyalty shown by Livingstone's servants who carried his remains out to the coast. It was inspirational, and made Britain proud to call Livingstone one of her finest.

Livingstone's legacy was enhanced when the *New York Herald* released Stanley's sensational news of finding Livingstone to the world. Stanley's subsequent serialising of his book reignited interest in both Livingstone as a man, and the work that he was trying to achieve. Without Stanley, Livingstone may have continued to fade into obscurity; because of Stanley, Livingstone would never be forgotten.

One immediate impact was a whole succession of books on Livingstone, which was unprecedented in those times. Livingstone's publisher, John Murray, could see the commercial advantages on capitalising on the public out-pouring of grief. He moved quickly and in December 1874, Murray with help from the Reverend Horace Waller, as editor, and Livingstone's son, Thomas, published *The Last Journals of David Livingstone, in Central Africa, from 1865 to his Death,* in two volumes, based on a large journal carried out by Stanley and pocket books carried back in a battered tin-case. Lieutenant Cameron had also found valuable documents in Ujiji, which he visited after overseeing the return of Livingstone's body to the east coast. These included fourteen pocketbooks, and a map that was a missing section of the Livingstone cartography of the region. Among the books were some seeds and geological specimens that Livingstone had collected and these too were sent back to England.

Waller had carefully edited out any inflammatory or offensive passages in Livingstone's journals, in collaboration with Susi and Chumah, that would denigrate the legend of Livingstone. The book received good literary reviews:

> The most artistic narrative would do far less to enhance the fame of Livingstone as an explorer and a man than these rude and simple diaries. Extending over more than seven years from his arrival at Zanzibar, in January 1866, to his death in the fen-country of Bangweolo on the 1st of May, 1873, they tell in plainest, sometimes in broken words, the hopes, disappointments, and results of his last efforts to fulfil the mission of his life.[3]

By June 1876, over 9,550 copies of the *Last Journals* had been sold.[4]

During the late 1880s shortened and cheaper versions of Livingstone's own books were sold to schools when the life and achievements of Livingstone became part of the national school educational curriculum. These books helped to cement Livingstone's heroic exploits in the public consciousness long after he was dead.[5]

Predictably many sought to cash in on the public's interest in other ways. A notable example was the way that Stanley sought his own public acclamation by marketing his association with Livingstone. He undertook wildly popular lecture tours in both Britain and the United States immediately on his return from finding Livingstone in Ujiji. His books were also released to huge successes; over 150,000 copies of *In Darkest Africa*, published in 1890, were sold. Stanley's and Livingstone's popularity was also due to the rapid growth of the circulation of newspapers, particularly in Europe and the United States. Bennett was very aware of the potential impact on circulation of his *New York Herald* if Stanley was successful in discovering Livingstone—and he was not disappointed with the result.

Businessmen were also quick to spot an opportunity surrounding Livingstone's celebrity status; and his image appeared on many consumer products, such as commemorative plates. In time Stanley also took advantage of his own celebrity status by being paid to endorse products.

Madame Tussaud's cannily seized on the commercial opportunity and barely three weeks after Stanley's news of his 'discovery' of Livingstone was transmitted to the world, they triumphantly presented a diorama of the meeting between Stanley and Livingstone. People poured in to see the moment recreated in wax, noting how lifelike the figures appeared.

The story and death of Livingstone was subsequently recounted and celebrated in public meetings, schools and churches across the world, and his story would not be eclipsed until the dramatic account of Scott and his fellow explorers' travails and eventual death in Antarctica on their return from the South Pole. Like Livingstone this event become the stuff of legend and Scott became a modern day schoolboy hero.

The Scots have continued to claim Livingstone as their own, conveniently forgetting that Livingstone had chosen to join the London Missionary Society. This pride was on public view at the opening of a massive exhibition on Livingstone at The Royal Scottish Museum in Edinburgh on 17 March 1913. There were 1,600 guests present, including Anna Mary Livingstone, who was by then the only surviving child.

This practice of celebrating Livingstone as a true Scot was again demonstrated during the latest exhibition at the National Museum Scotland, Edinburgh, the successor to The Royal Scottish Museum, when Rt Hon. Alex Salmond, MSP, First Minister of Scotland, described Livingstone as 'one of Scotland's great humanitarians' whose values were still shared by Scots today.[6] He went on to say: 'We can reflect on David Livingstone as exemplifying many of the best characteristics of Scotland. He had an internationalist outlook, an ambition to succeed, a passion for education and, perhaps most of all, a strong sense of solidarity and a deep sense of compassion.'

13.2 Missionary Work

There were many detractors about Livingstone's inability to get natives to give up their heathen ways and become Christians. After all, Livingstone only converted Sechele and had he not later relapsed back into his native ways? Livingstone thought it 'amusingly ludicrous'[7] to think about missionary work in this way. He did not see the number of converts as an accurate measure of the work that he and others were undertaking. After all the conversion of the soul was of vital importance only to the person making that commitment to the Kingdom of Christ, and it did not matter in the terrestrial world.

Livingstone also knew that the important thing was that the word of God was spread. He recognised that it was a long, slow game he was playing, and he was content and confident enough to strike out where others feared to tread. What increasingly irked him, particularly on his last visit to the Cape, was just how smug and comfortable many of the missionaries were. It seemed to Livingstone that they had lost their pioneering missionary spirit, and were refusing to go where the real need was, particularly amongst the tribes that were being persecuted by the Boers, and beyond. Livingstone summed up his feelings in a letter to Mary. 'Some find fault with everything, and comfort themselves by feeling they are better than I am because they would not do so & so. Their consciences are laid gently down by feeling their do-nothingism is better than my blundering do-somethingism. Well, we shall see.'[8]

He summed up this challenge to do something—and his personal satisfaction about progress he had made with his Bakwains—in a letter he wrote to his mother-in-law in 1855:

> There is a mighty difference between what I found them [the Bakwains] and what they now are. I found them as I now find the Makololo. And take the *worst* of your Kurumanites. From intimate knowledge of the three I am certain they stand thus: Kurumanites *bad*, Bakwains *worse*, Makololo *worst*. The morals of the Bakwains are very much elevated from what I found them.[9]

He also understood that he only had to sow the seed; even if it was amongst wild and dangerous native tribes. 'I thank God for allowing me to do what I did, though I may never see fruit.'[10] Before and after his death there were a number of young missionaries ready to seize the opportunities that Livingstone had identified, and as a result in places like Zambia today, there are an extraordinarily high number of people who identify themselves as active Christians.

There were others who were quick to point out that Livingstone had given up with proselytising and had instead turned to 'scientific exploration'. This was highlighted to Moffat when he was making a tour of France in 1877. In response

Moffat delivered a lecture refuting these nefarious claims about his son-in-law and his address was widely commented on at the time in the Paris press.[11] Moffat was not worried about these charges and neither would Livingstone have been, had he been around to hear them.

Despite the failure of the Universities Mission to Central Africa there were others that were keen to follow in Livingstone's footsteps. Another enterprising young Scot, Robert Laws, established the Free Church of Scotland's mission, aptly named the Livingstonia Mission, at Cape Maclear, in 1875, after David Livingstone. Laws moved the Mission twice until it was finally established on the highland plateau above Lake Nyassa in an area free from malaria.

Laws also linked the Mission with the Livingstonia Central Africa Company that was established in 1877. The company was set up by Scottish businessmen to co-operate with missions, but it operated on a commercial basis. The company's businesses included water transport on the lakes and rivers of Central Africa and trading.

Livingstone would have been pleased about the way that Laws copied his own plans, for Laws shrewdly involved Livingstone's former crew member on the HMS *Pioneer*, Lieutenant E. D. Young. Their ship, a steam vessel, was fittingly called the *Ilala* in recognition of the place where Livingstone had died. The Livingstonia Mission remains a thriving mission today.

The following year the rival Scottish Presbyterian Blantyre Mission was established and in 1888 began construction on the imposing St Michael and All Angels Church in Blantyre, in modern day Malawi.

13.3 Discoveries

The Victorian age was rich in the number of intrepid explorers who swarmed across the globe, for with success came fortune and fame, but there was a special fascination in those brave individuals involved in discovering the source of the Nile, since many considered it to be the holy grail of geographical discovery.

It is the numerous geographical discoveries that Livingstone is chiefly remembered for. The breadth of Livingstone's discoveries over some thirty years was staggering and made him one of the world's greatest modern explorers. He ranged over vast areas from the Cape to Lake Tanganyika, and traversed the Congo basin. His pioneering expeditions laid down the geographical foundations for many others to complete. Stanley determined the course of the Congo River, and numerous other Englishmen progressively filled in the detail of central Africa. The Dean of Westminster gave a sermon after Livingstone's burial dwelling on the importance of his discoveries and he enjoined his congregation to see God's work in Livingstone's exertions:

In few men has been developed in a stronger, more persistent form, that passion which we just now analysed, for penetrating into the unknown regions of the earth. His indomitable resolution has revealed to us, for the first time, that vast waste of Central Africa, which, to the contemplation of the geographer, has literally been transformed from a howling wilderness into the 'glory of Lebanon'. 'The parched ground' has, in his hands, 'become a pool, and the thirsty land springs of water'. The blank of 'Unexplored Regions' which, in every earlier map, occupied the heart of Africa, is now disclosed to us, adored with those magnificence forests; that chain of lakes, glittering (to use the native expression) like 'stars' in the desert; those falls, more splendid, we are told, even than Niagara, which no eye of man had before beheld—where, above the far- resounding thunder of the cataract and the flying comets of snow-white foam, and amidst the steaming columns of the ever-ascending spray, on the bright rainbows arching over the cloud, the natives had for ages seen the glorious emblem of the everlasting Deity—the Unchangeable seated enthroned above the changeable.[12]

Livingstone became aware of the importance of keeping detailed records and of the need to make accurate observations of latitude and longitude. Indeed Thomas Maclear had as early as April 1852 encouraged Livingstone to improve on this aspect of his explorations. The intensive debate between Burton and Speke about Lake Victoria being the source of the Nile largely centred on the fact that Speke did not have the equipment to conclusively prove that this was the case. Livingstone saw this debate first-hand and so successfully did he apply himself to the task of making accurate records that the Portuguese 'saw me in the Interior calculating Longitudes, they wondered why a "Doutor Mathematico" should pretend to be a missionary.'[13] The detailed maps, the precise geographical referencing and his extensive handwritten notes on language, customs, mores and flora and fauna make Livingstone's legacy such a rich and important one.

Livingstone substantially expanded the knowledge of the geography and awareness about the people of southern and central Africa, at a time when the world powers were becoming much more interested in building empires, gaining access to resources and opening up markets for their manufactured goods. Livingstone may not have always been the first European to have seen these places, but he was in the vanguard, particularly as the quality of his observations made his discoveries compelling from a scientific point of view. This knowledge enabled the western European empires to establish large colonies in Africa within fifty years of his discoveries.

Livingstone was famously wrong about the Nile, and was looking in quite the wrong place for it—deep in the Congo Basin. This is understandable given his long periods of isolation. At the Royal Geographical Society's session on 11 November 1872 it was already known that the water system that Livingstone was following forms part of the Congo; 'although the constant trending of the waters to the west haunted him with misgivings, still he clung tenaciously to his old belief that he must be upon the track of the Nile'.[14]

Livingstone discovered numerous geographical features, such as Lake Ngami, Lake Malawi, and Lake Bangweulu in addition to the mighty Victoria Falls. He also filled in details of Lake Tanganyika, Lake Mweru, and the course of many rivers, especially the upper Zambezi. However, there were limits as the furthest north he reached was the northern end of Lake Tanganyika, which was south of the Equator, and he did not penetrate the rainforest of the River Congo any further downstream than Ntangwe near Misisi.[15]

Despite these failures, Livingstone was transformed into a celebrity, together with a number of other explorers. The reason was, as Claire Pettitt has written— there was an unusual alliance of interests between the learned institutions, such as the Royal Geographical Society and the Royal Society, the press and the nation as a whole, whose pride, collectively, urged these explorers on.[16] Their interests included increased memberships, enthused congregations, and greater sale of newspapers.

13.4 Cessation of Slavery

One of Livingstone's greatest achievements was the attention that he gained about the slaving practices in both western and eastern Africa, describing it as the 'great open sore of the world'.[17] The offensiveness to his Christian principles and the truly horrific slaving scenes he witnessed first-hand motivated him. Writing about what he had seen in his diary in 1872, he noted:

> The sights I have seen, though common incidents of the traffic, are so nauseous that I always strive to drive them from memory. In the case of the most disagreeable recollections I can succeed, in time, in consigning them to oblivion, but the slaving scenes come back unbidden, and make me start up at dead of night horrified by their vividness.[18]

Livingstone's recollections can be described as being similar to a soldier suffering from post–traumatic stress disorder.

In 1833 the British House of Commons passed the Abolition of Slavery Act in all of Great Britain's colonies. Under this Act all slaves under the age of six were to be freed immediately while those over this age would first serve a four-year apprenticeship before being freed. William Wilberforce,[19] a determined and powerful proponent for the elimination of slavery, died suddenly, just three days after the Bill was passed by Parliament.

Most western European countries slowly enacted similar laws and policies and in 1836 the Portuguese Government issued a decree that abolished the slave trade.

While not as far reaching as the measures undertaken by Britain, the decree did limit the number of slaves that can be transported by colonists and committed the Government to punish Portuguese slave traders.

Great Britain continued to put pressure on the Portuguese Government to do more to stop the slave trade in Portuguese colonies. Finally and significantly, in 1842 Great Britain signed a comprehensive treaty with Portugal that gave British warships the 'Right of Search' of all ships in Portuguese waters when it was declared that the slave trade was an act of piracy. The treaty also authorised the capture of vessels equipped for slave trade and allowed for all liberated slaves to be given to the Government whose warships made the capture.

The slave trade was devastating. Estimates of the number of slaves taken from central and eastern Africa vary widely, but it may have been as high as eighteen million people enslaved. Livingstone wrote about the destruction of native communities that was brought about by slavery in his book, *Narrative of an Expedition to the Zambesi and its Tributaries*. He related that Colonel Rigby, formerly H.M. Political Agent and consul of Zanzibar, had told Livingstone that about 19,000 slaves from the Nyassa country alone went through the Zanzibar slave markets each year. Livingstone estimated that at best only one in five of all slaves captured survived the march to the coast; and across the whole of the Shire Valley he thought the average was nearer to only one in ten captured slaves ended up being sold in the Zanzibar slave market.

During his return visit to Britain in 1856-58, Livingstone very successfully raised the issue of the evil impact of slaving and in doing so encouraged abolitionists of the slave trade. This message was heard and understood at the highest levels of Government in Britain, including the Prime Minister, Lord Palmerston. Without such an appealing and effective spokesperson, those advocating for the abolishment of slaving may have had to wait much longer before their message was acted upon. In the meantime, much greater damage and dislocation of populations within central Africa would have occurred.

Despite all these formal measures the Portuguese and Arab slave traders continued to be active. The only difference was that the Royal Navy now had a policy of stationing men-of-war ships outside the ports of known slave markets, such as Loanda, to ensure slaving ships could not land and take their illegal cargo to the Middle East, Americas or wherever there was a market. As a result demand for slaves rapidly fell, as did the price. To illustrate, Livingstone was informed that before the appearance of the Royal Navy patrol, the established price for good young slaves near the coast ranged from seventy to eighty dollars per head. When Livingstone was in Loanda the price had fallen to ten to twenty dollars. The principal reason given by the local traders for the fall in price was due to the difficulty in 'exporting' slaves.[20]

The British Government's Commissioner, Edmund Gabriel whose presence in Loanda was mainly to monitor slave practices told Livingstone that in 1837 he had once counted thirty-nine slaving ships in Loanda harbour. When Livingstone was staying with Gabriel there were none in harbour although the odd slaving ship still occasionally slipped into port under the cover of darkness to take on its illicit cargo.

The role that Livingstone played in highlighting the loss and misery that the predations of slave traders were having, unseen in the interior of Africa, was universally acknowledged. Sir Bartle Frere, President of the Royal Geographical Society summed up this contribution when giving Livingstone's obituary:

> Ages may elapse before the full measure of his services to Africa can be accurately measured, for we may hope that by his lifelong labours a new era will be opened to all the Negro races of that continent, and no man can foresee the ultimate consequences of their enfranchisement.[21]

While Livingstone was battling through the savage interior of Africa, Kirk was continuing Livingstone's work to end the east African slave trade. As the new H.M. Political Agent and Consul for Zanzibar, he was in an excellent position to achieve this aim. As Kirk realised the key was to close the slave market in Zanzibar and for years he diplomatically negotiated with Sultan Seyyid Bargash, the ruler of Zanzibar, attempting to gain his trust by promising to help the Sultan to make more money from engaging in legitimate commerce.

It was a slow process, but on 5 June 1873, barely a month after Livingstone's death in Chitambo's village, the Sultan of Zanzibar was finally forced to sign an edict which made the sea-borne slave trade illegal and the slave market in Zanzibar was closed. The Sultan did so only under the threat of a British naval bombardment. In time missionaries erected the Anglican Cathedral Church of Christ on the site of the former slave market. Freed slaves were used in the construction of the cathedral, which was supervised by Bishop Edward Steere. To capture the poignancy of the place, they built the cathedral altar on the spot of the whipping tree. A window is dedicated to Livingstone, and the church's crucifix is made from the wood of the Mvulu tree from Chitambo, under which Livingstone's heart and other internal organs had been buried.

Unfortunately, despite the edict, the slave trade was diminished, but not extinguished as it continued furtively, particularly on the mainland where it was also illegal. Sadly it was to continue until the end of the First World War. In some cases former slaves found that their conditions had not improved when they were employed as labourers at extremely poor wages in spice plantations.

Despite this, significant progress in halting the slave trade was made, perhaps best summed up by his former assistant, Kirk, who wrote in 1921, shortly before his death:

> Had Livingstone only lived to see the results of our joint work—to see Nyasaland under British rule, happy and peaceful, and to know that after

twenty years of hard work at Zanzibar I had ended the slave trade, what a happy man he would be.[22]

So was Kirk, who was by then knighted and widely recognised as a diplomat and expert on Southern and Eastern African matters.

13.5 A Colonial Legacy

The information that Livingstone collected was studied and became useful in the Great Race for the partition of Africa by the Great Powers.

Most explorers and their backers during the great age of European discovery, commencing in the early eighteenth century, espoused a deep regard for the survival and welfare of indigenous peoples of the areas being discovered. These sentiments were, however, almost always accompanied by the certainty of the benefits of introducing a 'superior' European culture. Led by Livingstone, Speke and Burton, large parts of southern and central Africa were quickly opened up so that within a relatively short period of time after Livingstone's death, most of the map of Africa had been filled in.

Livingstone was an active proponent of commerce and missionary work going hand-in-hand, as he saw all too clearly the possibilities of fertile land, largely untapped natural resources and strong healthy people.

The Dutch, British, French, Portuguese, and in time the Belgians and Germans began to wrestle for control of land and resources. This global power play between nations started in earnest from 1881 and only ceased at the commencement of the First World War. In their haste, these imperial powers quickly invaded, occupied, annexed and colonised huge swathes of territory in Africa. During this period of imperialism it became known as the 'Scramble for Africa'. It enabled these countries to build powerful empires by exploiting the resources of these colonies using new technological developments. A distinguishing feature of these times was the autocratic rule of the colonies, backed up by military power and economic dominance.

Colonial imperialism also meant competing political and economic rivalries were played out in distant theatres, including Africa, and this system contributed to the successful maintenance of a balance of power between often difficult, greedy and fearful emperors and their advisors. It continued until an obscure event in Serbia provided the pretext for the World War that eventually raged across the fields of Europe and the lands of their colonies.

The friendship that Livingstone formed with Sechele survived the difficulties that arose following Sechele's Christian baptism. It also had an enduring benefit to Britain as Sechele, a clever native chief, saw that aligning his people with the British, the rising power in South Africa, would ensure his people were protected.

It did not take long for this to happen; on 31 March 1885 the Bechuanaland Protectorate was established by the United Kingdom in southern Africa. It became the Republic of Botswana on 30 September 1966. When the Protectorate was first established, the local Tswana rulers remained in power, and the British administration was limited to a police force to protect Bechuanaland's borders against other European colonial powers.

There was rarely much reflection on the true benefits that came with European sovereign claims over their African possessions. Nor was there much reflection on their obligations as visitors to new colonies and the rights of the indigenous peoples. In the case of Australia, in 1835 the governor of New South Wales, Major-General Richard Bourke proclaimed the doctrine of *terra nullius*. This stated that indigenous Australians could not sell or assign land, nor could an individual person or group acquire it, other than through distribution by the Crown. Despite prolonged protestation, it was not until 1992 that the High Court of Australia handed down its decision in the Mabo Case, declaring the doctrine of *terra nullius* to be invalid and the Court ruled in favour of the common law doctrine of aboriginal title.

The action of this governor was to reverberate around the world and in 1837 it led to the formation of the Aborigines Protection Society. This society had similar aims as its sister organisation, the Anti-Slavery Society, with which it merged with in 1909.

The impact of colonialism is still being played out today. One of Livingstone legacies was to call the great falls on the Zambezi River the Victoria Falls after Queen Victoria, but this name is today under dispute, led by Robert Mugabe, President of Zimbabwe who has progressively changed nearly all the former colonial names in Zimbabwe. The Zambian maKololo name for the falls is *Mosi-oa-tunya*, 'The Smoke that Thunders', whereas the Ndebele, on the Zimbabwean side, call them *aManzi Thungayo*, 'The Water that Rises Like Smoke'. It seems the only reason why the falls have not been renamed is because the Zambians and Zimbabwean's cannot agree on a new name.

As regards Livingstone himself, his statue on the Zambian side, twice the size of a normal man, peers at the Victorian Falls, a massive, passive, bronze memorial to his African endeavours. Inscribed on the base are three words: *Liberator. Explorer. Missionary.* The term *Liberator* is a strange epithet to apply to Livingstone because of its colonial implications. Robert Mugabe, for one has taken exception to it and he has reputably threatened to have the statue torn down if he is given the chance.[23]

13.6 The long-term Impact

Livingstone had been very clear from the outset that 'good' commerce and missionary work must go hand in hand if there was to be a lasting change. While this idea was not new, Livingstone took it up as a mantra and continued to expound upon this at every opportunity. The Zambezi Expedition had at the heart of its purpose this very idea; to see if there was a navigable route up the Zambezi where commerce, Christianity and civilisation could flourish.

In his lifetime, Livingstone was successful in encouraging other missionaries to take up his challenge, often with disastrous consequences. But he never said it would be easy. He was also a living testament that a white man could live in Africa although he continued to do so at the increasing cost to his health. Later missionaries did more carefully follow in his footsteps and in doing so, gradually opened central Africa up so that the natives could benefit from education and health care. In doing so they set the groundwork for the African states to be formed, governed by Africans for Africans. It is not too excessive to say that Livingstone's explorations laid the foundations for this occur.

British settlement followed in time. By the late 1890s British settlers were occupying areas around the Zambezi River, through the activities of the Chartered Company of South Africa. The publishing of a new book, *The Story of David Livingstone*, bound in catching scarlet cloth and sold for just a shilling by the Sunday School Union, London, helped to encourage the interest of potential settlers in relocating to this part of Africa.[24]

The establishment of the Livingstonia Central Africa Company in 1877 provided another example of British commercial activity. The company was headquartered in Glasgow and was managed by John and Frederick Moir. Their focus was on exploiting trade and transportation opportunities in central Africa, both to make a profit and to develop European influence in the area. In the spirit of what Livingstone had publicly advocated, the Moir brothers established a number of trading posts between Nyasaland down to the mouth of the Zambezi River. They also operated a number of steamboats on Lake Nyassa.[25]

There is no doubt that as a result of Livingstone's calm and forthright manner in dealing with the natives, the subsequent work of British colonial rulers was made easier, because of their association with Livingstone. This encouraged greater trade and more European settlement in central Africa than might have been the case.

When Livingstone was a missionary at Mabotsa he opined that natives must be educated and receive vocational training if the work of missionaries was to expand. Later he included vocation training and while he was dismayed at the abilities of some young natives who had received skills in woodwork, metalwork and other such essential skills, he was fully supportive of the idea that natives should receive proper training.

Paradoxically it was this fundamental change—access to education, work opportunities and healthcare—that enabled African leaders to have the confidence in time to shrug off colonial rule and take up the responsibility of governing their peoples. In many cases they were educated at missionary schools and were consequently at the forefront of leading these changes.

One of the reasons for Livingstone's relatively modern views was that he knew the value of a good education. In many of his letters to his children he continually extolled them to learn and work hard.

It also had to do with the times that Livingstone was living in. The evangelical and nonconformist movement in Britain during the nineteenth century, demonstrated by deep ructions with the Scottish Kirk, helped change the mind-set from the notion of the divine right of rule over the uneducated masses, based on nobility and privilege, to a realisation that all must share in the fruits of prosperity based on equality and fairness. This social change infused a more balanced and ethical Government policy, including how the Government treated the indigenous people that made up the British Empire. It also set the necessary conditions to enable African nations to progressively splinter off from the British Empire.

13.8 Memorials

Livingstone was much honoured during his lifetime including an honorary doctorate and freedom of various cities in his homeland. Livingstone was, and still is, revered in many places in southern and central Africa, as evidenced by the numerous memorials, institutions and place names celebrating his name and work. His image was even used on the Clydesbank one-pound note.

In time there were numerous memorials to him across Britain. The first statue of Livingstone in Britain was erected in 1876 in the Princes Street Gardens in Edinburgh. The statue was first proposed in 1874, a year after the reported death of Livingstone first arrived. Livingstone is shown standing over the lion he shot in Mabotsa, with his right arm extended, Bible in hand. Another statue was soon after erected in Glasgow in 1879.

As regards recognising his medical capabilities, The Livingstone Medical Mission, Scotland is but one example. Another is the Charing Cross Hospital where Livingstone had attended as a student. The enduring power of his name was used when 98 years after Livingstone's birth the Hospital announced it had plans to reopen a ward and name it after Livingstone. To achieve this aim, the Council of Charing Cross Hospital established a David Livingstone Million Shilling Fund, and invited the public to make a small donation.[26]

His life is best commemorated at The David Livingstone Centre in Blantyre. The Centre was opened by the Queen Mother in 1929, and is housed in the place in which he was born, on the site of the cotton mill in which he started his working life. John and Frederick Moir, the first managers of the African Lakes Corporation, also became the first governors of the David Livingstone Centre.

Outside of Britain, one of the places most closely associated with the explorer is Livingstone in Zambia. Located near Victoria Falls, it was the only colonial place name that was retained when the new Republic of Zambia was formed in 1964.

During his lifetime postcards of his image sold for a shilling and were collected and traded by a whole generation of boys and girls, in much the same way as footballer cards are traded today. There have been numerous books; one estimate is that there have been over 250 biographies published and numerous articles. In 1960 Ladybird Books published a book on Livingstone as part of their 'Adventure from History' series. Today, across Africa, Livingstone merchandise, safaris, camps and tours are still trading on his name.

The Mvula tree in Chitambo Village in modern Zambia where his heart and lungs were buried under was felled in 1929. The wood was cut up and pieces were used to make crucifixes in all shapes and sizes, from the large crucifix that hangs in the Cathedral in Zanzibar that was built over the old slave trading yards, to small crucifixes that could be hung around a believer's neck. There seemed to be no end of uses to which the Mvula wood could be put to commemorate the life—and death—of Livingstone.

Livingstone has also been the subject of theatre plays and film, including a 1930's Hollywood blockbuster starring Spencer Tracey, the motion picture *Livingstone, a Drama of Reality* starring M. A. Weatherall as Livingstone, and a 1997 National Geographic film, *Forbidden Territory, Stanley's search for Livingstone*. Numerous musical pieces were produced including a cantata, *Livingstone the Pilgrim* by the London Missionary Society. He also spawned a board game, *Across Africa with Livingstone*. The board game was manufactured by Chad Valley Co. Ltd., for the United Council of Missionary Education in the 1920s.

In spite of this legacy what best-defined Livingstone was his lack of concern for material wealth and his deep Christian faith and unyielding conviction in the power and sanctity of God. He had little time for decorations, titles and gifts for he was essentially a simple person, with a simple philosophy and values. This is made clear when he wrote in his journal:

> I place no value on anything I have or may possess, except in relation to the kingdom of Christ. If anything will advance the interests of the kingdom, it shall be given away or kept, only as by giving or keeping it I shall promote the glory of Him to whom I owe all my hopes in time and eternity.[27]

Livingstone was undoubtedly one of the greatest of all explorers and for a time there was no man more famous in Britain and perhaps in the world. He also had great human failings but the dramatic circumstances of his death ensured that he would be remembered. In the modern context, the important social role that

Livingstone played may have been the inspiration for the Kenneth Kaunda, first President of Zambia, to describe Livingstone, fittingly, as 'Africa's first freedom fighter'.[28] It is an appropriate epithet for this doughty, determined Scottish missionary and explorer.

Southern African Geography

In 1988 geologists studying the basalt rocks on the island of Grand Manan, New Brunswick, Canada, realised that similar basalt rocks existed in a mountain range of Morocco. This was the beginning of a profound understanding of how the Atlantic Ocean was formed about 200 million year ago[1] as more and more of the same basalt formations were found in countries ringing the Atlantic Ocean. What these deposits reveal is just how the Atlantic was formed; huge volcanic eruptions that caused the giant landmass Pangaea to split open. This allowed seawater to pour into the growing split; a process that continued over many millions of years of unceasing tectonic activity until the eastern and western sides were pulled and forced apart. Eventually, the southern edge of Pangaea was split asunder and the land that would eventually become known as either the Amazon or Congo was formed. On the southern African part, it is now known as the Etendeka Traps and the outer edge is delineated by the mighty Victorian Falls. It has a twin in the Amazon, known as the Parana basalts and includes the magnificent Iguaçu Falls.[2]

Modern day Zambia and Malawi lie on the great central African plateau with an average altitude, ranging between 1,000 and 1,300 metres above sea level. In the east and particularly around the Muchinga Escarpment, the land rises to about 2,000 metres above sea level. Moving east across the plateau, broad depressions occur which form the Kafue basin and the alluvial plains of the Zambezi in the west and the south (the Zambezi River today forms Zambia's southern boundary with Namibia and Zimbabwe); the Luangwa River in the east; and Lakes Bangweulu,[3] Mweru and Tanganyika in the north.

In addition to the physical features, the weather in southern Africa also contributed to the hardship that Livingstone had to face. In terms of rainfall distribution, there are just two seasons. However, if one considers temperature as well, there are in fact four seasons. These are called the cool season (June to August); hot season (September to October); rainy season (November to March); and the post-rainy season (April to May). During the post-rainy season, 'Guti' conditions will occasionally break the generally fair weather, when light, continuous rain or drizzle is experienced, carried by the south easterly winds prevailing over the sub-continent.

The equatorial belt of continental Africa receives the greatest rainfall because there is an area of low pressure at the surface covering the equator. The amount of rainfall decreases both northwards and southwards from this area. The northeast and southeast trade winds of the tropical areas converge in this belt because it is an area of low pressure. The convergence zone covers a large area, although it does have distinct northern and southern boundaries.

Meteorologists refer to this phenomenon as the Inter-Tropical Convergence Zone, or ITCZ for short. The equatorial low and the ITCZ move north and south over the year with the apparent movement of the sun. The sun is overhead the equator in March; reaches its most northern position in June; again comes down and crosses the equator in September; and reaches its southernmost position in December. Therefore from roughly July to January, the sun is moving south, bringing with it the ITCZ.

While the movement of the ITCZ is smooth and free along the east coast, its movement in the west is arrested. The obstruction is caused by the intervention of different circulation patterns forming in the summer months of the southern hemisphere. The geography of Africa is largely responsible for this, since the southern half of Africa is narrower than in the north and at the so called 'armpit' of Africa on the west coast, there is a temperature contrast between the cold sea surface and the adjacent warm and humid coastal land. The cold Benguela Offshore Current further accentuates the temperature contrast. This means that as the sun comes over the equator in September, heat lows form over the Congo region. A clockwise circulation pattern develops around this low. The south-easterly trade winds of the Atlantic turn clockwise and enter southern Africa as a westerly current. It does, however, veer over the Congo, becoming a northerly current and in doing so, enters Zambia as a moist, unstable air mass. This air mass is known as the Zaire Airmass (with the leading edge being called the Zaire Air Boundary) and is largely responsible for the thundershowers and convective cloud development that predominates in this sub-region. It is also this circulation that prevents the ITCZ from sliding down the west coast. As the hot season advances, the Angolan heat low intensifies while the Zaire Airmass becomes deep and starts spreading southwards and eastward into modern day Zambia. At the same time, the ITCZ is moving southwards. It is then the eastward movement of the Zaire Air Boundary and the north–south movement of the ITCZ and the intensity of convergence between the two air masses that influence the weather over the northern part of southern Africa during the rainy season. The Zaire Air Boundary and the ITCZ start withdrawing by about the middle of March–April and by the beginning of May, the ITCZ lies north of the border of Zambia.

The Livingstone Children

Livingstone and Mary had six children: Robert, Agnes, Thomas, Elizabeth, William and Anna Mary. At the time of his death Livingstone had four surviving children, as first Elizabeth, and then Robert had died. Of them only Agnes, William and Anna Mary married and had children of their own.

It was a time of great confusion for the Livingstone family after the funeral. Fortunately, to allay their financial concerns, the Prime Minister, William Ewart Gladstone, had successfully recommended to Queen Victoria, in his last official act as Prime Minister, that the children of Livingstone receive an annual pension of £200 per annum. The Government, under a new Prime Minister, Benjamin Disraeli, soon after made a further one off capital grant of £3,000 to the Livingstone family, as well as undertaking to pay for all the arrears of pay that was due to Livingstone's servants and followers. It was a popular response by the Government of the day.

The first issue that had to be dealt with was the will. Disturbingly there was a disagreement over which will to use in disposing of £9,000 that formed part of Livingstone's estate.[1] Agnes knew Livingstone's Scottish Agent, Sir James Young, had in his possession a document that she thought was a legal will. Livingstone had supposedly written the document about two months before his death near Lake Bangweulu. Young thought so too, but the family's English Agent thought it was not legally binding. But it was the disposal of Livingstone's personal effects that affected them the most. His daughter Agnes was reduced to writing to Mrs Webb, with whom she had stayed at Newstead Abbey during Livingstone's last trip to Britain. The pain is evident in her letter:

> Is not this too disgusting? Mr Waller has written to Mr Young telling him that there was a sale of Arrowsmith's effects and among them were all poor Papa's original maps. One of them was brought by Stamford, the map engraver, for a few shillings, if not pence and was the one which Arrowsmith altered to suit Cooley.[2]

Agnes Livingstone

His eldest surviving child was Agnes. She was born on 13 June 1847 in Chonuane and was 33 at the time of his death. Livingstone provided the first description we have of Agnes in a letter to his parents in July 1848 when Agnes, or Nannee was about fourteen months old. 'Nannee is a frolicsome little lady with black eyes & hair, always merry, generally wakening in the morning with a loud laugh before her eyes are open.'[3] This bright personality obviously appealed to Livingstone as two years later he wrote about her, 'When Nane [Agnes] wishes to plague him [Robert] she runs away with his hat on her head, calling to him, 'A re ee' (let us go). She has a wonderful stock of spirits.'[4]

Agnes became the de-facto head of the family. She had enjoyed a good relationship with her father throughout his lifetime, and during their time together at Newstead Abbey, Agnes became her father's closest companion, administrative assistant and confidante. It is clear from the interest that Livingstone took in Agnes that he fully reciprocated her affections.

Agnes married Alexander Bruce, of Edinburgh, on 27 July 1875. Her grandfather Moffat was able to attend the wedding[5] and her youngest sister, Anna Mary, was the chief bridesmaid. After the wedding the young couple moved to Lothian Vale in Edinburgh where Alexander had a job as a brewery manager. They had four children; two sons and two daughters. They later moved to a new house with the very upmarket address of 10 Regent Terrace in Edinburgh.

Bruce was an entrepreneurial Scot and in time acquired an estate near Magomero in Nyasaland where the UMCA had first tried unsuccessfully to establish a missionary centre.

Agnes died in 1912.

Thomas Steele Livingstone

Thomas was born on 7 March 1849 in Kolobeng, Bechuanaland (now Botswana). Livingstone thought he was 'a fine strong boy, in no way troublesome, for which although none of the trouble falls on me I thank him sincerely.'[6]

It seems that Thomas was always a favourite of Moffat:

> Thomas is a fine fellow. Has lighter hair & eyes than the others, and is always in good humour. His grandfather Moffat calls him a 'noble fellow, the finest infant he ever saw.'

Thomas studied in Glasgow with the Free Church ministry. He became seriously ill in 1872. Livingstone was still in Africa and Moffat, his grandfather whose own wife had already predeceased him, went and visited him. Unfortunately Thomas never fully recovered from this illness.[7]

Thomas moved to Alexandria in Egypt to recover his health and where he became a merchant. He harboured plans to explore areas in northern Africa in the way that his father had explored southern Africa. This did not materialise as he had hoped as his health did not improve, and by early March 1876 it was clear that he was dying. Thomas had in the meantime become engaged and when his fiancée, Mary Ralston, heard he had fallen ill, she and Mary Livingstone's sister, Helen Mary Vavasseur quickly travelled down from Naples to visit him in the Deaconesses' Hospital in Alexandria. They arrived early evening on 15 March 1876. His eyesight was failing and he could barely talk—little pieces of ice had to be placed into his mouth to enable him to speak. Tragically he died later that evening.

In a strange coincidence, the person who brought Livingstone's body back from Zambezi two years prior, Mr Laing, arrived in Alexandria on the *Brindisi Mail* the day before his burial. He knew Thomas and was one of his bearers at his funeral. After visiting Thomas's fiancée, Laing sailed that evening for Zanzibar.

The genial Thomas was wildly mourned, as evidenced by the large funeral procession of twenty carriages. He was a deep loss to Moffat as he frequently visited his grandfather when he could.[8]

William Oswell Livingstone

William, also known as Oswell or Zouga after the Zouga river where he was born, was the Livingstone's fifth child. He was born on 15 September 1851. William went to school at Gilbertfield, near Hamilton, Scotland. He accompanied the Livingstone Search and Relief Expedition led by Lieutenant Dawson in 1872. The expedition was abandoned after they met Henry Stanley at Bagamoyo, after Stanley was returning from his successful meeting with Livingstone.[9]

Livingstone was delighted to hear that Oswell had taken up the medical profession, when he became a medical student in Glasgow. Frere offered to assist him should he choose to practice in India, although Livingstone thought he should consider going to America.[10] Unfortunately Oswell was unsuccessful in his application to practice as a medical doctor.

Oswell married a Scottish girl, Catherine Jane Anderson on 18 May 1875[11] in Glasgow, although this date is different from that suggested by J. S. Moffat who attended the wedding in April 1875.[12] Both of his parents were by then dead, and only Moffat was able to attend. They had only one daughter, Kate Agnes Livingstone who was born in Glasgow, Lanark, Scotland in 1878.

Oswell fell ill and died young in St Albans, Hertford, in 1892, aged 41.

Anna Mary Livingstone

Anna Mary was the youngest of the six children and was born on 16 November 1858, seven years after William, in Kuruman. Mary was living in Kuruman patiently hoping to join Livingstone on the Zambezi Expedition.

Sadly for Anna Mary she came too late in Livingstone's life to have had the time to build a close relationship with her father. This tragedy was made worse when her mother died young and Anna Mary was farmed out to her elderly spinster aunts, Janet and Agnes Livingstone who cared for her in a loving way. Despite the brief time father and daughter had together, Livingstone tried to be a good father when he could. There is a touching photograph of them together, showing a young Anna Mary looking at her father with respect and awe.

Anna Mary attended Henry Longmaid's Quaker Girls' School in Kendal. She later spent two years in Weimar, Germany and in Nîmes in France. In 1881 she married Frank Wilson in Kendal, Westmoreland. Frank and Anna Mary Wilson initially worked for the Deep Sea Fisherman Society, They moved to London and then later Frank took up a job with the Church Missionary Society in Sierra Leone and became a pastor to the West Indian troops stationed there. He died of yellow fever in 1910.

Anna Mary and her husband gave a bronze tablet to Chitambo's village and it was erected in the village in July 1892 although by then the chief had relocated the village to a place about eight miles away. When a young explorer, Edward Grave, one of Stanley's officers, visited the village in 1894, coastal slave traders had reportedly stolen the tablet. Grave was presented with the letter that accompanied the tablet, dated 6 July 1892. The letter was written by Captain Bia and Lieutenant Franqui, the two Belgium Officers entrusted carry the tablet.[13]

Anna Mary and Frank had a daughter and a son.[14] Their son, Hubert Wilson, also went on to become a medical missionary with the United Free Church at Chitambo, where Livingstone had died, after serving as an officer in the Royal Ambulance Medical Corps during the First World War. Hubert also wrote a biography of his grandfather. Anna Mary visited Hubert and his sister Ruth in Chitambo in 1915, travelling north by train from Cape Town. *En route* she stopped off to see the mighty Victoria Falls.

Anna Mary lived on to a ripe old age of 81, dying in 1939 and is buried in Carnoustie, Scotland.

About the Author

Paul first began writing this biography *Dr Livingstone, Africa's Greatest Explorer,* while stationed in Lusaka, Zambia, when working on a United Nations Food and Agricultural Organisation programme in 1991–92. This role enabled him to travel extensively throughout southern and eastern Africa and in the course of these travels, he became fascinated by the continuing references and landmarks relating to Livingstone.

Paul has been involved in a number of expeditions around the world. These include a project advisor and sailor on two Royal Geographical Society approved expeditions. The first was the Borobudur Ship Expedition, 2003–04, sailing a reconstructed AD 700 ship from Indonesia to the Seychelles and then around to the Cape of Good Hope and up to Ghana. The second expedition was the Phoenician Ship Expedition, 2008–12, where a reconstructed 600 BC boat was sailed from Syria through the Suez Canal and around Africa and back to Syria, and then subsequently to London. He has also been involved in a number of other expeditions, including kayaking the Zambezi River down to the Mozambique border. Paul is a Fellow of the Royal Geographical Society.

Paul is a retired Colonel in the New Zealand Army, and most recently commanded a Regiment. He has also served with the Commando Regiment, Australian Special Forces, and the Queens Regiment, England. He attended the Canadian Militia Command and Staff College in Canada and has undertaken operational tours in Syria, South Lebanon and East Timor.

Paul is an investment banker and his career has spanned England, southern and eastern Africa, New Zealand and Australia. He has completed the Senior Executive Fellows Program at the Harvard University Kennedy School of Government, and has postgraduate and graduate degrees from the London School of Economics and Political Science, England, and Massey University, New Zealand.

Endnotes

Chapter 1: The Early Years

1. The boguera was the initiation ceremony into manhood.
2. *The Matabele Mission,* Letter 8, 16.4.1858, p.10
3. James McNair, p. XIV
4. The Reader, *The Graphic,* London, England, Saturday, 15.6.1889, Issue 1020.
5. Turkey red is a colour that was widely used to dye cotton in the eighteenth and nineteenth centuries. It was made using the root of the rubia plant, through a long and laborious process. In 1786 the British Government paid Louis Borelle and Abraham Henry Borelle "a Sum not exceeding Two Thousand Five Hundred Pounds be granted to his Majesty, to be paid to, upon a proper Discovery to be made by them, for the Use of the Public, of their Method of dyeing the Colour called Turkey Red upon Cotton in Hanks and in the Piece". Source: "Turkey Red in Blackley: A Chapter in the *History of Dyeing*", excerpt from Pro Memoria—Turkey Red Dyeing and Blackley, a manuscript by W. H. Cliffe.
6. House of Commons Papers, Volume 19. HMSO, 1856, p. 44.
7. The Reader, *The Graphic,* London, England, Saturday, 15.6.1889, Issue 1020.
8. Tomkins, p. 1.
9. David Livingstone Centre, 1857.
10. Blaikie, p. 9.
11. *Missionary Travels.*
12. "*Livingstone and the Exploration of Central Africa*", H. H. Johnston, p. 57.
13. *Missionary Travels.*
14. Blaikie, p. 12.
15. Blaikie, p. 14.
16. Karl Friedrich August Gützlaff (1803-1851), anglicised as Charles Gutzlaff, was a German missionary to the Far East, notable as one of the first Protestant missionaries in Bangkok, Thailand and for his books about China. In 1832 he became the first Protestant missionary to visit Korea. He dressed like a Chinese and took on a Chinese name. He served as interpreter for British diplomatic missions during the Opium Wars. Gutzlaff Street in Hong Kong was named after him. Source: Wikipedia, 22.11.2012.
17. Blaikie, p. 12.
18. The Andersonian University was founded from money gifted in the will of Professor John Anderson, of Glasgow who died in 1796. Source: *The Graphic,* London,

England, Saturday, 5.6.1880, Issue 549.
19. Blaikie, p. 16.
20. *Missionary Travels*.
21. Joseph Moore was a life-long friend of Livingstone. He also graduated from the London Missionary Society College, Ongar as a Reverend and was posted as a London Missionary Society missionary to Tahiti. He later returned to England.
22. Blaikie, p. 22.
23. Blaikie, p. 21.
24. David Gilkinson Watt (1817-91) was a life-long friend of Livingstone. He also graduated from the London Missionary Society College, Ongar as a Reverend and was posted as a London Missionary Society missionary in India (1840-5). He was on the Board of the London Missionary Society before becoming an independent minister in various parts of England.
25. Blakie, pp. 21-23.
26. R. Cecil to LMS 26.1.39, LMS Archives.
27. Seaver, p. 27.
28. Livingstone to Revd J. Arundel, LMS, SOAS, Ongar, 2.7.39, LMS Archives.
29. His son was Dr (later Sir) James Risdon Bennett, (1809-1891), M.D., LL.D., F.R.S., and President of the Royal College of Physicians, London. They were lifelong friends. Blaikie, p. 26.
30. Livingstone to G. Drummond 5.7.40, NLS.
31. *The Spectator*, Volume 13, p. 534.
32. The Niger expedition of 1841 was a largely unsuccessful journey in 1841 and 1842 of three British iron steam vessels to Lokoja, at the confluence of the Niger River and Benue River, in what is now Nigeria. It was mounted by British missionary and activist groups, with the backing of the British government. The crews of the boats suffered a high mortality from disease. Wikipedia, 21.11.2012.
33. Blaikie, p. 29.
34. Jeal, pp. 42-43.
35. Chamberlin, p. 12.
36. *Missionary Travels*.
37. Blaikie, p. 29.
38. Livingstone to Mrs N. Livingstone (undated), NLS.

Chapter 2: Missionary Expectations

1. Herodotus, *The Histories*, Book IV, [42-43], p. 248 (translated by Robin Waterfield). The author sailed on the Phoenician Ship Expedition 2008/12 which involved sailing a reconstructed 600 BC Phoenician trading vessel, built at the ancient Phoenician port of Arwad, from Syria through the Suez Canal and around Africa and back to Syria, and then subsequently from Syria to London. The purpose of the expedition was to re-trace the Phoenicians' route around Africa. The circumnavigation of Africa took twenty-six months and covered over 20,000 miles at sea.
2. Sitchuana was the way that Livingstone spelt it.
3. *The Zambian Collection*, Letter 3, 27.1.1841, p. 11.
4. *The Zambesi Doctors*, Letter 38, 4.2.1865, p. 99.
5. *The Zambian Collection*, Letter 1, 27.1.1841, p. 7.
6. *The Zambian Collection*, Letter 3, 27.1.1841, p. 12.

7. William Ross died at Likatlong 30th July 1863 at the age of 61. His death is commemorated in the Abernyte Church, Between Perth and Kinross, Scotland.
8. *David Livingstone Family Letters*, Volume One, Letter 31, 11.2.1846, p. 167.
9. *David Livingstone Family Letters*, Volume One, Letter 6, 13.7.1842, p. 60.
10. *David Livingstone Family Letters*, Volume One, Letter 31, 11.2.1846, p. 167.
11. Livingstone refers to it as Simon's Bay and today is known as Simonstown in False Bay, 23 miles south of Cape Town, South Africa.
12. *The Zambian Collection*, Letter 3, 5.3.1841, p. 13.
13. John Philip (1775-1851). He was a Minister of Union Chapel, Cape Town. He was also the author of *Researches in South Africa* (1828), a book that detailed the civil, moral and religious condition of the local tribes. He was eventually replaced in August 1844.
14. *The Zambian Collection*, Letter 4, 3.8.1841, p. 14.
15. *The Zambian Collection*, Letter 4, 3.8.1841, p. 14.
16. Hughes, p. 13.
17. Blaikie, p. 22.
18. Thomas Maclear, (1794-1879) was a medical doctor who was appointed in 1834 British Astronometer at Royal Observatory, Cape Town. He was later knighted for his services.
19. *David Livingstone Family Letters*, Volume One, Letter 2, 19.5.41 p. 34.
20. *David Livingstone Family Letters*, Volume One, Letter 1, 30.3.1841, p. 28
21. *The Zambian Collection*, Letter 4, 3.8.1841, p. 13.
22. *The Zambian Collection*, Letter 4, 3.8.1841, p. 13.
23. Robert Edwards (1795-1876) was born in Lancashire. He joined the LMS in 1823 as an artisan (carpenter). He served at two missions in the Cape Colony before going to Kuruman in 1831. Edwards and Livingstone founded the mission at Mabotsa. He was forced to leave Mabotsa in 1852 by the Boers and returned to the Cape Colony.
24. *David Livingstone Family Letters*, Volume One, Letter 4, 8.12.1841, p. 44.
25. *David Livingstone Family Letters*, Volume One, Letter 4, 8.12.1841, p. 46.
26. *The Zambian Collection*, Letter 5, 2.12.1841, p. 17.
27. *The Graphic*, London England, Saturday 12.9.1885, Issue 824.
28. *David Livingstone Family Letters*, Volume One, Letter 3, 29.9.1841, p. 40.
29. Edwards to Tidman, 8.12.1841.
30. Moselikatsi also known as Mzilikazi.
31. Bakhatla are also known as Bakgatla.
32. Jeal, p. 71.
33. *The Zambian Collection*, Letter 5, 2.12.1841, p. 17.
34. *The Zambian Collection*, Letter 5, 2.12.1841, p. 20.
35. Blaikie, p. 37.
36. Livingstone to LMS, 24.6.43 M.C. 36.
37. Blaikie, p. 41.
38. *David Livingstone Family Letters*, Volume One, Letter 4, 8.12.1841, p. 47.
39. *David Livingstone Family Letters*, Volume One, Letter 11, 21.8.1843, pp. 82-83.
40. Ransford, p. 35
41. Thomas Montague Steele, (1820-90). He was a British Army Officer and aide-de-camp to the Governor of Madras (1842-8) when he met Livingstone. He later became General Sir Thomas Steele.
42. *David Livingstone Family Letters*, Volume One, Letter 11, 21.8.1843, p.81.

43. Mebaloe Molehane was a member of a local tribe of Balala that lived around Kuruman. He was baptised David, became a deacon of a local church and accompanied Livingstone when he established Mabotsa. He was paid £12 per annum (Footnote: *David Livingstone Family Letters*, Volume One, Letter 13, 15.2.1844, p. 90).

44. *David Livingstone Family Letters*, Volume One, Letter 11, 21.8.1843, p.85.

45. Livingstone to LMS, 30.10.43, M.C. 49

46. Livingstone to Tidman, 23.05.56, Missionary Correspondence

47. Letter from Revd R. Moffat to LMS Directors, February 1844, extract from *The Lives of Robert and Mary Moffat*, J. S. Moffat, 1885, p. 245.

48. *David Livingstone Family Letters*, Volume One, Letter 12, 16.12.1843, p. 88.

49. Ransford, p. 34

50. Walter Inglis (1815-84). He was born in Scotland and joined the London Missionary Society in 1838.

51. William Ashton (1817-97). He was born in England and arrived in Kuruman with Moffat and Inglis in 1843. In served in Kuruman and other stations until 1876.

52. *David Livingstone Family Letters*, Volume One, Letter 12, 16.12.1843, p. 88.

53. *David Livingstone Family Letters*, Volume One, Letter 14, 27.4.1844, p. 95.

54. *David Livingstone Family Letters*, Volume One, Letter 14, 27.4.1844, p. 95.

55. *David Livingstone Family Letters*, Volume One, Letter 13, 15.2.1844, p. 90. There are number of conflicting dates about the lion attack. DL wrote to Robert Moffat on 15 February 1844 from Mabotsa and informed him about the lion attack. In his letter he makes reference to the event being "last Wednesday" so is probably likely to be the 7 February to allow time for a letter to arrive at Kuruman.

56. *David Livingstone Family Letters*, Volume One, Letter 13, 15.2.1844, p. 91.

57. Livingstone provided a much more graphic account of the incident in his book, *Missionary Travels*.

58. Letter from R. Edwards to LMS, SOAS, Africa A 1 21, Mabotsa, 28.1.1845.

59. *David Livingstone Family Letters*, Volume One, Letter 32, 11.3.1846, p. 176.

60. A cast of the bone is on display at the Scottish national memorial to David Livingstone, Blantyre.

Chapter 3: Marriage

1. Southafricanholiday.org.uk website.

2. *The Lives of Robert and Mary Moffat*, J. S. Moffat, 1885, p. 165.

3. Letter from Mary Moffat to Miss Lees of Manchester, 15.9.1830. Extract from *The Lives of Robert and Mary Moffat*, J. S. Moffat, 1885, p. 168.

4. Letter from Mary Moffat to Mrs Roby of Manchester, 1.10.1833. Extract from *The Lives of Robert and Mary Moffat*, J. S. Moffat, 1885, p. 179.

5. Letter from Mary Moffat to her Father, 14.4.1836. Extract from *The Lives of Robert and Mary Moffat*, J. S. Moffat, 1885, p. 207.

6. *The Lives of Robert and Mary Moffat*, J. S. Moffat, 1885, pp. 222-223.

7. Letter from Mary Moffat to Robert Hamilton, 25.11.1840. Extract from *The Lives of Robert and Mary Moffat*, J. S. Moffat, 1885, pp. 230.

8. *The Lives of Robert and Mary Moffat*, J. S. Moffat, 1885, p. 231.

9. The book was published by John Snow, Paternoster Row, London.

10. *The Lives of Robert and Mary Moffat*, J. S. Moffat, 1885, p. 244.

11. Letter from Revd R. Moffat to LMS Directors, February 1844, extract from *The*

Lives of Robert and Mary Moffat, J. S. Moffat, 1885, p. 247.

12. *David Livingstone Family Letters*, Volume Two, Letter 57, 16.5.1849, p. 55.
13. A section from the Almond tree is on display at the David Livingstone Centre, Blantyre, Scotland.
14. Buba was local Griqua trader (Methuen, p. 193).
15. *David Livingstone Family Letters*, Volume One, Letter 17, 12.9.1844, p. 105.
16. Livingstone to Tidman, 2.12.44, LMS 31.
17. Livingstone to D. G. Watt, 2.4.45, LMS Archives.
18. *David Livingstone Family Letters*, Volume One, Letter 16, 1.8.1844, p. 103.
19. *The Lives of Robert and Mary Moffat*, J. S. Moffat, 1885, p. 248.
20. *David Livingstone Family Letters*, Volume One, Letter 27, 1.10.1845, p. 153.
21. Livingstone to Revd D. G. Watt 13 February [1848], David Livingstone Letters & Documents 1841-1872.
22. *David Livingstone Family Letters*, Volume Two, Letter 55, 20.4.1849, pp. 32-33.
23. *David Livingstone Family Letters*, Volume Two, Letter 63, 5.2.1850, p. 77.
24. The letters are now lost.
25. *David Livingstone Family Letters*, Volume Two, Letter 85, 5.5.1852, p. 182.
26. *David Livingstone Family Letters*, Volume One, Letter 21, 14.5.1845, p. 113.
27. *David Livingstone Family Letters*, Volume Two, Letter 66, 28.7.1850, p. 99.
28. *David Livingstone Family Letters*, Volume Two, Letter 80, 29.11.1851, pp. 154-155.
29. *The Lives of Robert and Mary Moffat*, J. S. Moffat, 1885, p. 257.
30. *David Livingstone Family Letters*, Volume Two, Letter 83, 2.4.1852, pp. 176.
31. Letter from Mary Moffat to her Father, 17.3.1848, extract from *The Lives of Robert and Mary Moffat*, J. S. Moffat, 1885, p. 247.
32. *David Livingstone Family Letters*, Volume Two, Letter 79, 10.1851, p. 141.
33. *David Livingstone Family Letters*, Volume Two, Letter 81, 29.12.1851, p. 159.
34. *David Livingstone Family Letters*, Volume Two, Letter 83, 2.4.1852, pp. 171.
35. *David Livingstone Family Letters*, Volume Two, Letter 83, 2.4.1852, pp. 172.
36. *David Livingstone Family Letters*, Volume Two, Letter 63, 1.1849, p. 73.
37. *David Livingstone Family Letters*, Volume Two, Letter 106, 12.9.1855, p. 261.
38. *David Livingstone Family Letters*, Volume Two, Letter 107, 14.9.1855, p. 268 and footnote 1.
39. *David Livingstone Family Letters*, Volume One, Letter 20, 1.4.1845, p. 121.
40. Livingstone to Tidman, 24.6.43, LMS 23.
41. *David Livingstone Family Letters*, Volume One, Letter 21, 14.5.1845, p. 120.
42. *David Livingstone Family Letters*, Volume One, Letter 22, 6.6.1845, p. 129.
43. Livingstone to Tidman, 23.3.45, LMS 32.
44. *David Livingstone Family Letters*, Volume One, Letter 20, 12.5.1845, p. 118.
45. *David Livingstone Family Letters*, Volume One, Letter 20, 12.5.1845, p. 113.
46. *David Livingstone Family Letters*, Volume One, Letter 22, 12.5.1845, p. 123.
47. *David Livingstone Family Letters*, Volume One, Letter 20, 12.5.1845, Footnote 8, p. 113.
48. Livingstone goes on at some length in petty detail about the Edwards and others. *David Livingstone Family Letters*, Volume One, Letter 20, 12.5.1845, p. 114.
49. Tidman to Livingstone, LMS, SOAS, London, 29.10.1846.
50. *David Livingstone Family Letters*, Volume One, Introduction p.17 and footnote 2.
51. *David Livingstone Family Letters*, Volume One, Letter 38, 16.3.1847, p. 190.
52. *David Livingstone Family Letters*, Volume One, Letter 24, 13.8.1845, p. 142.
53. Livingstone suggests the correct pronunciation is 'Chonwaney'. *David Livingstone*

Family Letters, Volume One, Letter 29, 11.11.1845, p. 157.

54. Livingstone to Tidman, 24.6.43, MC 42-3.
55. *David Livingstone Family Letters*, Volume One, Letter 24, 13.8.1845, p. 138.
56. *David Livingstone Family Letters*, Volume One, Letter 24, 13.8.1845, p. 138.
57. *David Livingstone Family Letters*, Volume One, Letter 25, 5.9.1845, p. 143.
58. *David Livingstone Family Letters*, Volume One, Letter 28, 1.11.1845, p. 154.
59. *David Livingstone Family Letters*, Volume One, Letter 24, 13.8.1845, p. 141.
60. Henry H. Methuen was a naturalist and traveller. He wrote *Life in the Wilderness: or, Wanderings in South Africa* (1846).
61. *David Livingstone Family Letters*, Volume One, Letter 24, 13.8.1845, p. 142.
62. *David Livingstone Family Letters*, Volume One, Letter 26, 22.9.1845, p. 150.
63. One reason for not calling him Neil was his dislike for the name. It is customary for many tribes across southern and eastern Africa to call the parents after their first-born. This would mean Livingstone and Mary would be called Ra-Neil and Ma-Neil. The name for the boat used for the Zambesi Expedition was called Ma-Robert, in acknowledgement of Mary. *David Livingstone Family Letters*, Volume One, Letter 30, 17.1.1846, p. 160.
64. *David Livingstone Family Letters*, Volume One, Letter 30, 17.1.1846, p. 150.
65. *David Livingstone Family Letters*, Volume One, Letter 42, 14.10.1847, p. 233.
66. *David Livingstone Family Letters*, Volume Two, Letter 57, 16.5.1849, p. 55.
67. Tidman to Livingstone, 29.10.46, LMS Archives, Box 6.
68. *David Livingstone Family Letters*, Volume One, Letter 25, 5.9.1845, p. 145.
69. Livingstone to Tidman, 17.03.47, LMS 41.
70. *David Livingstone Family Letters*, Volume One, Letter 31, 11.2.1846, p. 165.
71. *David Livingstone Family Letters*, Volume Two, Letter 55, 20.4.1849, p. 35.
72. *David Livingstone Family Letters*, Volume One, Letter 34, 8.9.1846, p. 178.
73. *The Lives of Robert and Mary Moffat*, J. S. Moffat, 1885, pp. 254.
74. *David Livingstone Family Letters*, Volume One, Letter 35, 5.10.1846, p.182.
75. *David Livingstone Family Letters*, Volume One, Letter 38, 16.3.1847, p. 191.
76. *David Livingstone Family Letters*, Volume One, Letter 36, 27.10.1846, p.184.
77. *David Livingstone Family Letters*, Volume One, Letter 37, 15.3.1847, p. 187 and footnote 7.
78. *David Livingstone Family Letters*, Volume One, Letter 37, 15.3.1847, p. 187.
79. There is no agreement on the date of Agnes's birth. The Clan Moffat genealogy has her recorded as born on 13 June 1847. Livingstone added a postscript to a letter he wrote to his mother on 4.5.1847 but the date the postscript was added is uncertain. *David Livingstone Family Letters*, Volume One, Letter 39, 14.5.1847, p. 199.
80. "...the Natives have no hard g in their language she is usually called Nannee", *David Livingstone Family Letters*, Volume One, Letter 46, 5.7.1848, p. 246.
81. Letter from Mary Moffat to her Father, 17.3.1848, extract from *The Lives of Robert and Mary Moffat*, J. S. Moffat, 1885, p. 265.

Chapter 4: A Fresh Start

1. *David Livingstone Family Letters*, Volume One, Letter 41, 13.8.1847, p. 203.
2. *The Lives of Robert and Mary Moffat*, J. S. Moffat, 1885, pp. 271-272.
Friday was also known as Morukanelo and he later accompanied Livingstone and Oswell in the trip to discover Lake Ngami in 1850.
3. *David Livingstone Family Letters*, Volume One, Letter 41, 13.8.1847, p. 210.

4. *The Zambian Collection*, Letter 8, 13.2.1848, p. 26.
6. Livingstone to LMS, 1.11.48, LMS 44.
7. Completed in about July 1848. *David Livingstone Family Letters*, Volume One, Letter 46, 5.7.1848, p. 245.
8. *David Livingstone Family Letters*, Volume One, Letter 46, 5.7.1848, pp. 245-246.
9. *David Livingstone Family Letters*, Volume One, Letter 42, 29.9.1847, pp. 211-212.
10. *David Livingstone Family Letters*, Volume One, Letter 47, 11.8.1848, p. 250.
11. *The Zambian Collection*, Letter 8, 13.2.1848, p. 26.
12. Blaikie, p. 78.
13. "We had been on our previous picture night on the magicians of Pharaoh throwing down their rods." *David Livingstone Family Letters*, Volume One, Letter 42, 14.10.1847, p. 220.
14. .*The Zambian Collection*, Letter 9, 23.6.1848, p. 32.
15. *David Livingstone Family Letters*, Volume One, Letter 49, 10.1848, pp. 259-60.
16. *David Livingstone Family Letters*, Volume Two, Letter 53, 23.3.1849, footnote 20, p. 27.
17. Andries Hendrik Potgieter, known as Hendrik Potgieter (1792-1852) was a Voortrekker leader. He served as the first head of state of Potchefstroom from 1840 and 1845 and also as the first head of state of Zoutpansberg from 1845 to 1852. Wikipedia, 23.11.2012.
18. Lieutenant General Sir Henry George Wakelyn Smith, 1st Baronet of Aliwal GCB (1787-1860), known as Sir Harry Smith, was a notable English soldier and military commander in the British Army of the early 19th century. A veteran of the Napoleonic Wars, he is also particularly remembered for his role in the Battle of Aliwal (India) in 1846. Wikipedia, 23.11.2012.
19. Andries Wilhelmus Jacobus Pretorius (1798-1853) was a leader of the Boers who was instrumental in the creation of the Transvaal Republic, as well as the earlier but short-lived Natalia Republic, in present-day South Africa. Wikipedia, 23.11.2012.
20. *The Lives of Robert and Mary Moffat*, J. S. Moffat, 1885, p. 272.
21. *David Livingstone Family Letters*, Volume Two, Letter 50, 18.1.1849, pp. 8-9.
22. *David Livingstone Family Letters*, Volume Two, Letter 51, 31.1.1849, p. 16.
23. *David Livingstone Family Letters*, Volume Two, Letter 53, 23.3.1849, p. 20.
24. *David Livingstone Family Letters*, Volume Two, Letter 53, 23.3.1849, p. 21.
25. Letter from Mary Moffat to one of Her Children, 2.3.1849, extract from *The Lives of Robert and Mary Moffat*, J. S. Moffat, 1885, p. 275.
26. Letter from Mary Moffat to one of her Children, 2.3.1849, extract from *The Lives of Robert and Mary Moffat*, J. S. Moffat, 1885, pp. 275-276.
27. *David Livingstone Family Letters*, Volume Two, Letter 56, 4.5(?)1849, p. 41.
28. *David Livingstone Family Letters*, Volume Two, Letter 54, 11.4.1849, pp. 29-30.
29. *David Livingstone Family Letters*, Volume Two, Letter 54, 11.4.1849, p. 31.
30. *David Livingstone Family Letters*, Volume Two, Letter 56, 4.5(?)1849, p. 42.
31. *David Livingstone Family Letters*, Volume Two, Letter 57, 16.5.1849, p. 51 and footnote 7.
32. *David Livingstone Family Letters*, Volume Two, Letter 57, 16.5.1849, p. 50.
33. It is more generally known today as the Boteti River or the Botletle River.
34. *David Livingstone Family Letters*, Volume Two, Letter 60, 25.9.1849, p. 66.
35. Bakoba are also known as the Bayeiye.
36. McNair p. 29.
37. *David Livingstone Family Letters*, Volume Two, Letter 59, 17.9(?), 1849, p. 61.

38. *David Livingstone Family Letters*, Volume Two, Letter 59, 17.9(?), 1849, p. 61.
39. *David Livingstone Family Letters*, Volume Two, Letter 60, 25.9.1849, p. 65.
40. The Royal Geographical Society (RGS) was founded in 1830 to support commerce, industry and government. It sponsors numerous explorations to many parts of the world.
41. *David Livingstone Family Letters*, Volume Two, Letter 72, 4.12.1850, p. 116.
42. Schapera, pp. 70-71.
43. *David Livingstone Family Letters*, Volume Two, Letter 63, 5.2.1850, p. 74.
44. *David Livingstone Family Letters*, Volume Two, p. 81.
45. Oswell's biographer suggested that Livingstone had "been unable to resist the desire and opportunity of being the first too visit Sebitoane". *William Cotton Oswell, Hunter and Explorer,* William Edward Oswell, Volume I, p. 214.
46. *David Livingstone Family Letters*, Volume Two, Letter 65, 8.7.1850, p. 85.
47. Livingstone thought it was a paludal or malarial fever. *David Livingstone Family Letters,* Volume Two, Letter 65, 8.7.1850, p. 83.
48. *David Livingstone Family Letters*, Volume Two, Letter 66, 28.7.1850, p. 96.
49. *David Livingstone Family Letters*, Volume Two, Letter 65, 8.7.1850, p. 84.
50. *David Livingstone Family Letters*, Volume Two, Letter 65, 8.7.1850, p. 84.
51. *David Livingstone Family Letters*, Volume Two, Letter 66, 28.7.1850, p. 96.
52. She was named after Mrs Elizabeth Pyne of Ongar. *David Livingstone Family Letters*, Volume Two, Letter 72, 4.12.1850, p. 116, footnote 7.
53. *David Livingstone Family Letters*, Volume Two, Letter 68, 18.9.1850, p. 103.
54. *David Livingstone Family Letters*, Volume Two, Letter 67, 24.8.1850, pp. 100-101.
55. *The Lives of Robert and Mary Moffat,* J. S. Moffat, 1885, pp. 280-281.
56. *David Livingstone Family Letters*, Volume Two, Letter 73, 9.2.1851, p. 120.
57. *David Livingstone Family Letters*, Volume Two, Letter 70, 17.10.1850, p. 109.
58. *David Livingstone Family Letters*, Volume Two, Letter 71, 27.10.1850, p. 112.
59. The passage as quoted from a copy of the letter transcribed by Livingstone into his Journal.
60. *David Livingstone Family Letters*, Volume Two, Letter 76, 28.4.1850, p. 131.
61. "I am happy to say Mary reciprocates these sentiments." *David Livingstone Family Letters*, Volume Two, Letter 76, 28.4.1850, p 131.
62. Letter from Robert Moffat to Dr. Bruce, of Newcastle, March 1851, extract from *The Lives of Robert and Mary Moffat,* J. S. Moffat, 1885, p. 281.
63. Livingstone also noted that a rhinoceros had tossed Oswell twice and an elephant had run over him. *David Livingstone Family Letters*, Volume Two, Letter 81, 19.12.1851, p. 159.
64. *David Livingstone Family Letters*, Volume Two, Letter 77, 28.4.1851, p. 134.
65. *David Livingstone Family Letters*, Volume Two, Letter 78, 29.9.1851, p. 137.
66. *David Livingstone Family Letters*, Volume Two, Letter 79, 10.1851, p. 142.
67. McNair, p.32.
68. The Chobe River is also known as the Linyanti River, and is a tributary of the Zambesi River.
69. Letter from Robert Moffat to Dr. Bruce, of Newcastle, 30.10.1851, extract from *The Lives of Robert and Mary Moffat,* J. S. Moffat, 1885, p. 290.
70. McNair, pp. 34.
71. Schapera, p. 163.
72. They met on 21 June and Sebitoane died on 7 July 1851. *David Livingstone Family Letters*, Volume Two, Letter 78, 29.9.1851, p. 138.

73. *David Livingstone Family Letters*, Volume Two, Letter 79, 10.1851, p. 144.
74. MacNair, p. 34.
75. Livingstone described it as the Seseheke, a main branch of the Zambesi. *David Livingstone Family Letters*, Volume Two, Letter 79, 10.1851, p. 145.
76. *David Livingstone Family Letters*, Volume Two, Letter 78, 29.9.1851, p. 138.
77. *David Livingstone Family Letters*, Volume Two, Letter 79, 10.1851, pp. 149-150.
78. They were correct as the Quelimane river mouth is about 100 km (60 miles) north of the Zambesi river mouth.
79. *David Livingstone Family Letters*, Volume Two, Letter 78, 29.9.1851, p. 139.
80. *David Livingstone Family Letters*, Volume Two, Letter 81, 29.12.1851, p. 159.
81. Mambari were traders. In *Travels* Livingstone identifies them as members of the OviMbundu of Central Angola (p. 218).
82. *David Livingstone Family Letters*, Volume Two, Letter 79, 10.1851, p. 146.
83. *David Livingstone Family Letters*, Volume Two, Letter 79, 10.1851, p. 146.
84. This tribe were also known as WaiYao, Waiyau or just Yao.
85. *David Livingstone Family Letters*, Volume Two, Letter 79, 10.1851, p. 147.
86. *David Livingstone Family Letters*, Volume Two, Letter 79, 10.1851, pp. 147-148.

Chapter 5: The Journey to Loanda

1. *David Livingstone Family Letters*, Volume Two, Letter 63, 5.2.1850, p. 74.
2. The Xhosa Wars, also known as the Cape Frontier Wars, were a series of nine wars between the Xhosa people and European settlers, from 1779 to 1879, in what is now the Eastern Cape in South Africa. They are also known as "Africa's 100 Years War". Wikipedia, 22.11.2012.
3. Letter from Mary Moffat to her Father, 7.6.1851, extract from *The Lives of Robert and Mary Moffat*, J. S. Moffat, 1885, p. 285.
4. *David Livingstone Family Letters*, Volume Two, Letter 80, 29.11.1851, p. 155.
5. *David Livingstone Family Letters*, Volume Two, Letter 81, 19.12.1851, p. 158.
6. Revd Edwards Waring Oswell (1821-53). See *Oswell*, vol. I, p. 16. And vol II, p. 26.
7. *David Livingstone Family Letters*, Volume Two, Letter 81, 19.12.1851, pp. 158-159.
8. "We arrived here about a fortnight ago". *David Livingstone Family Letters*, Volume Two, Letter 82, 2.4.1852, pp. 167.
9. *David Livingstone Family Letters*, Volume Two, Letter 83, 2.4.1852, pp. 168.
10. Livingstone to Tidman, 17.3.1852, Cape Town, See Campbell p. 135.
11. Livingstone to Tidman, 17.3.1852, Cape Town, See Campbell p. 136.
12. *David Livingstone Family Letters*, Volume Two, Letter 83, 2.4.1852, pp. 172.
13. *David Livingstone Family Letters*, Volume Two, Letter 83, 2.4.1852, pp. 173.
14. Later Sir Thomas Maclear (1794-1879). *David Livingstone Family Letters*, Volume Two, Letter 83, 2.4.1852, pp. 173.
15. *David Livingstone Family Letters*, Volume Two, Letter 84, 26.2.1852, p. 179.
16. *David Livingstone Family Letters*, Volume Two, Letter 84, 26.2.1852, p. 179 and footnote 8.
17. *David Livingstone Family Letters*, Volume Two, Letter 84, 26.2.1852, p. 177.
18. The almost verbatim copy of the report had been sent to the Royal Geographical Society that afterwards appeared in the *Journal of the R.G.S.*, vol 22, 1852, pp. 163-173.
19. *William Cotton Oswell*, William Zoward Oswell, Vol, II, p. 2.
20. *David Livingstone Family Letters*, Volume Two, Letter 84, 26.2.1852, p. 177.

21. Letter from Dr. A. Tidman to Livingstone, 14 April 1852, as quoted in DL Family Letters, Volume One, p. 16.
22. *David Livingstone Family Letters*, Volume Two, Letter 83, 2.4.1852, p. 175.
23. He reached Kuruman about 29 August 1852. *David Livingstone Family Letters*, Volume Two, Letter 87, 20.9.1852, p. 184.
24. Pieter Ernst Scholtz had led the raid against Sechele, as apparently Pretorius was sick. *David Livingstone Family Letters*, Volume Two, Letter 92, 28.12.1852, p. 196.
25. *David Livingstone Family Letters*, Volume Two, Letter 87, 20.9.1852, p. 184 and footnote 2-3.
26. They destroyed books, medicines and surgical instruments worth upwards of £150, and carried off or destroyed furniture and other property of more than £185 value. *David Livingstone Family Letters*, Volume Two, Letter 87, 20.9.1852, p. 184 and footnote 3.
27. *David Livingstone Family Letters*, Volume Two, Letter 87, 20.9.1852, p. 184.
28. *David Livingstone Family Letters*, Volume Two, Letter 92, 19.12.1852, p. 194.
29. The Boers claimed only 3 men were killed 6 wounded although one of the wounded subsequently died. *David Livingstone Family Letters*, Volume Two, Letter 87, 20.9.1852, p. 185 and footnote 5.
30. Schapera, pp. 88-89.
31. In *Missionary Travels* Livingstone stated he left on the 14 December 1852 but returned to Kuruman with Sechele and set out again on probably 20 December 1852, *David Livingstone Family Letters*, Volume Two, Letter 92, 19.12.1852, pp. 193-194 and footnote 2.
32. In *Travels* (p. 120) Livingstone described him as "a man of colour", and have been previously employed by Oswell, and had accompanied both Oswell and Livingstone in their explorations to Lake Ngami (1849) and the first journey to the Makololo (1851). He now accompanied Livingstone in order to trade with the Makololo with goods supplied by Mr H. E. Rutherfoord of Cape Town. *David Livingstone Family Letters*, Volume Two, Letter 96, 6.2.1853, p. 212 and footnote 22.
33. The meeting took place on 15 January 1953. *David Livingstone Family Letters*, Volume Two, Letter 94, 14.1.1853, pp. 199-200 and footnote 4.
34. *David Livingstone Family Letters*, Volume Two, Letter 94, 14.1.1853, p. 200.
35. The tribe was the BaRolongboora Tshidi, then living near Mafeking. The Boers had requested their help in assaulting Sechele's tribe and when they refused the Boers subsequently returned an attacked them too. *David Livingstone Family Letters*, Volume Two, Letter 93, 29.12.1852, pp. 195-196 and footnote 5.
36. Schapera, pp. 100-101.
37. *David Livingstone Family Letters*, Volume Two, Letter 96, 6.2.1853, p. 213.
38. *David Livingstone Family Letters*, Volume Two, Letter 93, 28.12.1852, p. 197.
39. *David Livingstone Family Letters*, Volume Two, Letter 96, 6.2.1853, p. 207.
40. Schapera, p. 102.
41. The author made the return trip from Lusaka to Pretoria in an old Suzuki jeep without air conditioning during the summer of 1992.
42. "Chapman's Baobab" was named by a South African explorer by the name of James Chapman in 1861. This tree is about 26 metres in circumference at its base. This is the third largest tree in Africa. According to carbon testing it is about 4,500 to 5,000 years old.
43. Schapera, pp. 97-98.

44. *David Livingstone Family Letters*, Volume Two, Letter 94, 14.1.1853, p. 203 and footnote 17.

45. *David Livingstone Family Letters*, Volume Two, Letter 97, 16.9.1850, pp. 215-216.

46. *David Livingstone Family Letters*, Volume Two, Letter 97, 16.9.1853, p. 216.

47. Livingstone to Lt Col T. Steele, 20.9.1853, *David Livingstone Explorations into the Interior of Africa*, London Missionary Society and Thomas Clear, p. 292.

48. Sekeletu was Sebitoane's son. He died of leprosy in 1863. *David Livingstone Family Letters*, Volume Two, Letter 97, 16.9.1853, p. 216 and footnote 9.

49. *David Livingstone Family Letters*, Volume Two, Letter 97, 16.9.1853, pp. 216-217.

50. *David Livingstone Family Letters*, Volume Two, Letter 97, 16.9.1853, pp. 219-220.

51. *David Livingstone Family Letters*, Volume Two, Letter 97, 16.9.1853, p. 217.

52. *David Livingstone Family Letters*, Volume Two, Letter 97, 16.9.1853, pp. 217-218.

53. Livingstone to Lt Col T. Steele, 20.9.1853, *David Livingstone Explorations into the Interior of Africa*, London Missionary Society and Thomas Clear, p. 295.

54. *Missionary Travels*, p. 180.

55. Schapera p. 176.

56. António Francisco Ferreira de Silva (1817-90), who added "Porto" to his surname in commemoration of his birthplace, Oporto. Extract from his journals, titled *Viagens e Apontamentos de um Portuense em Africa,* were later published in Lisbon, 1942.

57. *David Livingstone Family Letters*, Volume Two, Letter 97, 16.9.1853, pp. 221.

58. Ferreira sold textiles, small porcelain objects and explosives bought and traded ivory, honey and rubber from the interior, which he meticulously recorded in his journals. These tomes (14 volumes in all) contained varied descriptions of geography, ethnography and anthropology of his region of Africa. Source: Wikipedia, 15.8.2012.

59. *David Livingstone Family Letters*, Volume Two, Letter 97, 16.9.1853, pp. 221.

60. *David Livingstone Family Letters*, Volume Two, Letter 97, 16.9.1853, pp. 221.

61. Said bin Sultan Al-Said (1797-1856) was Sultan of Muscat and Oman from 1804 to 1856. In 1834, he agreed to a treaty with the United States on very favourable terms. In 1837, he conquered the town of Mombasa, Kenya. In 1840, Said bin Sultan moved his capital from Muscat, Oman, to Stone Town, Zanzibar. In 1840, he sent a ship to the United States in an attempt to establish a trading relationship. Upon Said's death in 1856, his realm was divided: his third son, Thuwaini bin Said, became the Sultan of Muscat and Oman; and his sixth son, Sayyid Majid bin Said, became the Sultan of Zanzibar.62. *David Livingstone Family Letters*, Volume Two, Letter 97, 16.9.1853, pp. 221.

63. Letter from Robert Moffat to Dr. Bruce, of Newcastle, March 1851, extract from *The Lives of Robert and Mary Moffat*, J. S. Moffat, 1885, p. 297.

64. *The Lives of Robert and Mary Moffat*, J. S. Moffat, 1885, pp. 305-307.

65. Letter from Robert Moffat to Dr. Bruce, of Newcastle, 9.6.1855, extract from *The Lives of Robert and Mary Moffat*, J. S. Moffat, 1885, pp. 313.

66. Letter from Mary Moffat to Miss Braithwaite, 8.6.1855, extract from *The Lives of Robert and Mary Moffat*, J. S. Moffat, 1885, pp. 312.

67. Jean Frédoux had married Ann Moffat on 12.9.1850 in Kuruman. Ann was Moffat's second daughter. Frédoux was a French missionary who was killed in 1866, leaving his widow and seven children unprovided for.

68. Letter from Mary Moffat to Robert Moffat, 9.10.1854, extract from *The Lives of Robert and Mary Moffat*, J. S. Moffat, 1885, pp. 308-309.

69. The Portuguese 'founded' Kuito (also Cuito) in 1750. Kuito was built in the traditional headquarters of the Ovimbundu kingdom. The Ovimbundu were known for selling captives from neighbouring tribes to the European slave traders that made the area an ideal location for the slave business and brought colonists to the area. They later called it Silva Porto after António da Silva Porto who built his home embala Belmonte in the area. Source Wikipedia, 18.8.2012.

70. *David Livingstone Family Letters*, Volume Two, Letter 97, 16.9.1853, pp. 221 and footnote 23.

71. *David Livingstone Family Letters*, Volume Two, Letter 98, 28.9.1853, p. 222 and footnote 2.

72. *David Livingstone Family Letters*, Volume Two, Letter 98, 28.9.1853, p. 225.

73. *David Livingstone Family Letters*, Volume Two, Letter 101, 1.11.1853, p. 240.

74. *David Livingstone Family Letters*, Volume Two, Letter 102, 19.5.1854, p. 243.

75. *David Livingstone Family Letters*, Volume Two, Letter 101, 1.11.1853, p. 235 and footnote 18.

76. The man committing the adultery was a driver of Fleming's wagon. *David Livingstone Family Letters*, Volume Two, Letter 101, 1.11.1853, p. 232.

77. *David Livingstone Family Letters*, Volume Two, Letter 101, 1.11.1853, p. 235.

78. Macnair, p. 73.

79. *David Livingstone Family Letters*, Volume Two, Letter 102, 19.5.1854, pp. 245.

80. *Missionary Travels*, p. 279.

81. *David Livingstone Family Letters*, Volume Two, Letter 102, 19.5.1854, p. 245.

82. *David Livingstone Family Letters*, Volume Two, Letter 102, 19.5.1854, p. 243.

83. Macnair, pp. 96-97.

84. *African Journal*, p. 88.

85. *African Journal*, p. 104.

86. Macnair, p.109.

87. *David Livingstone Family Letters*, Volume Two, Letter 102, 19.5.1854, pp. 242-243.

88. Livingstone described him a "...a young half-caste Portuguese sergeant of militia, Cypriano di. Abreu." *Missionary Travels*, p. 365.

89. Livingstone referred to him as Antonio Rodrigues Neves, Cassange. *Missionary Travels*, p. 369.

90. *David Livingstone Family Letters*, Volume Two, Letter 102, 19.5.1854, pp. 246-247.

91. *David Livingstone Family Letters*, Volume Two, Letter 102, 19.5.1854, p. 246.

92. "Reach Ambaca, and have been mostly kindly recieved by the Commandant of the District, Senor Arsenio Pompilio Pompeo de Carpo, who speaks English", *Journal* 2.v.1854.

93. Macnair, p. 123.

94. Lieutenant Antonio Canto e Castro, a young gentleman whose whole subsequent conduct will ever make me regard him with great affection," *Missionary Travels*, p. 385.

95. Mary Livingstone to LMS, LMS Archives, SOAS, Glasgow, 1852.

96. Mary Livingstone to LMS, LMS Archives, SOAS, Hackney, February 1853.

97. Mary Livingstone to LMS, LMS Archives, SOAS, Winton Bridge, 19.10.1853.

98. Neil Livingstone to LMS, LMS Archives, SOAS, Burnbank Road, 24.6.1853.

99. Neil Livingstone to LMS, LMS Archives, SOAS, Burnbank Road, 25.6.1853.

100. Anna Mary Livingstone Reminiscences, undated. From the Neil Wilson Family collection.

101. Mary Livingstone to LMS, LMS Archives, SOAS, Winton, 14.12.1853.

102. Mary Livingstone to LMS, LMS Archives, SOAS, Kendal, 12.1.1854.

Chapter 6: The Trans-African Crossing

1. *David Livingstone Family Letters*, Volume Two, Letter 106, 12.9.1855, p. 265.
2. Blaikie, pp. 136-137.
3. Blaikie, p. 140.
4. *David Livingstone Family Letters*, Volume Two, Letter 103, 25.10.1854, pp. 249-250.
5. *David Livingstone Family Letters*, Volume Two, Letter 104, 8.11.1854, p. 256.
6. *Missionary Travels*, p. 419.
7. *David Livingstone Family Letters*, Volume Two, Letter 103, 25.10.1854, pp. 248-249.
8. *David Livingstone Family Letters*, Volume Two, Letter 102, 19.5.1854, p. 248.
9. *David Livingstone Family Letters*, Volume Two, Letter 103, 25.10.1854, p. 249.
10. *David Livingstone Family Letters*, Volume Two, Letter 105, 20.3.1855, p. 258.
11. The Jesuits were expelled on the orders of the Marquis of Pombal, (1699-1782) from all Portuguese territories in 1759. On 19 January 1759 the Marquis issued a decree sequestering the property of the Jesuit Society in the Portuguese dominions and in September 1780 he deported about one thousand Portuguese Jesuit fathers to the Pontifical States.
12. *Missionary Travels*, Chapter 20.
13. Pungo Andongo is a town in the district of Cuanza Norte and is about 180 miles east-south-east of Loanda.
14. The *Forerunner* was wrecked on 25.10.1854. *David Livingstone Family Letters*, Volume Two, Letter 106, 12.9.1855, p. 266.
15. Macnair, pp. 133-134.
16. *Missionary Travels* p. 431.
17. Macnair, p. 136.
18. Blaikie, pp. 145-146.
19. *Missionary Travels*.
20. *David Livingstone Family Letters*, Volume Two, Letter 106, 12.9.1855, p. 260.
21. *David Livingstone Family Letters*, Volume Two, Letter 106, 12.9.1855, p. 261.
22. *LMS Chronicle*, vol. 16, 1852, pp. 52 f., 122, vol 18, 1854, p. 131.
23. *David Livingstone Family Letters*, Volume Two, Letter 108, 26.9.1855, pp. 269-270.
24. *David Livingstone Family Letters*, Volume Two, Letter 108, 26.9.1855, pp. 271-272.
25. *David Livingstone Family Letters*, Volume Two, Letter 107, 14.9.1855, p. 268.
26. In Livingstone's *Journals* he is identified as Rya Syde ben Habib ben Salem who Livingstone met in Naliele on 12 December 1853. *David Livingstone Family Letter*, Volume Two, Letter 106, 12.9.1855, p. 265.
27. In 1991 the author was part of a small party that spent a week canoeing down the Zambesi River towards the Mozambique border. At one point they were chased by a bull hippopotamus and saw many, many large crocodiles.
28. Macnair, p. 157.
29. The author has visited Victoria Falls many times and because of the amount of vapour in the air, it is possible to see full circular rainbows.
30. Livingstone's *Journal*, 1855.
31. *David Livingstone Family Letters*, Volume Two, Letter 109, 1.3.1856, p. 277.
32. Livingstone had written to Tidman on 12.10.1855 explaining his intention to settle with the Makololo in the area north of Victoria Falls. Livingstone also noted to Moffat that he planned to settle north-east of Victoria Falls because the "farther

East for a certain distance, the more salubrious. The Upper parts of this country are very healthy." *David Livingstone Family Letters*, Volume Two, Letter 109, 1.3.1856, p. 278.

33. "Mary would I daresay like her tea service, and any preserves her mother may feel inclined to send had better be suited to her taste and not mine, for I am not fond of any." *David Livingstone Family Letters*, Volume Two, Letter 109, 1.3.1856, pp. 276-227.
34. Blaikie, p. 151.
35. Macnair, p. 165.
36. *Missionary Travels*, p. 604.
37. Livingstone to Tidman, 2.3.56, LMS 93.
38. *Missionary Travels*, p. 628.
39. Livingstone to Tidman, 2.3.1856, LMS 93.
40. *David Livingstone Family Letters*, Volume Two, Letter 110, 18.3.1856, p. 280 and footnote 5.
41. Macnair, p. 161.
42. *Journal of the Royal Geographical Society*, vol. 25, 1855, pp. lxxvi ff.
43. *Proceedings of the Geographical Society*, RGS, 18, 1873-74, p. 503.
44. Blaikie, p. 489.
45. *David Livingstone Family Letters*, Volume Two, Letter 110, 18 3.1856, p. 281.
46. *David Livingstone Family Letters*, Volume Two, Letter 111, 5.4.1856, p. 282.

Chapter 7: Return to Civilisation

1. *Missionary Travels*, p. 672.
2. Tidman to Livingstone, LMS, SOAS, 24.8.1855.
3. *David Livingstone Family Letters*, Volume Two, Letter 112, 1.6.1856, p. 286.
4. Livingstone to Tidman, 23.05.56, National Archives of Rhodesia and Nyasaland.
5. Livingstone refers to him as Sekuebu although elsewhere he is also known as Sekwebu. *David Livingstone Family Letters*, Volume Two, Letter 113, 17.8.1856, p 291.
6. *David Livingstone Family Letters*, Volume Two, Letter 112, 1.6.1856, p. 288.
7. *David Livingstone Family Letters*, Volume Two, Letter 114, 27.11.1856, p. 294.
8. *David Livingstone Family Letters*, Volume Two, Letter 115, 11.12.1856, p. 295.
9. Julie Anderson, *Looking for Mrs Livingstone*, pp. 224-225.
10. *David Livingstone Family Letters*, Volume Two, Letter 90, 11.1852, p. 192.
11. *David Livingstone Family Letters*, Volume Two, Letter 100, 2.10.1853, pp. 229-231.
12. *The Zambesi Doctors*, Livingstone's Letter to John Kirk 1858:1872, Letter 18, 2.6.1863 p. 64.
13. Mary Livingstone to LMS, LMS Archives, School of Oriental and African Studies, University of London, February 1853.
14. Blaikie, pp. 166-167.
15. *The Times*, 16.12.56.
16. Blaikie, p. 174.
17. Blaikie, pp.178–179.
18. David Livingstone, *The Great Heart of Africa*, Rev G.W. Smith, p. 117.
19. Sir Roderick Impey Murchison, 1st Baronet KCB DCL FRS FRSE FLS PRGS PBA MRIA (1792-1871) was a Scottish geologist who first described and investigated the Silurian system. In 1846 he was knighted, and in the same year he presided over

the meeting of the British Association at Southampton. During the later years of his life a large part of his time was devoted to the affairs of the Royal Geographical Society, of which he was in 1830 one of the founders, and he was president 1843-1845, 1851–1853, 1856–1859 and 1862-1871. He served on the Royal Commission on the British Museum (1847–49). Source: Wikipedia, 20.11.2012.

20. Livingstone to Sir R. Murchison, 22.12.56, Z.J. (I).xxii.

21. In another letter to his brother Charles Livingstone again repeated that he would like to write a travel book, "but when I reflect on what is necessary for such an undertaking I give up in dispair." *David Livingstone Family Letters*, Volume Two, Letter 96, 6.2.1853, p. 211.

22. *The Atlantic Monthly*, CXXX, 9.

23. John Arrowsmith (1780-1873) was an English Cartographer In 1810 he joined his uncle Aaron Arrowsmith in his mapmaking business in London. In 1821, they published a map of North America John Arrowsmith took over the business in 1839. In 1834 John published his London Atlas that was the best set of such maps then in existence. He followed the atlas with a long series of elaborate and carefully executed maps, those of Australia, America, Africa and India being especially valuable. Arrowsmith was one of the founders of the Royal Geographical Society and in 1863 he received the gold medal of the Society. Source: Wikipedia, 19.9.2012.

24. NAR, LI, 1.1.1, 654.

25. *The Times*, 17.12.56.

26. Livingstone to Sir R. Murchison, 15.4.57, Z.J. (I). xxiii-iv.

27. The house they rented in Hadley Green, London is now known as the Livingstone Cottage.

28. Board Minutes, LMS, Schapera M.C. xxv.

29. Blaikie, p. 182.

30. *Missionary Travels*.

31. Captain John Washington (1800-1863) was an officer of the Royal Navy, He was appointed Hydrographer of the Navy, and held this position from 1855-1863. He was also a founder member of the Geographical Society of London and an enthusiastic supporter of African exploration. He was in charge of supplies etc. for the Zambesi Expedition. Appointed Rear Admiral in 1862.

32. *The Zambesi Doctors*, Letter 4, 22.1.1858, p. 34.

33. Dr John Kirk (1832-1922). Born Forfarshire, Scotland. He was a Scottish physician and naturalist and later a British administrator in Zanzibar. Later knighted, *The Zambesi Doctors*, p. 2.

34. Charles Livingstone (1821-1873).

35. *The Illustrated News of the World*, Saturday, February 27, 1858, No. 4 – Vol. I, p. 50.

36. *The Zambesi Doctors*, Letter 1, 4.1.1858, pp. 29-30.

37. *The Zambesi Doctors*, Letter 3, 21.1.1858, p. 32.

38. (John) Thomas Baines (1820-1875). Born in King's Lynn, Norfolk, Baines was apprenticed to a coach painter at an early age.

39. According to Blaikie Mr. James Young provided the account of the meeting. "*The Personal Life of David Livingstone*", Blaikie, Chapter XI.

40. *The Illustrated News of the World*, Saturday, February 27, 1858, No. 4 – Vol. I.

41. "*The Personal Life of David Livingstone*", Blaikie, Chapter XI.

Chapter 8: The Zambesi Expedition

1. *The Zambian Collection*, Letter 19, 6.2.1858, p. 50.
2. *The Zambesi Doctors*, Letter 10, 18.3.1858, pp. 40-47.
3. Richard Thornton's letter was dated 16 April 1858, obviously prepared before Kirk's letter. *The Zambian Collection*, Letter 21, 16.4.1858, pp. 51-52.
4. *The Lives of Robert and Mary Moffat*, J. S. Moffat, 1885, p. 328.
5. John Smith Moffat (1835-1918) was the fourth son of Robert Moffat. Livingstone paid him to establish a mission to the Makololo 1859-65.
6. From a paper written in pencil by Anna Mary, 1874, From the Neil Wilson Family collection.
7. Livingstone to George Grey, Steamer, *Pearl*, 10.5.1858. Grey Letters, Vol 25. GL: L30(2), p. 6
8. The Zambesi River has three main distributaries, Kongone, Luabo and Timbwe, all of which are obstructed by sand bars at various times of the year.
9. *The Zambian Collection*, Letter 22, 21.6.1858, p. 53.
10. *The Zambian Collection*, Letter 23, 25.8.1858, p. 54.
11. Commander Norman Bernard Bedingfeld R.N. (1824-1894). After leaving the Zambesi Expedition he continued to serve with the Royal Navy. He was promoted to Captain on 15 April 1862 and retired as a Captain from the Royal Navy on 31 March 1877.
12. *The Zambian Collection*, Letter 26, 2.4.1859, p. 58.
13. Routledge, p. 64.
14. *The Zambian Collection*, Letter 26, 2.4.1859, p. 58.
15. *The Zambian Collection*, Letter 24, 17.9.1858, p. 55.
16. Livingstone letter to Captain Washington, R.N., Admiralty, 13.11.1859. The National Museum of the Royal Navy, Portsmouth, MSS 120.
17. *Medical Aspects of Dr Livingstone's Zambesi Expedition, 1858 1864*, A. J. Larner, 1969.
18. Shupanga is also spelt Shupunga. I have used Shupanga.
19. *The Zambesi Doctors*, Letter 12, 21.7.1858, p. 54.
20. *The Zambesi Doctors*, Letter 13, 25 8.1858, p. 56.
21. *The Zambian Collection*, Letter 23, 25.8.1858, p. 54.
22. *The Zambesi Doctors*, Letter 12, 21.7.1858, pp. 54-55.
23. *Lost Explorers*. Wright, Ed (2008). Murdoch Books. ISBN 978-1-74196-139-3.
24. *The Zambian Collection*, Letter 24, 17.9.1858, p. 56.
25. The middle Zambezi ends where the river enters what was known as the Kebrabassa although Livingstone initially called them 'Koara-basa', formerly the site of dangerous rapids but in 1974, Lake Cahora Bassa (also spelled Cabora Bassa) was created by the construction of the Cahora Bassa Dam. Source: Wikipedia, 6.9.2012.
26. *Last Journals*, Vol I, p. 347.
27. *The Zambian Collection*, Letter 26, 2.4.1859, p. 59.
28. *The Zambian Collection*, Letter 26, 2.4.1859, p. 60.
29. Livingstone to George Greg, River Shire, 1.6.1859. Grey Letters, Vol 25. GL: L30 (6), p. 30.
30. Livingstone to Grey, River Shire, 1.6.1859. Grey Letters, Vol 25. GL: L30 (6), p. 33.
31. Malawi is the third-largest lake in Africa.
32. *The Zambian Collection*, Appendix III, 26.10.1861, pp. 179-182.

33. *The Zambian Collection*, Letter 39, 2.12.1862, p.77 & Appendix IV, 26.10.1861, pp. 183-185.
34. The Protectorate underwent a number of title changes; in 1893 it was changed to the Central African Protectorate, then Nyasaland Protectorate in 1907, in 1953 the territories of Rhodesia, Northern Rhodesia and the Nyasaland Protectorate were united as the federation of Rhodesia and Nyasaland before finally in 1964, Nyasaland officially became the Republic of Malawi. Wikipedia, 2.08.2012.
35. On 13 September 1866 Livingstone identified the point where Dr. Roscher reached the lake was at Leséfa. *Last Journals*, Vol I, p.101.
36. Dr Albrecht Roscher (1836-1859) was a German naturalist and explorer. He was active in East Africa 1858-1860. The local chiefs later identified his assailants and they were deported to Zanzibar where they were executed. *Last Journals*, Vol I, p. 47.
37. *The Zambian Collection*, Letter 29, 1.11.1859, p. 64.
38. *The Zambesi Doctors*, Letter 14, 17.10.1859, p. 58.
39. Livingstone to George Grey, Shire, 20.10.1859. *Grey Letters*, Vol 25. GL: L30 (9), p. 45.
40. *The Zambesi Doctors*, Letter 14, 17.10.1859, p. 59.
41. *The Zambian Collection*, Letter 29, 1.11.1859, p. 64.
42. Loafsugar is sugar that comes in the form of a solid block, rather than as a granulated substance.
43. *The Zambesi Doctors*, Letter 17, 6.11.1859 p. 62.
44. The Kongone was a recognised entry point into the Zambesi River from the sea.
45. *The Zambian Collection*, Letter 30, 28.1.1860, p. 65.
46. Charles James Meller, (1836-69). He was appointed Surgeon to the Zambesi Expedition, 1861-62.
47. Charles Frederick Mackenzie, (1825-62). Anglican clergyman who was consecrated Bishop at George's Cathedral, Cape Town, on 1 January 1861 and was appointed to lead the Universities' Mission to Central Africa. He died of fever.
48. Henry de Wint Burrup, (1831-62). Anglican minister and member of UMCA. Died of fever.
49. Horace Waller. (1833-96). Member of UMCA and later editor of Livingstone's *Last Journals*.
50. *The Zambesi Doctors*, Letter 3, 21.1.1858, p. 33.
51. *The Zambian Collection*, Letter 32, 14.5.1861, p. 68.
52. Tshibisa is also known as Chibisa.
53. Livingstone refers to them as a "detached portion of a tribe called Ajawa". *The Zambian Collection*, Letter 34, 11.1861, p. 71.
54. *The Zambian Collection*, Letter 33, 7/9.11.1861, p. 70.
55. Routledge, p. 87.
56. Routledge, p. 87.
57. Lake Nyassa is the southernmost lake in East Africa's Great Rift Valley system. Today it is bordered in the east by Mozambique, to the south and west by Malawi and to the north by Tanzania. http://www.encyclopedia.com/topic/Lake_Nyasa. aspx#1-1E1:Nyasa-La-full.
58. http://world-geography.org/lakes/417-lake-malawi.html.
59. Livingstone said they were called either Mazite or Mazatu. Mazitu is a Bisa word that means 'those who come from nowhere' that was applied to the invaders. *The Zambesi Doctors*, Livingstone to Sir George Grey, 15.11.1861 p. 160.

60. Lake Nyassa is estimated to contain up to 1,000 freshwater fish species and 99 per cent of the fish are thought to only occur in the lake. *Livingstone's Lake,* Geographical, Magazine of the Royal Geographical Society, September 2012, pp. 46-52.
61. They arrived on 2 September and left on 27 October 1861. Routledge, p. 91.
62. *The Zambesi Doctors,* Livingstone to Sir George Grey, 15.11.1861 p. 160.
63. *Looking for Mrs Livingstone,* Julie Davidson, p. 243.
64. Anna Mary Livingstone Reminiscences, undated. From the Neil Wilson Family collection.
65. John Crawford Wilson (1834-85), Royal Navy Commander of the HMS *Gordon.* He provided valuable assistance to the Zambesi Expedition, 1861-2.
66. *The Zambian Collection,* Letter 35, 19.2.1862, pp. 72-73.
67. *Livingstone's Lake,* O. Ransford, p. 118.
68. *The Zambesi Doctors,* Letter 50, 8.6.1865, p. 117.
69. James Young (1811-83) had been Livingstone's chemistry teacher at Anderson's College, Glasgow in 1839. He had discovered the how to extract paraffin (Kerosene) from coal-shale. He established the Paraffin Light and Mineral Oil Company and made a fortune. He was one of Livingstone's trustees and financially supported Livingstone.
The Zambian Collection, p. 202.
70. *The Zambian Collection,* Letter 35, 19.2.1862, p. 73.
71. *Livingstone's Lake,* O. Ransford, p. 121.
72. See Editor's note. *Last Journals,* Vol I, p. 176.
73. John Kirk Diary, 27 April 1962.
74. In 1896 it was reported that Mary's grave was "well looked after by the officers and men of the British gunboats stationed on the Zambesi and Shire Rivers, but the headstone, which bears inscriptions in Portuguese and English, is slowly but surely falling into a state of decay." Greater Liverpool, *The Graphic,* Saturday 25.1.1896, Issue 1365.
75. *Livingstone's Last Journey,* R Copeland, p. 14.
76. *The Zambian Collection,* Letter 37, 5.11.1861, p. 75.
77. *The Lives of Robert and Mary Moffat,* J. S. Moffat, 1885, pp. 355.
78. *Daniel Livingstone, Travels,* Edited by Dr James I. McNair, Heron Books, pp. 32-33.
79. *The Zambian Collection,* Letter 38, 19.11.1862, p. 76.
80. *The Zambian Collection,* Letter 46, 22.12.1863, p. 87.
81. *Last Journals,* Vol I, p. 32.
82. *Last Journals,* Vol II, p. 74.
83. Baron Karl Klaus von der Decken (1833-1865). Following military service, von der Decken travelled to eastern Africa in May 1860. He explored the region around Lake Nyasa only a year after David Livingstone had been the first European to reach the area. The following year, von der Decken set out from Mombasa to survey the Kilimanjaro massif. He later visited Madagascar and the Mascarene Islands. In 1865, he visited Somalia and became one of the first Europeans to explore the lower reaches of the Jubba River, on board the small steamship. Source: Wikipedia, 10 September 2012.
84. The Geological Society website, 10.9.2012
85. *The Zambesi Doctors,* Letter 43, 22.4.1863, p. 82.
86. *The Zambesi Doctors,* Letter 44, 30.4.1863, p. 84.
87. *The Zambesi Doctors,* Letter 18, 2.6.1863 p. 64.

88. Lord John Russell (1808-82). Foreign Secretary 1859-65 and Prime Minister 1865-66.
89. "This has not been unlooked for by me." *The Zambesi Doctors*, Letter 19, 5.7.1863 p. 65.
90. *The Zambesi Doctors*, Letter 21, 8.8.1863 p. 71.
91. *The Zambesi Doctors*, Letter 19, 5.7.1863 p. 65.
92. *The Zambesi Doctors*, Letter 19, 5.7.1863 p. 65.
93. Sir George Grey, K.C.B. (1812-98). High Commissioner and Governor of Cape Colony from 1854-61. He was relieved of his post in 1859 for encouraging the federation of South African states without Government approval but was reinstated in 1860.
94. *The Zambesi Doctors*, Letter 44, 30.4.1863, p .84.
95. *The Zambesi Doctors*, Letter 21, 8.8.1863 p. 71.
96. Bishop William George Tozer (1829-1899) had been consecrated in Westminster Abbey on 2.2.1863. He replaced Bishop Mackenzie as the second Missionary Bishop to Central Africa and leader of the Universities' Mission to Central Africa.
97. Livingstone also spelt it Morumbala. *The Zambesi Doctors*, Letter 45, 5-7.1863?, p. 86.
98. *The Zambesi Doctors*, Letter 21, 8.8.1863 p. 70.
99. Drawn from an article from *The Guardian* 28 June 1899.
100. Livingstone had to pay 30 pounds to cover his debts. *The Zambesi Doctors*, Letter 45, 5-7.1863? p. 85.
101. *The Zambesi Doctors*, Letter 21, 8.8.1863 p. 72.
102. *The Zambesi Doctors*, Letter 19, 5.7.1863 p. 66.
103. Livingstone named the five in a letter to Kirk: Kanyai, Peoso, Arimasau, Ropa and Mandzu (the slave). The Zambesi Doctors, Letter 21, 8.8.1863 p. 72.
104. A fathom was equivalent to about six feet of cloth. *Last Journals*, Vol I, p. 39.
105. *The Zambesi Doctors*, Letter 22, 9.12.1863 p. 75.
106. The author saw these routes marked by palm trees during his travels in Northern Zambia in 1990s.
107. *The Zambesi Doctors*, Letter 22, 9.12.1863 p. 75.\
108. *The Zambesi Doctors*, Letter 47, 10.2.1864, p.88.

Chapter 9: Return to Britain

1. One of the native boys was Chuma, who was to remain with Livingstone for the rest of his explorations and eventually accompany Livingstone's body back to England.
2. Livingstone named then in a letter to Kirk as "Pennell, Collyer and John Reid – with seven Zambesians, quite raw fellows." *The Zambesi Doctors*, Letter 23, 28.7.1864, p. 78.
3. *The Zambesi Doctors*, Livingstone's Letter to John Kirk 1858:1872, pp. 8-9.
4. The author was a member of the Borobudur Ship Expedition 2003/04. The ship was a reconstructed 8th-century Indonesia trading vessel. The purpose of the expedition was to prove that it would have been possible for traditionally built double outrigger vessels (dating back to early 8th Century AD as depicted at the Borobudur Temple, Indonesia) to have sailed around the Cape of Good Hope and as far as West Africa—a migration that some commentators believe was made by ancient Indo-Malay peoples.

5. This was a useful contact for Livingstone to make, as Sir Bartle Frere later became President of the Royal Geographical Society.
6. *The Zambesi Doctors*, Letter 23, 28.7.1864 p. 78.
7. Royal house names in Europe were therefore generally taken from the father; in cases where a queen regnant married a prince of another house, their children (and therefore subsequent monarchs) belonged to the house of the prince consort. Thus Queen Victoria belonged to the House of Hanover, but her male-line descendants belong to the house of her husband Albert, which is Saxe-Coburg and Gotha, a branch of the House of Wettin. The name was changed to Windsor in 1917. Source: Wikipedia, 12.9.2012.
8. Anon, 1863: 'The East African Mission' (reprinted from *The Examiner*), *The Times*, 20.1.1863, 5e.
9. *Lost Explorers*. Wright, Ed. (2008). Murdoch Books. ISBN 978-1-74196-139-3.
10. *The Zambesi Doctors*, Letter 23, 28.7.1864 p. 78.
11. *The Zambesi Doctors*, Letter 23, 28.7.1864 p. 79.
12. George Douglas Campbell Argyll, 8th Duke of Argyll (1823-1900). He was a liberal politician and the British Secretary for India, 1868-74.
13. *The Zambesi Doctors*, Letter 52, 26.9.1864, p. 96.
14. *The Zambesi Doctors*, Letter 51, 2.9.1864, p. 96.
15. The *Zambesi Doctors*, Letter 53, 8.10.1864, p. 97.
16. *The Times*, 14 & 19.9.1864.
17. *The Zambesi Doctors*, Letter 33, 8.12.1864, p. 94.
18. *The Zambesi Doctors*, Letter 51, 2.9.1864, p. 95.
19. The manuscript was published by D. & C. Livingstone, *Narrative of an Expedition to the Zambesi and its Tributaries, etc.* by John Murray, Albemarle, 1865.
20. The Memorandum of an Agreement was dated 21.12.1864 and signed by both Livingstone and Charles and witnessed. *The Zambesi Doctors*, Appendix V, Memorandum, 21.12.1864, p. 186.
21. *The Zambesi Doctors*, Letter 44, 27.3.1865, p. 108.
22. *Livingstone and Newstead*, A. Z. Frazer, Murray, 1913, p. 89.
23. *The Zambesi Doctors*, Letter 52, 30.7.186, p. 120.
24. *The Zambesi Doctors*, Letter 55, 9.10.1864, p. 98.
25. Charles Livingstone (1821-1873). When Charles was invalided home from the Zambesi Expedition he went and joined his family in America. His health would not, however, allow of his resuming ministerial duties, and after writing out his journal, he came to England to assist Livingstone in preparing the work on the Zambesi for the press. He died near Lagos on 28.10.1873 of African fever.
26. *The Zambesi Doctors*, Letter 58, 30.11.1864, p. 100.
27. *The Zambesi Doctors*, Letter 60, 7.1.1865, p. 102.
28. *The Zambesi Doctors*, p. 13.
29. The facts as recorded by Livingstone were wrong as The Battle of Richmond took place on 29-30.8.1862. *The Zambesi Doctors*, Letter 59, 4.1.1865, p. 102.
30. The Battle of Darbytown and New Market Roads was an engagement between Union and Confederate forces during the American Civil War, which took place on October 7, 1864, in Henrico County, Virginia, as part of the Richmond-Petersburg Campaign. Source: Bla'an'tir's Ain Website, 17.9.2012.
31. "Take Robert with me if he gets off." *The Zambesi Doctors*, Letter 60, 7.1.1865, p. 102.
32. Livingstone letter to C. B. Adderley, 18.5.1865.
33. *The Zambesi Doctors*, Letter 106, 18.5.1865, p. 134.

34. *The Zambesi Doctors*, Interlude in Great Britain, p. 92.
35. A Buruli ulcer is an infectious disease caused by Mycobacterium ulcerans. The genus also includes the causative agents of tuberculosis and leprosy. The early stage of infection is characterised by a painless nodule, necrotising lesions developing in the skin, and occasionally in adjacent bone, as the disease progresses. Source, Wikipedia, August 2012.
36. Royal Geographical Society "Twelfth Meeting, Monday Evening, 11 May 1863". *Proceedings of the Royal Geographical Society* of London 7 (3): 108–110.37. Sir Samuel White Baker, KCB, FRS, FRGS (1821-93) was a British explorer, officer, naturalist, big game hunter, engineer, writer and abolitionist. He also held the titles of Pasha and Major-General in the Ottoman Empire and Egypt. He served as the Governor-General of the Equatorial Nile Basin (today's South Sudan and Northern Uganda) from 1869-73. He established it as the Province of Equatoria. He is remembered as the discoverer of Lake Albert, and an explorer of the Nile and interior of central Africa, and for his exploits as a big game hunter in Asia, Africa, Europe and North America. Baker wrote a considerable number of books and published articles. Source; Wikipedia: 17.9.2012.
38. *International River Basin Organizations in Sub-Saharan Africa*, Robert Rangeley (1994). World Bank Publications. ISBN 0-8213-2871-9, p. 54.
39. Recent exploration, as described in Joanna Lumley's Nile, 7-8 p.m., ITV 1, Sunday 12 August 2011, related that an exploring party went to a place described as the source of the Rukarara tributary. They hacked a path up steep jungle-choked mountain slopes in the Nyungwe forest and found (in the dry season) an appreciable incoming surface flow for many miles upstream. This new source means the Nile has a new length of 4,199 miles (6,758 kilometres).
40. *The Zambesi Doctors*, Letter 49, 13.5.1865, p. 115.
41. *The Zambesi Doctors*, Letter 108, 25.5.1865, p. 136.
42. *The Zambesi Doctors*, Letter 72, 13.2.1865, p. 112.
43. *The Zambesi Doctors*, Letter 49, 13.5.1865, p. 115.
44. *The Zambesi Doctors*, Letter 111, 20.6.1865, p. 138.
45. *The Zambesi Doctors*, Letter 50, 8.6.1865, p. 118.
46. *The Zambesi Doctors*, Letter 50, 8.6.1865, p. 118.
47. From a paper written in pencil by Anna Mary, 1874, collection Neil Wilson.
48. *The Zambesi Doctors*, Letter 10, 10.8.1865, p. 143.
49. *The Zambesi Doctors*, Letter 50, 8.6.1865, p. 118. His book, *Narrative of an Expedition to the Zambesi and its Tributaries*, by David & Charles Livingstone was published by John Murray in the autumn of 1865
50. *The Zambesi Doctors*, Letter 121, 19.8.1865, p. 114.

Chapter 10: In Search of the Source of the Nile

1. Robert Lambert Playfair, (1828-99) was Her Majesty's Consul and Political Agent of Zanzibar, 1863-67.
2. *The Zambesi Doctors*, Letter 125, 31.12.1865, p. 152.
3. *The Zambesi Doctors*, Letter 126, 1.1.1866, p. 153.
4. *The Zambesi Doctors*, p. 16.
5. *The Zambesi Doctors*, Letter 57, 1.1.1866, p. 133.
6. *Last Journals*, Vo1 I, p. 1.
4. The term sepoy came into use in the forces of the British East India Company in

the eighteenth century, where it was used for various categories of native soldiers. Initially it referred to Hindu or Muslim soldiers without regular uniform or discipline. It later generically referred to all native soldiers in the service of the European powers in India. Close to ninety-six percent of the British East India Company's army of 300,000 men were native to India and these sepoys played a crucial role in securing the subcontinent for the company. Source: Wikipedia, 18.9.2012.

8. A Havildar is in military terms, a non-commissioned officer in the Indian army, equivalent in rank to sergeant.
9. *Britain and Slavery in East Africa*, Moses D. E. Nwulia, p. 155.
10. *The Zambesi Doctors*, Letter 123, 29.9.1865, p. 150.
11. William Sunley. The French presence in Mayotte from 1843 stimulated the British to establish a consul in Anjouan in 1846. They appointed Sunley Consul (1846-65) who owned a sugar plantation and used slave labour.
12. *The Zambesi Doctors*, Letter 125, 31.12.1865, p. 152.
13. The Comoro Islands or Comoros is an archipelago of volcanic islands situated off the southeast coast of Africa, to the east of Mozambique and northwest of Madagascar. *The Zambesi Doctors*, Letter 109, 6.6.1865, p. 137.
14. *Last Journals*, Vol I, p. 9.
15. *Livingstone and the Exploration of Central Africa* Harry Johnston Chapter XVII, p. 297.
16. *The Zambesi Doctors*, Letter 49, 13.5.1865, p. 115.
17. *Last Journals*, Vol I, p. 8.
18. *Last Journals*, Vol I, p. 9.
19. *Last Journals*, Vol I, p. 7.
20. *The Zambesi Doctors*, Letter 128, 7.3.1866, p. 155.
21. *The Zambesi Doctors*, p. 17.
22. Rovuma is also spelt Ruvuma River. I have chosen to use the spelling Rovuma in this book.
23. *The Zambesi Doctors*, Letter 49, 13.5.1865, p. 116.
24. Livingstone refers to it as Mikindany. *Last Journals*, Vol I, p. 11.
25. *Last Journals*, Vol I, p. 11.
26. *Last Journals*, Vol I, p. 16.
27. *Last Journals*, Vol I, p. 13.
28. *Last Journals*, Vol I, p. 19.
29. *The Zambesi Doctors*, Letter 130, 24.8.1866, p. 157.
30. *Last Journals*, Vol I, p. 35.
31. *Livingstone and the Exploration of Central Africa*. Harry Johnston Chapter XVII, p. 297.
32. *Last Journals*, Vol I, p. 36.
33. *Last Journals*, Vol I, p. 42.
34. *Last Journals*, Vol I, p. 42.
35. *The Zambesi Doctors*, Letter 130, 24.8.1866, p. 157.
36. *Last Journals*, Vol I, p. 80.
37. *Last Journals*, Vol I, pp. 70-71.
38. *Last Journals*, Vol I, p. 72.
39. *Last Journals*, Vol I, p. 74.
40. *Last Journals*, Vol I, p. 75.
41. *The Zambesi Doctors*, Letter 129, 20.5.1866, p. 156.
42. *The Zambesi Doctors*, Letter 130, 24.8.1866, p. 157.

43. *Last Journals*, Vol I, pp. 90-91.
44. *Last Journals*, Vol I, p. 95.
45. *Last Journals*, Vol I, p. 100.
46. *Last Journals*, Vol I, pp. 108-109.
47. *Last Journals*, Vol I, p. 112.
48. *Last Journals*, Vol I, p. 114.
49. *Last Journals*, Vol I, p. 115.
50. *Last Journals*, Vol I, p. 116.
51. Kirk Range. This is a plateau in southwestern Malawi, extending in a north-south direction and skirting the southwestern shore of Lake Nyasa and the western border of the Shire River valley. The northern scarp overlooks the Central Region Plateau, while the southern limits merge into the lower Shire Highlands. The plateau's height decreases in a southerly direction, from 5,500 feet (1,676 m) at Dedza to 1,400 feet (425 m) in the Blantyre area. The plateau is dotted hills, such as Dedza Mountain (7,120 feet [2,170 m]) and the hills of Chirobwe and Mvai. Source: Encyclopaedia Britannica, 19.9.2012.
52. *Last Journals*, Vol I, pp. 123-124.
53. *Last Journals*, Vol I, p. 124.
54. Livingstone referred to the gum-copal tree as Masuko Mochenga. *Last Journals*, Vol I, p. 136.
55. *Last Journals*, Vol I, p. 141.
56. *Last Journals*, Vol I, p. 148.
57. *Last Journals*, Vol I, pp. 149-150.
58. *Last Journals*, Vol I, p. 150.
59. *The Zambesi Doctors*, Letter 130, 24.8.1866, p. 160.
60. *Last Journals*, Vol I, p. 155.
61. Lilongwe Plain, known also known as the Central Region Plateau is the largest continuous tableland in modern day Malaŵi. It covers an area of 9,000 square miles (23,310 square km) and is bordered by the Chimaliro Hills and Viphya Mountains on the north, the Great Rift Valley on the east, the Dwangwa River on the west, and the Kirk and Dzalanyama ranges on the south. The highlands, rising out of the east-central area, have a gently undulating surface with heights varying from 2,500 feet (760 m) to 4,500 feet (1,400 m). The broad valleys of the Lilongwe, Bua, and Dwangwa rivers traverse the region in an east-northeast direction. Their tributaries spread out in nadambo (bogs). Source: Encyclopaedia Britannica, 19.9.2012.
62. *The Zambesi Doctors*, Letter 130, 24.8.1866, p. 159.
63. *Last Journals*, Vol I, p. 172.
64. *The Zambesi Doctors*, Letter 130, 24.8.1866, p. 160.
65. Dr John Stenhouse (1809-80) gave Livingstone some waterproof inventions. Stenhouse was a chemist and inventor of waterproof fabric and shoes, patented in 1861. *The Zambesi Doctors*, Letter 130, 24.8.1866, pp. 160-161.
66. *Last Journals*, Vol I, p. 173.
67. *Last Journals*, Vol I, p. 175.
68. *Last Journals*, Vol I, p. 177.
69. *The Zambesi Doctors*, Letter 130, 24.8.1866, p. 161.
70. *Last Journals*, Vol I, p. 181.
71. *Last Journals*, Vol I, pp. 182-183.
72. *Last Journals*, Vol I, p. 183.
73. *Last Journals*, Vol I, p. 184.
74. Also called Tshitapangwa. *Last Journals*, Vol I, p. 184.

75. *Last Journals*, Vol I, p. 200.
76. *Last Journals*, Vol I, p. 204.
77. *Last Journals*, Vol I, p. 209.
78. Nsama is also refered as Msama.
79. *The Zambesi Doctors*, Letter 58, 12.9.1867, p. 137.
80. *Last Journals*, Vol I, p. 224.
81. *Last Journals*, Vol I, p. 216.
82. *The Zambesi Doctors*, Introduction, p. 17.
83. Susi told Waller that the nickname arose when Tipo Tipo (sometimes called Tippoo Tib by Livingstone) stood over the booty taken from Nsama, he said "Now I am Tipo Tipo", which means "the gatherer together of wealth". *Last Journals*, Vol I, p. 230.
84. This is a title given to the chief and according to Livingstone means 'General'. There had been six Kazembe before the one that Livingstone met. Livingstone also spelt it as Cazembe. *Last Journals*, Vol I, p. 224.
85. Mazitu was a tribe of Zulus who had settled in the area south of Lake Nyassa.
86. Lord Edward Henry Stanley, 15th Earl of Derby (1826-73), British Foreign Secretary 1866-8.
87. Routledge, p. 119.
88. *Last Journals*, Vol I, p. 110.
89. Routledge, p. 120.
90. *The Zambesi Doctors*, p. 19.
91. *Last Journals*, Vol II, p. 74.
92. Kezembe was also known as Casembe or Mwata Kazembe. I have adopted to use Kazembe.
93. Routledge, p. 108.
94. Routledge, p. 110.
95. Draft letter to The Right Honourable the Earl of Clarendon, Town of Caseme, 10.12.1867. *Last Journals*, Vol I, pp. 261-262.
96. *Last Journals*, Vol I, p. 253.
97. Sorghum is also known as dura
98. *Last Journals*, Vol I, p. 271.
99. *Last Journals*, Vol I, pp. 278-279.
100. *Last Journals*, Vol I, p. 279.
101. *Last Journals*, Vol I, p. 283.
102. *Last Journals*, Vol I, p. 286.
103. *Last Journals*, Vol I, p. 288.
104. *Last Journals*, Vol I, p. 306.
105. These people originally came into the area as traders but after defeating an attack by the Mazitu, became the new local power in the area. They gave their allegiance to the Sultan of Zanzibar and were much impressed by Livingstone's letters from the Sultan. *Last Journals*, Vol I, p. 311.
106. *Last Journals*, Vol I, p. 308.
107. Livingstone called it Mpabala in his journals. *Last Journals*, Vol I, p. 316.
108. The Chambeze River is today known as Chambeshi.
109. The Luapula River is known today as Luyua River.
110. *Last Journals*, Vol I, p. 324.
111. Claudius Ptolemy (AD 90-168). Greek-Roman mathematician and geographer of Alexander, Egypt. In his *Geography* he states that the source of the Nile rises from two sources in the 'Mountains of the Moon' near the equator, the western source

flowing through the Lake 'Coloe" before joining the eastern at Meroe.

112. A burn is a Scottish expression for a stream.

113. *The Zambesi Doctors*, Letter 133, 8.7.1868, p. 165.

114. Livingstone spelt it using both Manyuema and Manyema. I have adopted Manyuema unless it appears in a direct quote.

115. *Last Journals*, Vol I, p. 346.

116. *The Zambesi Doctors*, Letter 133, 8.7.1868, p. 165.

117. Livingstone wrote, "Syde bin Habib is said to have amassed 150 frasilahs of ivory = 5250 lbs., and 300 frasilahs of copper = 10,000 lbs. *Last Journals*, Vol I, p. 337.

118. *Last Journals*, Vol I, p. 327.

119. *Last Journals*, Vol I, p. 341.

120. *Last Journals*, Vol I, p. 348.

121. *Last Journals*, Vol I, p. 358.

122. *Last Journals*, Vol II, pp. 1-2.

123. *Last Journals*, Vol II, p. 2.

124. *The Zambesi Doctors*, Letter 134, 10.1869, p. 166.

125. Unyanyembe is also referred to as Unyembe. It was a halfway settlement on the great Arab caravan road from the coast to the interior. *Last Journals*, Vol II, p. 6.

126. *The Zambesi Doctors*, 1858:1872, Letter 59, 30.5.1869, p. 138.

127. *The Zambesi Doctors*, Letter 59, 30.5.1869, p. 138.

128. *The Zambesi Doctors*, Letter 59, 30.5.1869, p. 139.

129. *The Zambesi Doctors*, Letter 59, 30.5.1869, p. 139.

130. It is unclear how his letter got carried back to England although it is likely Stanley took it with him and delivered it to Waller.

131. *The Zambesi Doctors*, 1858:1872, Letter 59, 30.5.1869, p. 138.

132. *Last Journals*, Vol II, p. 10.

133. *Last Journals*, Vol II, p. 11.

134. *Last Journals*, Vol II, p. 20.

135. *The Zambesi Doctors*, Letter 60, 2.11.1870, p. 141.

136. *The Zambesi Doctors*, Letter 60, 2.11.1870, p. 141.

137. Moenekus was also called Moenékuss. He was the paramount chief of the Manyuema. *Last Journals*, Vol II, p. 16.

138. *Last Journals*, Vol II, p. 27.

139. *The Zambesi Doctors*, Letter 134, 10.1869, p. 168.

140. *The Zambesi Doctors*, Letter 134, 10.1869, p. 166.

141. In 1874, the New York Herald, in partnership with Britain's *Daily Telegraph*, financed Stanley on another African expedition to trace the course of the Congo River to the sea. Stanley used sectional boats to pass the great cataracts separating the Congo into distinct tracts. After 999 days, on 9 August 1877, Stanley reached the mouth of the Congo River. Starting with 356 people, only 114 had survived the expedition, of whom Stanley was the only European. Source: Wikipedia, 19.9.2012.

142. *The Zambesi Doctors*, Letter 60, 2.11.1870, p. 140.

143. *The Zambesi Doctors*, Letter 135, 24.11.1870, p. 169.

144. Livingstone gave the latitude of the Binanga Hills as about 3° 30' S. lat.

145. *Last Journals*, Vol II, p. 32.

146. *Last Journals*, Vol II, p. 33.

147. *Last Journals*, Vol II, p. 37.

148. Despatches, No.1, David Livingstone to Lord Stanley, Bambarre, November 15,1870.

149. *Last Journals*, Vol II, p. 40.

150. *Last Journals*, Vol II, p. 39.

151. *Last Journals*, Vol II, p. 43.
152. *Last Journals*, Vol II, p. 47.
153. *Last Journals*, Vol II, pp. 47-48.
154. "Buruli ulcer disease – Mycobacterium ulcerans infection". Health Topics A TO Z. Retrieved 2010-12-24.
155. *Last Journals*, Vol II, p. 55.
156. *Last Journals*, Vol II, pp. 61-62.
157. *Last Journals*, Vol II, p. 76.
158. *Proceedings of the Geographical Society*, 15, 1870-71, RGS, p. 207.
159. *Last Journals*, Vol II, p. 86.
160. *Last Journals*, Vol II, p. 95.
161. *Last Journals*, Vol II, p. 86.
162. *The Zambesi Doctors*, Letter 137, 6.1.1872, p. 172.
163. Peter Beard the owner of this previously unpublished letter of 5 February 1871 to Horace Waller made the letter available to the public in July 2010. It is the first nineteenth-century British literary work to be captured and enhanced with the multispectral imaging process.
164. "David Livingstone letter deciphered at last; Livingstone's Letter from Bambarre Four-page missive composed at the lowest point in his professional life". Associated Press. 2 July 2010. Retrieved 2 July 2010 http://cmclibrary.org/livingstoneletter/.
165. *Last Journals*, Vol II, p. 105.
166. *Last Journals*, Vol II, p. 108.
167. *Last Journals*, Vol II, p. 110.
168. *Last Journals*, Vol II, p. 122.
169. *Last Journals*, Vol II, p. 118.
170. *Last Journals*, Vol II, p. 154.
171. *Last Journals*, Vol II, p. 124.
172. *The Zambesi Doctors*, Letter 61, 25.3.1871, p. 146.
173. *Last Journals*, Vol II, p. 124.
174. *Last Journals*, Vol II, p. 135.
175. *Last Journals*, Vol II, p. 139.
176. *Livingstone's 1871 Field Diary. A multispectral critical edition*, an 80-page document can now be read in its original form. It took 18 months of work to decipher. The British Academy and the US National Endowment for the Humanities funded the project.
177. *Last Journals*, Vol II, pp. 153-154.
178. *Last Journals*, Vol II, p. 154.
179. Routledge, p. 115.
180. *Last Journals*, Vol II, p. 156.

Chapter 11: An Encounter with Stanley

1. *Henry M. Stanley's American Lectures*, 1872, pp. 8-9.
2. The reader is encouraged to read Tim Jeal's book, *Stanley: The Impossible Life of Africa's Greatest Explorer*. Jeal explores Stanley's flawed character that seems all the more brave and humane for his ambition and insecurity, virtue and fraud. His self-control in the wilderness becomes even more remarkable considering the secrets he was hiding.
3. Christmas Books, *The Graphic*, London, England, Saturday, 26.12.1874, Issue 265.

4. *Henry M. Stanley's American Lectures*, 1872, p. 5.
5. Livingstone noted in his journal it was £4,000 and presumably Stanley must have told him the amount. *Last Journals*, Vol II, p. 156.
6. http://www.smithsonianmag.com/history-archaeology/Henry-Morton-Stanleys-Unbreakable-Will.html#ixzz25QDIIbvb.
7. *Last Journals*, Vol II, p. 156.
8. David Livingstone, *The Penny Illustrated Paper and Illustrated Times*, London, England, Saturday, 13.7.1872, p. 29. Issue 564.
9. *Henry M. Stanley's American Lectures*, 1872, p. 11.
10. In *Stanley: the Impossible Life of Africa's Greatest Explorer*, Tim Jeal calls the remark "probably the most famous phrase in the history of journalism". But there's no mention of it in Stanley's diary or letters. Livingstone's journal doesn't refer to it either. And so it's a phrase, Jeal concludes, that was "almost certainly never uttered".
11. The shirt is on display at the David Livingstone Centre, Blantyre.
12. *The Zambesi Doctors*, Introduction, pp. 22-23.
13. *Last Journals*, Vol II, p. 156.
14. Desptaches, No.2, Dr Livingstone to the Earl of Clarendon, Ujiji, November 1, 1871.
15. Also referred to as Luisizé. *Last Journals*, Vol II, p. 159.
16. They arrived in Unyanyembe on 18 Feb. 1872.
17. These journals were later published in two volumes as Livingstone's *Last Journals*.
18. Herodotus (484-425 BC), Greek author of *The Histories*. In book Two, 27, he wrote that he was told by the scribe who kept the treasures of the Goddess Athene (Romans called her Minerva) in the Egyptian city of Sais, that the Nile rose from fountains between two conical mountains called Crophi and Mophi and that half the water flowed north to Egypt and half south into Ethiopia (or the interior of Africa).
19. These boatmen were Mbundu speaking people called Mokantju.
20. *The Zambesi Doctors*, Letter 137, 6.1.1872, p. 172.
21. *Henry M. Stanley's American Lectures*, 1872, p. 11.
22. *Last Journals*, Vol II, p. 169.
23. *Last Journals*, Vol II, p. 169.
24. *Last Journals*, Vol II, p. 169.
25. *Last Journals*, Vol II, p. 170.
26. Granville George Leveson Gower, 2nd Earl Granville (1815–1891), was a British Liberal statesman. In a political career spanning over 50 years, he was thrice Secretary of State for Foreign Affairs. Following Lord Clarendon's death on June 27, 1870 he was appointed Foreign Secretary, Source: Wikipedia, 6.12.2012.
27. Stanley Henry M., *How I Found Livingstone; travels, adventures, and discoveries in Central Africa, including an account of four months' residence with Dr. Livingstone. 1871.*
28. Desptaches, No.4, Dr. Livingstone to Earl Granville, Ujiji, November 14, 1871.
29. *Last Journals*, Vol I, Introduction, p. iv.
30. Routledge, p. 121.
31. Waller refers to it as the Livingstone Relief Expedition. *Last Journals*, Vol II, p. 204.
32. *Proceedings of the Geographical Society*, 16, 1871-72, RGS, p. 436.
33. Despatches, Inclosure in No.4, Dr. Livingstone to Dr. Kirk, Ujiji, October 30, 1871.
34. Henry Morton Stanley, Journal, 10 July 1872. Quoted in Jeal 2007, pp. 133 and 1.

35. Livingstone Letter to Sir Thomas Maclear and Mr. Mann, Ujiji, 17.11.1871. Published in *Proceedings of the Geographical Society*, 17, 1872-73, RGS, p. 72.
36. To give an example just how popular these lectures were, Stanley gave lectures on 3rd, 4th, 6th, 7th 11th, 13th and 14th December 1862 at the Steinway Hall, New York.
37. *Henry M. Stanley's American Lectures*, 1872.
38. Letter given to Stanley by Livingstone, Unyanyembe 14.3.1872. *Henry M. Stanley's American Lectures*, 1872.
39. *Henry M. Stanley's American Lectures*, 1872, p. 9.

Chapter 12: The Final Chapter

1. *Last Journals*, Vol II, p. 174.
2. *Last Journals*, Vol II, p. 182.
3. *Last Journals*, Vol II, p. 190.
4. *Last Journals*, Vol II, p. 188.
5. Mabruki was also known as Nathaniel Cumba.
6. *Last Journals*, Vol II, p. 205.
7. *Last Journals*, Vol II, p. 195.
8. *Last Journals*, Vol II, p. 237.
9. Anna Mary Livingstone to Livingstone, Elmbank House, Hamilton, 12.10.1872.
10. *Last Journals*, Vol II, p. 238.
11. Bangé or hemp was widely smoked by the inland tribes.
12. *Last Journals*, Vol II, p. 247.
13. *Last Journals*, Vol II, p. 252.
14. *Last Journals*, Vol II, p. 256.
15. Kalongosi River is also referred to as the Kalongwesé. *Last Journals*, Vol II, p. 256.
16. *Last Journals*, Vol II, p. 259.
17. *Proceedings of the Geographical Society*, 17, 1872-3, RGS, p. 323.
18. *The Man Who Met Livingstone*, Kittermaster, Broadcast, p. 1.
19. Kittermaster, 10.1950, p. 22.
20. *Last Journals*, Vol II, p. 289.
21. *Last Journals*, Vol II, p. 291.
22. *Last Journals*, Vol II, p. 294.
23. *Last Journals*, Vol II, p. 297.
24. Molilamo is also referred to as Lulimala. *Last Journals*, Vol II, p. 303.
25. Chitambo is also known as Tshitambo. I have used the former spelling.
26. Ulala is also known as Ilala. I have used the former spelling.
27. The memorial is 5 km south of the Lulimala, 10 km south of the edge of the floodplain, and 40 km from the edge of the permanent swamps.
28. *Last Journals*, Vol II, p. 307.
29. Source: Wikipedia, 26.8.2012.
30. *Last Journals*, Vol II, p. 307.
31. *Last Journals*, Vol II, p. 307.
32. *Last Journals*, Vol II, p. 308.
33. It was subsequently suggested he may have died from acute splenitus. *Last Journals*, Vol II, p. 316.
34. A Mvula tree is also known as a Mpundu tree.
35. The date of 1 May 1873 is the accepted date of Livingstone's death. J. Desmond

Clark: "David Livingstone Memorial at Chitambo's", The Northern Rhodesia Journal, Vol 1 No 1, 1950.

36. Letter from Tom S. Livingstone to Anna Mary Livingstone, Alexandria, Egypt, 30.6.1873. From the Neil Wilson Family collection.

37. Verney Lovett Cameron (1844–1894) was an English traveller in Central Africa and the first European to cross equatorial Africa from sea to sea. He was born in Dorset, England. He entered the Royal Navy in 1857, served in the Abyssinian campaign of 1868, and was employed for a considerable time in the suppression of the East African slave trade. This experience led to his being selected to command an expedition sent by the Royal Geographical Society in 1873, to assist Dr Livingstone. He was also instructed to make independent explorations, guided by Livingstone's advice. Soon after the departure of the expedition from Zanzibar, Livingstone's servants were met bearing the dead body of their master. Cameron's two European companions turned back, but he continued his march and reached Ujiji, on Lake Tanganyika, in February 1874, where he found and sent to England Livingstone's papers. Cameron spent some time determining the true form of the south part of the lake, and solved the question of its outlet by the discovery of the Lukuga River. From Tanganyika he struck westward to Nyangwe, the Arab town on the Lualaba previously visited by Livingstone. This river Cameron rightly believed to be the main stream of the Congo, and he endeavoured to procure canoes to follow it down. In this he was unsuccessful, owing to his refusal to countenance slavery, and he therefore turned south-west. After tracing the Congo-Zambezi watershed for hundreds of miles he reached Bihe and finally arrived at the coast on 28 November 1875, being the first European to cross equatorial Africa from sea to sea. Source, Wikipedia, 28 February 2013.

38. Lieutenant Cameron to the Secretary of the Royal Geographical Society, Unyamyembe, October 16th, 1873. *Proceedings of the Geographical Society*, 18, 1873-74, RGS, p. 177.

39. *Proceedings of the Geographical Society*, 18, 1873-74, RGS, p. 177.

40. For example, the Graphic printed a full account of Livingstone's life in its Saturday issue on 31 January 1874. Stanley provided the account. David Livingstone, *The Graphic*, London, England, Saturday, 31.1.1874, Issue 218.

41. *A "Body" of Evidence*, J. D. Livingstone , 2012, p. 1.

42. From a paper written in pencil by Anna Mary, 1874, From the Neil Wilson Family collection.

43. *The Lives of Robert and Mary Moffat*, J. S. Moffat, 1885, p. 395.

44. William Frederick Webb (1829-99). Was an army officer who enjoyed hunting in Bechuanaland. *David Livingstone Family Letters*, Volume Two, Letter 97, 16.9.1853, p. 216.

45. From a paper written in pencil by Anna Mary Livingstone, 31.5.1874, From the Neil Wilson Family collection.

46. *Proceedings of the Geographical Society*, 18, 1873-74, RGS, p. 511.

Chapter 13: Livingstone's Legacy

1. Last Journals, Vol I, p. 100.
2. Tim Jeal, *Livingstone*, p.163.
3. Livingstone's Last Journals, *The Graphic*, London, England, Saturday, 19.12.1874, Issue 264.

4. *The Livingstone Legend*, p. 193.
5. *The Livingstone Legend*, p. 195.
6. Rt Hon Alex Salmond, MSP 2012 Christmas message, 23.12.12.
7. *David Livingstone Family Letters*, Volume Two, Letter 110, 18.3.1856, p. 279.
8. *David Livingstone Family Letters*, Volume Two, Letter 107, 14.9.1855, p. 268.
9. *David Livingstone Family Letters*, Volume Two, Letter 108, 26.9.1855, pp. 272-273.
10. *David Livingstone Family Letters*, Volume Two, Letter 108, 26.9.1855, p. 273.
11. *The Lives of Robert and Mary Moffat*, J. S. Moffat, 1885, p. 403.
12. Wreath laying Ceremony to Commemorate the Bicentenary of the Birth of Dr David Livingstone. From a sermon preached at Westminster Abbey by the Very Reverend Arthur Penrhyn Stanley, Dean of Westminster on 19.4.1874, being the Sunday after Livingstone's burial.
13. *David Livingstone Family Letters*, Volume Two, Letter 104, 8.11.1854, p. 256.
14. *Proceedings of the Geographical Society*, 17, 1872-73, RGS, p. 12.
15. *Map of Livingstone's Travels*, National Museums of Scotland. The map is online at www.scran.ac.uk but a subscription to the site is required to view it.
16. *Dr. Livingstone, I Presume?* Claire Pettitt.
17. *Last Journals*, Vol I, Introduction, p. x.
18. *Last Journals*, Vol II, p. 212.
19. William Wilberforce (1759-1833) was an English politician and philanthropist. He headed the parliamentary campaign against the British slave trade for twenty six years until the passage of the Slave Trade Act of 1807. In later years, Wilberforce supported the campaign for the complete abolition of slavery. He resigned from Parliament in 1826 because of poor health but continued pressing for the abolition of slavery. The Slavery Abolition Act was finally passed in 1833 that abolished slavery in most of the British Empire.
20. *David Livingstone Family Letters*, Volume Two, Letter 104, 8.11.1854, pp. 252-253.
21. *Proceedings of the Geographical Society*, 18, 1873-74, RGS, p. 511.
22. Cited in Mathews 1921, 11, Kirk Papers: Fo. 52.
23. *When a Crocodile eats the Sun*, Godwin, pp. 107-108.
24. The book was published by the Sunday School Union, 57 Ludgate Hill, E.C. London. *The Penny Illustrated Paper and Illustrated Times*, London, England, Saturday, 25.4.1896, pg. 269, Issue 1822.
25. The Livingstonia Central Africa Company was renamed African Lakes Corporation in 1894. A rail link established in 1908 reduced the importance of the steamers; company focused on its Mandala stores, and established an automotive business Mandala Motors in 1924, which grew to include 11 countries in Africa. It was later absorbed by the British South Africa Company, and operated general stores known as Mandala, but in 1982 was re-registered as The African Lakes Corporation plc. Wikipedia, 31 August 2012.
26. Lloyd George and the Hospitals, *P.I.P.: Penny Illustrated Paper*, London, England, Saturday 27.5.1911, pg. 690, Issue 2609.
27. *A History of Christian Missions*, Neill. p. 315.
28. Kenneth D. Kaunda, President of Zambia made the comment when he commemorated the centenary of Livingstone's death in Chitambo in May 1973.

Appendix 1: Southern African Geography

1. *Atlantic, A Vast Ocean of a Million Stories*, Simon Winchester, p. 43.

2. *Atlantic, A Vast Ocean of a Million Stories*, Simon Winchester, p. 47.
3. Livingstone frequently spelt Bangweulu as Bangweolo. I have chosen to use the older spelling of Lake Bangweolo. Lake Bangweolo was also known as Lake Bemba.

Appendix 2: The Livingstone Children

1. *The Zambesi Doctors*, Livingstone's Letter to Kirk 1858:1872, Appendix: Letter *Agnes Livingstone to Mrs Webb of Newstead Abbey*, 29.9.1874, p. 164.
2. *The Zambesi Doctors*, Livingstone's Letter to Kirk 1858:1872, Appendix: Letter *Agnes Livingstone to Mrs Webb of Newstead Abbey*, 29.9.1874, p. 164.
3. *David Livingstone Family Letters*, Volume One, Letter 46, 5.7.1848, p. 246.
4. *David Livingstone Family Letters*, Volume Two, Letter 55, 20.4.1849, p. 33.
5. *The Lives of Robert and Mary Moffat*, J. S. Moffat, 1885, p. 398.
6. *David Livingstone Family Letters*, Volume Two, Letter 55, 20.4.1849, p. 33.
7. *The Lives of Robert and Mary Moffat*, J. S. Moffat, 1885, p. 385.
8. *The Lives of Robert and Mary Moffat*, J. S. Moffat, 1885, p. 401.
9. Blaikie, W.Garden, *The Personal Life of David Livingstone*, 1880 and *The Livingstone Family Tree, 1725-1986*, compiled by David Livingstone Wilson, c. 1988. (Available from the Livingstone Memorial in Blantyre, Scotland.)
10. *The Zambesi Doctors*, Letter 137, 6.1.1872, p. 172.
11. Wikipedia, 7 August 2012.
12. *The Lives of Robert and Mary Moffat*, J. S. Moffat, 1885, p. 397.
13. *Glave's Journey to the Livingstone Tree*, E. J. Glave, The Century: a popular quartet 52 (30): 1896, p. 780.
14. Wikipedia, 7 August 2012.